EARLY DUTCH

SETTLERS

OF

MONMOUTH COUNTY

NEW JERSEY

EARLY DUTCH

SETTLERS

OF

MONMOUTH COUNTY

NEW JERSEY

BY

GEORGE C. BEEKMAN

Southern Historical Press, Inc.
Greenville, South Carolina

This volume was reproduced
from a personal copy located in
the Publishers private library

Please direct all correspondence and book orders to:
SOUTHERN HISTORICAL PRESS, Inc.
1071 Park West Blvd.
Greenville, SC   29611
southernhistoricalpress@gmail.com

Published Freehold, NJ 1901
ISBN #978-1-63914-322-1
Printed in the United States of America

PREFACE.

When the publication of these articles on the Early Dutch Settlers of Monmouth was begun in The Freehold Transcript, I had no idea they would develop to such length.

Several of the articles written for the weekly issues of this newspaper read all right therein, but now, gathered together in book form, they appear fragmentary and disconnected.

A great deal of time and labor by more than one person has been devoted to gathering material from public records, family papers, tombstone inscriptions, and other original sources of information. Much of this is comprised in short notes and small type, and, by putting these compilations in book form they will be accessible for reference. For there is much work to be done before a full genealogy can be written of either the Conover, Hendrickson, or Schanck families.

The illustrations are chiefly old dwelling houses erected by the early settlers or their sons. The buildings are disappearing before the march of improvement and the decay of time, and in another generation not one will probably be left. Some are of the Dutch style of architecture, others of the English, but they show the radical difference of the two races in character. I have been unable to procure the likeness of any of our pioneer settlers, and therefore was compelled to select persons of the present generation, who bear in form or features a strong family resemblance to their parental ancestors. These selections have been made by myself, and solely for the above reason.

Among these pictures are four members of different generations of the same family, all closely connected by ties of blood. Each generation shows a marked difference, yet a family likeness can be detected in all of them. G. C. B.

Freehold, N. J., August 7, 1901.

RECORDS OF THE CONOVERS, SCHENCKS AND VANDERVEERS.

Roelof Martense Schenck was born at Amersfoort, Province of Utrecht, Holland, in 1619, and came to New Amsterdam with his brother Jan, and sister Annetje, in 1650. In 1660 he married Neeltje, daughter of Gerrit Wolphertse VanCouwenhoven, who was a son of Wolfert Garretson VanCouwenhoven, who came from Amersfoort aforesaid to America in 1630 with the Dutch emigrants who settled Rensselaerwick, near what is now Albany in the state of New York. Soon after his marriage to Neeltje Conover (as the name is now spelled) he settled permanently at Flatlands, Long Island, where his wife had been born.

His will was made September 4, 1704, proved August 3, 1705, and is recorded in Book 7, page 209, in Surrogate's office of the county of New York. This will with other information concerning him and many of his descendants, is published in a book compiled by Capt. A. D. Schenck U. S. A., published in 1883 and entitled "Ancestry and Descendants of Rev. William Schenck."

The will of his son Garret, who settled in Monmouth county, N. J., is also published in this work; it was executed January 12, 1739, proved October 7th, 1745, and is now on record in the office of Secretary of the state of New Jersey.

Roelof Martense Schenck devised all his real estate to his eldest son Martin, who married June 20th, 1686, Susanna Abrahamse Brinckerhoff. He bequeaths to his two youngest sons, Garret and Jan, and to his six living daughters, Jonica, Maryke, Margaretta, Neeltje, Mayke and Sara, and the two children of his deceased daughter Annetje, sixty and a half pounds each, and makes these legacies chargeable upon the real estate devised to his eldest son.

His two sons, Garret and Jan, settled in Monmouth county about 1695. Their names appear in our court and other public records soon after this date. They and their wives were among the first communicants of the Marlboro Dutch church, as now called. Garret Schenck married Neeltje Coerten VanVoorhees at Flatlands, L. I., and died September 5, 1745, on the farm known as the Rappleyea farm at Pleasant Valley in Holmdel township, now occupied by Theodore R. Thorn.

He names in his will five sons, viz:— Roelof, who married Eugentje VanDorn; Koert, who married Mary Peterse VanCouwenhoven, and died on his farm near the present village of Marlboro in 1771. Garret, who married Jannetje Williamse VanCouwenhoven and died on the homestead farm in Pleasant Valley, February 14, 1792; John, who married for his first wife Ann Couwenhoven, and died February 13, 1775; Albert, who married first Caty Conover, second, Agnes VanBrunt, and died May 21, 1786.

Mary, one of Garret Schenck's daughters, married Hendrick Smock and died in 1747, leaving six sons and two daughters surviving her.

Altje, another daughter, married Tunis VanDerveer and had six sons and three daughters.

A third daughter married for her first husband Hendrick Hendrickson and for her second Elias Golden.

The Smocks and Vanderveers, now so numerous in Monmouth county, are principally descended from these sons of the above named Schenck sisters.

Jan Schenck, the brother of Garret, was born at Flatlands, L. I., February 10, 1670, married there in 1691 his cousin, Sarah Couwenhoven, who was born at the same place January 6, 1675. He died January 30, 1753, on the farm now owned by Edgar, son of the late Hon. George Schenck in Pleasant Valley. His wife died January 31, 1761. Three of Garret and Jan Schenck's half sisters married the three VanCouwenhoven brothers, who were the first settlers of this name in Monmouth county, viz:

First. Cornelius Williamse VanCouwenhoven, born at Flatlands, L. I., November 29, 1672, married there September 8, 1700, Margaretta Schenck and died May 16, 1736, on his farm adjacent to the farms of Garret and Jan Schenck in Pleasant Valley. On pages 82 and 82½ of the old town book of Middletown township is the record of their cattle marks as follows:

"June ye 24, 1696, then Garret Schenck, Cornelius Couwenhoven and

Peter Wicoff gave their ear marks to be recorded."

"Garret Schenck, his ear marks, a fork on top of left ear and a piece cut aslope of the upper or foreside of the right ear, making the ear both shorter and narrower. Recorded to his son."

"Cornelius Couwenhoven, his mark is a fork on the right ear and a small cut in on the underside of the left ear. Recorded to his son."

"Peter Wicoff, his ear mark is a hole through the right ear and a piece cut aslope off the upper or foreside of the left ear, making the ear both shorter and narrower."

"April 25, 1698, John Schenck, his ear mark is a crape of the top of the near ear and a half penny on each side of same ear."

Second. Albert Williamse VanCouwenhoven, born at Flatlands, L. I., December 7, 1676, married there about 1701 Neeltje Schenck and died in Monmouth county July 7, 1751.

Third. Jacob Williamse VanCouwenhoven, born at Flatlands, L. I., January 29, 1679, married there November 12, 1705, Sarah Schenck and died at Middletown, Monmouth county, December 1, 1744.

Thus a very close relationship, both by blood and intermarriage, existed between the two Schenck brothers, and the three Conover brothers who first settled here, and who are the ancestors of all who now bear those names in Monmouth county.

The name VanCouwenhoven, as the Dutch language yielded very slowly but surely to the English tongue, underwent several changes both in spelling and pronunciation. Our early court and church records show some of these changes. The "Van" was dropped and name spelled Couwenhoven or Kowenhoven. Then Cowenhoven, next Covenhoven or Covenoven, and finally Conover.

This family have been in America nearly three centuries. As the original progenitor came here in 1630, another generation, or 32 years from present date, will complete this period since the Conover tree was first planted in the new world. Very few families in the United States of Netherland blood can show such an ancient lineage, about which there can be no doubt. Neither can any family show greater fidelity in their obedience to the Scriptural injunction "to increase and multiply in the land." If all the male and female descendants of Wolphert Garritson VanCouwenhoven now in the United States could be gathered together in one place it would be a mighty multitude.

Neither do I know of any of this name who has been convicted of any infamous crime. Their family history is remarkably free from all dishonorable stains. While none of them have achieved fame as authors, ministers, presidents, generals, or millionaires, yet on the other hand they have generally occupied respectable positions, led useful lives, and been good citizens. That is, the Conovers are not found at either extreme of the social scale but on the safe middle ground. During the stormy days of the Revolution I do not know of a single Conover, Smock, Schenck, or Vanderveer in Monmouth county who was a Tory. On the contrary, so far as I can learn, they were all sturdy, uncompromising patriots. Many of them, like Captain Jacob Covenhoven, Colonel Barnes Smock, Captains John and William Schenck and Tunis Vanderveer, did yeoman service both in council and battle for their country. During the late war of the rebellion the records of our state show that over 50 Schencks and over 70 Conovers served in the New Jersey regiments. I, therefore, can sincerely say that I do not know of any family of Dutch descent who have a better right to celebrate the year 1930, the tricentennial of their residence in America (now only 32 years off) than the Conovers and their kinsmen among the Smocks, Schencks and Vanderveers. They can then sing with gusto and truth the following verses and no one can question their right to do so, or the propriety of such a tricentennial jubilee.

Ye sturdy Dutchmen, now arise,
  Stand up in a row,
For singing of the ancient times,
  We're going for to go;
When this fair land on every hand
  Was peopled by the Dutch,
And all the rest however blest,
  They did not count for much.

Of centennial celebrations,
  We've had some two or more;
These upstarts of an hundred years,
  But one find in their score,
And tho' they boast a mighty host,
  "Four Hundred," brave and fair;
We quietly look in History's book
  And fail to find them there.

      Chorus.
I am a Van, of a Van, of a Van, of a Van,
  Of a Van of a way back line;
On every rugged feature
  Ancestral glories shine,
And all our band in kinship stand,
  With all that's old and fine.
I'm a Van, of a Van, of a Van, of a Van,
  Of a Van of a way back line.

TRAITS OF CONOVER CHARACTER. FANCIFUL ORIGIN OF THE NAME.

I have sometimes heard the inquiry, what does "Covenhoven" mean in the Low Dutch language? This question I cannot answer, although many years ago, I heard a gentleman of this family give the following explanation:

He said that in the early settlement of Long Island, a Hollander with a long jaw-breaking name, had taken up his residence near Gravesend. His nearest neighbors were English people, who had followed Lady Deborah Moody from Massachusetts Bay. They were unable to understand his Dutch talk any better than he understood their foreign speech. Neither were they able to pronounce his name. Near his house he had erected on four posts an old fashioned oven. Such ovens were quite common in Monmouth county fifty years ago. They had a level brick bottom, some three or four feet wide, and eight or ten in length. This was arched over with brick. Light dry fuel, like old fence rails, was placed in the oven and fired. When the wood was consumed and the oven thoroughly heated, the bread, pies or other things to be baked, were shoved in with a long handled iron shovel. The door was then closed until the articles were thoroughly done. This Hollander also owned a cow, which had been brought over from his old sea-home, and was a highly prized animal in those early days. One cold winter's night, a pack of hungry wolves approached very close to his dwelling. Their fierce howling frightened the cow, so that she broke out of the shed, and ran wildly around the house. Coming in contact with the oven on four posts she kicked it over. This incident was talked about by the English neighbors who, unable to pronounce his name, described him as the man whose cow kicked over, or went over the oven. This was soon abbreviated into "Cow-and-oven," or "Cow-n-hoven," This is doubtless a fanciful explanation. Like those given by Washington Irving in his Knickerbocker History of New York, of the meaning or origin of Dutch surnames, based on the erroneous idea, that Dutch names have a meaning like English words of "idem sonans."

Although this old "VanCouvenhoven" name has been often changed, yet the genuine Conovers retain in a marked degree the physical and mental characteristics of the Batavian and Frisian race from which they spring. That is, where they have not intermarried too often with French, Irish, English or other foreign people.

The real Couvenhoven, whose Dutch blood is unadulterated, is generally a fine looking specimen of the "genus homo." Robust and well proportioned in person, square shouldered and deep chested, with ruddy complexion, light blue eyes and sandy hair. Bluff in manner, sincere and frank in expression of his opinions, honest in his dealings and grim and tenacious in resolution. Trickery, deceit and show he detests, and would rather be underestimated than overestimated by other people. He wants the substantial things of this life and not the mere show or appearance of things. That is, he would choose anytime a square meal of pork and potatoes, rather than a fine or fashionable suit of broadcloth, with jewelry to match, on an empty stomach. Such are some of the traits of the genuine Couvenhoven, if a true descendant of the first Hollanders of this name. And there ought to be many genuine Conovers in Monmouth. The late Rev. Garret C. Schenck told the writer that there have been 150 marriages in Monmouth county since 1700 where both the bride and groom were of this name. The three brothers who settled here, must have been men of marked individuality, great vigor, and force of character. For a century after their settlement, or in 1800, their respective descendants were spoken of as three separate or distinct branches or families.

The late Samuel Conover, who was twice sheriff of Monmouth county, often remarked that there were three kinds of Conovers, and distinguished as the "Lop-eared" Conovers, the "Big-foot" Conovers and the "Wide-mouth" or "Weasel" Conovers.

The lop-eared variety were so called because of their protuberant ears, set at right angles with the head. They were noted for their up-to-date farms.

substantial buildings and good strong fences. Their crops in the rear of their farms were as well cultivated and looked as good as those next to the public highway, for none of them liked "Presbyterian" farming, as they called it. They liked to set a good table with full and plenty on it, and the "wayfaring man," if half decent in looks, who happened to come along at meal time, was never denied a seat at their table.

The "Big-foot" Conovers, although sadly lacking in the standard of beauty which prevails in the Celestial empire, are nevertheless a fine looking people. Some of the most handsome men and most beautiful women ever raised in Monmouth county can be found among the different generations of the big-foot variety. They, too, liked good big farms, solid and comfortable buildings for man and beast, with well filled barns, well stocked cellars and smoke houses, with true friends and neighbors to gather around the blazing fire, and partake of the good cheer of their homes.

The "Wide-mouth" or "Weasel" Conovers, were generally tall and wiry men. Polished and polite in manners, smooth and pleasant in speech, and very well groomed in appearance and dress. Fond of fast horses and elegant carriages, of fashionable clothing and expensive jewelry. This variety of the Conovers were also very successful in horse trading, in running for office and also occasionally in "bucking the tiger" when led into it by bad company. In fact they were at home in any business which required diplomacy or extra finesse.

How this description given by Sheriff Sam Conover tallies with the real facts the reader can judge for himself. I merely repeat the current gossip without vouching for its accuracy. Although I can safely say that so far as successful horse trading and office getting goes, nobody has ever beat the Couvenhovens in Monmouth county, unless it is the Hendricksons, Schencks, Smocks or Vanderveers, who are really nine-tenths Conover by blood and intermarriage for some 300 years.

THE WILL OF JAN SCHENCK, AND SOME OF HIS DESCENDANTS.

Jan Schenck, who settled on and owned the farm now owned by Edgar Schenck in Holmdel township, was a VanCouwenhoven on his mother's side. He likewise married an own cousin, Sarah Couwenhoven, who was a sister of the three brothers of this name, who all married Schenck wives and settled in Monmouth county.

His will was executed September 7th, A. D. 1746, proved June 3rd, 1753, and is now on record in the office of Secretary of State at Trenton, N. J., in Book F of Wills, pages 262, etc.

The following is a true copy of this will:

In the name of God Amen:

The seventh day of September in the twentieth year of the Reign of our Sovereign Lord George the Second by the grace of God over Great Britian King, etc. Annoq Domni one thousand seven hundred and fourty-six, I, John Schenck, Sen., of Middletown in the County of Monmouth and Eastern Division of the Province of New Jersey, yeoman, being in health of body and of sound and perfect mind and memory thanks be given to God; therefore calling unto mind the mortality of my body and knowing that it is appointed for all men once to Die, do make and ordain this my last will and Testament. That is to say Principally and first of all I give and recommend my Soul into the hands of God that gave it, and my Body I recommend to the Earth to be buried in Christian like and decent manner at the discretion of my Executors hereafter mentioned, nothing doubting but at the General Resurrection I shall receive the same again by the mighty power of God; and as touching these wordly things and Estate wherewith it has pleased God to bless me in this life, I give, Devise and Dispose of the same in manner and form following. Viz: Imprimis I Will and positively Order that all my Debts and Funeral charges be paid and fully discharged in convenient time after my Decease by my Executors hereafter mentioned. Item: I give and bequeath to Sarah, my dearly beloved wife (and hereby order that she shall have) the full and sole use and possession and benefit of all and singular my Estate Real and Personal after my decease of what nature or kind soever or wheresoever the same may be found to be belonging to me, by any way or means whatever the use benefits and profits thereof, and every part and parcel thereof to be received by and belong unto her for and during her natural life. That is to say for the support of herself and maintenance of my loving son John Schenck, so long as my above said wife's natural life shall continue. Item: I give, bequeath and Devise unto my aforesaid son, John Schenck, after the decease of my aforesaid loving wife, Sarah Schenck, all and singular my Lands and Tenements, meadows and Rights

DANIEL SCHENCK

DANIEL P. SCHENCK

JOHN C. SCHENCK

JOHN L. SCHENCK

to Lands and meadows that I shall die possessed of or that shall by any way or means belong unto me at the time of my decease; the same immediately after the decease of my aforesaid wife, to be received held possessed and Enjoyed by my said son, John Schenck, his heirs and assigns forever, to his and their own proper use, benefit and behoof forever. He performing, fulfilling and paying what is hereinafter by me appointed for him to pay and discharge as legacies to his brothers and sisters as follows: Viz: It is my will and desire and I do hereby order that my said son, John Schenck, shall pay unto my two sons, Roelof and Peter, and their seven sisters in equal portions the sum of four hundred and fifty pounds current money of the Province aforesaid at eight shillings the ounce; the one half in two years and the other half in five years after the Decease of the longest liver be it either me or my wife; that is twenty-five pounds to each of my said nine children at two years and twenty-five pounds more to each of them at the end of five years after the decease of the longest liver of us two; that is me and my wife. I do further order and it is my will and desire that the fifty pounds that falls to my daughter Sarah be equally divided between my said Daughter Sarah and all her children, as well as those she had by Johannes Voorhees, as those she had by Hendrick Voorhees; also in case of the Death of either of my two sons or seven daughters or that one or more of them should die before they have received their part of the said sum of four hundred and fifty pounds, then my will and desire is and I do hereby strictly charge and order that the share or part thereof that should be paid to such so Dying shall be by my said Son John, paid to the Heirs of their Body or Bodies them surviving; also it is my will and desire that after the decease of the longest liver of us two; that my said son John shall have his outfit of my movable Estate in quantity and quality equal with his Brothers and Sisters as they had of me when they left me, and if any of my movable Estate be then left, I will and devise it may be equally divided between all my children. And in case my said Son John Dies before he is seized and possessed of the said Estate in fee simple, then I give and bequeath the same to my two sons and seven daughters, viz: that the whole Estate given as above said to my said Son John shall be sold to the highest bidder amongst my children, and the money thence arising shall be equally Divided amongst my two Sons and seven daughters in the same manner as the aforesaid four hundred and fifty pounds is to be Divided in every respect whatever. But it is my Will and Desire anything herein contained to the contrary notwithstanding that my said Son John at the time of his Decease have issue of his Body, lawfully begotten altho it be before he is in actual possession; that if his Ex. shall perform in every particular what is herein by me ordered; that then the whole Estate given to him as aforesaid shall be and remain to his lawful Heirs and assigns forever. Item: I Give and bequeath unto my Son, Roelof Schenck, the sum of Ten pounds money at eight shillings to the ounce with interest, to Barr him of further Claims to my Estate or part thereof either Real or Personal as Heir-at-Law or otherwise (except what is herein before given and bequeathed to him) the sum of Ten pounds to be paid to him by my Executors in convenient time after my Decease. And lastly I do hereby make, ordain, constitute and appoint my beloved wife, Sarah Schenck, and my loving Son, Roelof Schenck, Executrix and Executor of this my last Will and Testament hereby utterly disallowing, revoking and disannulling all and every other former Testament, Wills, Legacies and Bequests and Executors by me in any wise before named willed and bequeathed, ratifying and confirming this and no other to be my last Will and Testament.

In witness whereof I have here unto Set my Hand and Seal, this day and year above written.   JAN SCHENCK. [L. S.]

This Will contained in two half side sheet of paper, the one of fourty-seven lines, the other of fourty-one lines without any alterations or interlinations was signed, sealed and pronounced by the said Jan Schenck, to be his last Will and Testament in Presence of Roelof Couvenhoven, Garret Schenck, Tho. Craven.

The foregoing is a true copy Executed by
       THO. BARTOW.

Jan Schenck and his wife were buried in the old Schenck and Couvenhoven burying ground, which lies at the corner of the farms of Edgar Schenck, Theodore R. Thorne and Henry Conover, about half a mile from Holmdel village and near the turnpike to Keyport. This graveyard has lately been cleared up and put in order by Mrs. Lydia Hendrickson Schenck Conover, daughter of the late Daniel P. Schenck, and widow of Dr. Charles A. Conover of Marlboro. It was a very creditable work for which she deserves commendation. She has also devoted much time and labor to tracing up an accurate record of the descendants of Jan Schenck from church records, inscriptions on old tombstones, and private family papers scattered through many farmhouses in Holmdel and the adjacent townships. She has thus completed a genealogy which can be depended on for accuracy. I am indebted to her for nearly all the dates of births, deaths and marriages contained in this paper. She has accomplished a work which will be more appreciated in the future than though she had erected a costly monument of marble over their graves. She has honored the memory of a virtuous, hardy and industrious race of men and women, who laid the foundation of the solid respectability and prosperity which their descendants have so long enjoyed in Monmouth county and elsewhere in the United States where they have settled.

Some of the descendants of the two Schenck brothers who settled here over two centuries since, like Gen. Robert C. Schenck of Ohio, Admiral Findlay

EARLY DUTCH SETTLERS OF MONMOUTH.

Schenck and others, have left names famous all over our country for ability and patriotism.

Jan Schenck by his wife, Sarah Couwenhoven, had the following children:

Roelof, b. February 21, 1692, married Geesie, daughter of Sheriff or Capt. Daniel Hendrickson; d. January 19, 1766.

Sarah, b. 1696, married May 16, 1721, Johannes Voorhees of New Brunswick, N. J. Second husband, Hendrick Voorhees of Freehold township.

Altje, baptized May 25, 1705, married Chrystjan VanDooren, d. 1801.

Rachel, b. February 19, 1709, is said to have married a Boone of Kentucky.

Maria, b. August 8, 1712, married Jacob VanDooren and died October 31, 1756.

Leah, b. December 24th, 1714, married December 17th, 1735, Peter Couwenhoven and died March 14, 1769.

William, baptized April 13, 1718, died young.

Jannetje, baptized April 12, 1719, married Bernardus Verbryke, who is said to have settled at Neshaminy, Pa.

John, b. June 27, 1722, married June 28, 1750, Nellie Bennett; d. December 24, 1808.

Antje, b.——married Arie VanDooren.

Peter, b. ——married first Jannetje VanNostrand, second, Jannetje Hendrickson.

John, to whom the father devised all his real estate, lived and died on the homestead farm in Pleasant Valley.

John Schenck, by his wife, Nellie Bennett, who was born November 29, 1728, and died June 1st, 1810, had following children all born on the farm in Pleasant Valley:

*John Schenck, b. June 19, 1752.

Chrineyonce, b. September 18, 1753, died young.

*William, b. March 30, 1755.

Ida, b. February 1, 1757.

Sarah, b. February 13, 1759, married Ruliff, son of Hendrick Schenck and Catharine Holmes, her own cousin, December 22, 1774; d. April 13th, 1811.

Chrineyonce, b. December 29, 1760, married November 20, 1793, Margaret Polhemus; d. March 15, 1840.

Peter or Ogburn, b. May 27, 1763, married Anna Ogden.

Nellie, b. January 13, 1765, married October 20, 1785, Joseph H. Holmes; died June 5, 1838.

Annie, b. November 15, 1766, married December 28, 1786, Denyse Hendrickson.

Mary, b. January 23, 1769; d. May 12, 1772.

Daniel, b. April 1, 1771, married October 13, 1793, Catharine Smock; d. August 9, 1845.

Mary, b. April 19, 1775, married John O. Stillwell, March 25, 1806; died September 29, 1864.

---

*John and William, the two oldest sons above removed to Ohio and settled there.

DUTCH TENACITY AS SHOWN BY THEIR LOVE FOR THEIR CHURCH.

Roelof Schenck, the eldest son of Jan Schenck and Sara Couvenhoven, his wife, had no real estate devised to him under his father's will although he was appointed one of the executors. The reason of this was that he had acquired a large tract of land at and in the vicinity of what is now Bradevelt station, Marlboro township, then a part of Freehold township. The younger son John, had doubtless remained at home working on his father's farm. He was 28 years old when he married Nellie Bennett. When his father's will was executed he was unmarried, while the eldest son Roelof, had been married some thirty years, and had eight children and also grandchildren at this time.

His dwelling house stood near the site of the Brick Church, about two or three hundred yards south of the public road, which now passes by the Brick Church, and about 500 yards east of the railroad track. The buildings are now all gone. The lands owned by him in this vicinity are now cut up into several large and valuable farms, some of which are still owned and occupied by his descendants on the female side.

Rev. Theodore W. Wells in his memorial address at Brick church, speaks of this Roelof Schenck, and states he was called "Black Roelof" and noted for his great physical strength. He was also the person who selected the site of the church edifice, where it has remained to this day, by carting the first load of building stones to the spot. On page 308 in "Old Times in Old Monmouth" are several references to this Roelof Schenck, who was quite a noted business man in his day and active in church work.

The first two Schenck brothers, Garret and Jan, were among the first organizers and supporters of the Dutch church in Monmouth county. Their names appear on the early records, both as elders and deacons.

The majority of their descendants down to the present day have generally sustained this church or the churches which have sprung from it.

They have been married, their children baptized and their funerals solemnized by the clergymen of the Dutch church. Many of them sleep their last sleep in the yard adjacent to the Brick Church, as the tombstones show.

Rev. Theodore W. Wells has given us a full history of the successive pastors of this church, but the history of the congregation is yet to be written. When it is, the Schencks and their kinsmen among the Hendricksons, Vanderveers, Conovers and Smocks, will occupy the most conspicuous places. And I assert without fear of contradiction that the progress and prosperity of the Dutch church in America is due to the stability and tenacity inherent in the Dutch character, rather than to any excellency in the church government or its polity, and ability of its trained clergymen.

In fact the clergymen of this denomination committed a great blunder when they dropped the name "Dutch" and called themselves the "Reformed Church." This name is applicable to the Episcopalians, Quakers or any other of the many protestant sects, and has no particular meaning.

Instead of resisting the detraction, ridicule and abuse, which originated in England, and was based on conflicting interests, commercial rivalries and national prejudices, which prevailed during the reign of Charles II, and which saturated all English literature of that period, they weakly yielded to it.

This denunciation of Holland and the Republican government and citizens of that country was increased, through the bitter malice and rank partizan feeling which prevailed in England during the reign of William of Orange. As Macauley in his history of England has shown, every effort was made by the adherents of the Stuart dynasty and the papists to stir up English hate and prejudice, by denouncing and ridiculing the "Dutch" in order to overthrow their "Dutch King" and the Stadholder of the Dutch Republicans.

This spirit was caught up by writers in America and eagerly imitated until the word "Dutch" became synonymous with all that was vile, cruel, brutal and cowardly. Instead of resisting these slanderous charges and falsehoods, and upholding the right and truth as could have been done, the "Shepherds of the Church" pusillanimously surrendered the old historical name, and the glorious past which belonged to it. A respectable body of the laymen of this denomination strongly objected to this change, but before the matter was fairly understood by the lay element, the "disgraceful deed was done." It has been the lay element of this denomination which has upheld and perpetuated this church in the United States, and their consent should have been obtained before the "standard" or "flag" was pulled down.

This fact is shown by the history of each separate church, for the history of one, in its general features, is the history of all which have come down from the last century.

The following article is from the pen of Judge John Fitch, giving an account of the old Dutch church at Schodack Landing, Rensselaer county, N. Y. The writer is a lineal descendant of the Colonial governor of Connecticut of same name, and, I am informed, of unmixed English descent.

Like Macauley and Motley, he rises above the narrow prejudices and supercilious arrogance and self righteousness which characterize so many English writers and their servile imitators in New England, when they write of Holland or its people. We have had lately a specimen of this same spirit in the English papers when they speak of Paul Krueger and the Dutch farmers of South Africa or Boors, as they so frequently call them. Judge Fitch does not hesitate to give others such credit as they justly deserve even when it impairs the extravagant claims of the "Pilgrim Fathers" to all that is great and grand in the early history of our country. The following is a true copy of Judge Fitch's article:

"About the year 1637 the Dutch began the first settlement on the east side of the Hudson river, between the mouths of Kinderhook creek and a point about opposite the present city of Albany, then a mere trading post. The principal settlement was on the present site of the village of Schodack Landing. The first thing they did was to build a log church at the landing. It was located near the site of the present burying ground: This was the origin of the church now in existence at Mutzeskill, which is either the third or fourth edifice.

"It was regularly incorporated in 1788 by the name of 'The Ministry, Elders and Deacons of the Reformed Protestant Dutch Church at Schodack.' In 1810 the church edifice was removed back from the Hudson river about two and a half miles to Mutzeskill, where it still remains.

"The Hollanders were then, as their descendants are now, firm, reliable Christians—few or no infidels among them. The descendants of these men are today more free from cant, hypocrisy and "isms" than are the descendants of the English. Comparatively few, if any of Holland descent, stray away from the path of rectitude and virtue or the protestant faith of their fathers; while the English become Presbyterians, Methodists, Baptists, Catholics, and frequently what all decent people despise, skeptics or religious reformers, which is another name for hypocrites or infidels. Such has been the experience of those who have observed the fate of the Dutch, Presbyterians, Methodists and Baptists of the vicinity of which I speak.

"One of the reasons why the Hollanders have so long retained and maintained their foothold and standing in the valley of the Hudson and also along the Mohawk is because of their tenacity and firmly fixed moral and religious principles, temperate habits and homely and disinterested virtues. They do not run about, emigrate from place to place, and are not continually on the go, jump and run. They are not yearly movers, are not easily moved from their fixed residences, but are stable in all their ways.

"The residence of the Hollander can be very readily distinguished from that of other nationalities, because his residence once selected, the location becomes his home and at once he sets to work to improve it. Buildings, fruit trees, gardens and shrubbery are put up, planted, looked after and cared for.

"The fences are in a still better condition, and the farm is more carefully cultivated than the farms of those who are moving from place to place and who never, as it were, live anywhere long. The Hollander has been true to his country's principles of liberty and religion and he has steadily adhered to the Reformed Dutch church here in the State of New York. The Protestant religion holds its own firmly imbued in the mind of the Hollander.

"It is a singular fact that when a Reformed Dutch church is established, it is there to stay. In very few instances has a Dutch church been abandoned when once fairly established in the valley of the Hudson.

"It lives, prospers and holds its own although surrounded by Catholics, Methodists, Episcopalians, and other persuasions. The Dutch church did its full share and more in spreading the cause of our Saviour from 1637 to 1785 than all the other persuasions in the colony of New York.

"Time has rolled on, but still the distinctive mark of the Hollander remains. The church at Schodack Landing may be said to be the mother church of the Dutch churches on the east bank of the Hudson river."

This account comes from a man whose judicial experience, associations and English descent place it above all suspicion of bias or partiality. By simply changing name of church and location, it is applicable to the First Dutch church of Monmouth county, as well as other old churches in New Jersey of this denomination.

The same kind of people founded and sustained them, and the same results have followed. Our forefathers from Holland had real practical faith and trust in God. They believed He cared for them in the wilderness of the New World, surrounded by the fierce Mohawk warriors, the perils, diseases and hardships of their pioneer life, as He had in their memorable struggle of 80 years with Spain and the popish hierarchy. This church of their fathers had been born "amidst perils, tears and blood;" its countless martyrs were subjected to all the cruelties and tortures Spanish malice, treachery and bigotry could inflict or the inquisitors could invent, and their deeds of courage, sacrifice and endurance have never been excelled in the annals of human history. The persecution of the Puritans in England or of the Presbyterians in Scotland were but child's play compared to the wholesale massacres and tortures of the Dutch people by that Spanish Nero, Philip II, and that fiend incarnate, the Duke of Alva. Instead of weakly yielding to the abuse, ridicule and detraction which had been heaped on the "Dutch," "The Shepherds of the Church" should have repelled with indignation the mere suggestion of dropping the "historic name." Instead of being ashamed they should have gloried in their name, and with united hearts and voices raised to heaven the anthem:

"From out the sea, O Motherland,
Our fathers plucked thy billowy strand;
 As from the deep,
 Where treasures sleep,
The pearl rewards the daring hand.

And when far angrier billows broke,
Of bigot hate and war's fell stroke,
 Our sires withstood
 This sea of blood,
With hearts no tyrant's hand could yoke.

The thrift that wrought, like Moses' rod,
A path where man had never trod;
 That highway kept,
 By storm unswept,
A land unpromised yet from God.

A land where genius flamed with power,
Where learning earned its glorious dower,
 Where commerce sped
 With boundless tread,
And art bloomed forth in beauteous flower.

A land where knowledge grew for all,
Where conscience knew no gyve or thrall;
 Where exiled bands
 From other lands,
Bore truth, that made old errors fall.

That land can well afford to be
The theme of Irving's pleasantry;
 And toss the jest
 From off its crest,
As off it tossed the mocking sea.

Our hearts untraveled high expand.
To read thy record strangely grand;
 With tongue aflame,
 We call thy name,
And proudly own thee, Motherland."
—Vedder.

Roelof Schenck not only owned the lands around what is now the Marlboro Brick church, but he lived and died in his dwelling house near this spot. He also married the daughter of Daniel Hendrickson, who was one of the principal organizers of the Dutch church of Monmouth county, and one of its earliest elders. His name and the name of his wife, Catharine VanDyke, appear among communicants of this church as early as 1709. Daniel Hendrickson came from Long Island and settled on the farm now owned by his great-great grandson, Hon. William Henry Hendrickson at Holland in Holmdel township. He was the first person of Holland descent to hold the office of high sheriff of this county, and he was also an officer of the county militia. He was very active in all church work, and often conducted service on the Sabbath in absence of any regular clergyman. The late Rev. G. C. Schenck had in his possession a sermon printed in Dutch language which had been written and delivered by this Daniel Hendrickson.

Roelof Schenck married Geesie, one of his daughters, and Jonathan Holmes married Tuniche, another daughter. Their names also appear among communicants of this church on pages 86-87 of Wells' memorial address. Roelof Schenck and Jonathan Holmes, his sons-in-law, were appointed executors of his will and settled up his estate. Hendrick, a son of Roelof Schenck, married Catharine, a daughter of Jonathan Holmes, his own cousin, and his and her children were therefore doubly the grandchildren of this Daniel Hendrickson.

Roelof Schenck and his wife, Geesie Hendrickson, together with their son, Hendrick Schenck, and his wife, Catharine Holmes, are all buried in the Schenck-Couwenhoven burying ground in Pleasant Valley, Holmdel township.

ROELOF SCHENCK AND HIS DESCENDANTS.—A WOMAN OF GREAT BUSINESS CAPACITY.

Roelof Schenck, by his wife, Geesie Hendrickson, had the following children:

Sarah, b. May 22, 1715, married December 1, 1731, Joseph VanMater or VanMetteren, as spelled on records of the Marlboro Brick church. He was a son of Kriin or Chrineyonce VanMater and Nelly VanCleaf; his wife Sarah, died September 1, 1748.

Katrintje, baptized March 19, 1717, died young.

Kalrya or Catharine, baptized December 21st, 1718, married first, Simon DeHart, second, Peter Couwenhoven.

Jan, b. January 22, 1721, married November 26, 1741, Jacomintje Couwenhoven; died January 27th, 1749.

Daniel, baptized May 26, 1723, died September 20, 1747.

Neeltje, b. September 10, 1724, married October 13, 1744, Garret Couwenhoven; died March 25, 1800.

Engeltje, baptized April 28, 1732.

Hendrick, born July 29, 1731, married his own cousin, Catharine, daughter of Jonathan

Holmes and Tuniche Hendrickson, his wife, and died August 24, 1766, at the early age of thirty-five years. Catharine Holmes, his wife, was born May 11, 1731, died May 12, 1796. It is said she married a second husband, one John Schenck, of Penns Neck.

Roelof Schenck made his will April 10, 1765, proved March 3, 1766, and is now on record in Secretary of State's office at Trenton in Book 1 of Wills, page 93, etc.

He describes himself as a resident of Freehold township, which then included that part of Marlboro township where he resided. He gives to his grandson, Ruliff, his land at the Point. To his grandsons, Ruliff and Cornelius, the plantation he bought of Peter Voorhees. To his daughter, Nelly Couwenhoven, one hundred acres of land near the church. All the rest of his lands called Timber Neck, he devised in fee to his son, Hendrick, subject to payments of legacies amounting in all to eleven hundred and twenty pounds as follows: To his granddaughter, Geesie Schenck, £280. To his six grandchildren, the children of his daughter, Catharine Couwenhoven, viz: Simon DeHart, Geesie DeHart, Jacob Couwenhoven, Ruliff Couwenhoven, Mary Couwenhoven and John Couwenhoven, £280, share and share alike. To his three grandchildren, the children of his daughter, Sara VanMater, £280, share and share alike. To his daughter, Nelly Couwenhoven, £280. He also speaks in this will of the children of his deceased son, John. Hendrick Schenck, his son, and Garret Couwenhoven and Peter Couwenhoven, two of his sons-in-law, are appointed executors. The will is witnessed by William Tice, Cornelius Couvenhoven and John Tice.

This Roelof Schenck was a noted man in his day and did considerable business for others in the way of settling estates, etc. He served as foreman of the grand jury at the October term, 1754, of our county courts, and his name also appears quite frequently in public matters.

Hendrick Schenck, his son, died within a year after his father. His will was made August 23, 1766, proved September 12, 1766, and is recorded in Secretary of State's office at Trenton in Book 1 of Wills, page 105, etc.

He devises to his only son, Ruliff, all his personal and real property, subject to use by his wife of half profits of his real and all profits of his personal property until all his children arrive at age. After this a fixed amount has to be paid annually to the widow, and she was also to have use of one room in the dwelling house so long as she lived. This will was evidently made while the testator was sick and just before his death. The injustice of some of the provisions made trouble, and it is a warning that an important matter like the making of a will should not be deferred until a man is on his death bed. To make a fair and judicious will requires all the faculties of a well man. When a man's mind is clouded by sickness and his time is short, it is impossible to make a will which is just to all concerned. Such wills generally make trouble. The devise of all his real and personal estate to his son Ruliff, was further subjected to the payment of £160 to each of his four daughters, as they came of age. He appoints his uncle, John Schenck, of Middletown township, and Daniel Holmes and Obadiah Herbert of Freehold township, executors. The same persons witness his will as witnessed his father's will the preceding year.

On the fly leaf of an old English Bible still in existence, and which the writer has seen, is this inscription:

"Ann Holmes, her book, given her by her mother, Caty Schenck, July 10th, 1792."

Then below is the following entry:

"Presented to Ann Crawford by her aunt, Ann Holmes, 1815."

Between the Old and New Testament is a record of the births of the children of Hendrick Schenck and Catharine Holmes, his wife, as follows:

"Rulif Schenck was born April 17, 1752."
"Sarah Schenck was born May 26, 1755."
"Mary Schenck was born March 17, 1757."
"Jonathan Schenck was born July 19, 1761."
"Catharine Schenck was born March 7, 1762."
"Eleanor Schenck was born March 17, 1764."
"Ann Schenck was born June 14, 1766."

Of these children Sarah and Jonathan died young.

Ruloff Schenck, the only surviving son, married December 22, 1774, his own cousin, Sarah, daughter of John Schenck and Nellie Bennett, his wife, of Pleasant Valley, and died October 12, 1800. His wife was born February 13, 1759, and died April 13, 1811. They are buried in the old Schenck and Couwenhoven burying ground heretofore described.

Mary married Jacob Couwenhoven, who was known as "Farmer Jacob" on account of his well cultivated and productive farm. It is said that he was the most handsome man of the day in Monmouth county.

Catharine remained single.

Eleanor was married January 27, 1797, by Rev. Benjamin Bennett to George Crawford of Middletown Village and died there May 17, 1850. Her husband was born December 5, 1758, and died July 10, 1834. They are both interred in private family burying ground on the Crawford homestead at Nutswamp.

Ann married Jonathan or John Holmes and died without issue.

Eleanor Schenck and her husband, George Crawford, had the following children, all born on the homestead in Middletown Village:

Mary, born January 12, 1800, married November 20, 1817, William W. Murray, and is buried by the side of her husband in graveyard of Baptist church at Middletown Village.

Ann, born February 22, 1801, married February 12th, 1833, by Rev. Doctor Milledoller to Rev. Jacob TenBroeck Beekman; died at homestead where she was born and had always lived, May 18, 1876; interred by side of her husband in Fairview cemetery.

Adaline, born February 16, 1803, married John Lloyd Hendrickson and is buried by her husband in private family burying ground on the farm where she lived and died at Middletown Village.

Eleanor, born January 26, 1805, died December 22, 1823, unmarried; interred by her father and mother in Crawford burying ground.

In Book K of Deeds, pages 380, etc., Monmouth clerk's office, is the record of a deed from John Schenck, surviving executor of Hendrick Schenck, deceased, to Catharine, the widow of Hendrick Schenck, deceased. This deed is dated February 25, 1785, and consideration named therein as £1,000. The land is described as situated in Freehold township (now Marlboro) and as part of a tract of land formerly belonging to Roelof Schenck, deceased, and by him devised to his son, Hendrick. After a particular description by chains and links, a general description is given as one hundred and ninety acres, bounded northwardly by Ruliff Schenck's land, westwardly in part by lands belonging to Dutch congregation and in part by lands of James VanKirk, southwardly by Jacob Couwenhoven's lands and eastwardly by Garret Couwenhoven's lands. Thus it appears that the widow, although cut off by her husband's will from all interest in his real estate except the use of one room in the dwelling house, yet in 20 years thereafter, obtained the absolute ownership of that part of his real estate on which the house and outbuildings stood.

containing 190 acres. This is the same farm which Hendrick S. Conover, son of Tunis Conover, inherited and which he sold to John McClellan within the memory of many now living. It is now owned by a son of the late Ruliff Hendrickson of Freehold.

Catharine Holmes Schenck, the widow, is said to have been a woman of great energy and business capacity. She made her will December 12, 1795. It was proved May 31, 1796, and is on record in secretary of state's office at Trenton.

She gives her only son, Ruliff, (to whom his father had devised nearly all his property) five shillings. The above homestead farm of 190 acres, she devises in fee to her three youngest daughters, Catharine, Eleanor and Ann share and share alike. She gives her eldest daughter, Mary, wife of Jacob Couwenhoven, £200. She gives to her daughters, Catharine and Eleanor, her two negro slaves, Jack and Jude, and her old negro, Brom, who is to be kept on the farm and supported for life by her two daughters. Her negro woman, Elizabeth, she gives to her daughter, Ann Holmes. Her large looking glass and a smaller one with all her tables are given to Catharine and Eleanor, and her third looking glass to her daughter, Ann. All residue of her movable property is to be equally divided between her three youngest daughters, whom she also appoints executrices.

This will is singular for that period because of the appointment of females to settle the estate. She must have held advanced ideas on the rights of women. Daniel Herbert, Thomas Herbert and Daniel Peacock were subscribing witnesses to the will. Her daughter Catharine never married but occupied the homestead farm until her death. She also became the sole owner of the farm. A deed dated January 13, 1816, recorded in Book Y of Deeds, pages 814, etc., Monmouth clerk's office, shows that Ann Holmes, one of the three daughters to whom the mother devised this farm, had died intestate and without children, leaving three sisters, Mary Couwenhoven, Catharine Schenck and Eleanor Crawford and the children of their brother Ruliff Schenck, who had died October 12, 1800, as her heirs at law. By the above deed Eleanor Crawford and husband released all their interest in said real estate to Catharine Schenck. This Catharine Schenck died unmarried June 5, 1816, and is interred by her father and mother in the Schenck-Couwenhoven burying ground, Pleasant Valley. Her will was made

May 7, 1816, proved July 1, 1816, and is recorded in surrogate's office of Monmouth county in Book B of Wills, page 10, etc. She gives to her four nieces, Mary, Ann, Adaline and Eleanor, daughters of her sister, Eleanor Crawford, all her beds, bedding, wearing apparel and household furniture except a Dutch cupboard, to be equally divided between them. She gives her nephew, Garret, son of her sister, Mary Couwenhoven, $500. She gave her four nieces above named $700 each to be paid in one year after her decease. She gives the Dutch cupboard to her nephew, Hendrick, son of her sister, Mary Couwenhoven. She also devised to him the 190 acre homestead farm together with all residue of her real and personal property, in fee subject to payment of above legacies. She also appoints her nephew, Hendrick Couwenhoven, sole executor. This Hendrick Couwenhoven was married March 31, 1805, to Ann B. Crawford. One of his daughters, Rebecca, married Tunis Conover and was the mother of William I. Conover, who still (1898) owns and resides on the farm where his parents lived, in the township of Marlboro, near the Brick church.

CHRINEYONCE SCHENCK AND HIS DESCENDANTS. PROBASCO AND POLHEMUS FAMILIES.

Chrineyonce Schenck was a man well known throughout Monmouth county in his day. Many ancedotes are told of his peculiarities and of his grim ways, and great physical strength. His voice was very deep and gruff, and when angry or in earnest, it deepened into a roar, or as an enemy remarked, "Like the savage growl of a bear with a sore head." He was very bluff and open in the expression of his opinions, and in his likes and dislikes. His grim manner and gruff words were, however, wholly superficial for no man was more kind and considerate to his wife, children and friends than he.

A well authenticated story is told of him by a lawyer who was an eye witness of the incident. He was foreman of a jury impanneled in a very important civil case tried in the Freehold court house. Among the prominent lawyers employed by the plaintiff was one of the Stocktons from Trenton or Princeton. The defendant was a poor man and had some unknown and young attorney to represent him. The plaintiff was a man of great wealth, and notorious for his shrewd and unscrupulous methods of getting other people's property. Mr. Stockton was selected to sum up the case and had, of course, the closing speech. After speaking an hour with great ability and eloquence, tearing the arguments of his young opponent all to tatters, he noticed that the foreman of the jury was leaning over in his chair with his arm upraised and his head resting on his open hand with his eyes closed. Thinking he was asleep and provoked by his supposed inattention, he abruptly stopped. Turning to the court, he pointed his finger at Mr. Schenck and said in an angry tone, "May it please the Court, there is but little use to argue this case to a sleeping juror." In an instant Chrineyonce Schenck sprang to his feet; raising himself to his full height he thundered out in his deep gruff voice: "I am not asleep. I have heard all the evidence and have made up my mind from it as my oath requires, and I want you all to understand, that no lawyer by his smooth gab can persuade me to find a verdict for a scoundrel." Angry and disconcerted by this vehement explosion, Mr. Stockton not only lost his temper, but the thread of his argument and after stumbling along for a few minutes in an incoherent manner he sat down.

Another anecdote is related of Chrineyonce which shows his great bodily strength and the mighty grip of his right hand. He was attacked by a large and savage bull dog. As the brute sprang at him he seized him by the throat, and lifting him clear of the ground held him out at arm's length and choked him to death.

As the family records show Chrineyonce Schenck and his son, John C., married Polhemus wives. This family is also of Dutch descent, although like Lupardus, Antonides, etc., they bear a Latin name. In that case you can generally find that the family is descended from a clergyman of the Dutch church, sent out in early times by the Classis of Amsterdam. It was quite common for scholars in that age to select a

Front view of old dwelling on the farm of Garret Schanck, the pioneer settler, in Pleasant Valley, N. J.

Photograph taken by Mrs. L. H. S. Conover in summer of 1900.

Rear view of old dwelling on the farm of Garret Schanck, the pioneer settler, in Pleasant Valley, N. J.

Photograph taken by Mrs. L. H. S. Conover in summer of 1900.

Latin name, which expressed what their surname meant in Dutch.

The Polhemus family in Monmouth and Somerset counties are descendants of Rev. Johannes Theodorus Polhemus, who had been a minister at Itamaca in Brazil before coming to the New Netherlands in 1654. He preached at Flatbush in the morning and at Brooklyn and Flatlands in the afternoon of each Sunday until 1660. When Brooklyn obtained a minister in 1665 Dominie Polhemus ceased to be connected with the church at Flatbush, and removed to Brooklyn where he died June 9th, 1675, the worthy and beloved pastor of that church.

Among the freeholders and residents of Flatbush, L. I., published on page 147, Vol. 3, O'Callagan's Documentary History of New York, we find in the year 1698 the name of Daniel Polhemus who is credited with six children, and Stoffel or Christopher Probasco, who also had six children. These two names, Probasco and Polhemus, have long been identified with the agricultural progress of that territory now included in Atlantic township, this county. They have stood in the front ranks of the successful and prosperous farmers of this county in the years gone by. The appearance of the buildings and orchards on the old Polhemus homesteads at Scobeyville and the Phalanx today bear silent, but undisputable testimony to their industry, economy and intelligence. Generally speaking the past generations of this family have been zealous and consistent church members. As I understand, a son of Daniel Polhemus above mentioned at Flatlands, named Johannes, married in Brooklyn, Annatie, daughter of Tobias TenEyck, and settled on a tract of land at what is now Scobeyville. Their names appear among the early communicants of the Marlboro Brick church. They had three sons, Daniel, Tobias and John. Tobias removed to and settled in Upper Freehold township and is the ancestor of all now bearing this name in that part of our county.

Daniel married Margaret, daughter of Albert Cowenhoven and Neeltje, his wife, hereinbefore mentioned and had three sons, John, Albert and Tobias. John Polhemus married Mary, daughter of Cyrenius VanMater and Abigail Leffert his wife, and one of their daughters, Margaret, married Chrineyonce Schenck above mentioned. She lived to a great age, and was very fond of talking about her youthful days. She would often tell how she and her sister went to church. She said they "rode and tied" and "tied and rode." "What is that, grandma?" her little grandchildren would ask. "Well, my dears," she would say, "we all liked to go to church, but the roads were poor and roundabout; no bridges over the streams and swamps, mere bridle paths. Father let my sister and myself have a horse to ride. One would mount and ride about a mile, while the other walked, then she would dismount and tie the horse to a tree and walk on. When the other sister came up to the horse she would untie him, get on and ride on a mile before the sister who was walking, then dismount, tie the horse and walk on, so alternately walking and riding they reached the church, and in the same way returning home." This was to "ride and tie."

Hon. Daniel Polhemus VanDorn, whose mother was a daughter of Daniel Polhemus, who owned and lived on the homestead at Phalanx, in Atlantic township, says he often heard his grandfather tell the story of his father, Tobias Polhemus' incarceration in the old sugarhouse prison during our revolutionary war. It happened that Garret Wyckoff of this county, was a prisoner at the same time. He was a warm friend of Tobias Polhemus. It happened that he had often entertained at his home a peddler who resided in New York city. This man hearing of their wretched situation managed to introduce from time to time provisions to Garret Wyckoff, who generously shared them with Mr. Polhemus. This timely supply barely saved them from starvation. So emaciated did they become that Mr. Polhemus, when released, could span his waist with his two hands. He said more Americans were killed by disease and starvation in this prison and the prison ships than fell in battle from bullets of the enemy.

Among the citizens of this county who have borne the Polhemus name, were two who commanded extraordinary respect and regard, Dr. Daniel Polhemus, who practiced medicine at Englishtown and died there March 1, 1858, and Henry D. Polhemus, who was Surrogate of this county from 1833 to 1848. David S. Crater, our present Surrogate, told the writer that the records show that he was strict, accurate and methodical; in short, one of the best surrogates the county ever had. He was a man of fine appearance, very pleasant and gentlemanly and almost idolized by the people of Monmouth county. He belonged, however, to the Somerset branch.

The reader will notice how the names

"Tobias" and "Daniel" appear from generation to generation as Christian names. This fact was noticed over a century ago by some unknown rhymnster, who put his observations into the following doggerel, which has been remembered because it expresses a truth, although the poet's name is forgotten:

By Koert or Ruliff, a Schenck you may know,
Chrineyonce or Cyrenius with VanMater doth go.
Garret or Jacob is a Couwenhoven name,
From generation to generation always the same.

Tobias or Daniel, without feathers or fuss,
Marks the kind and gentle Polhemus.
Simon and Peter a Wyckoff does show,
Nor will they deny 'till a rooster doth crow.

Whether the present and future generations will continue to use those old names, is uncertain, for we are living in a transition age when change seems to be in the very air. Old customs and well established principles are overturned for the mere sake of change or something new.

Chrineyonce, son of John Schenck and Neeltje Bennett, his wife, married November 20, 1793, Margaret Polhemus, who was born March 11, 1766, and died January 13, 1857. Their children were:

Mariah, b. February 2, 1795, married Garret Rezo Conover, a well known farmer who lived near Edinburg in what is now Atlantic township. She died December 5, 1830.

John C., b. June 2, 1797, died August 22, 1799.

Ellen and Eliza were twins, b. March 2, 1799. Eliza died in infancy. Ellen married Jonathan I. Holmes and died September 17, 1877.

Margaret, b. May 12, 1800, died March 10, 1835, unmarried.

John C., b. June 6, 1803, married Margaret Polhemus and died August 13, 1858.

Daniel Polhemus, b. May 12, 1805, married first November 30, 1831, Lydia H. Longstreet, who was born December 18, 1809, and died April 7, 1838; married second Mary Conover, October 10, 1843. She was born June 8, 1822, died April 4, 1890. He died December 29, 1864.

Abigail, b. April 28, 1808, died May 30, 1825, unmarried.

Daniel Polhemus Schenck and Lydia H. Longstreet, his first wife, had the following children:

Ellen L., b. November 2, 1832, married July 3, 1860, Stacy P. Conover, and died without children, August 18, 1890. Her husband was born June 5, 1828, and died on his farm near Wickatunk station, Marlboro township, August 18, 1896. He was a man of fine presence, commanding stature, with pleasant, genial manners and was well known throughout New Jersey and New York city. He was deeply interested in and always attended the meetings of the New York Holland society.

Chrineyonce, b. February 21, 1838, died February 17, 1839.

By his second wife, Mary Conover, he had the following children:

Lydia Hendrickson, b. July 30, 1846, married December 6, 1870, Dr. Charles A. Conover, a physician who settled at Marlboro. He was born February 13, 1842, died November 2, 1882, without children.

John C., b. February 21, 1848, married December 6, 1871, Charlotte L. Conover, who was born September 28, 1849.

Eliza V., b. January 5, 1850, married January 7, 1874, Henry D. VanMater, who was born August 11, 1851.

Margaret Polhemus, b. March 27, 1854, married December 20, 1875, William H., a son of the late Tunis VanDerveer DuBois, one of the most successful and prosperous farmers in the township of Marlboro, during the greater part of his life. William H. DuBois was born February 9, 1851, and has two children by this marriage, viz: Jennie S. and Daniel Schenck.

John C. Schenck and Charlotte L. Conover, his wife, have had the following children

Mary C., b. October 26, 1872, married August 7, 1896, William Lefferts Brown.
John L. C., b. May 14, 1874, married November 23, 1897, Matilda C. Carson.
Nellie L., b. October 18, 1875.
Abbie M., b. January 9, 1879.
LuEtta H., b. July 30, 1883, died July 21, 1885.
Mabel I., b. December 23, 1886.
Florence A., b. September 7, 1887.

So far as this branch of the family is concerned we find no divorces, scandals or grass widows. Neither do we find any member but what has been a producer and helped build up farms, making many blades of grass grow where few had grown. Nor one who has lived out of public office by politics but all by the sweat of their brow as tillers of the soil.

RULEFF SCHENCK AND HIS DESCENDANTS.
SOME OF THEIR PECULIAR TRAITS.

As has been stated before, Ruleff, the only surviving son of Hendrick Schenck and Catherine Holmes, his wife, married December 22, 1774, his first cousin, Sarah, daughter of John Schenck, who lived and died on the homestead farm in Pleasant Valley. Ruliff Schenck lived and died on his farm adjacent to Bradevelt station, and was buried in the Schenck Couwenhoven burying ground. His children were:

Nellie, b. August 24, 1775, married January 18, 1795, Thomas Shepard or Shepherd. They removed to and settled in Ohio.

Hendrick, b. June 13, 1777, died single December 27, 1812.

Mary, b. June 15, 1779, married July 1, 1798, Elias Conover, died December 17, 1851. She was buried by her husband and sons in the yard of Brick church. They were the parents of three sons, viz:

John E., who owned and lived on the farm lying west of Marlboro Brick church, formerly the parsonage farm of this church.

After his death his son, Daniel P. Conover, owned and occupied it. He was well known to present generation and only died lately.

Hendrick E., who lived the latter part of his life in the town of Freehold, was well known to all our citizens for his quiet, unobtrusive manners and his irreproachable life and conduct. He owned two of the finest farms in Marlboro township, one of which includes the famous "Topanemus" burying ground. He left only one son, John B. a licensed lawyer of this state and at one time chosen freeholder of this township. He was also an elder of the Presbyterian church of Freehold.

Ruliff E. Conover lived and died on his farm in Marlboro township, now owned and occupied by his son, Holmes R. Conover, who married Ada B., the daughter of John Buckelew and his wife, Mary A. Griggs. Ruliff E. Conover had three other sons who are now deceased. They were:

Elias R., who married Mary Ann Wyckoff and left one son, Peter Wyckoff, who still owns the farm where his father lived, adjacent to Holmes R. Conover's farm.

John R., who married Mary Jane VanKirk, and Hendrick R., who married Anna Gussie VanWickle. The last two sons died childless.

John R., b. May 3, 1781, married Margaret, daughter of Roelof P. Schenck and Elizabeth Gordon, his wife; died August 14, 1858.

Because of his stout, broad and barrel like form he was called "Chunky John Schenck." He was also famous for his original ideas, independent ways, mechanical skill and inflexible resolution. One of his daughters married Hon. William Spader of Matawan. at one time lay judge of the Monmouth county courts and well and favorably known throughout this county. He left three sons surviving him, John, Daniel and Providence, who lived on the homestead farm he devised to them. None of them married. They were men who thought and acted for themselves without regard to the usages and customs of other people. Strictly honest and truthful in their dealings, they gave employment to many men and made their money out of the soil. They were a great deal better and more useful citizens than many of the "Quid Nuncs" who talked about them behind their backs and anticipated the judgment of Heaven on them after they were dead. Some of the people who thus condemned them, had beams as big as a "telephone pole" in their eye compared with the mote in John's, Daniel's and Providence's eyes.

Jonathan R., b. December 15, 1782, married Sarah Peacock, died January 16, 1864, leaving one son, Elias, who lived and died on his father's farm in Marlboro township. Many anecdotes are also told of this Jonathan R. Schenck.

Katherine, b. November 25, 1785, married December 16, 1806, Peter VanKirk; died March 31, 1871. John VanKirk, who now owns and occupies the farm adjacent to "Old Scots Burying Ground" and who married a daughter of the late

John Segoine of Smithburg, is a grandson.

Sarah, b. August 16, 1787, married January 6, 1807, Garret I. Conover, died August 16, 1875.

Jacob, b. August 12, 1789, died November 15, 1790.

Jacob, b. September 13, 1793, died unmarried December 22, 1859. He devised his farm which lay between the farms of his two brothers, John R. and Tylee, to the two youngest grandsons of his sister Mary, wife of Elias Conover, viz: Hendrick R. and Holmes R. Conover. Holmes R. quit claimed to his brother Hendrick, who devised it to his widow in fee simple. She now owns it.

Lydia, b. June 25, 1795, married April 4, 1815, Garret Schenck. They removed to and settled in the state of Ohio.

Anne, b. November 26, 1797, married September 27, 1814, J. Schuyler Walter, died May 8, 1874.

Tylee, b. October 27, 1799, married Eleanora, a daughter of John Schuyler Schenck, died June 24, 1854, leaving two daughters surviving him, both of whom married Asher H. Holmes, who now occupies the homestead farm in Marlboro township. The house which Tylee Schenck built is still standing and is very pleasantly situated on a knoll, on the west side of the turnpike from Freehold to Matawan. The barns and outbuildings are among the best in the county, and kept cleaner than some people's dwellings. The dwelling house and grounds are particularly noticeable for the neat and orderly condition they always present. John R. Schenck, Jonathan Schenck and Tylee Schenck are all buried in the yard of the Brick church. Hendrick Schenck and Jacob Schenck are buried in the old yard in Pleasant Valley where their forefathers are all buried.

The house in which John R. Schenck lived was planned and built by him and is yet standing. It has probably been talked about and excited more curiosity than any dwelling house ever erected in this county. The stairway was constructed from a solid log and the whole house put together in the most durable and solid manner. A great fence some twelve feet high surrounded the house. The palings were fastened with bolts and screws.

While John R. Schenck never meddled in other people's business, neither did he permit anyone to interfere with him. He strongly objected to any one shooting or killing birds, rabbits or other game on his premises. He insisted that life was as dear to them as to the hunters who killed them.

A German from New York City not knowing his character, came one day on his farm with dog and gun. Mr. Schenck, hearing a report of the gun, went to him and told him to go off, as he allowed no shooting on his farm. The German refused to go, whereupon he was told that if he shot a single bird or rabbit on that farm he would be shot. This threat was greeted with a laugh of derision and to show his utter contempt, he proceeded at once to shoot and kill a robin. Hardly had the report of his gun died away when Mr. Schenck fired a load of shot in his legs. As he fell Mr. Schenck said "Now you know how a bird feels and if you ever shoot another on these premises I will shoot higher." The wound was not serious, but after this the wild game was not molested on that farm.

The lightning struck and burned his barns for two successive years. He then erected small barns in different fields all over his farm. When the next thunder shower came over he stood in his doorway and shaking his clenched hand at the sky exclaimed "Strike away, you can't hit more than two this time." Some of his superstitious neighbors talked a great deal about this incident and accused him of defying "High Heaven" and forthwith adjudged him to be a "very wicked man." Mr. Schenck was a man of strong rugged sense and knew that electricity like the winds and frost, was an element of nature and when he thought he had circumvented their destructive forces he naturally exulted over it. It is also said that he succeeded in inventing "a perpetual motion machine." I cannot say as to this, although he was remarkably skillful and ingenious in the use of tools. This talent seems a natural one with the Schencks. As much so as singing or music is a talent with a Smock, and physics or medicine is with a Vanderveer.

Very few Smocks but are natural singers or musicians, or as was said by another many years ago:

"A hardy Smock who cannot sing
Is rare as a bird without a wing,
A brass bell that will not ring."

Among the stories told of his brother, Jonathan R. Schenck, is the following: He had a tombstone made and put up with inscriptions all complete except the date of his death. He selected a quiet spot on his farm for its location. He would often go out and look at it. One day a neighbor came along and asked why he had put up a tombstone

The dwelling house of John Polhemus, son of Daniel and Margaret Polhemus, at Scobeyville, N. J.

Headstone at grave of Catherine Schanck in Schanck-Covenhoven Yard.

Photograph taken in 1899.

before he was dead: "For begad you see, when I die my boys may get at loggerheads and then the rascally lawyers will get them into law, and use up all my property, and so you see poor old Jonathan won't get any tombstone, at all, at all, you see, for begad, unless I put it up myself and so make sure of it."

The third surviving son of Jan Schenck and Sara Couwenhoven, his wife, as heretofore stated, was Peter. By his first wife, Jannetje VanNostrand or VanOstrandt, he had the following children:

Williamtje, baptized August 29, 1731, died young.
Jan, baptized June 10, 1733.
Williamtje, haptized April 6, 1735, married Elbert Williamson.
Sara, baptized July 17, 1737.
Peter, baptized February 24, 1740.
Mary, baptized April 25, 1742.

I think this son Peter, was the justice of the peace whose name appears frequently in our court records during and after the revolutionary war. I am not sure, however, of this.

By his second wife, Jannetje Hendrickson, (maiden name) widow of Roelof Jacobse Couwenhoven, whom he married in 1747, he had the following children:

Roelof P., baptized January 22, 1749, married Elizabeth Gordon.
Jannetje, baptized July 28, 1751, married John Walter, December 5, 1769.
Leah, baptized November 9, 1755.
Francyntje, baptized March 7, 1762.
Antje, baptized September 30, 1763, married Garret Conover.

Jan, son of Roelof Schenck, (black Roelof) and Geesie Hendrickson, his wife, married November 26, 1740, Jacominkey, daughter of Cornelius Couwenhoven and Margaretta Schenck, his wife. He died June 27, 1749, before his father. Their children were:

Roelof, baptized September 19, 1742.
Cornelius, baptized October 12, 1744.
Sara, baptized September 21, 1746.
Geesie, baptized October 23, 1748.

THE MASTERFUL CHARACTERISTICS OF THE DUTCH WOMEN.

While speaking of the men of these Dutch families, we must not forget the women. The woman was indeed the "King Pin," or rather the "Queen Pin,' around whom the whole family life, past, present and future revolved. The old Roman historians, when describing the Teutonic tribes, often mention, as something very singular, the consideration and respect shown by these "Barbarians" to their women, that they were treated as the equals and in some cases as the superiors of the men. In important affairs the women were not only consulted but were entrusted with the management of them. Sometimes they led the men in battle. Among the Orientals and Latin races, females were treated as the inferiors of the males; as untrustworthy and on the level with children. They were caged in harems among the Orientals, and secluded behind barred windows and doors among the Spaniards, Italians and other Latin peoples. The Batavians or Fresians, from whom the Netherland people spring, belonged to the Teutonic race, and their regard and respect for women was a national characteristic. During the long war with Spain the Holland women often fought in the front ranks, side by side with their fathers, brothers, sons and husbands.

During the sieges of some of the cities when people fell dead from starvation in the streets, and when it seemed as if human beings could not endure further suffering, the women encouraged the men to hold out and suffer death before surrendering to the hated Spaniard. Another trait of the Dutch women which is always noticed and commented upon by travellers through Holland, is their extreme cleanliness. Sweeping, washing, mopping and scrubbing form a passion with them.

Cleanliness is said to be next to godliness. If this saying is true then the Holland woman must "take the cake" for superlative piety. Among the farm houses scattered through Pleasant Valley, Atlantic, Marlboro and other townships and occupied by the descendants of the Dutch, these same traits have been noticed about the women folks. To soil the kitchen floor was deemed a serious matter, and the men in some houses were required to take off their boots or shoes before stepping over the sill of the kitchen door.

House cleaning two or three times a year was a solemn and important work, especially so, if it was suspected that a bed-bug had effected an entrance into the domicile. Then the "huisvrouw" was up in arms. An angry frown marred her usually placid features and her tongue clattered all day like the machinery in a grist mill, giving commands, orders, and urging "all hands" to the work of hunting out and exterminating the pestiferous insects. The house, from foundation to turret, was deluged with floods of water and soap-suds, so that the men folks had no dry place where they could place their feet. They thereupon retreated to the barn or wagon house to get a little peace and comfort, from the fierce rushing to and fro of the angry vrouw and the ceaseless clatter of her tongue. The bed clothes were also inspected with a microscopic eye. The bedsteads all taken apart, the furniture all moved, the carpets all taken up, and beat and beat and beat, and then hung on a line outdoors for the free winds to blow away what little dust there was left. In short, the whole house was turned topsy turvy and there was no rest, peace or comfort for anybody, but more especially for the unfortunate bed bug, who wished he had never been born. After the whole house had thus been deluged and scrubbed, if the vrouw still suspected there was yet a solitary bed bug lurking in a deep crack of the floor or walls, she brought up her heavy artillery in the shape of scalding water and bed-bug poison, and poured that into his hiding place, until the miserable insect gave up the ghost. Then and not till then, did "order reign in Warsaw." After the whole house had been thoroughly swept and garnished and white wash applied from cellar to garret and the furniture all polished and varnished, returned to its usual place, were the "men folks" allowed any peace or comfort. The long exile was then over and once more the "good man" of the house could comfortably sit in his chair by the chimney corner and smoke his pipe. Among these families the real "boss" was the vrouw.

The very name "huisvrouw" means the "woman of the house or home." Her authority was absolute in the home. No one dared to dispute her edicts, for a woman can scold with more terrific effect in the Low Dutch language than in any other. A true story is told of a Mrs. Benjamin Van-Cleaf or Cleef which will illustrate the power and authority of the wife. During the early part of the present century many of our school teachers were Irishmen. They were paid by the parents of the children. It was greatly to their interest to have all the children sent it was possible to get. This Irish teacher taught school at or near the old Tennent church. Benjamin Van-Cleaf lived some two or three miles from the school house and had a large family of boys and girls, all of whom were under eighteen years of age. The Irishman had no personal acquaintance with him, but hearing about his family called at his residence in order to persuade him to send his children to his school. A colored man, who had long been a slave in Mr. VanCleaf's family, came to the door and upon his inquiring for the master of the house, was informed that he was not at home. Thinking he could learn something from the old negro the Irishman slipped a silver shilling in his hand, and then asked how he could induce Mr. VanCleaf, the boss, to send his children to the school in question. "Ah," said the old slave, "you go an' see de vrouw. She is de real boss. Mr. VanCleaf is only called de boss. You git on de right side of de vrouw fust an' you hab no trouble den." The shrewd Irishman took the darkey's advice and secured all the children.

To show the respect and regard in which the women were held, look at our court records of criminal cases in Monmouth county for the past two centuries, and I doubt if you could find a single case where a white man of true Dutch descent, has ever been indicted for striking or beating his wife. At least I have never seen or heard of any such case. The vrouw was the ruler of the home and inmates. The parlor was her throne room, a place kept sacred from all common uses. Closed and darkened, except when respectable company came or when the damsel of the house was visited by an approved suitor for her hand. Here before the open fireplace, in which the fire cheerily blazed and sent its dancing light and genial warmth through the room, the young couple took their seats on each side of the hearth to spend the long winter evening, in courtship.

The young "Lochinvar" would gradually hitch his chair nearer and nearer to the blooming and blushing fraulein, if she did not move away, his chair, before the long winter evening wore away, would get very close to hers, and before he hardly realized it he was tied hand and foot in the matrimonial knot. His liberty was gone. He was engaged After the wedding feast the parlor was sternly closed to him, for he was one of the family and only entitled to the same usage.

The huisvrouw with her store of household linen, her heavy blankets, home woven, her patchwork quilts, with more colors than Joseph's famous coat, and many other household articles were also prepared and laid away to start her daughter in housekeeping.

The parlor was the trap in which many a roystering, devil-may-care, hot-headed young Dutchman was caught in the marriage noose and compelled to settle down as a sedate, meek and docile married man. Thenceforth he was ruled by the vrouw and his mother-in-law. Yet his lot was by no means an unhappy one. The great majority of the Schencks, Conovers, VanCleafs, VanBrockles, Gulicks and others of the Van name, had wives of unadulterated Dutch blood, on the farms of Monmouth county during the past generations, and were truly described as follows:

"She will do him good and not evil all the days of her life."

"She seeketh wool, and flax, and worketh willingly with her hands."

* * * * *

"She riseth also while it is yet night, and giveth meat to her household, and a portion to her maidens."

"She stretcheth out her hand to the poor; yea, she reacheth forth her hands to the needy."

* * * * *

"She looketh well to the ways of her household, and eateth not the bread of idleness."

"Her children arise up, and call her blessed; her husband also, and he praiseth her."

THE SIX CONOVER BROTHERS AND FOUR CONOVER SISTERS.

In one of my former articles I inadvertently stated that the three Conover brothers who married Schenck wives were the only original settlers of this name. I should have said that they were the only brothers who married in the Schenck family, and were likely the first ones to come here with the two Schenck brothers. As a fact there were six Conover brothers and four sisters, who were all born in Kings county, Nassau Island, as Long Island was then called, and removed to Monmouth county.

They were the children of William Gerritse Cowenhoven, who resided for a number of years in Brooklyn. He was a magistrate there in the years 1661-62-64, and a deacon of the Dutch church in 1663. From there he removed to Flatlands. His name appears as a resident and freeholder of that place, on the assessment rolls of 1675-83-93. He was also an elder of the Dutch church there in 1677. Nov. 1, 1709, he sold his farm at Flatlands to his son William, and is supposed to have spent his declining years among his ten children in Monmouth county.

William Gerritse Couwenhoven was born in year 1636. He married for his first wife Altje, daughter of Joris Dirckse Brinckerhoff. On 12th of February, 1665, he married his second wife, Jannetje, daughter of Pieter Monfoort. By his first wife he had two sons.

Garret.

Joris, or George, who married Alletta Luyster, or, as spelled on Brick church records, Altige Luyster, where they became communicants in 1731.

By his second wife he had eleven children:

Altje, b. Dec. 14, 1665, married Cornelius VanAertsdalen.

Neeltje, b. Dec. 7, 1667, married John Pieterse Wyckoff.

Peter, b. Feb. 12, 1671, married Patience, daughter of Elias Daws.

Cornelius, b. Nov. 20, 1672, (according to Teunis G. Bergen), married Margaretta Schenck, Sept. 8, 1700. According to inscription on his tombstone in the Schenck-Couwenhoven burying ground, Pleasant Valley, he died May 16, 1736, aged 64 yrs., 5 mos., 17 days. This would place his birthday back in 1671. As his brother Peter is said to have been born in 1671, there is a mistake either in Mr. Bergen's record or in the tombstone record. His wife, Maragreta, as spelled on her tombstone, died Dec. 6, 1751, aged 73 yrs., 9 mos., 27 days.

Sarah, b. Jan. 6, 1675, m. Jan Schenck.
Albert, b. Dec. 7, 1676, m. Neeltje Schenck.
Jacob, b. Jan. 29, 1679, m. Sarah Schenck.
Jan, b. Apr. 9, 1681, m. Jacoba VanDerveer.
Annatie, b. Apr. 13, 1683, m. Aert Williamson.

William, b. Mar. 7, 1686, m. Annatie Lucasse Voorhees.

Jacomina, b. Dec. 28, 1689, m. Elbert Williamson.

Garret, William and Altje were the only ones who did not come to Monmouth county. Cornelius, Jacob and

Albert came first, then Peter, Jan and Joris. Sarah and Neeltje, of the daughters came first, as their names appear among the communicants of the Brick church as early as 1709, while their sisters, Annatie and Jacomina appear in 1717.

Joris or George Couwenhoven, who married Alletta or Altje Luyster, although the eldest of all the sons who came to Monmouth, was the last one to come. He evidently had children born before he took up his residence in this county. The Brick church records show the baptism of the following children of George Couwenhoven and his wife, Aletta Luyster.

Elizabeth, b. Mar. 18, 1725. She married May 7, 1747, John Smock, and died May 7, 1812. She and her husband are interred in the Smock burying ground, on the farm formerly owned by Peter R. Smock, the father of ex-sheriff Rulief P. Smock, in Holmdel township.

John Smock and Elizabeth Smock had the following children:

Mary, b. Mar. 20, 1748.
Hendrick, b. Dec. 31, 1749.
Joris, b. June 9, 1751, died young.
Joris, b. Dec. 22, 1754.
Neeltje, b. Nov. 21, 1756.
Sara, b. July 30, 1758.
Caterina, b. Apr. 27, 1760.
Johannes, b. Jan. 19, 1764.
Roelif, b. Nov. 20, 1769.

In Book E of Deeds, page 226, Monmouth clerk's office, is record of a deed dated Dec. 9, 1712, from Capt. John Bown, merchant, of Middletown township, to Johannes Smock, late of Staten Island, New York, for 230 acres in Middletown township and four acres of salt meadow at Shoal Harbor. Ramenessin brook is called for as one of the boundaries of the 230 acre tract.

Joris Couwenhoven had the following children baptized after Elizabeth, wife of John Smock:

Cornelius, bapt. July 2, 1727.
Daughter, not named, bapt. Jan. 1, 1729.
Peter, baptized Mar. 31, 1731.

We also find in these records a Garret Couwenhoven and his wife, Sarah Traphagle (Traphagen), had a son named Joris, baptized Oct. 26, 1746. Aletta Luyster appears as sponsor. As this Garret Couwenhoven cannot be accounted for among the children of the other brothers, and the coincidence of name also agreeing with Joris Couwenhoven's family, we think it reasonable to say that he was a son of Joris Couwenhoven and his wife, Aletta Luyster, born prior to their removal to Monmouth county.

In Book H of deeds, page 152, Monmouth Clerk's office, is record of a deed dated May 6, 1729, from John Antonides, miller, and Johanna, his wife, of Freehold township, to George Couwenhoven, yeoman, of Middletown township, for 105 acres in Freehold township. This is about all the definite information the writer has of Joris Couwenhoven.

As to the other five brothers, who took up their residence in Monmouth county the records are clear and certain. I will take them up in the order of their respective ages.

Peter Couwenhoven married Patience, daughter of Elias Daws, and is said to have settled somewhere in what is now Manalapan township. His Dutch Bible, a very precious book to him, is now in the possession of Mrs. Lydia H. S. Conover, who has kindly furnished me with names and dates of births of his children as follows:

Hannah or Johanna, b. Sept. 26, 1695, m. John, a son of Rev. Vincentius Antonides, a Dutch clergyman, sent out by Classis of Amsterdam to supply the churches in Brooklyn, Flatbush and Flatlands. The quarrel between him and Rev. Bernardus Freeman, who had been commissioned by Lord Cornbury as pastor of these same churches fills many pages of the early history of teh Dutch churches in Kings county, L. I.

Jane, b. July 28, 1697, married ―――― Williamson.
Alice, b. Sept. 28, 1699, died young.
Mary, b. July 25, 1701, m. Koert Gerritse Schenck.
William, b. July 11, 1703, m. Mary Calyer or Colyer and died May 3rd, 1777. Mary, his wife, died January 30, 1777, in her 70th year. Both were buried in Tennent church cemetery.
Altje, b. May 21, 1705, m. Jan. 16, 1730. Her cousin, William Williamson, who was born Feb. 18, 1709, died April 22, 1788. He was a son of Aert Williamson and Annetie Couwenhoven, his wife.
Elias, known in after life as "Ensign Elias," was born Sept. 12th, 1707, m. Williamsee, daughter of John Wall, died Dec. 25, 1750. His wife died March 24th, 1759, aged about 58 years. Both are interred in the Schenck-Couwenhoven burying ground, Pleasant Valley.
Neeltje, b. Sept. 2, 1709.
Peter, b. June 27, 1712, married his cousin, Leah, Janse Schenck, and removed to state of New York.
Anney, b. Sept. 29, 1714, m. John Longstreet, son of Adriaan Langstraat and Christina Janse, his wife. He was baptized Jan. 13, 1712, and married Anne Couwenhoven Dec. 17, 1746.

Pieter Couwenhoven, the father of these ten children, made his will March 15, 1743. It was proved April 23, 1755, and is on record at Trenton, N. J., in Book F of Wills, page 259, etc. He names in this will his wife, Patience, his sons Peter, William and Elias, whom he also appoints executors, and his daughters, Hannah Antonides, Jane Williamson, Mary Schenck, Aeltje Williamson and Ann Longstreet. He was an active member of the Dutch church and served as elder in 1711-21. I do not know where he is buried.

His son Elias, called "Ensign Elias," who married Williamsee Wall, was the father of Col. John Couwenhoven, who was born March 8, 1734, married Eleanor Wyckoff and died April 21, 1803. He is interred in yard of Marlboro Brick church. He represented Monmouth county in the Provincial Congress of this state and was a member of Council of Safety during years 1775-76. He seems to have been one of the trusted leaders of the people in Monmouth county, at the very beginning of the stormy days of our Revolutionary war. The following resolutions representing the views of the patriots in Freehold township are closely associated with his name, if indeed he was not the author and mover of them.

It required great courage and devotion to the people's cause for a man at that time to speak out so plainly.

At a meeting of the freeholders and inhabitants of the township of Lower Freehold, in the county of Monmouth in New Jersey, on Monday, the 6th day of June, 1774, after notice given of the time, place and occasion of the meeting.

RESOLVED, That it is the unanimous opinion of this meeting, that the cause in which the inhabitants of the Town of Boston are now suffering, is the common cause of the whole continent of North America, and that unless some general and positive measures for the public safety be speedily entered into, there is just reason to fear that every province may in turn share the same fate with them; and that, therefore, it is highly incumbent on them all to unite in some effectual means to obtain a repeal of the Boston Port Bill, and any other that may follow it, which shall be deemed subversive of the rights and privileges of free born Americans. And that it is also the opinion of this meeting, that in case it shall appear hereafter to be consistent with the general opinion of the trading towns and the commercial part of our countrymen, that an entire stoppage of importation and exportation from and to Great Britain and the West Indies, until the said Port Bill and other acts be repealed, will be really conducive to the safety and preservation of North America and her liberties, they will yield a cheerful acquiesence in the measure and earnestly recommend the same to all their brethren in this province.

RESOLVED moreover, That the inhabitants of this township will join in an association with the several towns in the county and in conjunction with them, with the several counties in the province (if we doubt not, they see fit to accede to this proposal) in any measures that may appear best adapted to the weal and safety of North America and her loyal sons.

Then follows the names of the seven persons appointed as a committee of Freehold township to carry said resolutions into effect. Among them appears the names of Hendrick Smock and Capt. John Couwenhoven.

A month later still stronger resolutions were passed, and we find his name again among the committee. Also in the proceedings of the Congress of New Jersey of the years 1775-76 we find his name prominent. He was the great grandfather of late Hon. Charles H. Conover, who was during the seventies, one of the lay judges of our county courts and who resided on the old Couwenhoven homestead farm in Marlboro township, still (1898) in the family ownership. He was a gentleman of reserved and retiring manners, but upright and faithful in the discharge of private and public duties, and consistent and reliable in his business dealings.

The writer for several years was brought in close contact with him, and learned to respect him for many excellent traits of mind and heart.

ODDITIES AND PECULIARITIES OF THE DUTCH PEOPLE AND THEIR DESCENDANTS IN MONMOUTH.

To understand the character and peculiarities of the different races and people who settled these United States, it is necessary to consider the nationality from which each one springs. Children of the same parents often differ greatly in appearance and conduct. Sometimes they inherit the physical or mental traits of a remote progenitor, but we may generally expect them to exhibit more or less of the characteristics of the nation from which they originate. Today we have in our country representatives of all the races and nations of the world. Never before in all times, was there such a heterogeneous population. But among them all there is no people who have more distinct and marked characteristics than the Hollanders. They belong to a very ancient race, whose known history goes back to the days of Julius Caesar and Pompey. In the battle of Pharsalia the Batavians took a prominent part, as we learn from Roman history. The Hollanders are a people who have ever acted and thought for themselves. They have never been imitators or sycophants. On the contrary, they are truly said to be the oddest people in Europe. Everything in Holland is different from what it is in other countries. Even their morsel of territory is neither water nor dry land. Only by the most herculean labors has it been wrested from the ocean, and by unceasing vigilance is it preserved from the constant assaults of the waves. The reader, therefore, can easily see how likely it is for strangers, who travel hastily through the country to make many mistakes in describing or understanding such a people. We are all apt to estimate others by our own experience. The venal man loudly asserts that "every man has his price." The honest man falls an easy victim to the plausible talk of the "confidence man."

The English writers and those of the same school in America, often describe the Dutch as a plegmatic people, as slow, sluggish or torpid. It is true that they are a quiet, grim and taciturn people. It would be strange if they were not, when we recall the wonderful achievements of the little country, about the size of New Jersey, and ever in danger of inundation. "That beats the Dutch" has become a proverb, when some skillful or remarkable work has been done. The love of truth and justice is said to be a national trait. As a fact there is less crime in Holland, according to her population, than in any other European country. They have especially prized liberty and independence. That industry, so noticeable in Holland, where even the dogs are trained to work, is based on this intense love of "independence."

They know, as was said of old by the wise king of Israel, that there can be no true and permanent independence without industry. The primeval curse still continues that man must earn lasting bread by "the sweat of his brow" and not by spoils taken in Wall street or watering railroad stocks or patent medicines. To avoid, however, the charge of partiality, or exaggeration, I will quote from the writings of a Frenchman and an Englishman, for the writers of both of these nations have been very keen to see the faults and failings of the "Low Dutch." "If this is not true, you can call me an Englishman," is an expression very often used by certain English writers, except you must substitute Dutchman for Englishman. But it shows their animus and the lofty contempt and scorn.

The following is from the pen of Henri Alphonse Esquiros, entitled, "Dutch at Home." "It has long been remarked how naturally a pipe hung from a Dutch mouth; and most local habits are based on hygenic conditions of climate. Beneath the foggy sky of the Netherlands, a necessity was felt to produce smoke against smoke. It is a sort of local homeopathy. Some physical writers have asserted that tobacco smoke befogged the intellect; but this observation is contradicted by the Dutchmen, who live in a climate of smoke and whose minds are more precise, positive and clear in their details, than those of any other people.

"In Holland we find what thinkers born in periods of moral agitation never attain, and what Dante sought—peace. It is not rare to notice in little wayside hostelries, the inscription, "Pax Intrantibus." We might say that life is like the water in their canals, it does not flow. Be it illusion or reality, it seemed to us that the hours strike here more slowly than in France, and are ushered into life with a song. The whole character of old Holland is found in these solemn peals, in those aeolian voices which the fathers heard, and which the sons will hereafter hear.

"At Utrecht, a thoroughly protestant town, the chimes played a hymn according to the Reformed ritual. This Puritan gentleness, the notes of which the beels dash out in the air harmonizes with the calm and reposed hues of the scenery. The gardens which border the water are kept up. gravelled and raked with extreme care, and trees loaded with fruit ofter pleasing variety to the slightly monotonous character of the verdure." According to this French writer, contentment and peace prevail among the people of this land, and each one is not trying to exceed or beat his neighbor, or discontented because some one else has a few more dollars than he has. Peace, quiet and contentment, while easily mistaken for, are very different from the apathy and stupidity which come from ignorance and sluggishness. The bustle, excitement and hurry which mark life in America is unknown in Holland. The same slow and sure walk and talk, although modified by modern environments, may be seen in their genuine descendants in America. Washington Irving, in his so called Knickerbocker History of New York has seized upon this trait as one of the principal themes for his pleasantry, ridicule and caricatures. Other English writers have done the same, forgetting that the shallow brook ever makes more noise than the deep and silent river. English austerity and stolidity can be well contrasted with Dutch phlegm and grimness. Occasionally an English writer appears who is able to see some merit in other nations. The following is taken from the London Times of October 23rd, 1888, and is supposed to have been written by an author who has shed his "cockney shell" and dropped his "Lion's skin." He speaks first of the great preparations being made in Holland to celebrate the 75th anniversary of their liberation from French domination, and the re-establishment of their national independence, and then goes on to say:

"No nationality in the world has earned its liberties more worthily than the Dutch or has more right to something of self glorification on the score of it. The land on which it dwells is, if not its own creation, its salvage. Without indefatigable efforts this morsel of territory would have been a barren salt marsh. Human enterprise has reclaimed and guards it and has converted the whole into one of the most productive regions in Europe. Not only has it turned an expanse of foggy unwholesome fens into a vast model farm, but it has built prosperous cities and filled them with the products of art and civilization. The Dutch race has stretched its hands everywhere and the earth is full of evidence of its courage and foresight.

The surprising history of its influence and affluence is essentially connected with its stubborn determination to be independent. It defied the powers of nature, it compelled the old world and the new to pay it tribute; it made itself learned and accomplished, because it felt that it was performing the work for and by itself.

In the history of its rise and fortunes, the maintenance of its independence, with the briefest intervals, is a continual marvel. Swiss independence, with all its great deeds cannot match the tale of the vitality of Dutch Freedom.

A highland people occupies defensive strongholds and has little to provoke covetousness. The Dutch inhabit a country which can be overrun in a week, and perpetually has been overrun. "The Dutch have taken Holland" is a byword the world over, and has been for generations past.

By their industry they rendered it long ago desirable and a constant temptation to those powers who coveted wealth. They have accumulated within its territory incalculable riches, not only of gold and silver and precious stones, but masterpieces of art, ingenuity and patient industry. They also endowed it with a network of valuable external dominions, apparent prizes of their conqueror.

Their maritime enterprise, distant colonies, great mercantile marine, laden with the precious products of the earth, were so many additional temptations to the unscrupulous powers of Europe, who not only hated and feared their Republican and Democratic proclivities, but looked on their little country and small population as easily subjected. In the midst of numberless dangers Dutch independence seems to have borne a charmed life. When they proclaimed their independence of the great Spanish Empire, until then invincible, the first coin struck bore the picture of a ship without sails, masts or rudder, a mere hulk tossing on the mountainous waves of a storm dashed ocean, with the words "In God We Trust." This truly expressed their desperate straits, and that they realized that deliverance could only come from Him Who holds the world in the hollow of His hand.

Feudalism, instead of quenching, like the cruelties of Alva and the tortures of the inquisition, invigorated their love of liberty and independence. While Europe languished under the burden of thousands of petty despots, Holland throve under its counts; Burgundian, Spanish and French rule passed over it, without stifling its free spirit. The oath of the ancient Frisians that "The Frisians would be free as long as the winds of Heaven blow," seems to have been kept in letter and spirit by their descendants. Under a variety of forms of government, the essence of Dutch independence has gone on many centuries, pertinaciously immovable. Only in 1795 was there any serious risk of an extinction of Dutch nationality. Had France employed its armed authority over the country for the simple benefit of the Dutch people, and the building up of a true Republican government, objects which had induced a large part of the Dutch people to co-operate in assuming the French rule, the contagion of French Democratic ideas might have ended in absorbing Holland permanently in the French republic.

Bonaparte's dynastic ambition opened their eyes to the fact that they were regarded as a conquered nation and were in chains to a tyrant, who sought to aggrandize himself at the expense of his wife, his friends, his allies and his country.

For the uplifting of himself as Emperor he abolished the Batavian republic and after four years of his brothers' mock reign incorporated the province of Holland as part of his empire. Up to this time Holland troops and Holland officers, like VanDamm, had served him faithfully. In his disastrous invasion of Russia some of the Holland regiments had perished almost to a man in the performance of duty. Thenceforward it was a mere question of time when the deceived and betrayed people of Holland would throw off the yoke of this Corsican soldier, and assert their independence. The field of Leipsic gave them this opportunity. A month later the Dutch nation declared itself once more free and summoned the Prince of Orange home to lead the movement. Circumstances then aided Holland in its deliverance and in shaking off the French yoke which the Hollanders themselves had originally co-operated in adjusting. Coincidences were equally favorable when its troops marched with those of Marlborough and Eugene. It profited by the great league which William III constructed from the vantage ground of the English throne. Queen Elizabeth and Valois and the Bourbon Kings of France had all helped in its struggle for existence against Philip II but the nationality, too, was constantly on the alert and ready.

Generally it has been the heart and soul of the international combinations for resistance to a crushing monopoly of powers in Europe. European liberties owe yet more to the uncontrollable Dutch love of independence than Dutch independence owes to European succor. The Dutch race are not especially conciliatory, any more than is supposed to be the English. Frequently it has shown itself harsh, as Belgium found between 1814 and 1830. Englishmen have had cause to accuse it of commercial rapacity and exclusiveness. Its handful of people and morsel of territory ever in danger of being swallowed up by the sea, has ever been throughout a palpable and visible unit, which it has been impossible for European countries to ignore and entirely possible for them to obey."

This tribute from a foreign Englishman shows certain characteristics of the Dutch and which their descendants in America should naturally possess. The Dutch farmers of the Transvaal in Africa have exhibited the same spirit in their determined efforts to preserve their independence, and the Dutch settlers of Monmouth showed the same spirit during our revolutionary war.

CORNELIUS COUWENHOVEN OF PLEASANT VALLEY AND HIS CHILDREN.

Cornelius Couwenhoven seems to have been the first one of this name who actually settled in Monmouth county, but there is evidence that one or more of this family had long been familiar with the territory and the Indian inhabitants. As early as 1663 we hear of a Jacob Couwenhoven, who owned a small sloop and who traded with the Indians for venison and furs. The trade with the Indians for peltries and furs was very profitable and extensively carried on by the early Dutch settlers. The Albany records contain an account of an attempt made in 1663 by certain of the English people at Gravesend and other Long Island towns to purchase lands of the Indians, known as the Navesinks, and who occupied part of what is now Monmouth county. The Dutch authorities hearing of this, sent an officer and a few soldiers in a vessel to prevent it. When the boat reached the southern point of Staten Island, opposite the mouth of the Raritan river, they met Jacob Couwenhoven in a small sloop. He informed them that he had been out trading for venison, also that a number of the Navesink and Raritan Indians had gathered at a place about three miles up the Raritan, and that the English, in an open sloop, the day previous had gone up the river to meet them. From this it appears that Jacob Couwenhoven had made former trips across the bay and was well

House erected by Cornelius Covenhoven, the pioneer settler, on his farm at Pleasant Valley in the early part of the eighteenth century.

Photograph taken by Mrs. L. H. S. Conover in summer of 1899.

The ruins of the early home of Cornelius Covenhoven, who married Mary Hendrickson, and called his place "Carroway"
(near Keyport, N. J.)

Photograph taken by Mrs. L. H. S. Conover in July, 1898.

enough acquainted with the Indian inhabitants to distinguish those who lived in what is now Monmouth county from those who lived on the Raritan river. It is more than probable that the ownership of vessel property and the continuance of this traffic with the Indians would remain in the family. The emigration of the Dutch people from King's county, Long Island, to Somerset, Middlesex and Monmouth counties between 1695 and 1730 was quite large. Several vessels must have been employed to transport their household effects, agricultural implements and stock over the water.

Cornelius Couwenhoven, it is said, owned a sloop which he named the "Carroway." It sailed between the East River and some landing, either up Matawan or Waycake creek. His son, William, afterwards owned the boat and no doubt made trips from the Monmouth shore to New York and Kings county whenever there was a necessity for it. In this way an intercourse was kept up with the old people and goods and passengers transported back and forth. I think it likely that sometimes the first settlers, prior to 1709, may have had some of their children baptized in the Dutch churches of Kings county. There was no regular Dutch church minister in Monmouth county until 1709, and, although there may have been an occasional visit by a licensed clergyman, there was no such thing as regular services. It is to be remembered that our early Dutch settlers lived on isolated clearings with the primeval forest all around them. There were no schools for their children. They learned to speak the Dutch language from family intercourse. The children also would hear the uncouth talk of the negro slaves, the broken English of the wild Indians, and the talk of the ignorant Englishman or Frenchman who occasionally visited their home. Thus they gradually fell into a dialect which was impure Dutch, mingled with many English words wrongly pronounced and wrongly spelled. Take the christian names of the children born after 1700 as spelled in their wills or private family records, and you can see how far they had drifted away from the correct Dutch spelling of their own names. We can hardly conceive today the many disadvantages our pioneer settlers labored under.

Cornelius Couwenhoven by his wife, Margaretta Schenck, had the following children:

William, born July 20, 1700, married first Jannetje, daughter of Peter Wyckoff, and Williampe Schenck, his wife. Second Antje, daughter of Daniel Hendrickson and Catharine VanDyke, his wife, and widow of William, son of Jacob Couwenhoven.

He died November 10, 1755, leaving a will dated September 29, 1755, proved December 22, 1755, and recorded in Book F of Wills, page 305, etc., secretary of state's office. He appoints his brother Roliph, and his son-in-law, Matthias "Cownover," as he spells the name, executors. He speaks in this will of his father-in-law, Peter Wyckoff. He signs the will "William C. Kouwenhoven" and describes himself of Carroway, Middletown township. As stated before "Carroway" was the name of his sloop and he called his place by the same name. He only names one son, Cornelius, and two daughters, Williamtie and Catharine, in this will.

Roeleff, born April 12, 1710, married Sarah, daughter of Cornelius Voorhees, and Maritje Ditmars, his wife, and died December 12, 1789.

In Book G of Deeds, page 31, Monmouth clerk's office, is a record of a deed from Alexander Laing of Scotland, Great Britain, to Hendrick VanVoorhies of Flatlands, Kings county, Nassau Island, for such was then the name of Long Island. A tract of land at Topanemes, Freehold township, containing 250 acres is conveyed by this deed. I think this Cornelius Voorhees was a brother of the Hendrick VanVoorhies named in the deed and who actually settled on this land, but I am not certain.

Annetje.
Jannetje, married in 1731, Aris, son of John Vanderbilt and Ida Suydam, his wife.

One of the earliest records we have of the Suydams in Monmouth is in Book G of Deeds, page 74; a deed dated April 1st, 1729, from Thomas Williams to Hendrick Suydam of Flatbush on Long Island, for a tract of land in Freehold township. Then in the same book of deeds, pages 139-141, from Lewis Morris of Manor of Morrisania, in Province of New York, to Ryke Hendrickse, Dominicus Vanderveer, Daniel Polhemus, Jacob Hendrickse, Auke Leffertse, Stephen Coerten and Johannes Polhemus, all of Kings county on Long Island, for a tract of land known as "Fifteen hundred acre tract," bounded on one side by Swimming river, dated May 17, 1709. This Jacob Hendrickse and Ryke Hendrickse were really Suydams, but in accordance with the Dutch custom, they were given their christian names and their father's christian name with "se" or "son" annexed. This clearly appears from a deed recorded in Book H of Deeds, page 211, Monmouth clerk's office, dated June 6, 1727, wherein Ryk Hendrickson Suydam of Flatbush, Kings county, L. I., conveys to John VanMeeteren (VanMater) of Middletown township, Monmouth county, N. J., all that tract of land in Middletown township bounded west by Dominicus Vanderveer, east by Anken Leffertson, south by Swimming river and north by 'heirs of Quryn (Kriin) VanMeeteran (VanMater) and known as No. 4, containing 152 acres. Daniel Polhemus of Flatlands, L. I., by a separate deed conveyed his share to Johannes Polhemus.

Altje, married William, son of first Jacob VanDorn and Marritje Bennett, his wife.

In Book H of Deeds, page 325 we find record of a deed dated December 23, 1689, from John Reid of Hortencia, Monmouth county, to Richard Salter of same county for part of Hortencia. The tract begins where west Branch comes into Hop brook at a place called Promontoria; on page 327 of same book we find record of assignment of same deed from Richard Salter to Adrian Bennett and Jacob VanDorn of "Gawanus," Kings county, L. I. This is dated April 2, 1697.

Again on page 329 of Book H of Deeds is record of a deed from Aria Bennett and Barbary, his wife, of Freehold township, to Jacob VanDorn of same township, dated February 14, 1707, and conveys the undivided one-half of a 200 acre tract in Freehold township, beginning at a corner of Albert Cowenhoven's land and being same premises conveyed to said Bennett and VanDorn by John Bowne May 17, 1700. Also another tract adjacent to this also conveyed to them by John Bowne. I am not sure whether this Aria Bennett was the same person as Adrian Bennett or another. The above deeds however, show the time when the VanDorns and Bennetts came into this county and the place they came from on Long Island.

Leah.
Sarah.
Neeltje, married July 2, 1741, Benjamin, son of Benjamin VanCleaf and "Hank" Sutphin, his wife.

In Book H of Deeds, page 222, is a record of a deed dated May 4, 1725, from John Job of Freehold township to Lawrence VanCleve and Isaac VanCleve of Gravesend, L. I. On our old records the VanCleaf name is spelled many different ways, VanCleaf, VanCleve, etc. This deed, however, shows about what time this family came into the county. In Book G of Deeds, page 50, is record of a deed dated December 6, 1718, from John Johnston of New York City, to Jacob Sutvan (for so the name is spelled) yeoman, of Kings county, L. I., for a tract of land containing 333 acres at a place called "Wemcougak in Freehold towns'hip." Topanemus Brook, Middle Brook and John Craig line are called for as boundaries in the description. This "Sutvan" was no doubt a "Van Sutphen," for so the name is spelled in old records of Kings county, L. I.

Mary, baptized December 24, 1710.

The first Dutch church of Monmouth had been regularly organized with a stated pastor, one Joseph Morgan, in 1709, and so we have a record of the children baptized from this time.

Rachel, baptized November 2, 1712.
Margaret, baptized December 5, 1714.
Jacometje, baptized November 23, 1717, married November 26, 1741, Jan Roelefse Schenck.

The youngest child by this marriage was named Geesie after her paternal grandmother. She married May 9, 1765, Aurie, son of second Jacob VanDorn and Maria Schenck, his wife. Aurie VanDorn was born September 14, 1744, died July 14, 1830.

Caterina, baptized June, 1720, married December 22, 1741, Daniel Hendrickson.

Cornelius Couwenhoven, the father of these thirteen children, made his will November 22, 1735, proved June 22, 1736, recorded in office of secretary of state at Trenton in Book C of Wills, page 107. He mentions the names of all of the above children, but the spelling differs considerably from mine. For instance he spells "Jacomintje" "Yacominsky," and "Jannetje" "Yannikie."

He devises to his son William the land sold to him by William Bowne by deeds dated March 1, 1704, and January 20, 1705, one for 94½ acres, and the other 62 acres, and also 120 acres released to him by Daniel Hendrickson, Garret Schenck, John Schenck and Peter Wyckoff, dated July 10, 1716.

Cornelius Couwenhoven and his wife are buried in the Schenck-Couwenhoven burying ground. The inscription on his tombstone shows that 'he died May 16, 1736, aged 64 years, 5 months and 17 days. His wife, Margaretta Schenck, died December 6, 1751, aged 73 years, 9 months and 27 days.

ALBERT COUWENHOVEN AND HIS TWELVE CHILDREN.

Albert Couwenhoven came from Flatlands, L. I., to Monmouth county, and settled on lands in the township of Freehold (now Marlboro) where Mr. Selah Wells now resides. We find his name and that of his wife, Neeltje or Eleanor Schenck, daughter of Roelof Martense Schenck, and his second wife, Annetje Wyckoff, among the communicants of the Brick church in 1709. His Dutch Bible is still in existence with dates of the births of all his sons and daughters entered in his own handwriting. He had the following children:

William, b. March 7, 1702, married Libertje, daughter of Benjamin VanCleaf and Hank Sutphen, his wife. She was baptized May 19, 1705.

He settled in what is now Manalapan township, and left a will recorded in the office of the Secretary of our state.

Ruliff, b. September 8, 1703, married Antje, daughter of Jan Strycker and Margaretta Schenck, his wife. She was baptized December 20, 1708.

Antje, b. August 21, 1705, married Abraham Polhemus, supposed to be of the Somerset county or Long Island people.

Jannetje, b. September 30, 1707, married Joseph Coernel.

Altie, b. January 20, 1709, married Hendrick, son of Hendrick Hendrickson. He was born November 11, 1706, and died July 28, 1783.

In Book G of Deeds, page 59, Monmouth county clerk's office, is record of a deed from Tunis Covert of Freehold township, to Cornelius VanBrunt and Hendrick Hendrickson of New Utrecht of Long Island, for 203½ acres and 96½ acres in Freehold township. On pages 61-62 of same book is record of a deed dated May 1, 1719, from Abraham Emans of Freehold township, to Hendrick Hendrickson and Jaques Denys of New Utrecht, L. I., for a tract of 96 acres in Freehold township. It therefore appears that there were other Hendricksons who purchased land in Monmouth county, besides Daniel and William who came here prior to 1700 and settled on lands at what is now Holland in Holmdel township. The early Dutch settlers were in the habit of visiting once or twice a year their old homes in Kings county, L. I. And mariages likely occurred between the young people here with the young people in Long Island. The Dutch generally preferred to marry among their own people, and it was not often that any of them were caught by the "daughters of Heth," or the sons of the Philistines.

Margaret, b. February 15, 1711, married December 8, 1731, Daniel, son of Johannes Polhemus. He was born in 1706 and died September 26, 1763. She died June 7, 1780.

Both are buried in the family burying ground of the Polhemus family at Scobeyville, Atlantic township.

Sarah, b. June 21, 1714, married May 19, 1737, Johannes, son of Benjamin VanCleaf and Hank Sutphen, his wife. He was baptized June 3, 1711.

Peter, b. October 12, 1716, married May 19, 1740, Wiliampe, daughter of Hendrick VanVoorhees and Jannetje Jansen, his wife. She was born January 25, 1722, died August 12, 1803. He died October 1, 1771; interred in yard of Marlboro Brick church.

Nellie, b. February 7, 1719, died unmarried August 22, 1738. Buried in Schenck and Couwenhoven burying ground.

Garret, b. June 16, 1721, married November 8, 1742, Sarah, daughter of Hendrick VanVoorhees and wife aforesaid.

Jan, b. February 18, 1723, married October 19, 1744, Catherine, daughter of Hendrick VanVoorhees and wife.

Cornelius A., b. October 29, 1728, married in 1750 Antje, daughter of William Williamson and Antje Couwenhoven, his wife. She was born September 13, 1730, and died September 14, 1757, and was buried in Wyckoff I'ill grave yard, near Freehold. He married for his second wife, July 12, 1770, Mary Logan, who was born August 9, 1748, and died May 2, 1831.

The Logan family is now extinct in Monmouth county. Cornelius Couwenhoven died January 23, 1802, leaving a last will proved before Caleb Lloyd, Surrogate of Monmouth county, April 15, 1802, and a true copy of same is given hereafter. Cornelius and his second wife are buried in the Schenck and Couwenhoven burying ground. He had a son named Cornelius, born May 18, 1771, who married Elizabeth, a daughter of Harmon Conover and Phoebe Bailey, his wife, died December 20, 1814. He was also buried in the Schenck Couwenhoven burying ground. His oldest son was named John C. Conover, born November 10, 1797, married December 3, 1820, Elizabeth, a daughter of John A. Vanderbilt and Mary MacKildoe. She was born September 11, 1804, and died January 30, 1860. He was the last owner of the Albert Couwenhoven homestead. He died November 26, 1852, and this farm then passed out of the family.

Albert Couwenhoven and his wife, the parents of the above named twelve children, were buried in the Schenck and Couwenhoven burying ground. He left a last will which is herewith given. Following it is the will of his son Cornelius.

WILL OF ALBERT COUWENHOVEN.

In the name of God Amen, I, Albert Covenhoven, of Freehold, in the county of Monmouth and province of East New Jersey, yeoman, being, thro' the abundant mercy and goodness of God, tho' very sick and weak in body, yet of a sound and perfect understanding and memory, do constitute this my last will and testament, and desire it may be received as such. Imprimis: I most humbly bequeath my soul to God, my maker, beseeching his most gracious acceptance of it thro' the all sufficient merits and mediation of my most compassionate Redeemer, Jesus Christ, who gave himself to be an atonement for my sins, and is able to save to the uttermost all that come unto God by Him; seeing he ever liveth to make intercession for them, and who I trust, will not reject me, a returning penitent Sinner, when I come to Him for mercy. In this hope and confidence I render up my soul with comfort, humbly beseeching the most blessed and glorious Trinity, one God, most Holy, most Merciful and Gracious, to prepare me for the time of my dissolution, and then to take me to himself into that peace and rest and incomparable felicity, which he has prepared for all that love and fear his Holy name, Amen! Blessed be God.

Imprimis: I give my body to the earth, from where it was taken, in full assurance of its resurrection from thence at the last day.

As for my burial, I desire it may be decent, without pomp or state, at the discretion of my executrix and executor hereinafter named, who, I doubt not, will manage it with all requisite prudence. As to my wordly estate, it is my will, and I do hereby order, that in the first place all my just debts and funeral charges to be paid and satisfied out of my movable estate.

Item: I give and bequeath unto Eleanor, my dearly beloved wife, all my whole estate, both real and personal, for her own proper use, benefit and behoof, as long as she remains my widow and no longer.

Item: I give and bequeath unto my eleven well beloved children (viz: William, Ruluf, Anna, Jane, Alice, Margot, Sarah, Peter, Jarratt, John and Cornelius), after the death or widowhood of my dearly beloved wife, all my whole estate, both real and personal, as goods, chattels, lands and tenements, to be equally divided amongst them (my eleven dearly beloved children aforementioned) (viz: William, Ruluf, Anna, Jane, Alice, Margot, Sarah, Peter, Jarratt, John and Cornelius, to them and each of them and their heirs and assigns forever) so that each of them or each of their heirs and assigns hath the eleventh part of my whole estate as above mentioned.

Item: I give and bequeath unto my well beloved son, William, the sum of three shillings as a gift (acknowledging him to be my oldest child) and to be paid to him in a convenient time after my decease. I likewise constitute, make and ordain my dearly beloved wife, Eleanor, and my well beloved kinsman, William Covenhoven, son of Cornelius Covenhoven, my only and sole executrix and executor of this my last will and testament. And I also hereby utterly disallow, revoke and disannul all and every other former testaments, wills, legacies and executors by me in any way before this time, named, willed and bequeathed, ratifying and confirming this, and no other to be my last will and testament. In witness whereof I have hereto set my hand and seal this sixth day of September, in the year of our Lord one thousand seven hundred and forty-eight (1748).

Signed, sealed, published and declared by the said Albert Covenhoven, as his last will and testament in the presence of us, the subscribers (viz:)

"My will and desire is that my well beloved son, Jarratt, have the use of one hundred pounds for ten years, whenever he wants it. This was writ before signing and sealing it being forgot to be mentioned."

    ALBERT COVENHOVEN. [L. S.]

Jan Covenhoven,
Matteys Piterson,
William Williamson.

Be it remembered that on the third day of October, in the year of our Lord one thousand seven hundred and forty-eight, the within witnesses, Jan Covenhoven, Matteys Piterson and William Williamson, personally came before me, Thomas Bartow, duly authorized to prove wills and qualify executors in New Jersey, and they being duly sworn on the Holy Evangelist did depose that they were present and saw Albert Covenhoven, the testator within named, sign and seal the within written testament and heard him publish, pronounce and declare the same to be his last will and testament and at the day thereof the said testator was of sound mind and memory to the best of their knowledge, and as they believed, and that they each signed as a witness in the testator's presence.

    THOS. BARTOW.

Be it also remembered that at the same time Eleanor Covenhoven, the executrix within named, personally came before me and was sworn to the due execution and performance of the within will and testament according to law.

    THOS. BARTOW.

Probate granted by Governor Belcher in the usual form. Dated Oct. 3rd, 1748.

    THOS. BARTOW, Pr. Reg'sr.

The wife of Albert Covenhoven was Neeltje, Dutch for Eleanor or Nelly, daughter of Roelof Schenck of Flatlands, L. I., by his second wife, Annetje Wyckoff.

WILL OF CORNELIUS A. COVENHOVEN.

In the name of God Amen This Eleventh Day of September In the year of Our Lord One Thousand Seven hundred and Ninety-three I Cornelius Covenhoven of The Township of Freehold in The County of Monmouth & State of New Jersey Yeoman Being In health of Body and of Perfect Sound & Disposeing Mind and Memory Praised be Almighty God for the Same, Considering the frailty of Nature and Knowing it is appointed for all men To Die Do Make & Ordain This My Last Will and Testament In the following Manner and form—First I Recomend·My Soul To God Who Gave it Trusting for Salvation In & Through the alone Merits of My Ever Blessed Redeemer· Jesus Christ and as to my Body I recomend it To the Earth To be Interred at the Discretion of My Executors hereinafter named Nothing Doubting but at the General Resurrection I Shall Receive the same again by the Mighty Power of God And as Touching Such Worldly Estate wherewith it Hath Pleased God To Bless me in This Life I Do order, Give & Dispose of The Same in the following Manner—Imprimis I Do order That my Executors Do pay all my Just Debts & Funeral Expenses Out of my Moveable Estate which I may Leve at the time of My Decease —Item I Give & Bequeath To my Loveing Wife Mary Dureing her Widdowhood a Comfortable Liveing as Usual With My Son Cornelius on My said Farm and have the Use of one Room with a Fire Place and Fire wood Brought to her Door one Good Feather Bed & Furniture and One Negro Woman Named Jane so Long as She shall Remain My Widdow and in Case my Said Wife Should Remarry my will is that my said wife have the sum of fifty pounds paid her by me Son Cornelius Current money of the City of New York as all Moneys in this my Will are to be Taken & Esteemed To be, And one feather Bed & furniture In Lieu of her Dower or Thirds—Item I Give and Bequeath To my Daughter Sarah an Out Sett Equal in Vallue To the Out Sett I Gave my Daughter Nell To be Delivered to her by my Executors out of my Moveable Estate at the Time of My Decease. Item—I Give Devise & Bequeath To my Son Cornelius Covenhoven all the Remainder of My Estate Both Real & Personal Wheresoever, To him his Heirs and Assigns forever Provided he Performs & fulfills all the other Matters & Things herein Injoined him in this My Will, (Excepting My Covered Waggon & Horses & Harness & the Remainder of My Horses & Cattle and Such Moveables That I may have and Negroes at the time of My Decece To be Equally Divided amongst my Children, To wit: William, Nelly, Allice, Cornelius & Sarah or their Children) Item it is My will That my said Son Cornelius Do pay the sum of Six Hundred pounds money aforesaid In Manner folling To Wit To allow a Good & Sufficient Support out of said sum for my Son Albert And after the Decease of my Self, my wife and my Son Albert, Whatever Part of said Six Hundred pounds Shall be Remaining Shall be Equally Divided Between my four Children William, Nelly, Allice & Sarah or their Children And Lastly I Do Hereby Nominate, Constitute & appoint My brother in Law, Stoffel Logan & my friend Tobias Polhemus, Executors of this my Last will & Testament Utterly Revokeing & Disannuling all other Wills by me heretofore Made Rattifying & Confirming this & no other to be my last Will & Testament Note the word (form) and the word (of) & the word (Sarah) being Interlined Before Sealing & Delivery hereof

CORNELIUS A. COVENHOVEN.

Signed Sealed pronounced & Declared To be his Last Will & Testament In the Presence of
Garret Covenhoven
Ruth Covenhoven
Joseph Throckmorton

JACOB COUWENHOVEN AND HIS ELEVEN CHILDREN.

Jacob Couwenhoven married at Flatlands, L. I., November 12, 1705, Sarah Schenck, who was baptized in the Dutch church at Brooklyn, December 18, 1685. She too was a resident of Flatlands, and the couple had doubtless known each other from earliest childhood. Jacob Couwenhoven received such education as the schools in Brooklyn at that time could give, and also such as he could pick up from chance associations with the traders, merchants, sailors and emigrants who frequented the harbor of New York. Like his brother Cornelius he is said to have owned a sloop, which made trips from Brooklyn across the bay to the Monmouth shore. It is likely that this was the same boat and owned jointly by two or more of the six Conover brothers. For one boat of this kind would be amply sufficient to transport all their families, goods, chattels and stock, from the shore of the East river over to Monmouth county, and also to take back such peltries, venison and other articles they had to sell and for which a demand existed in the New York markets.

Jacob Couwenhoven, by his wife, Sarah Schenck, had the following children, all of whom are supposed to have been born in his dwelling house which stood on the north side of the street through Middletown village, somewhere between the location of the present Baptist church and the Hartshorne burying ground.

Jannetie, b. December 10, 1706.

Annetje, b. February, 1708, married John, son of Daniel Hendrickson and Catherine VanDyke, his wife.

Daniel Hendrickson, a son of this couple, married Nelly or Eleanor VanMater. She was born August 4, 1735, and died February 12, 1828, and is buried in the Hendrickson burying ground on the farm of the late George Crawford Hendrickson in Middletown village. A son of this last couple, John, born June 13, 1773, married Mary, daughter of John Lloyd, and died in January, 1807. He was the father of the late Charles I. Hendrickson, of John Lloyd Hendrickson and Daniel Hendrickson, who owned the farm now occupied by the Morfords at the eastern end of Middletown village and opposite to the farm owned by his brother, John Lloyd Hendrickson, in his lifetime.

William, b. February, 1710, married Antje, daughter of Daniel Hendrickson and Catherine VanDyke, aforesaid.

She was baptized December 30, 1711. The records in secretary of state's office at Trenton, show that letters of administration on his estate were granted October 17, 1742, to his widow, Ann, his brother Ruliph, and his brother-in-law, William Hendrickson. The Brick Church records show that he had two children baptized, viz: Daniel, March 30, 1737, and Jacob, October 14, 1739. His widow married March 17, 1744, for her second husband William, son of Cornelius Couwenhoven, of Pleasant Valley, and who has been heretofore mentioned as "William C. Kouwenhoven of Carroway." By this last marriage she had three children, (1st) Cornelius, baptized April 7, 1746, married Mary, daughter of Hendrick Hendrickson and Neeltje Garretse Schenck, his wife, and died October 10, 1806; (2nd) Catherine, baptized April 16, 1749; (3rd) Williampe, who married Martin or Matthias Couwenhoven, a brother of her mother's first husband and hereinafter particularly described.

Ruliph, b. March 1, 1712, married August 12, 1741, Jannetje, daughter of Daniel Hendrickson and Catherine VanDyke, his wife, aforesaid.

The church records show the following children baptized: Sarah, baptized February 21, 1742; Daniel, January 15, 1744, and Catherine, February 16, 1746. Letters of administration on his estate were granted to Peter Couwenhoven, (brother) William Hendrickson, (brother-in-law) and Tunis Denyse, or Denise. His widow married for her second husband Peter Janse Schenck, as has been already mentioned, together with the names of her children by this last husband

Jacob, b. February 1, 1714, married December 21, 1742, Margaret, daughter of William Couwenhoven and Arriantje Bennett, his wife. The marriage license was granted November 16, 1742.

Garret, b. November 5, 1716, married October 12, 1744, Neeltje, or Eleanor, daughter of Roelof Schenck and Geesie Hendrickson, his wife, died December 9, 1797.

He owned quite a large tract of land in what is now Marlboro and Holmdel townships. Part of this land is still (1898) in the ownership and occupation of his lineal male descendants. The two farms near Taylor's Mills in Holmdel township, where Daniel D. Conover and Garret Rezo Conover lived about 40 years ago and where their sons now live, is part of the tract. The family burying ground is on the farm owned by Daniel D. Conover and near the dwelling house. It is especially noticeable for the care, neatness and good taste which it always shows. Here Garret and his wife and many of his descendants are buried.

Peter, b. December 14, 1718, died January 14, 1719.

Peter, baptized May 29, 1720, married Catherine, daughter of Roelof Janse Schenck and Geesie Hendrickson, his wife, and at that time widow of Simon DeHart.

Garret and Peter Couwenhoven are the two sons-in-law named as executors in Black Roelof Schenck's will. Also see pages 317-18, Old Times in Old Monmouth.

John, b. May 17, 1722, married Mary, daughter of Arie VanDorn and Antje Janse Schenck, his wife.

Martin, as spelled in will but Matthias elsewhere, b. 1725, married Williampe, daughter of "William C. Kouwenhoven of Carroway," and Antje Hendrickson, his second wife, and the widow of his oldest brother, William.

This Matthias Couwenhoven lived on a farm on the right side of the road from Ogbourns Corner to Middletown, just east of the Golden farm. There is an old Conover burying ground on the Golden farm near the line, which would show that the Conovers owned all the land around this burying ground at one time.

The Matthias Conover interred in the Baptist church yard at Middletown and whose tombstone shows that he died

House of Daniel Polhemus Schanck on his farm in Pleasant Valley, N. J.
Photographed in summer of 1900.

Part of Schanck-Covenhoven Cemetery in Pleasant Valley, N. J.
Photographed by Mrs. L. H. S. Conover in the winter of 1900.

September 28, 1842, aged 80 years, 2 months and 5 days, and the Ruliph Conover, interred near him, who died June 12, 1873, aged over 85 years, are I believe descendants of the above named Matthias Couwenhoven.

There was also another child named Sarah but I can find no record of her except in her father's will.

Jacob Couwenhoven made his will July 5, 1743. He appoints his sons, Ruliph, Garret and Jacob, executors, and they all qualified. He mentions in his will six sons, Martin, (Matthias) Ruliph, Jacob, Garret, Peter and John, one daughter, Sarah, three grandsons, Daniel Hendrickson and Jacob Hendrickson and Daniel Couwenhoven, and one granddaughter, Sarah Couwenhoven. This grandson, Daniel Hendrickson, I think became sheriff of Monmouth county during the revolutionary war. He was the grandfather of the late Charles I. Hendrickson who owned the farm on the north side of Middletown street, between the lands of the late Dr. Edward Taylor and the Murray homestead, now owned by his son, John S. Hendrickson.

Jacob Couwenhoven in his will describes himself as a yeoman and a resident of Middletown. I have not been able to find out where he was buried. He owned a large tract of land, and it is likely he was buried somewhere upon that as was then the custom.

According to tradition current among the descendants of his son, Garret, at Taylor's Mills, he provided all of his seven sons with a farm. Of course such traditions are very uncertain and unreliable, but they sometimes contain a few grains of truth. I do not know whether there is any truth in this tradition, but only repeat what is said. And this is the story handed down among the descendants of his son Garret, who as everybody knows, are among the most respectable citizens of Monmouth county, and whose everyday word is better than a good many people's oath on the Bible. They have been informed and so understand from talk of their forefathers, that Jacob Couwenhoven's seven sons owned and occupied the following farms:

William had the farm where Daniel G. Conover lived, and now or lately owned by Edward Hopping in Middletown township.

Ruliph owned lands where the late Ezra Osborne lived and the farm adjacent on the west or north side of the highway from Balm Hollow to the John Golden farm.

Matthias owned the lands on the opposite side of this highway. The private family burying ground of the Conovers on this land supports this claim.

Jacob owned the farm of the late John Eastman.

Garret owned what was in after years known as the farm of "Farmer Jacob Conover" and the farms of Daniel D. Conover and Garret Rezo Conover, near Taylor's Mills in Holmdel township. The last two are still (1898) in family ownership.

John owned the farm known as the Murray homestead in Middletown village together with lands adjacent, now part of the Morford farm and of John S. Hendrickson's farm.

Peter owned the "Garret VanDorn farm" on the south side of Middletown street, now owned by the son of the late Azariah Conover.

Jacob Couwenhoven is said to have been a large, well proportioned man, bluff and straightforward in manners and hospitable and obliging to all who sought shelter under his roof or aid at his hands. It will be noticed that there were several marriages between his children and Daniel Hendrickson's children. This man was quite a near neighbor, living where his great grandson, Hon. William H. Hendrickson, now lives at Holland or the Luyster neighborhood, as sometimes called.

Garret, one of Jacob Couwenhoven's sons, married Netty or Eleanor, daughter of Black Roelof Schenck, and had the following children:

Jacob, b. June 19, 1746, married April 25, 1771, Mary, daughter of Hendrick Schenck and Catherine Holmes, his wife.

He was known as "Farmer Jacob," and the farm he lived on was considered the model farm of that day in Monmouth county. He left two sons, Hendrick, who married Ann B. Crawford and whose descendants are named in "Old Times in Old Monmouth." Garret, who married Alice, daughter of Tobias Hendrickson and Rebecca Coward, his wife, of Upper Freehold township. A daughter of this couple named Rebecca H., born in 1805, married Thomas Meirs and was the mother of Collin B. Meirs, born September 7, 1833, on the old Meirs homestead in Upper Freehold township, and who was auditor of Monmouth county for seven years, and now one of the first citizens of Upper Freehold township.

Ruleph, b. Novembr 8, 1747, married June 22, 1773, Anna, daughter of Garret Coertse Schenck, and Nelly Voorhees, his wife.

Sarah, b. January 3, 1749, married John Lloyd and died September 8, 1773.

She is buried in the Conover family burying ground on the Daniel D. Conover farm near Taylor's Mills. One of her daughters, Mary, married John Hendrickson, son of Daniel Hendrickson and Eleanor VanMater, his wife, before mentioned. She is buried in the Hendrickson burying ground at Middletown village and the tombstone at her grave states that she died July 11, 1865, aged 92 years, 8 months and 24 days. She was the mother of the late Charles I. Hendrickson of Middletown village.

Daniel G., b. January 20, 1750, married February 9, 1786, Margaret Reseau, (often spelled Rezo). She was born February 23, 1763, and died December 26, 1823.

Daniel G. Conover lived and died on the homestead farm near Taylor's Mills and is buried in the family burying ground on this farm. After his death the land was divided between his two sons, Daniel D. Conover and Garret Rezo Conover, whom many persons now alive remember. Garret married as before stated, Mariah Schenck. Daniel D. married May 26, 1825, Mary, daughter of Garret G. Vanderveer, and died October 22, 1861. He was a genial, hearty man and endeavored to make everything pleasant to all with whom he came in contact. His hospitality was unlimited, if the roof of his house was left. His widow, who was born February 21, 1806, is still living on the homestead with their son, Garret. She is remarkably active and hale for one so near the century mark. Hon. William V. Conover, who occupied the farm left him by his father, Tylee Conover, on the north side of the Shrewsbury river, opposite Red Bank, and who died a few years ago, was a grandson of the above named Daniel G. Conover and Margaret Reseau, his wife

Gachey, b. February 5, 1753, married first Hendrick P., son of Peter Albertse Couwenhoven and Williampe Voorhees, his wife.

Anne, b. May 21, 1754, married July 13, 1785, Isaac, son of second Jacob VanDorn, and Maria Janse Schenck, his wife, and died June 11, 1843.

She and her husband are buried in the Episcopal church yard at Middletown village. They were the parents of Garret VanDorn, who was born May 31, 1789. He married Williampe, daughter of Hendrick P. Couwenhoven and Gachey Couwenhoven, his wife, above mentioned, his cousin. She was born January 1st, 1793, and died on the VanDorn homestead at Middletown village, January 31, 1874. She and her husband are buried in the Episcopal church yard at Middletown aforesaid.

Garret VanDorn died childless and intestate. He was well known throughout Monmouth county, being gentle and placid in disposition, without an enemy in the world, he was respected and liked by all who knew him. He left a large estate with no debts beyond funeral expenses and charges of his last sickness. Yet this estate has remained unsettled down to the present day. It is the "Jarndyce vs. Jarndyce" case of Monmouth county. It shows how an estate involved in no law suits and no debts, can be dragged through the courts for years. A true history of this estate would be of great interest, not only to the relatives interested but to the public at large, so that we all might know "how not to do it," while making great pretension of doing, settling and distributing. A more honest man never lived than Garret VanDorn and no man ever left property freer from all claims and litigation than he. Yet the estate became entangled and has been left unsettled, although more than forty years have passed away since administration was granted to Williampe, his widow. She, of course, depended on and wholly trusted others to do the business.

The seventh child of Garret Couwenhoven and Neeltje Schenck, his wife, was Mary, born April 5, 1756, died young.

Garret, b. September 15, 1758, died unmarried.

John, b. May 23, 1760, married August 22, 1778, Jane, daughter of Garret Coertse Schenck and Nelly Voorhees, his wife, died May 11, 1802. He was buried in the yard of the Marlboro Brick church. His widow married August 20, 1812, her second husband, John H. Schenck, and died November 5, 1836.

John Conover and Jane Schenck, his wife, were the parents of the following children:

Elias, b. August 10, 1779, married July 1, 1798, Mary, daughter of Ruliff H. Schenck and Sarah Schenck, his wife.

They were the parents of John E., Ruliff E. and Hendrick E., already mentioned in a former article.

Garret I., b. March 31, 1785, married January 6, 1807, Sarah, daughter of Ruliff H. Schenck and Sarah Schenck, his wife, died May 12, 1829.

He owned and occupied the farm where Gideon C. McDowell now lives in Marlboro township.

Jane, b. September 10, 1789, married October 23, 1805, Jonathan R. Gordon, son of Ezekiel Gordon, and died June 1, 1831. Her husband was born March 16, 1785, died May 13, 1830.

Sarah, b. — married March 14, 1803, Albert VanDorn.

Nelly, b. — married December 7, 1796, George Morris.

There were two other children who died young.

There were, of course, other descendants of Garret Couwenhoven and Neeltje Schenck, his wife, but I have not the dates of their births, marriages and deaths and therefore do not name them, but the record I give will enable all who can go back to their grandfathers, to fix their family descent without any mistake. Garret Couwenhoven, the progenitor of this line of Conovers, is said to have been a hearty, whole-souled man. That he resembled in a marked degree his father, and because of his tall well proportioned form and his handsome appearance, attracted notice wherever he went. He is also said to have taken great interest in and care of his children; that he endeavored to train them to habits of sobriety, economy and industry, and judging by results after all these years his descendants seem to have profited by his efforts, for with very few exceptions they seem to have been among our principal citizens down to the present day. As his children grew up and left the old homestead to make their way in the world, he is said to have advised them in plain words, but in the spirit and intent expressed in the following verses:

"You're going to leave the homestead, Jacob,
  "You're twenty-one today,
And the old man will be sorry, Jacob,
  To see you go away.
You've labored late and early, Jacob,
  And done the best you could;
I ain't a going to stop you, Jacob,
  I wouldn't if I could.

The years, they come and go, my boy,
  The years, they come and go;
And raven locks, and tresses brown,
  Grow white as driven snow.
My life has known its sorrows, Jacob,
  Its trials and troubles sore;
Yet God, withal, has blessed me, Jacob,
  'In basket and in store.'

But one thing let me tell you, Jacob,
  Before you make your start,
There's more in being honest, Jacob,
  ' Twice o'er than being 'smart.'
Though rogues may seem to flourish, Jacob,
  And sterling worth to fail,
Oh! keep in view the good and true;
  'Twill in the end prevail.

And don't be mean or stingy, Jacob,
  But lay a little by
Of what you earn; you soon will learn
  How fast 'twill multiply.
So when old age comes creeping on,
  You'll have a goodly store
Of wealth to furnish all your needs,
  And maybe something more.

There's shorter cuts to fortune, Jacob,
  We see them every day,
But those who save their self respect,
  Climb up the good old way.
'All is not gold that glitters,' Jacob,
  And makes the vulgar stare,
And those we deem the richest, Jacob,
  Have oft the least to spare.

Don't meddle with your neighbors, Jacob,
  Their sorrows or their cares;
You'll find enough to do, my boy,
  To mind your own affairs.
The world is full of idle tongues,
  You can afford to shirk;
There's lots of people ready, Jacob,
  To do such dirty work.

And if amid the race for fame
  You win a shining prize,
The humble worth of honest men,
  You never should despise.
For each one has his mission, Jacob,
  In life's unchanging plan;
Though lowly be his station, Jacob,
  He is no less a man."

THE YOUNGER OF THE SIX CONOVER BROTHERS AND HIS CHILDREN.

This was the youngest of the six Conover brothers, who removed from Flatlands, L. I., to Monmouth county, N. J.

In Book G of Deeds, page 162, Monmouth county clerk's office, is the record of a deed dated October 3rd, 1705, from John Bowne, merchant of Middletown township, to John Covenhoven, yeoman of Flatlands, Kings county, L. I., for the consideration of £300 two tracts of land, one containing 94 acres and the other 215 acres, in the township of Freehold, (now Marlboro) and conveyed. In the description it is stated that these two tracts lie together and are bounded on the east by lands of Jacob VanDorn and Aria (Adrian) Bennett. On page 165 of the same book of deeds is record of a deed dated October 15, 1709, from Jacob VanDorn of Freehold township to John Covenhoven of the same place, for a tract of 38½ acres, adjacent to the two tracts above mentioned and between them and other lands of said VanDorn. These two deeds show that John Covenhoven had removed from Long Island and was actually settled in Monmouth county some time between 1705 and 1709. The lands described in the above deeds, or the greater part of them, have been continuously in the possession of the descendants of Jan Couwenhoven from that date to the present year of our Lord, 1898.

Peter G. Conover, the well known and highly respected farmer of Marlboro township, was born, lived and died on this homestead. He was a grandson of the said Jan Couwenhoven. John Lyall Conover, who now owns and occupies these lands, and who is one of the first farmers of Monmouth county, is a son of the late Peter G. Conover. Lafayette Conover and Stacy P. Conover, lately deceased, who owned and occupied valuable farms in the same vicinity, were also sons of Peter G. Conover and great grandsons of the original settler, Jan Couwenhoven. Jan Couwenhoven made his will November 23, it was proved December 29, 1756, and is on record in the office of the secretary of the state of New Jersey, in Book F of Wills, pages 392, etc. He names in this will seven sons, viz: William, Garret, Cornelius, Peter, John, Jacob and Dominicus. He appoints as executors his son Garret, his cousin Roelof Schenck, (Black Roelof) and his cousin Garret, son of Koert Schenck; only his son Garret qualifies. This will is witnessed by David Williamson, Cornelius Couwenhoven and Elbert Williamson.

All his sons except Garret removed from Monmouth county to Penns Neck and from there his sons, Cornelius, Peter and Jacob, emigrated to the state of Kentucky. Peter is said to have removed from Kentucky to the state of Illinois. It is also said that he had a daughter Tryntje, who removed with her three brothers to Kentucky. Dominicus married Mary Updyke. His will, dated January 23, 1778, at Princeton, N. J., is on record in Book 20 of Wills, page 194, etc., at Trenton, N. J. He names in this will the following sons: John, William, Garret, Levi and Peter. He devised his farm at Penns Neck to his sons, Levi and Peter.

The records of Marlboro Brick church show only the following children of Jan Couwenhoven baptized:—Trinke, baptized, October 30, 1709; Cornelius, baptized April 6, 1712; Peter, baptized December 5, 1714; Jan, baptized April 12, 1719; child un-named, baptized June 7, 1724.

Garret, his youngest son as supposed, was born on the old homestead in Marlboro township April 27, 1726, and resided there until his death, November 1, 1812. He is buried in the yard of the Marlboro Brick church, and his age, inscribed on his tombstone, is 86 years and 6 months. He married first Neeltje, daughter of Benjamin VanMater and Elizabeth Laen, his wife, and had by her five children. He married second Antje, daughter of Peter Janse Schenck and Jannetje Hendrickson, his wife. She died April 5, 1803, aged 49 years, 7 months and 2 days. By his second wife he had the following children:

Eleanor, b. December 13, 1787, married Hon. Lafayette Schenck.

Ruins of the old grist mill of Cornelius Covenhoven at Carroway, near Keyport, N. J.

Photographed July, 1898.

View of Cornelius Covenhoven's milldam and pond at Carroway, near Keyport, N. J.

Photographed July, 1898.

Mr. Schenck at one time represented Monmouth county in the New Jersey Assembly. He lived and died on the farm now (1898) owned and occupied by his youngest son, Lafayette Schenck, in the township of Atlantic. He was also the father of the late Rev. Garret Conover Schenck, the well known clergyman of the Dutch church, and who died only a few years ago. As Eleanor Conover was, on her mother's side, a descendant of Jan Schenck, and her husband, Lafayette Schenck, was a descendant of Garret Schenck, the Dominie was a lineal descendant of the two Schenck brothers who first settled in this county.

Jane, b. November 9, 1789.
Ann, b. September 1790, married first William Schenck, second Theodore Rue.
John, b. December 17, 1791, married Ann Smock.
Peter G., b. January 2, 1797, married November 10, 1819, Charlotte, daughter of John Lyall, and died May 21, 1886.

During his long life of nearly four score and ten years he lived in peace with all men and was respected by everybody for his integrity. His name is mentioned in a case decided by the supreme court of New Jersey back in the year 1825. This decision is found in Third Halstead, New Jersey Reports, pages 90 to 116. His name is brought in through his marriage in the Lyall family and in a brief account of this family and some of their connections. It seems to have been an important case, for the decision fills thirty-six solid pages of this book. Four of the greatest lawyers of that day in New Jersey appear for the parties. Robert Stockton and George Wood for the plaintiff, and Garret D. Wall and L. H. Stockton for the defendant. George Wood subsequently obtained a national reputation as a lawyer.

This case turned upon the construction of the will of Eleanor Lyall, who had bequeathed a farm of 108 acres at Nut Swamp, Middletown township, to Fenwick Lyall. Fenwick Lyall sold and conveyed this farm to Richard Crawford for the sum of $4,390. After Fenwick's death it was claimed that he only had a life right under his mother's will. The Supreme court in their long opinions sustained this construction. Fenwick Lyall and John Lyall are interred in the Lippitt burying ground at Middletown village. Peter G. Conover, by his wife, Charlotte Lyall, had the following children:

John Lyall, who married Abbie M. Bishop and now occupies the old homestead.

Lafayette, who married Elizabeth, daughter of William Schenck and Abbey Polhemus, his wife.

William Schenck was a son of Roelof P. Schenck, or Long Ruly, as called, and a brother of Antje Schenck who married Garret Conover above mentioned, the grandfather of Lafayette Conover.

Stacy P., who married Ellen L., daughter of Daniel P. Schenck.
Garret, married Mary L. Hulse, (formerly Hulshart.)
Charles, died young.
Ann Eliza, married David Baird.
Eleanor, married Alfred Conover. They are the parents of the well known lawyer, John L. Conover of this county.
Emma, married Ferdinand Hyers.

Three other children, Amanda, Jane and Eugene, died young

In this connection I might say that Garret Conover by his first wife, Neeltje VanMater, had a son named Garret who married Mary, daughter of the third Garret Schenck. He owned and lived on the farm where the late John W. Herbert lived in Marlboro township, adjacent, I think, to the farm of the late Stacy P. Conover. He built the brick house yet standing where Judge Herbert lived until his death. Another Garret H. Conover, son of Hendrick P. and Ghacey Conover, his wife, owned and occupied the adjacent farm where Joshua Smith now lives, and a Garret I. Conover owned and occupied the farm where Gideon C. McDowell resides. This Garret I. Conover was a son of John G. Conover (a brother of farmer Jacob Couwenhoven), born May 23, 1760, and married August 22, 1778, Jane, daughter of Garret Koertse Schenck and Nelly Voorhees, his wife, and who died May 10, 1802. Garret I., the son, was born March 31, 1785, married a daughter of Ruliff H. Schenck and died May 12, 1829. His brother Elias, born August 10, 1779, was the father of Hendrick E. Conover, so well known to the people of Freehold, and who died only a few years since and hereinbefore mentioned with his brothers. John E. and Ruliff E.

These three farmers all had the same walnut tree for a beginning corner. The people of this vicinity in speaking of these three Garret Conovers, made up a simple little rhyme which serves to identify and distinguish them. It ran thus:

The farms of the Garret Conovers, three:
Garret H., Garret I. and Garret G.,
All butted up to a walnut tree.

The walnut tree, I understand, was cut down a few years ago and a slab from it presented to all the descendants of the three Garrets who could be reached, as a relic.

Jacoba Vanderveer, the wife of Jan Couwenhoven and ancestress of this Conover line, was born at Flatbush, L. I. She was baptized April 29, 1686, and was a daughter of Cornelius Janse Vanderveer and his wife, Trintje, daughter of Gillis DeMandeville. Cornelius Janse Vanderveer came from Holland to America in the ship Otter, February, 1659. In 1677-8 he purchased a farm at Flatlands, L. I., where he settled. One of his daughters, Neeltje, married Daniel Polhemus. He also had a son, Dominicus, baptized November 16, 1679. This Dominicus Vanderveer was associated with Daniel and Johannes Polhemus, Auke Lefferts or Leffertson, Ryck Hendrickson Suydam, Jacob Hendrickson Suydam and Stephen Coerten in a purchase of a tract known as the 1500 acre tract on Swimming river from Lewis Morris in 1709. This Auke, or Aukey Lefferts was the progenitor of the Leffertson or Lefferts family in Monmouth county. He was born April 4, 1678, married May 29, 1703, Marytje TenEyck, a sister I think, of Johannes Polhemus' wife. He died November 26, 1769, and is interred in the Polhemus family burying ground at Scobeyville. Of these purchasers only Johannes Polhemus and Auke Leffertson actually settled. The old deeds for the purchase and subsequent transfer from Daniel Polhemus to Johannes Polhemus are still in the possession of the Polhemus family at Phalanx, Atlantic township. In Book I of Deeds, pages 450, Monmouth county clerk's office, is record of a deed from Cornelius Vanderveer of Middletown township to John Covenhoven of Freehold township, dated September 18, 1789. In this deed Cornelius Vanderveer states that he is a son of Dominicus Vanderveer and for the consideration of £1332 he conveys a tract of 330 acres in Shrewsbury township, lying on both sides of the public road leading from Tinton Falls to Colts Neck and between Swimming river and Fall river or brook, being a part of the Manor of Tinton, conveyed by Edward Antill and Anne, his wife, to Cornelius Vanderveer, March 27, 1741, the grandfather of said Cornelius, the grantor in this deed.

There is also record of a deed dated June 2, 1712, in the Monmouth county clerk's office from Stephen Warne of Middlesex county to Tunis Vanderveer and Cornelius Vanderveer of Flatbush, Kings county, L. I., for a tract of 350 acres in Freehold township. The Middle brook of Topanemes, the South brook of Topanemes and the line of John Baird's lands are mentioned in the description. The above named Tunis and Cornelius Vanderveer were sons of Dominicus Vanderveer. These deeds show when and how the Vanderveers first came into Monmouth county.

Tunis Vanderveer, above named grantee, married about 1723, Aeltje, daughter of Garret Schenck of Pleasant Valley, and settled on part of the above tract. It has been in this family ever since. David Arthur Vanderveer, who now owns and occupies it, is a lineal descendant of Tunis VanDerveer and Altje, Schenck, his wife. They had a son Tunis, born April 19, 1739. He had a son John, born April 4, 1763, married February 18, 1789, Anna Bowne. They were the parents of ten children. Among them were Joseph I., born January 9, 1790, and married Jane Smock; and David I., born April 19, 1806, married February 13, 1828, Mary, daughter of William Covenhoven and Janet Davis, his wife. Joseph I. Vanderveer was a wellknown and a very popular man through Monmouth county, "Uncle Josey Vanderveer," as he was generally addressed. He had two or three horses stolen one night from his stable. Single handed and in his everyday clothes he started out the next morning to find them. His pursuit led him through the state of New Jersey, city of Philadelphia. lower counties of Pennsylvania into the state of Maryland, where he found and captured the thieves and brought his horses back home. His courage, perseverance and determination shown in this adventure was talked of and told for many years afterwards. His brother, David I. Vanderveer, lived and died on the old homestead in Freehold township. His death occurred July 23, 1884. He left four children surviving him:—

Hannah Matilda, married February 5. 1851, David Clark Perrine, who was born at Clarksburg, Millstone township, October 20, 1816.

He was the well known merchant of Freehold who made the "Big Red Store" famous in this part of New Jersey. Their only son, David Vanderveer Perrine, the leading merchant of Freehold, has deepened and widened the business his father established.

William Conover, b. July 22, 1831.

Farmhouse now (1901) on the Jan Covenhoven farm, near Wickatunk, N. J., and still owned and occupied by the descendants of the pioneer settler.

Photograph taken by Mrs. L. H. S. Conover in the summer of 1900.

Old house on Murray homestead in village of Middletown, N. J., occupied and owned by Jacob Covenhoven during the latter part of the eighteenth century.

Photographed in the summer of 1900 by Mrs. L. H. S. Conover.

He removed to and settled in Ohio, where he still lives.

John D., b. September 28, 1836, married November 30, 1859, Jane Ann, daughter of John Henry Vanderveer and Jane Smock, his wife.

David Arthur, b. June 23, 1844, married November 2, 1865, Eleanor G., daughter of Tunis Vanderveer Schenck.

He resides on the old homestead where his forefathers settled nearly two centuries ago. Thus both in the history of Jan Couwenhoven and of the Vanderveer family in which he married we find they have held to the present day the lands in Monmouth county on which they first settled. This speaks well for their stability, conservatism and contentment with things as found. No family in Monmouth can show a better record in this respect. In this connection I may add the late Col. Elias Conover of Middletown, and Joseph Conover, father of the late William W. Conover of Red Bank, and of Sidney Conover, are descendants of the above named Jan Couwenhoven and Jacoba Vanderveer, his wife.

REASONS WHY THE NEW YORK HOLLANDERS MIGRATED TO NEW JERSEY.

It may seem strange why the VanDorns, VanPelts, VanAmacks, (Aumocks) VanSiclens, (Sickles) and other Dutch people left the towns and villages of New York, and the society of their relatives and friends between 1690 and 1720, when there was so much unoccupied land close by, just as fertile and cheap as that in Monmouth, Middlesex and Somerset counties, N. J.

Monmouth county at that time was reached from Long Island by sailing vessels, generally small sloops. They, of course, were dependent on the winds and tides. In calms or contrary winds a sloop might be two or three days in making the passage. In the winter when the bay was covered with floating ice or disturbed by violent storms, no passage was possible.

The few people who then resided in Monmouth county were of a different race and language and had nothing in common with these Dutch people from Long Island. The country here was little more than a howling wilderness. No roads which deserved the name, but mere tracks through the primeval forests over the old Indian paths, very few bridges, no schools or churches of their language and faith. In short, none of the conveniences of civilized life.

To understand this migration it is necessary to take a brief glance at the political and social conditions of affairs in the province of New York. Just before 1690 the great revolution had occurred in England, which drove King James into lasting exile, and placed on the throne of Great Britain the Stadholder of the Dutch Republic, William of Orange. Everything in England was in confusion, and they had no information or time to consider the affairs of a little colony like New York some three thousand miles away. When the news of this great revolution was received in New York, the old officials who had been appointed under King James were naturally supposed to be his adherents. The Dutch population were well satisfied to have a man of their own race and country, like William of Orange, as their sovereign. In fact, for the first time since the piratical seizure of New Netherlands, in the interest of this same King James, then known as the Duke of York, were the Dutch people really satisfied with English rule.

At suggestion and with support of many of the Dutch and English people, particularly those in Kings county, L. I., and New York City, a man named Jacob Leisler was chosen to administer temporarily the government of New York until communication could be had with the government of Great Britain. This, of course, would require from four to five months with the sailing vessels of that time.

An Englishman named Richard Ingoldsby, who had been identified with the old officials appointed under King James, backed by the aristocratic clique who had previously controlled the provincial government, attempted also to rule. In this they were defeated by the Leisler party and some of the leaders, like Nicholas Bayard, had been imprisoned. Jacob Leisler was a plain, sincere man, without any experience in political intrigue or duplicity. He was also without ability to manage public matters of such magnitude or at such a critical period. He was, however, a zealous protestant and an enthusiastic supporter of William of Orange, the revolutionary king.

He took every possible way to have King William and Queen Mary proclaimed the legitimate sovereigns of Great Britain at all the principal villages and towns of New York. On the 4th of March, 1690, he sent an order to one John Langstaff or Longstreet of East Jersey, directing him with the aid of the principal freeholders and inhabitants of the place to proclaim William and Mary king and queen of England, Scotland, France and Ireland, according to the form used, at chief towns of East Jersey, with all the solemnities usual on such occasions. This was done at the villages of Middletown and Shrewsbury, some time in the month of March, 1690, for they were the principal towns in this part of East Jersey. This action on the part of Leisler proves the utter falsity of the charge afterward trumped up by his enemies, that he was the ringleader of a Dutch plot to subvert the English government. Finally on the 19th of March, 1691, an Englishman named Henry Sloughter duly commissioned as Royal Governor, arrived in New York. He was entirely unacquainted with the people and the true situation of public matters. He naturally fell into the hands of the old English politicians and relied on them for all information. Many of these men were the bitter political and personal enemies of Leisler. They looked upon him as an upstart and the leader of the common people who had pushed himself forward, contrary to usage, precedent or aristocratic connections.

At their suggestion, made for a sinister purpose, Sloughter appointed Ingoldsby to demand from Leisler the surrender of the fort and the disbandment of his military forces. Surprised at such a messenger and suspecting a trick, Leisler at first refused but finally when convinced that the new governor had really deputized him, he surrendered up the fort without any resistance. Leisler, his son-in-law, Jacob Millbourne, and several of his principal officers, were at once arrested and thrown in prison. Sloughter, who was a mere thing of putty, was persuaded by these conspirators to call what was designated a special court of Oyer and Terminer to try these prisoners. Leisler and Millbourne, knowing that their conviction and death was a foregone conclusion with this packed tribunal, refused to sanction the farce by a "plea of guilty" or "not guilty," but stood "mute" as it was then called.

This so-called court, with indecent haste, found them guilty and sentenced them to death by hanging, mutilation of their corpses and confiscation of all their property. Sloughter, however, seems to have had a little idea of what was proper, for under date of May 2nd, 1691, he writes to Lord Inchiquin in England. After informing him of the "conviction of Leisler and his accomplices" by a court of Oyer and Terminer, adds "I am not willing to proceed but upon extreme necessity and until his majesty shall have information and his pleasure be known." If Sloughter had pursued this course the colonial history of New York, and his own memory would have been saved from a disgraceful stain.

The arch conspirators, however, well understood that a review of Leisler's case by intelligent and disinterested men, would defeat their vindictive purpose. They at once took measures to change the governor's intention. We have no sure means of knowing what private representations they made to him, although many grave and scandalous rumors and reports were circulated among the people. We have, however, the records of their public proceedings, made up by them in the best shape they could put it. The following is their record, on the 14th of May, 1691, at a council held at Fort William Henry, New York:

"Present: Governor Henry Sloughter, Frederick Phillips, William Nicolls, Nicholas Bayard, Stephen VanCortlandt and Gabriel Monville, of the council."

Then they go on to say that Governor Sloughter inquires "what is best for the peace of the country, as he was about to go to Albany" (then a trip of about two weeks). With one voice, showing previous collusion, they replied, "that to prevent insurrection in the future and to preserve the governor's authority, it was absolutely necessary that the death sentence against Leisler and Millbourne be forthwith executed."

At this time there was not the least danger of insurrection yet with this bold lie, they induced the governor to sign the death warrant. Two days later, such was their haste, May 16, 1691, Jacob Leisler and Jacob Millbourne were strangled to death in the city of New York. They both met their death like christians and brave men. They asserted their innocence to the last and declared that what they had done was for the protestant religion and in the interest of King William and Queen Mary. Thus was consummated one of the darkest crimes in the annals of the State and colony of New York.

We cannot now realize the deep anger and lasting resentment aroused among the friends and supporters of Leisler, particularly in Kings county, L. I., where he had a numerous following.

These men never forgot or forgave the aristocratic clique which with bitter malice and false pretenses had hunted these men to death. It affected and influenced the politics of New York down to the revolutionary war, when the "dangerous Democratic ideas," which Ingoldsby spoke of in one of his communications as being at the bottom of the Leisler troubles, were triumphant. The whole case, however, came before the English government a few years later. In 1695 an act was passed by the House of Lords and Commons and approved by the King, righting this foul injustice so far as was possible. This act is entitled 6 & 7 William III, Anno 1695. The following is the last section of the act.

"That said conviction, judgment and attainder of Jacob Leisler and Jacob Millbourne, deceased, and Abraham Governeur, and any of them, be and are repealed, revoked, made and declared null and void to all intents and constructions whatsoever, as if never made."

This was a sweeping and full vindication of those victims to partizan malice and personal hate on the part of the government of Great Britain. It restored to their families the property that had been confiscated. At about this time the celebrated Minister of New England, Rev. Increase Mather, writes under date of January 20, 1696:

"I am afraid that the guilt of innocent blood is still crying in the ears of the Lord against you. My Lord Bellmont said to me 'that he was one of the committee of Parliament who examined the matter, and those men, (Leisler and Millbourne) were not only murdered but barbariously murdered.' However, the murdered men have been cleared by the King, Lords and Commons, etc."

If such was the opinion of disinterested men, far removed from the scene of the troubles, the reader can judge how deep and bitter was the anger of the friends and supporters of Leisler and the relatives of the other men imprisoned and convicted with him. Many of these men were alarmed. If Leisler and Millbourne could thus be executed and their property seized what security is there for any of us? was a natural inquiry. The young men about to leave home and make a settlement elsewhere looked around to see if there was some place where they would be safe, where laws would be equitably administered and where there would be full liberty of conscience or religious worship. New Jersey was then governed by the proprietors. They had offered liberal terms to all persons who would settle on their lands, for without inhabitants their lands were worthless. Some of these proprietors, like the merchants in London, were influenced solely by mercenary considerations. Others, like William Penn and Robert Barclay, by philanthropic and conscientious motives. Robert Barclay of Aberdeen, Scotland, had been made governor of New Jersey. He was famous as a scholar and writer and for his philanthropy. He was a son of Robert Barclay, who at one time had served as a soldier under Gustavus Adolphus of Sweden, but in after years became a convert to the Friends. He is celebrated by John G. Whittier in his poem entitled Barclay of Ury. He had brought up his son in the tenets of the Quakers or Friends. It was through this son that many of the persecuted covenanters and Presbyterians had been released from prison and directed to New Jersey. These prominent Friends were for several years the managing or controlling men in the government of New Jersey. This fact was known far and wide, and it was a guarantee that full religious freedom would be allowed in New Jersey and fair laws enacted and equitably and justly enforced and construed. The Quakers themselves had suffered bitter persecution and their doctrine of peace and non resistance, etc., was an assurance to all that no persecution would occur under their government, as indeed was the case. William Penn's name too, was a tower of strength. A Hollender, too, named Arent Sonmans, and his son, Peter Sonmans, after his death, was a proprietor and owned thousands of acres in Somerset and Monmouth counties. He was well known to his countrymen in New York and used his influence to direct the current of immigration to those counties. But it was the bitter discontent with the government of New York caused by the judicial murder of Leisler and Millbourne and the confidence in the men who controlled the government of New Jersey, which induced so many of the young men to remove from the towns and villages of New York and settle in Monmouth, Middlesex and Somerset counties. This chapter in the colonial history of New York has never had the attention and consideration it deserved. It led to serious and far reaching results. Bayard and VanCortland, who had been so active in this injustice and outrage, were connected by blood with the patroons of New York. The wealth, influence and power of these men were used to suppress and smother as far as they could this disgraceful deed. They then controlled public matters almost as completely as Bill Tweed did in his day. Therefore, men were afraid to speak out and call things by their real names. Like the railroad corporations and Standard oil corporation and others of like character they had patronage and power. They could reward or punish. Thus ambitious men who wanted office, selfish men who wanted money, society men who wanted introduction and timid or cowardly men afraid of injury, and all the rest who were governed by self interest and cool calculation, did not speak out, but wound, turned and twisted their way so as to keep in with both factions or parties. Right, too, on the heels of the Leisler difficulty came the interference of Lord Cornbury with the church. His arbitrary efforts to establish Episcopacy and his assumption of power over other denominations deepened the discontent with the government of New York. The quarrels and contention and troubles in the Dutch churches of Kings county, L. I., from 1705 to 1714 and the government interference with them also disgusted the Smocks, VanBrunts, Luysters and other Dutch people and sent the young men over to New Jersey where they at least could worship as they pleased.

CONFLICT BETWEEN LEWIS MORRIS AND THE PEOPLE OF MIDDLETOWN.

Jacob VanDorn, as the name is now spelled, with his brother-in-law, Arie (Adrian) Bennett, removed from what is now a part of Brooklyn, then known as Gowanus, to Monmouth county in the year 1697 or 98, just two centuries ago. He married about 1694 Marytje, (Maria or Mary) a daughter of Arian Williamse Bennett and Angenietje VanDyke, his wife, who then resided at Gowanus. Jacob VanDorn became a communicant in the Dutch church of Brooklyn in 1695. Our records in the Monmouth County Clerk's Office show that John Reid, a Scotchman, who was quite prominent in public affairs of this county between 1690 and 1720, and who was a faithful agent for some of the Scotch proprietors, conveyed to Richard Salter, by deed dated December 23, 1689, recorded in Book H of Deeds, page 325, part of his land called Hortencia, lying principally in what is now Marlboro township and likely running over into what is now Holmdel township, for Freehold township in 1689 had not been set off from Middletown township. In this deed it is stated that the lands conveyed begin where "West Branch comes into Hop brook at a place called Promontoria." John Reid, who was an intelligent and prudent man, had doubtless satisfied the Indians and also procured a legal title from the proprietors of East Jersey for this tract of land prior to his transfer to Salter.

Under date of April 2, 1697, Salter assigns this deed to "Adrian Bennett and Jacob VanDorn of Gowanus, Kings county, Island of Nassau," (Long Island). This assignment is recorded in Book H of Deeds, page 327, and was a very singular method to convey real estate. The number of acres is not stated. It appears that Bennett, VanDorn and Salter were thrown together by this business transaction and that Salter must have gained the good will and friendship of those two men by his fair and kind treatment of them; for only a year or two later we find Bennett and VanDorn resisting the sheriff of the county, John Stewart, and preventing him from arresting Salter. Our court records show that for their action in this matter they brought upon themselves the vengeance of the notorious Lewis Morris of "Tintern Manor," as he or his uncle, the first Lewis Morris, had named it. This place is now known as Tinton Falls, in Monmouth county.

The minutes of the courts of Monmouth county in clerk's office, for the year 1700, shows the following record entered at the instance of, and no doubt dictated by, Lewis Morris himself, for a new clerk, Drummond, also a Scotchman, had just been appointed and he had no experience in making up the court records. The following is a correct copy of this record:

"A Court of Inquiry held at Shrewsbury for the county of Monmouth, the 27th day of August, 1700.

    Lewis Morris, President.
    Samuel Leonard,
    Jedediah Allen,   } Justices.
    Samuel Dennis,
    Anthony Pintard,

The Grand Jury of Inquiry for present service were these:

John Reid, (a Scotchman).
Jeremiah Stillwell, Alexander Adams,
John Slocum, Thomas Webley,
Thomas Hewett, Patrick Cannon, *
Abiah Edwards, James Melven, *
John West, Peter Embley, *
John Leonard, Samuel Hopenge,
William Layton, William Hoge.

Those marked with star (*) are Scotchmen.

After taking the oath Lewis Morris charged them. We have no record of what he said, but judging by his other writings, when angered, it was a violent harangue for the jury to indict Jacob VanDorn, Arie Bennett and the other persons who had resisted his pet sheriff, John Stewart, also a Scotchman. The jury were almost, outside of John Reid, the foreman, and the other Scotchman, made up of his retainers and henchmen in Shrewsbury township. The justices, also, who set with him had all been lately appointed at his suggestion by the Scotch governor, Andrew Hamilton. In plain words this jury was packed by Lewis Morris for the express purpose of indicting Jacob VanDorn, Adrian (Arie) Bennett and others of the Middletown people. They soon returned the following indictment, which had probably been drawn up by Lewis Morris himself and given to some of his agents on this grand jury. The following is a true copy of this indictment:

"August ye 27th, 1700.—We, jurors present Richard Salter, John Bray, James Stout, David Stout, Benjamin Stout, Cornelius Compton, William Bowne, Thomas Hankinson, Jacob VanDorn, Arian Bennett, Thomas Sharp, Benjamin Cook, Robert James, Thomas Estill and Samuel, a servant of Salter, for riotously assembling on the 17th of July and assaulting John Stewart, High Sheriff, and Henry Leonard, in the path near house of Alexander Adams and beat and greviously wounded these said persons, took their swords from them, carried them away and kept them to the value of five pounds, money of this province, in breach of the peace and terror of the king's liege people. Signed in behalf of the rest by
        JOHN REID, Foreman."

We have an account written by two of the most respected and honest citizens of Middletown township at the time of this occurrence which throws a different light on this subject. There is nothing in our early records to throw the least smirch upon the characters of Andrew Bowne and Richard Hartshorne. They were straightforward, honest men, who tried to do their duty in a plain unostentatious manner. They commanded the respect of all the people of Middletown. Even Lewis Morris with his abusive tongue and malicious heart, could say nothing worse of them than that one was an Anabaptist and the other a Quaker and that they had defeated a bill to tax the people for the maintenance of the Episcopal priests and prelates, as in England.

True copy of Andrew Bowne and Richard Hartshorne account of this trouble from pages 327-8-9 of Vol. II, New Jersey Archives.

"East Jersey, Middletown ye 23d July, 1700, &c.—Yours of 6th of April last come to our hands, it being the first we received from you, for which we thank you; but could have wished you had sent us a more certain account of the settlement of the government, which, never so much as now, wants to be settled Since the departure of Mr. Slater, Col. Hamilton [the usurping Governor at that date] hath put Mr. Morris [Lewis Morris of Tinton Falls] into commission of his council and justice, believing him to be the only man that can make the province submit to him as governor, without the king's approbation, and in order to effect it they turned out an Englishman who was sheriff and put in a Scotchman, [John Stewart, who resided in what is now Eatontown township], who they thought would obey them without reserve. And it is said Morris has given out that he will carry his point in making the people submit to Col. Hamilton or he will embrue the province in blood. In order to which they seized upon several persons intending to force them to give security for their good behaviour, which one of them refused to do, and so continued in the sheriff's custody. This the people took greviously, it being harvest time, and they had given out warrants to seize Richard Salter and others. And the sheriff [John Stewart with warrant issued by Lewis Morris, Justice] had like to have taken him. Which some of his neighbors understanding went and met the sheriff [John Stewart with his deputy, Henry Leonard], banged him, broke his head and sent him packing, upon which, as we are informed, the people resolved to meet on Friday, the 19th day of July, in order to go and fetch home him that was in the sheriff's hands, upon which Morris and Leonard, [Lewis Morris and Samuel Leonard] dispatched an express [man on horseback to ride fast] for Governor Hamilton [he then resided at Burlington City] who immediately came to them, [at Tinton Falls]. They pressed about fifty men [Morris' henchmen in Shrewsbury township and his Scotch contingent around Freehold, likely] and came on 19th of July [only two days after Sheriff John Stewart and Henry Leonard had been thrashed] in arms [with guns and other weapons] to Middletown [the village] and came to the ordinary [the tavern or public house, which then stood where George Bowne's dwelling now, 1898, stands] and there inquired for said Salter and one Bray [John Bray]. Then they marched off [went back to Tinton Falls]. The people of Middletown [township] were assembled to the number of about 100 [another account says about 150 men] but without arms, only sticks [mild term for clubs] yet had it not been for the persuasion of some much in the public favor there would have been broken heads if not further mischief, the said justices having persuaded the person in the sheriff's hands to give security for his good behavior the day before this meeting. In this position things stand in this county and we believe that throughout the province, including the Scotch, there is six to one against owning Col. Hamilton Governor, and almost all bitterly against Morris, whom they look upon as the first man [as indeed he was] that opposed government.

ANDREW BOWNE,
RICHARD HARTSHORNE,
One of ye Council."

Some of our local Newark historians have in their one-sided efforts to eulogize Lewis Morris, spoken in a slighting way of Captain Andrew Bowne. There is no evidence to justify this in our early records. He was a plain, outspoken, sincere man who always stood four square in his tracks. He could not cajole or flatter like Lewis Morris when he wanted favors, neither could he abuse in bitter fashion his opponents, like Morris. He had no such command of vituperative language, but what he said he meant, and he was always consistent. Those who knew him best (his neighbors of Monmouth county) respected him, while Lewis Morris was detested for his arbitrary and unscrupulous efforts to further his own interests even when he sat as judge of our county courts. He was constantly in law suits, during the years running from 1692 to 1698, and his influence and that of his cousin, Lewis Morris, of Passage Point, who was also a justice, gave him a decided advantage over the people he sued. The attempt of Governor Hamilton and Lewis Morris to overawe and intimidate the people of Middletown by an armed body of men failed. It ought to have been evident to them that the people of Middletown would not submit. They were distinctly informed to this effect and had warning of what would happen and what did happen at Middletown village on the 25th of March, 1701.

This record of that court as it stands on the minutes in the clerk's office was evidently entered at the dictation of Lewis Morris, who was then presiding judge of the county courts. This record represents the people of Middletown as breaking up this court, taking Governor Hamilton and the county officials prisoners, out of sympathy with a self confessed pirate, who had served under the notorious Capt. Kidd, and in order to rescue him from the officers of the law. This was a grave and serious charge and one very likely to be noticed and punished by the English government. Piracy, however, was an offense outside of the jurisdiction of the Monmouth courts as it occurs on the high seas and it is cognizable only in Admiralty courts. So Lewis Morris failed to bring upon the people of Middletown the vengeance of the home government. He however, sent a certified copy of the court record to the English government backed up by a long communication. He also wrote about the same time to the Bishop of London saying that the people of Middletown were the "most ignorant and wicked people on earth and have no such thing as church or religion among them." He also, a short time after his captivity at Middletown, went to England, in order to accomplish his vindictive or ambitious designs.

Jacob VanDorn and Arie Bennett, although indicted and harassed for some time by the officers, were never brought to trial, for the proprietors of New Jersey surrendered the next year (1702) their right of government to the English crown. Lord Cornbury and other new officials came into power who ignored entirely all the old disputes and quarrels.

This old record, while unexplained, throws a dark shadow on the characters of Jacob VanDorn and Arie (Adrian) Bennett, but when real facts are understood, it appears that they stood up manfully without regard to consequences to protect their friend, Richard Salter, and resist the tyrannical and illegal acts of a usurping governor and his pretended officers of the law. It speaks well for their resolution, courage and intelligence.

JACOB VAN DORN AND HIS DESCENDANTS.

Between 1697 and 1701, Jacob VanDorn became the sole owner in fee of 675 acres of land in what is now Holmdel and Marlboro townships. This tract lies west of Pleasant Valley, and was joined on the east by lands of Jan Schenck and on the west by part of lands of Albert Couwenhoven. It runs from the southwest corner of Pleasant Valley over to what is now called Hillsdale, near Bradevelt station and the Brick church. This is a small valley running west from Pleasant Valley. Jacob VanDorn's land included all this valley and ran up into the hills on each side. It was covered with the primeval forests and undrained swamps when he settled there. At the northwest corner of the original 675 acres is a tract of woodland now (1898) owned by Hon. Daniel P. VanDorn of Freehold, which has come down to him by descent from the first Jacob VanDorn, the pioneer settler.

Jacob VanDorn erected his first dwelling, probably a log cabin, on the rising ground or knoll where the residence of the late Thomas Ely stands, just west of the mill pond and on the north side of the road from Holmdel to the Brick church. Over this road the VanDorns, Schencks, Couwenhovens and Hendricksons, of Pleasant Valley and vicinity, travelled every Sunday to attend services at the First Dutch church for over one hundred years. After a few years the log house gave way to a more substantial and convenient dwelling, erected on the same site. Here Jacob VanDorn lived and died. On the stream which flows down from the hills, only a stone's throw east from his residence, Jacob VanDorn built a dam and erected a grist mill as early as 1714, if not earlier. This mill was a great convenience to the settlers for four or five miles around, and it shows that Jacob VanDorn was a practical, energetic man, who understood the needs of that community. This mill remained on the same site until 1829, when Sheriff John J. Ely, who was then the owner, erected a new mill about 200 yards further down the stream, where it still remains and is now known as Ely's mills near Holmdel village. Jacob VanDorn died between April 24, 1719, and March 21, 1720. I do not know where he is buried, unless on his farm, as was then the custom. He was quite young at the time of his death, and most of his children were minors. His wife, Marytje Bennett, survived him many years, and is said to have been an excellent woman and a most devoted mother. Jacob VanDorn left a last will executed in 1719. He devised half of his lands and half of his mill to his eldest son, Aure, or Arie, and the other half to his fourth son, Jacob. He also directs them to pay £75 to each of his other children except Isaac, his youngest son, who is to have £37 more than the others. Aure and Jacob VanDorn married sisters, daughters of their nearest neighbor, Jan Schenck, and run the mill together. After Aure's death in 1748 or '49, his only son, Jacob, occupied his part of the mill and the lands. He died unmarried September 9, 1785, and then Jacob Couwenhoven, son of his sister, Mary VanDorn* who married John Jacobse Couwenhoven of Middletown village, came into the ownership of it. Jacob Couwenhoven erected a large and commodious dwelling on the site where Jacob VanDorn had erected his log house and his second dwelling. This house, although remodeled and latered, is still standing and bids fair to outlast the showy and flimsy buildings of today. Jacob Couwenhoven died April 28, 1815, and left the real property to his sons, Aaron, Ruliph and Isaac, who lost it, and in the year 1822, it was bought by Sheriff John J. Ely, and has been since occupied by his two sons, William and Thomas Ely, and their heirs. Under the first Jacob VanDorn's will, the western half of the 675 acres adjacent to Hillsdale was as-

---

*Mary VanDorn and John Jacobse Couwenhoven had the following children:
Jacob, baptized January 19, 1752.
Antje, baptized January 18, 1753; died young.
Saartje, baptized June 15, 1755, married May 1, 1779, Joris Smock, who was born November 24, 1754, and died December 7, 1834. His wife died March 30, 1794.
Arie, baptized April 13, 1760.
Catrena, baptized April 30, 1764.
Antje, baptized September 5, 1773.

signed to and occupied by his fourth son, Jacob VanDorn, and on this he lived and brought up his family.

The eldest son, Jacob, who afterward owned and resided on the eastern half of the VanDorn homestead and ran the mills, married three times and had fifteen children. His first wife, Arriantje Couwenhoven, was baptized September 25, 1746, and was the daughter of Jacob Jacobse Couwenhoven, and Margaret Couwenhoven, his wife, who was a daughter of William Couwenhoven and Arriantje Bennett. By this wife Jacob Couwenhoven had the following children:

John, married November 25, 1789, Ann VanBrunt.
Jacob, married September 26, 1799, Catharine Schenck.
Margaret, married February 18, 1798, Schuyler Schenck.
Mary, who died unmarried, and always retained a room in the dwelling house where Thomas Ely lived, and where her father died.

By his second wife, Eleanor Smock, whom he married December 29, 1782, he had:

Elizabeth, married February 9, 1803, Daniel, a son of Dominie DuBois.
Anne, married November 18, 1806, Sidney Denise, who was baptized January 30, 1788, and was a son of Judge Denyse Denyse and Catharine Schenck, his wife, a sister of Capt. John Schenck, the famous patriot soldier of Pleasant Valley.

By his third wife, Nelly Schenck, whom he married December 10, 1788, he had:

Ellen, married April 3, 1811, Peter Schenck.
Ruliph, married first, Ellen VanCleaf, second, Maria VanCleaf, daughters of Joseph VanCleaf and Nelly Schenck, his wife.
Aaron, married a Miss Bray.
Jane, married February 3, 1820, Peter Garretson.
Isaac, married Alche Bennett, daughter of John W. Bennett and Elizabeth VanMater, his wife.
Sarah, married John French.
Caty, married John Frost.
Arinthia, died unmarried.
Peter, died when a little child.

Jacob Couwenhoven's will was made April 24, 1815, proved June 22, 1815, recorded in Book A of Wills, pages 703, in Monmouth county Surrogate's office.

The second Jacob VanDorn built a good and substantial dwelling on his half of his father's lands about 1753. When Jacob died, his son, Peter VanDorn, lived there, brought up a large family and died there. Then his son-in-law, Elisha Holmes, occupied the house and part of the 317 acres originally assigned to second Jacob. Many of the old people now living remember Elisha Holmes.

The first Jacob VanDorn, by his wife, Marytje Bennett, had ten children, all of whom were reared on the homestead at Holmdel, viz:

Arie or Aure (sometimes confounded with and spelled Aaron in English) his oldest son, was born about 1695 in Gowanus, (Brooklyn) married about 1730, Antje, daughter of Jan Schenck and Sara Couwenhoven, his wife, and died September 4, 1748, and is buried in the Schenck-Couwenhoven grave yard. His tombstone gives his age as 52 years and 8 months. His wife survived him for a number of years. He had one son, Jacob, baptized January 1st, 1734, and died September 9th, 1785, unmarried, aged 52 years, 9 months and 9 days; interred by his father. He had four daughters, viz:

Mary, baptized March 31, 1731, married John Jacobse Couwenhoven of Middletown village.
Sarah, born about 1736, died unmarried.
Ann, baptized March 25, 1738, married Cyrenius VanMater, who lived near Stone Hill, north of Colts Neck.
Neeltje, or Eleanor, baptized May 16th, 1742, married first Hendrick Smock of Freehold township, and second Garret Hendrickson of Middletown township; interred in Schenck-Couwenhoven yard. She died February 13, 1834, aged 90 years, 10 months and 8 days.

Engeltje, (Angelina) born about 1697, and about 1718 married Roelof, son of the first Garret Schenck and Neeltje Voorhees, his wife. Her husband was known as "Brewer Roelof" Schenck to distinguish him from his cousin, "Black Roelof" Schenck. He resided on a farm lying on the northwest side of Pleasant Valley, adjoining that of his father-in-law on the north. This couple had eleven children. Some of them settled in Somerset and Hunterdon counties and there cleared farms and raised families. Some in each generation went further and further west, and ever opening up the wilderness for farm lands, until now their descendants are found in all the northern tier of states to the Pacific ocean. And wherever they settled in the west, if sufficiently numerous to control public sentiment, (and it did not take very many of them to do this) we hear of no cowardly and horrible tales of lynching helpless and lonely prisoners in jail, but the orderly administration of the law, that no one should suffer death unless first proved guilty before a fair jury.

Wherever they went they took their Bibles, their homely virtues, plain ways and industrious habits. And while they never claimed any holiness and perfection from all sins, and never boasted of being Pilgrims or the sons of Pilgrims, and above earthly things with all their hopes fixed on a crown of gold and harp in Heaven, yet they tried to live without wronging other people in word or deed, to improve and build up the country and start their children on an honest and industrious path in life.

Christyjan, (Christain) baptized September 17, 1699, married Altje, daughter of Jan Schenck and Sarah Couwenhoven, his wife.

She was baptized May 25th, 1705, and died at Middlebush, Somerset county, N. J., in 1801. It is said that when 95 years old she rode every Sunday when the weather permitted to the Dutch church at New Brunswick six miles from her home.

Christian VanDorn removed from Monmouth to Somerset county about 1723. He purchased a tract of 525 acres in the north side of the present Amwell road at Middlebush. He let his younger brother, Abraham, who also came at a later date to Middlebush, have 166 acres on the north of the 359 acres which he retained.

Abraham VanDorn is said to have served as sheriff of Somerset county, 20 consecutive years, and was highly respected for his business qualities. In 1752, while Rev. John Leydt was pastor of the Dutch church at New Brunswick, Christain and Abraham VanDorn were both in the consistory, one as deacon and the other as elder. They followed in their father's steps. He was the first deacon of the Dutch church in Monmouth, when the church was organized in 1709, and his son Abraham was the first child baptized after the installation of Joseph Morgan, the pastor, by Rev. Bernardus Freeman, from Long Island.

Christain VanDorn, by his wife, Altje Schenck, (sometimes spelled Alchy) had 17 children, all of whom grew up, married and had large families, except one named Roelof. At the time of her death, 1801, Altje Schenck VanDorn had 17 children, 129 grand, 200 great grand and six great great grandchildren, in all 352 descendants. For the names of Christain VanDorn's children, whom they married and where they settled, and some account of their descendants, see an article by Hon. Ralph Voorhees, on the VanDorn family in Somerset county in August, 1873, number of "Our Home," a monthly magazine then published by A. V. D. Honeyman at Somerville, N. J., pages 337 to 342.

Wilhelm (William) VanDorn, born about 1701, married Altje, daughter of Cornelius Couwenhoven and Margaret Schenck, his wife, of Pleasant Valley, and died young without children. His widow married for her second husband Cornelius Middach.

Jacobus (Jacob) VanDorn, born January 21, 1703, baptized in Brooklyn April 27th, 1703, married first Marytje, daughter of Jan Schenck and Sarah Couwenhoven, his wife. This made three sisters of this Schenck family who married into this VanDorn family. Marytje Schenck was born August 8, 1712, and died October 31, 1756.

Jacob VanDorn married a second wife, Rachel, daughter of Garret Schenck and Neeltje Voorhees, his wife, also of Pleasant Valley, and a cousin to his first wife. She was at this time the widow of Guysbert Longstreet of Squan (Manasquan). Jacob VanDorn died February 26, 1779, on the western half of his father's lands, containing about 317 acres. He had by his first wife seven sons and three daughters of whom more hereafter.

Augenietje, baptized March 29, 1705, married about 1729, William Wyckoff, who lived near Monmouth court house or Freehold village. This couple had five sons and six daughters. One of their sons, Jacob Wyckoff, born 1730, and died March 5, 1812, married Sarah Couwenhoven, granddaughter of Jacob Couwenhoven of Middletown, and who is named in his will. She was born 1733 and died August 25th, 1796. Their son William, was a colonel in the Revolutionary war and was the father of Nathaniel Scudder Wyckoff, one of the principal farmers and land owners in what is now Manalapan township, during the early part of the present century. Another son of William Wyckoff and Augenietje VanDorn was Peter Wyckoff, who was a guide or aid to General Washington at the battle of Monmouth, and was also the grandfather of the famous "Chevelier Henry Wyckoff," once editor of the Democratic Review. Some of the descendants of this William Wyckoff and Augenietje VanDorn settled in Louisiana and others at Easton, Pa. The late Col. Wyckoff who fell at the head of his regiment in the battle of Santiago, Cuba, is said to be a descendant of this Easton branch.

Katrintje (Catharine), born 1707, married a Cornelius Wyckoff, supposed to be from Long Island or Somerset county.

Brom, (Abraham) baptized October 20, 1709, being the first child baptized in the Dutch church of Monmouth. His father was a deacon at this time. He removed to Somerset county, N. J., and settled on the north part of the tract purchased by his brother, Christain VanDorn, at Middlebush. He became sheriff of Somerset county, and one of the leading and influential men of that day. Whom he married I am unable to say, but it is said he married a Forman. *

Peter, baptized September 2, 1701, and was drowned at Shoal Harbour, (now Port Monmouth) when a young man and unmarried.

Isaak (Isaac) baptized March 13, 1715. He remained a bachelor and lived near the old VanDorn homestead and carried on a tannery, shoemaker shop and country store.

Jacob VanDorn, the fourth son above named, owned and occupied under his father's will, about 317 acres, the western half of the tract next to Hillsdale. He built the dwelling house where Elisha Holmes resided until his death. In 1745, while sick, he executed a will now in possession of Hon. Daniel P. VanDoren of Freehold.

He afterward recovered and lived many years, or until 1779. He had other children born after this date, so he cut off his signature from this will and so cancelled it. He probably made a later will. With exception of his signature the paper remains unaltered. It shows, however, exactly what children he then had, what disposition he intended of his property and also what friends he trusted to look after his minor children and carry out his wishes. In short, he speaks for himself in this will and I think it important that a copy should be preserved in print. It will interest his numerous descendants now residing in many states of our union.

True copy of second Jacob VanDorn's will made in 1745, and afterward cancelled by him:

"In name of God, Amen. I, Jacob VanDorn of Freehold, in the county of Monmouth and Eastern Division of the Province of New Jersey, Yeoman, this 28th day of May, A. D. 1745, being very weak in body but of sound and perfect mind and memory, do make, ordain and constitute this my last will and testament as follows, viz:

Imprimis: I resign my soul into the hands of God, my great and glorious Creator, who gave it me, and my body to the earth in hopes of a glorious resurrection at the last day through the merits of my blessed redeemer, Jesus Christ our Lord, to be buried at the discretion of my executors hereinafter mentioned. And as for my temporal estate, which God, in mercy hath given to me, my will and desire is that my funeral charges first be paid, and all my other just and lawful debts discharged and the remainder to be disposed of as follows, viz:

Item: I give unto my loving wife so long as she shall remain my widow, full possession of the farm I now live on with everything belonging to it; and if she should marry again, I give unto her £100 of this currency at 8 shillings the ounce to be levyed out of my movable estate.

Item: I give unto my eldest son named Jacob, three and one quarter parts of my estate; it being divided into sixteen equal parts (viz: all my estate both real and personal).

Item: I give unto my second son named John, three sixteenths parts of my estate, both real and personal.

Item: I give unto my third son named William, two and three quarters of sixteenth parts of my estate, both real and personal.

Item: I give unto my fourth son named Isaac, two and one half of the sixteenth parts of my estate, both real and personal.

Item: I give unto my daughter named Sarah, two and one quarter of the sixteenth parts of my estate, both real and personal.

Item: I give unto my youngest son named Aure, two and one quarter of the sixteenth parts of my estate, both real and personal. My will and desire also is, that if any of the above named children should die, having no legitimate issue, their portion to be equally divided between the surviving children.

My will and desire is that my executors hereinafter named, and I give them full power and authority, if my widow should marry again, so to dispose of the remainder of my estate, as may be by them esteemed the most advantageous for my children, And if any of my said children be under age at that time to bind them out to such trades as they shall see most suitable, paying each their several portions as soon as they shall arrive at the age of twenty-one years, or as the payments shall come in, if they shall sell the said estate.

Item: I do hereby nominate, ordain and constitute Roelof Schenck, the son of John Schanck, and William Wyckoff of said Freehold, executors of this, my last will and testament."

Signed, sealed and delivered in the presence of
JOHN BRAY,
ISAAC VAN DORN,
JACOB SCHENCK.

---

*In the grave yard of Old Scots burying ground we find a tombstone inscribed "Eleanor, wife of Abraham VanDorn, daughter of Jonathan and Margaret Forman, who died May 22, 1733, aged 20 years." Jonathan Forman married Margaret Wyckoff and became a communicant of the Dutch church in 1714. His wife no doubt brought up her children according to Dutch manners and customs and so the Forman children, like the Holmes, became Dutchmen through intermarriage with a more vigorous and sturdy race. I think his daughter Elinor married this Abraham VanDorn, who removed to Somerset county, but he lost her almost as soon as he married her, according to the inscription on this tombstone.

Jacob VanDorn had by his first wife, Maritje Schenck, the following children, all of whom were raised on the western part of the homestead tract:

Jacob, born January 15, 1731, died October 19, 1761, unmarried.

John, born January 6, 1733, married about 1756, his cousin, Augnitje, daughter of Roelof Schenck and Engeltje VanDorn, his wife. He removed to and settled at Peapack about 1760, and had sons Jacob, William and Roelof, and a daughter Ann.

William, born December 3, 1736, married first Rachel, daughter of Guysbert Longstreet of Squan, (now Manasquan) and Rachel Schenck, his wife. She died about 1765 and he afterward married Mary Hunt. He removed to Peapack and had sons, Jacob and Gilbert, and perhaps others. He died October 4th, 1816.

Isaac, born January 24, 1739, and died October 5, 1749.

Sarah, born February 20th, 1741, married about 1761, John Antonides of Dutch Lane, at East Freehold, and had ten children.

Aure, (sometimes mistaken for Aaron) born, September 14, 1744, married May 9, 1765, Ghacy, youngest daughter of Jan Roelofse Schenck and Jacomyntje Couwenhoven. She was born February 14, 1748, and died February 3, 1820. She was named after her father's mother, Geesie Hendrickson, wife of Black Roelof Schenck, but as the younger generations lost knowledge of the Dutch language they would spell Dutch names according to sound, so "Geesie" became "Ghacy," "Antje" became "Onchee," "Altje" "Alchy," etc., etc. This couple had known each other from childhood, for the homesteads lay near each other. Aure VanDorn and Ghacy, or Geesie Schenck, his wife, removed to Peapack and settled there. They raised a large family of children. General Earl VanDorn, who was killed in the Confederate service during the war of the Rebellion, was a descendant of this couple and not of Aaron, son of Christain VanDorn, as erroneously stated in a foot note to one of Judge Voorhees' articles in "Our Home" magazine of Somerville, N. J. See foot note on page 339 of "Our Home," in the year 1873.

Mary, born November 3, 1746, married John Schenck of Penns Neck. He was a captain in the Revolutionary war.

Isaac, born March 14, 1752, married July 3, 1784, Anne, daughter of Garret Couwenhoven and Neeltje or Eleanor Schenck, his wife, who was born May 21, 1754, and died June 11, 1843. Isaac VanDorn died at Middletown village where he lived, on the farm his only son, Garret VanDorn, lived and died on, as has been heretofore mentioned.

Peter, born July 4, 1755, married January 9, 1777, Jannetje, daughter of Elbert Williamson and Williamptje Schenck, his wife.* Jannetje Williamson was baptized July 12, 1758. Peter VanDorn lived in the home his father built and occupied his lands and raised a large family of seven sons and four daughters. Among his sons was one named William who married a daughter of Daniel Polhemus at Phalanx, purchased a farm in the present township of Marlboro about 1816, where he resided until his death. He left surviving him one son, Hon. Daniel P. VanDoren, now, (1898) residing in Freehold, and who still owns his father's farm, and one daughter, Jane, who married the late John Rue Perrine, who was among the first farmers of Manalapan township during the greater part of his life.

Ann, born October 27, 1756, married Lewis, son of Thomas Thompson, who then owned the old stone house on the west side of the turnpike from Freehold to Smithburgh, (now Elton, formerly Clayton's corner). This property was owned by Achsah Hendrickson, wife of Enoch Hendrickson, for many years. Since her death one Hartman has bought it. The private family grave yard of the Thompsons is on the farm.

This Lewis Thompson was a zealous and active loyalist during the revolutionary war. In courting and visiting his wife near Pleasant Valley he had become familiar with all the roads and byways and also with the customs and habits of the Dutch settlers there.

---

*Children of Peter VanDorn and Jannetje (Jane) Williamson, his wife.

Mary, born February 21, 1778, married Rulif Smock.

Jacob, born October 13, 1779, married Gitty Jane Schenck.

Elbert, born November 14, 1781, married Sarah Cowenhoven.

Williampe, born April 3, 1784, married Dr. Benjamin DuBois, son of Dominie DuBois.

Ann, born January 30, 1786, died young.

John, born November 28, 1787, married Mary Cowenhoven.

William, born March 2, 1790, married Catharine Polhemus, died September 2, 1850. His wife died the day previous. Both were buried at the same time in the yard of Brick church.

Isaac, born July 13, 1792, married Eleanor Hankinson, died August 16, 1858.

Peter, born April 15, 1794, married first Catharine DuBois, second Elizabeth VanDerveer. He died February 20, 1877.

Arthur, born July 29, 1797, married Harriet VanCleaf.

Jane, or Jannette, born April 29, 1799, married Elisha Iolmes. She died September 27, 1837, aged 37 years, 7 months and 27 days. She was buried by her husband in the Schenck Couwenhoven yard.

Sarah, born May 31, 1803, married Pierson Hendrickson, who carried on business for many years at Tinton Falls.

Captain John Schenck, the famous partizan leader, resided on an adjoining farm, now occupied by his grandson, David Schenck, and near the Van-Dorn's. A reward of fifty guineas had been offered for his capture or death by the British. There were several midnight raids made by the Tories and British to capture him. Three different times these bands surrounded his house between midnight and daybreak to capture him. He generally slept out in the woods or if in his house he had scouts outlying who brought him instant word of the approaching enemy.

On one of these occasions the Tories were guided or led by this Lewis Thompson, who had married among his near relatives and neighbors. Knowing the country, Thompson managed so well that Captain Schenck barely escaped in his night clothes from a rear window and concealed himself by lying down in a wheat field behind his house. It was in June and the wheat stalks were high enough to hide a man lying down, but so near was he that he could plainly hear them talk and their threats to his wife, and recognized this Lewis Thompson. When war ended Lewis Thompson with his wife removed to Nova Scotia. After remaining there many years and learning that the old bitterness and anger had died away, they came back to visit their relatives. While visiting his wife's people at Holmdel he went one day into a country store kept by one of his wife's relatives. While there Captain John Schenck happened to enter. As soon as his eye fell on Thompson, he turned to the storekeeper, saying "Either that Tory rascal must go out or else I will. The same roof can never cover us both, and if I go out I shall never step foot on your premises again if I live a hundred years."

Knowing that Captain Schenck would do just what he threatened, and that he would lose the custom of his large family connections, he turned to Thompson saying "You must get out of my store and never enter it again." So Thompson left. He died before his wife, leaving several sons and daughters. One of his sons became a lawyer and settled at Somerville, N. J. His mother went there to live with him after her husband's death, and died there at an advanced age.

Van Doren Marriages From Brick Church Records.

Joseph VanDoorn and Femmetje Wyckoff, Aug. 5, 1739.
Antje VanDoorn and Jan Clerk, Dec. 29, 1721.
Arie (or Aure) VanDoorn and Geesie (Ghacy) Schenk, May 9, 1765.
Catharine VanDoorn and Hugh Newel, Nov. 1, 1773.
Isaac VanDoorn and Anne Covenhoven, July 3, 1785.
Jacob VanDoorn and Gitty Schenck, Feb. 4, 1802.
Williampe VanDoorn and Benjamin DuBois, Feb. 16, 1803.
Albert VanDoorn and Sarah Covenhoven, March 14, 1803.
John VanDoorn and Mary Covenhoven, Jan. 30, 1809.
William VanDoorn and Catharine Polhemus, Nov. 28, 1815.
Arthur VanDoorn and Harriet VanCleaf, Jan. 6, 1817.
Peter VanDoorn and Catharine DuBois, March 4, 1817.
Jane VanDoorn and Elisha Holmes, Feb. 17, 1819.
Garret VanDoorn and Willampe Covenhoven, Feb. 24, 1821.
Sarah VanDoorn and Pearson Hendrickson, Aug. 7, 1823.
Margaret VanDoorn and Joseph D. Vanderveer, Jan. 13, 1834.
Peter VanDoorn and Elizabeth Vanderveer, Jan. 26, 1836.
Jacob VanDoorn and Eliza Jane VanMater, Dec. 5, 1837.
David VanDoorn and Mary H. Crawford, Dec. 25, 1824.

From Inscriptions on Tombstone in Private Family Burying-ground on the Daniel D. Covenhoven Farm Near Taylor's Mills.

Mary VanDoorn, d. March 16, 1877. 88 yrs., 5 mos., 2 days.
Her husband, John VanDoorn, d. June 25, 1864. 76 yrs., 6 mos., 27 days.
Peter Covenhoven, d. Feb. 12, 1857. 54 yrs., 10 mos.
His wife, Sarah VanDoorn, d. Aug. 6, 1873. 70 yrs., 3 mos., 12 days.

From Christ Church (Episcopal) Grave Yard, Middletown Village, N. J.

Isaac VanDorn, d. May 7, 1831; age 79 yrs., 1 mon., 12 days.
His wife, Anne Garretse Covenhoven, d. June 11, 1843; age 89 yrs., 21 days.
Their son, Garret VanDorn, b. May 31, 1789, d. Aug. 6, 1856.
His wife, Williampe Covenhoven, b. Jan. 1, 1791; d. Jan. 31, 1874.
William, son of Isaac and Anne VanDorn, d. Mar. 1, 1817, age 21 yrs., 8 mos., 4 days.
Mary VanDorn, daughter of Isaac and Anne VanDorn, d. Mar. 13, 1805; age 17 yrs., 3 mos., 22 days.
Jacob, son of Isaac and Anne VanDorn, d. May 30, 1808; age 22 yrs., 8 mos., 4 days.

From Brick Church Cemetery.

Peter VanDoorn, Sen., d. Apr. 18, 1834; age 78 yrs., 9 mos., 14 days.

His wife, Jane Willemsen, (daughter of Elbert Willemsen and Willempe Schenck) d. Jan. 28, 1845; age. 86 yrs., 6 mos., 23 days.

Peter VanDoorn, d. Feb. 20, 1877; age 82 yrs., 10 mos., 5 days.

His wife, Elizabeth Vanderveer, d. Mar. 2, 1862, age 59 yrs., 12 days.

Isaac VanDoorn, d. Aug. 16, 1858; b. Mar. 13, 1793. A soldier of the war 1812.

His wife, Elleanor Hankinson, b. Mar. 28, 1805, d. Mar. 28, 1888.

Peter A. VanDoorn, d. Jan. 17, 1876; age 71 yrs., 5 mos., 20 days.

His wife, Elizabeth Kernaghan, d. Mar. 5, 1869; age 58 yrs., 5 mos., 23 days.

Sarah VanDoorn, wife of John Patterson, d. Oct. 23, 1852; age 22 yrs., 1 mo., 24 days.

William VanDoorn, d. Sept. 2, 1850, b. Mar. 2, 1790.

His wife, Catharine Polhemus, b July 16, 1797, d. Sept. 1, 1850.

This last was a double funeral. In death they were united as in life. The fine monument in yard of Brick Church over their graves tells briefly the story.

Among the well known and honored citizens of Monmouth who have borne the VanDorn name was Rev. Luther Halsey VanDorn, a lineal descendant of Christain VanDorn and Altje Schenck, his wife, of Somerset county, heretofore spoken of. He was pastor of the old Tennent church seventeen years. The children he baptized and the young couples he married, are now old men and women scattered through the township of Manalapan and those adjoining. They remember, however, Dominie VanDorn's plain, earnest ways and talk, and the sincere interest he took in all that concerned their welfare. After he left Tennent he had charge of two churches in New York City, and then was called to a church at Montville, N. J. In the latter years of his life when his head was silvered and his shoulders bowed with the infirmities of age, he was pastor of the Dutch church at Middletown village, in this county. Here he "died in harness." While a man of reserved and rather stiff manners outwardly, he had a kind and sensitive heart, keenly alive to ingratitude, slights or insults, and very sympathetic for the troubles and sorrows of others. While he had his own share of the troubles, cares and trials which fall on a country minister of this denomination and also of domestic affliction, he bore them with that reticence and dislike of every public exhibition of either joy or grief, hereditary in his family and race. When trouble and bereavement came to others—his parishioners and neighbors—he was remarkably tender and sympathetic in his efforts to console and comfort them, but in a very plain and homely manner. The writer once saw him, when an old man and a little while before his death, break down in public, and cry like a child, while attempting to console the members of a family lately bereaved by death. The writer heard him in the pulpit a short time before his decease. The one idea which ran like a thread through his discourse, was that the mystery of life was as great as the mystery of death, and that both were controlled by the Creator. That the highest wisdom as well as practical judgment in everyday life, dictated entire trust or faith in the Creator, who did all things well, and had promised that "At evening time it should be light." I cannot recall his words which seemed prophetic of the end so soon to come to him, when he lay cold and still in his parsonage at Middletown.† His ideas, however, were identical with those expressed in the following verses:

"We know not what it is, Dear, this sleep so deep and still;
The folded hands, the awful calm, the cheeks so pale and chill;
The lids that will not lift again, though we may call and call;
The strange white solitude of peace, that settles over all.

We know not what it means, Dear, this desolate heart pain,
The dread to take our daily way, and walk in it again,
We know not to what sphere, the loved who leave us, go.
But this we know, our loved and lost, if they should come this day—
Should come and ask us "What is life?" Not one of us could say.
Life is a mystery, as deep as ever death can be;
Yet, oh! how sweet it is to us—this life we live and see.

Then might they say—those vanished ones, and blessed is the thought;
"So Death is sweet to us, Beloved, though we may tell you naught;
We may not tell it to the Quick, this mystery of Death—
Ye may not tell us if ye would, the mystery of Breath.'

The child, who enters Life, comes not with knowledge or intent,
So those who enter Death, must go as little children sent;
Nothing is known—but I believe that God is overhead,
And as life is to the living, so death is to the Dead."

†Rev. Luther I. VanDorn was sixty-two years old when called as pastor of the Middletown Dutch church. It was through his request that the new parsonage was erected on the opposite side of the street from the church edifice, and he was the first pastor to occupy it. In October, 1876, he was suddenly called away and his wife followed him February 25, 1881. Both are interred in Fairview cemetery. It was his wish to end his days and be buried in Monmouth county, for here his forefathers had lived, and numerous kinsmen sleep their last sleep beneath the soil of this county, and so it was.

SOME ACCOUNT OF LEWIS MORRIS AND HIS DOINGS IN MONMOUTH COUNTY.

The names of Jacob VanDorn, Daniel Hendrickson and Arie, Aure or Adrian Bennett appear prominently on the first records of the First Dutch church of Monmouth, not only as the organizers and first communicants in 1709, but as the deacons and elders, at this time or a few years after. The fact that Daniel Hendrickson had served as sheriff of this county, and had also conducted religious services among his own people, prior to the coming of Joseph Morgan as a regular pastor, would indicate that he was a trusted leader of the Dutch settlers, and a man in whose good judgment and integrity they confided.

There is, however, another record, which, if facts therein stated are really facts, casts an ugly stain, not only on their characters as professing christians, but as ordinary law abiding citizens.

The minutes of the Court of General Quarter Sessions of the Peace for the years 1700 and 1701 now in the Monmouth county clerk's office, contain entries not only accusing Jacob VanDorn and Arie (Adrian) Bennett as has heretofore been stated, but also accusing Daniel Hendrickson with refusing to serve as grand juror, defiance of the judges to their faces, or, as the record has it, open contempt and misbehavior in court. These men, also as residents of the old township of Middletown, and members of the militia, and from their sympathies and associations, are further implicated in the general charge against the citizens of this township of breaking up by violence, a court which convened at Middletown village March 25, 1701, making prisoners of Andrew Hamilton, the governor of New Jersey, Thomas Gordon, the attorney general, Lewis Morris, president of the council, and presiding judge of the Monmouth courts, together with the associate judges and the county officers, and keeping them under guard at Middletown four days. During this time there was no head to the government of New Jersey, and no officers to administer the law in Monmouth county. That all these outrageous and rebellious acts were committed for the sole purpose of releasing a pirate, one of Capt. Kidd's men, from the custody of this court.

John Johnstone, a Scotchman, who a few years before had been presiding judge of the Monmouth courts, and who was a zealous partizan of Governor Andrew Hamilton, wrote the following letter the next day:

March 26, 1701.
To the Council of New Jersey:

Honorable Gentlemen.—Yesterday Governor Hamilton, with four of the justices of this county, met at Middletown, for holding the Court of Sessions, as appointed by the acts of assembly of this province, when they had opened court, and begun the trial of one, who confessed himself, one of Kidd's men, several of the people of Middletown, who for that purpose, had appointed a training of the militia, and being in arms, came into the house where the court was sitting and forcibly rescued the prisoner. The governor and justices commended the sheriff and constables to keep the peace, and in the scuffle two of the foremost of the fellows were slightly wounded. There being seventy or eighty men, and the governor and justices, without force, they were by this multitude made prisoners; and are by them, kept under strict guards. This is not a thing which happened by accident, but by design. For some considerable time past there, some of the ringleaders kept, as I am informed, a pirate in their houses, and threatened any that would offer to seize him. Gentlemen, I thought it my duty to inform you of this, and to beg your assistance to help the settling our peace or to take the government upon you until his majesty's pleasure be known.

I am, your honors, most humble servant,

JOHN JOHNSTONE.
Monmouth, East Jersey, March 26, 1701.

The gravamen of the accusation in Dr. Johnstone's letter, as well as that in the court record of this occurrence, is that the Middletown people were associated and in sympathy with sea robbers, and committed all this high handed ruffianism to aid a pirate to escape from the faithful officers of the law, whom they illtreated and imprisoned, while the criminal was set at liberty.

Lewis Morris, soon after, in a communication to the Lords of Trade in

England, makes the same charge: That the wicked people of Middletown were guilty of rank rebellion, for the purpose of delivering a pirate from the clutches of the law. It was very common in that age for the politicians and others interested, to accuse the high officials of the American provinces on the Atlantic coast and the West Indies, of harboring or protecting pirates and illegal traders and sharing in their plunder. See Vol. II N. J. Arch., pages 150-55, 277-89, and 358-62.

The following is from a communication of Edward Randolph to authorities in England dated March 24, 1701, (the day before the outbreak at Middletown village). Speaking of East Jersey and West Jersey he writes "They are all in confusion for want of government, and humbly pray to be taken under his majesty's immediate protection and government. They likewise receive and harbor pirates." †

The ideas are very similar in all these communications and records and looks like concerted action. The Randolph letter is dated one day before and the Johnstone letter one day after the Middletown people captured the governor and his officers; but as it required some six weeks for a sailing vessel to reach England in that day, it was easy to antedate a letter two or three days, and then perhaps it might be a week or two before it could be sent.

Lewis Morris that same spring went to England, and carried with him a certified copy of the record from the minutes now in our clerk's office. It was a well settled maxim of the English law, that the facts set out in a court record must be accepted as true. Morris, therefore, calculated that his charge against the people of Middletown would be received as true by the government in England, and he would also be on hand to influence their action. He must have felt keenly the indignities to which he had been subjected, for he was a very proud and egotistical man. The excitement and feeling which prevailed at the Peace meeting in Middletown some hundred and sixty odd years later, was tame alongside of this attack on the governor of the province and the officers of the county.

We find Lewis Morris of Tinton Falls in London the following summer. He sends a communication to the Lords of Trade dated at London, August 4, 1701. Among other matters he writes:

†Vol. II N. J. Arch., page 360.

"Their endeavors had the effect they proposed as appears by the several records (No. 1, 2, 3, 4, 5) now laid before your Lordships. And to consummate the work so well begun and successfully carried on, they did on the 25th of March, 1701, rescue a pyrate, one of Kidd's crew, from the bar, seize the governor and justices as by record No. 6, does more at large appear."

This "record No. 6," was a certified copy from the minutes of the sessions of Monmouth county, of the court held at Middletown village March 25, 1701, which had been written up after their four days captivity at Middletown had ended, under supervision of Hamilton and Morris. Morris further writes:

"I have laid before your Lordships the truth of fact, as your Lordships, by comparing the names of the petitioners of East Jersey with the names in the records of the several riots committed in the province, will find these riots to be made by those persons who are now your petitioners. Especially, that remarkable riot, or rather rebellion, committed on the 25th of March, and by record No. 6 appears, which I now lay before your Lordships as a complaint, and beg those persons may have an exemplary punishment."

We thus see that Lewis Morris not only took the trouble of making a voyage to England, but used all his ability to bring the heavy hand of the English government on the Middletown people as rebels and abettors of piracy. He persisted with indefatigable malice in his efforts to punish them, even after Queen Anne, in her instructions to Lord Cornbury, had enjoined him to let the old quarrels and fights between the proprietors and people die out unnoticed. § Also see Morris' letter of September 29th, 1702, pages 504-5-6, Vol. II N. J. Archives. The vindicative feelings shown by him would indicate that there is some truth in the traditions of this uprising at Middletown, that after Lewis Morris was taken prisoner, he was tied to the whipping post in front of the block house, with a bunch of rods fastened on his back.

Lewis Morris had also grossly libeled the people of this part of Monmouth in a letter written to the Bishop of London, who was a man of influence with the English government, and by virtue of his office in the Church, a member of the House of Lords. This letter is published in full on pages 8 and 9 of Whitehead's eulogy of Lewis Morris, entitled "Papers of Governor Lewis Morris."

§Vol. II N. J. Arch., p. 508, section 6; Vol. III N. J. Arch., p. 71.

"Middletown was settled from New York and New England. It is a large township. There is no such thing as a church or religion amongst them. They are, perhaps, the most ignorant and wicked people in the world. Their meetings on Sunday are at the public house, when they get their fill of rum and go to fighting and running of races."

Capt. Andrew Bowne, a Baptist, together with many others of this sect, had met for religious services for many years previous to this time. Richard Hartshorne, a consistent Quaker, and others of this belief, are all included in this sweeping condemnation. So are Garret and Jan Schenck, Peter Wyckoff, Daniel Hendrickson, Jacob VanDorn and the Couwenhovens, who had all brought over from Long Island to Monmouth, their brass clasped Dutch Bibles, and tried to follow in everyday life the teachings therein. Some of these old Bibles are yet in existence and the pages show by the wear, that they were in everyday use for many years, or until the Dutch tongue was lost by their descendants.

The first pioneer settlers of Monmouth from Rhode Island and Gravesend, were men and women who had been persecuted and driven out of New England, because of their conscientious adherence to Baptist and Quaker convictions. It is true that many of them were dead at this time, but their children had become men and women and tried to follow in their footsteps. Knowing all this, Lewis Morris represented to the great Prelate of the Church of England, that they were the most degraded and evil-minded of all the inhabitants of this earth, and of course would naturally associate with cut-throats and robbers, and oppose such a godly and good churchman as Lewis Morris.

This charge of abetting pirates to escape from the officers of the law was a most serious one. Piracy was a high crime and punishable by English law with death on the scaffold. Capt. Kidd had been arrested only a short time before. Assisting a man accused of being a "Red Seaman," as they then called pirates, to escape was to become an accessory to the crime, and liable to same penalty. To break up a court and imprison the judges, who represented the King of England, was rank rebellion and an unpardonable crime like treason.

In view of these dark and evil accusations against the pioneer settlers of the old township of Middletown, whose descendants are now found among the most respectable citizens of this county and state, and in nearly all the other states of our union, it becomes important to understand the characters and interests and feelings of the leaders of the contending parties and factions of that time.

Only in this way can we ascertain whether these charges are true, or only trumped up for political ends or to gratify private vengeance. It is also a very interesting and important period in our colonial history, for it ended the Proprietary government and brought about a new era in our history.

When the last of the perfidious and false-hearted Stuarts was kicked out of England, and the Dutch king of "Glorious Memory" ascended the throne the principles of religious toleration which had long prevailed in the republic of Holland, together with personal liberty, were established for the first time in England and her colonies, by constitutional law. It was the great revolution of 1688, the most important era in English history.

The commercial interests of Holland had long demanded the suppression of piracy, and the interests of the great merchants of England, whose commerce was then next to the Netherlands, demanded it for the same cause. William of Orange used all his power in this direction, and caused laws to be enacted by the English Parliament of the most severe character against this crime.

In obedience to these laws and the earnest efforts of William of Orange to enforce them, the Lords of Trade sent the following order to the New Jersey proprietors and their officials in control of the provincial government: "That no Pirate or Sea-Robber be anywhere sheltered or entertained under the severest penalties." This order was dated "February 9th, 1696-7 ‖," some three years before "Moses Butterworth," one of Captain Kidd's men, came to New Jersey.

At this period, and for many years thereafter, merchant vessels bound for distant seas were manned and armed like men-of-war, for there was often more fighting than trading. The waters of the East Indies and the China and Malay coasts swarmed with ferocious and savage pirates. No ship in those far-off waters was safe from capture unless well armed and manned with a large crew of fighting men.

Morocco, Algiers, and other barbarous powers on the northern coast of

---

‖ Vol. II, N. J. Archives, p. 134-136.

Africa had long made piracy a business. The capture and enslavement of white Christians was a legitimate and profitable enterprise, according to their code of morals.

The Netherland republic had for a long time previous to the landing of their Stadtholder and his Dutch troops at Torbay, tried to suppress these sea-robbers of the Mediterranean, while Charles II of England had encouraged and aided them to injure the commerce of Holland.

After 1688, under the rule of the Dutch king, common sense and common honesty began to guide the policy of the English government for the first time, since great Cromwell's death. The maritime nations of Europe, jealous of each other, and rivals in commercial colonization, were in this age almost constantly at war, and privateers were used to prey on each other's merchant ships. These privateers and armed merchant vessels when in the Pacific or Indian oceans, or along the American Atlantic coast, did not hesitate to attack and capture vessels of another nation, even when at peace, if they thought the spoils warranted the risk. News in those days traveled slowly and even if such atrocities were heard of from the other side of the world, witnesses to the facts would be lacking for "Dead men tell no tales."

The American coast, particularly the Spanish Main, as called, was a favorite cruising ground for these half-pirates and half-privateers or armed illegal trading ships. Under the strong and resolute guidance of the Dutch king from the vantage ground of the English throne, the old policy of the Holland republic was thoroughly and energetically supported by England, to root out and exterminate these pests of trade and commerce ¶. The readers of colonial history will remember how common it was in this age to accuse colonial officers with harbouring pirates and sharing in their plunder. The charge was easily made if the pirate ships happened by chance or design to run into some bay or harbor, whether the governor knew it or not; so if a pirate crew or part of them slipped into New York or Philadelphia to spend their gold in wild orgies or carousels, the blame would be cast on the governor of harboring them, even if he had no knowledge of it. This charge was readily believed in England, for had they not been dumping their vagabonds, thieves and adventurers into the American colonies for many years, and what better could be expected? To disprove such complaints and charges required an expensive and long voyage across the Atlantic ocean, with witnesses and legal delays and expensive lawyers to fee. Finding how credulous the English government was in entertaining and acting on these accusations, and how fatal it was to the political life of a colonial governor or other officer, it soon became a favorite weapon of the politicians or office seekers of that time, to make this charge of "harboring and entertaining pirates" when they wanted to "down" some obnoxious officer, or get his place for themselves or friends. This same charge was made against Governor Andrew Hamilton to the Lords of Trade under date of May 20, 1702, by William Dockware and Peter Sonmans, as follows:

"His (Hamilton) encouraging and protecting pirates and receiving money from them, particularly Merick and Elson, two of Averries' crew, who together with several others, lived under his government unmolested 'till afterward seized by his successor, (Basse) and by him delivered to the governor of New York **."

Under date May 2, 1700, Governor Hamilton writes as follows:

Since my arrival (December, 1699), I have taken four pirates into custody that came from Madagascar. Their names are James How, Nicholas Churchill, Robert Hickman and John Eldridge. Eldridge's treasure is in the hands of Col. Quarry of Philadelphia. If the other three have any, it is hid in the woods, or elsewhere, for there is none to be found about them. How is a sensible man, and I presume if he is promised a pardon, can make considerable discoveries. I shall, pursuant to His Majesty's orders to my Lord Bellomont, (governor of New York with admiralty jurisdiction) deliver up to

---

¶ Capt. Kidd, at this date (1701), was in prison in England awaiting trial for piracy. The English people were all agog over the thousand rumors about his horrible crimes on the high seas. His conviction and execution was a foregone conclusion. The commercial interests of England demanded a victim to serve as an example or "scare-crow" to intimidate the sea rovers who infested the ocean. Capt. William Kidd happened to be the first one who put in an appearance at the wrong time for himself. At an earlier day when the Stuarts ruled or at a later day he would have been welcomed as a hero, like Jamison when he got back to England from his piratical expedition against the Dutch farmers of the Transvaal.

** N. J. Archives, Vol. II, p. 471.

his Excellency the before named persons and what treasure I can at any time discover, belonging to them or any such people, who, I am sensible are a pest among mankind.

Your Most Humble Servant,

ANDREW HAMILTON,

May, 1700.

This letter proves that Hamilton knew that the courts of New Jersey had no jurisdiction over this crime. Only admiralty courts could try offences committed on the high seas like piracy, and the governor of New York was vice admiral and there was admiralty court in that province. For this reason the New Jersey officials were ordered to send all pirates taken in this province to Bellomont, the New York governor. This is just what Hamilton writes he will do, and this was his only duty in the premises. The county courts of Monmouth had no more jurisdiction over piracy or other crimes committed outside of its territory, than they have today. Only criminal offences committed within the county boundaries can be tried in the county courts.

Besides, Hamilton resided at Burlington, in Burlington county, and any examination to see if there was probable cause to believe him guilty and so hold him, could have been taken before a justice of that place. In the above four cases Hamilton does not bind any of the four men to appear before the high court of Common Right at Perth Amboy or any of the county courts of sessions. Neither does he take any examination before a justice or himself, but writes that in pursuance of King William's orders he will deliver up the four pirates to Governor Bellomont of New York. This was all he was required to do and all he could do in such cases.

How then, can we explain his action at Middletown village in the case of Moses Butterworth, Capt. Kidd's man, as he admitted?

If he confessed his guilt there was no necessity for any examination to ascertain if there was probable cause to deprive him of his liberty. And why bind over a "self-confessed pirate" to appear before a county court at a remote place in the woods, as Middletown village was then situated, when it could just as well have been done before Hamilton himself at Burlington.

His duty at the most in such crimes was merely that of a committing magistrate. And what necessity was there for Hamilton as governor to preside formally at the remote courts of Monmouth, when Lewis Morris or Capt. Samuel Leonard, two of his council, were fully capable of transacting all the court business. All these questions can be answered, and the old settlers of Middletown, like Daniel Hendrickson, Jacob VanDorn, William Hendricks, and others cleared of this accusation that they broke up a court to rescue a "Pyrate" and were "the most ignorant and wicked people in the world."

This "pirate business" was a device or scheme of Lewis Morris, Hamilton, Leonard and others to throw blame on their political opponents, and put them in false position, or "hole," as modern politicians call it. They also wanted to hide the real issues involved, and particularly such questions as would cause the proprietors to lose the right of government over New Jersey. This pirate, Moses Butterworth, was "a good enough Morgan" for their purposes, but like all other frauds and deceptions they overreached themselves, when they put on record that he was a "self confessed pirate" and when this court had no jurisdiction either to try or punish him, even if he had been "Bloody Blackbeard" in person.

SAYINGS AND DOINGS OF LEWIS MORRIS OF MONMOUTH AND ELSEWHERE.

Andrew Hamilton had served as governor of New Jersey from 1692 to 1697, when he was superseded by Jeremiah Basse, an Englishman. The proprietors wrote from England that Hamilton was dismissed, not for any fault, but because all Scotchmen were debarred by a late act of parliament, from holding offices of trust or profit in an English colony.

The people of Middletown were very jubilant over this news, for they had long been governed, much to their disgust, by Scotch officials. They not only regarded the Scotch as foreigners, but felt that they had been transferred wrongfully to the control of these strangers. These Scotch officials also represented the proprietors and pushed them for "quitt rents."

The Middletown people had not only procured a patent for the territory of Monmouth with right of local government, from the authorized agent of the Duke of York (for it was clearly within Nicoll's instructions) but they had actually paid out their hard cash, and occupied the lands before any notice was given of the transfer of New Jersey to Berkeley and Carteret.

The pioneers of Monmouth had expended £369½, or $1,847 in buying out the Indians' title to part of what is now Monmouth county. If this money had been put out at interest at 6 per cent, and the interest invested each year from 1667 to 1898, it would now amount to more than the assessed valuation of the real estate in "Newasincks, Navarumsunk and Pootapeck Necks," as they called the lands so bought of the red men.

Besides, $1,847 was a large sum of money for men living in the wilderness of the new world in that day to raise. Money was then very hard to get. They were also obliged to make many journeys through Rhode Island and Long Island, to persuade men to subscribe for these expenses and to migrate to this region, and so make up the number their patent required.

They were subjected to trouble and expense of transporting their families, stock and goods across the water. To survey, lay out lots and roads, clear lands, build cabins, plant crops, protect stock and crops from wild animals, and themselves from the savages, required the hardest physical labor with their few and rough tools. Nearly everything was done by the hardest physical toil. For the most part they were uneducated men and women, yet they had to organize townships, enact local laws, establish courts and elect officers. They had no go betweens like clergymen, physicians, undertakers, and lawyers, but did their own praying, their own doctoring, and burying their own dead. After all this trouble, expense and hardship, they are suddenly told that their patent is worthless, and some people whom they had never heard of, not only own their lands but have the right to govern them. That these new and strange owners of the soil, and the rulers of the inhabitants thereof, are called Proprietors, "such a name as we simple creatures never before heard of" they frankly say. They are called upon to swear allegiance and obedience to these "unheard-of" rulers, and to pay them rent for their lands and betterments. Nobody offers to repay them for the money laid out for the Indian title, the true American lords of the soil. Their time, labors, and improvements are all owned by somebody else, and they are required to pay rent to them as tenants.

Three separate proclamations came from Charles II, King of England, that they must submit and obey Berkeley and Cartaret or their assigns, or be punished by the severest penalties of the law. They are told by the agents of the Lord Proprietors, that they must pay rent for the lands they occupy and render due obedience, or their goods will be distrained, and they prosecuted by law as mutineers or rebels.

Their reply to these demands can be found in the old township book of Middletown, and it is well worth reading, for it was the first declaration of independence uttered on the American continent. The substance is that they "will stick to their patent" and may God defend the right.

Their treatment was unjust, but the blame falls on that royal scoundrel

Charles Stuart, and his false-hearted brother known in history as the Duke of York, and later as James II of England. Richard Nicolls had full authority from the Duke of York to grant the Monmouth patent under his general instructions. The principal under such circumstances was bound by the acts of his agent, before the authority was revoked, and before notice was had of any transfer by the principal. The Duke of York made the transfer or assignment of New Jersey to Berkeley and Cartaret, after Nicolls had sailed from England, and before any notice of their successful robbery of the New Netherlands from the Dutch in time of peace. Berkeley and Cartaret had never expended a single cent or did one stroke of work for this land. They were the sycophants and toadies of Charles II, and his boon companions in his midnight orgies and daylight adulteries.

Every principle of equity demanded that Nicolls' grant, followed by actual purchase from the true owners, and settlement, without notice of a secret prior transfer, if such was the fact, should have been upheld, if there was any justice in the laws of England.

It would today in any equity court of these United States. It is very questionable whether the grant to Berkeley and Cartaret was really prior in point of fact. Charles II and his brother, James II, respected neither the rights of their own subjects in England, or of anybody else, except the King of France and the Pope of Rome. To antedate a charter of this kind would be a small trifle in their eyes. Besides, who would dare question it or call them to account? Surely not the poor people in the wilds of America three thousand miles away. The character of Charles II has been truly portrayed by Gilbert Burnet, Bishop of Salisbury, who lived during his reign, in the book called "History of His Own Time." He compares Charles to Tiberius, the infamous Emperor of Rome. But what could be expected of a so-called King, who dragged the poor bones of Great Cromwell from the grave, and suspended them on a gibbet. When Cromwell was alive he never dare look him in the face, but when dead he takes a contemptible savage revenge on his corpse. A man who would do such an act would not hesitate to rob a friendly nation of their territory, or his own subjects of their rights, by dating back a document like the charter of New Jersey. Neither would a man like the Duke of York, who fostered, upheld and pushed on George Jeffrey, the judicial wholesale murderer, Tom Boilman, and John Graham of Claverhouse, "the three heroes of his reign," hesitate at such a small matter as ante-dating a transfer of wild lands across the Atlantic.

James II, not his tools and creatures, is responsible for the horrors which followed Monmouth's rebellion in 1685, and which followed his efforts to establish prelacy in Scotland. So this falsehearted, cruel tyrant is responsible for the proprietary government of New Jersey and their ownership of the soil. The last has been a curse and a wrong to our people in Monmouth county from the day it was granted, down to the day within our memory, when they sold land under Shark river at public sale for a song, and took up lands on the coast next to Belmar, Spring Lake, and other places, clouding titles by wholesale, and selling them for insignificant sums of money, compared to their real value. Yet we find certain American historians of the New England type who try to justify Charles II. "The king can do no wrong," for he rules by divine right, seems ingrained in the minds of people who worship aristocracy and royalty. "These be thy gods, O Dudes and Dudesses!" Today, however, such superstitious, slavish, and snobbish ideas have no influence with sensible people who have any conscience and respect the right of their fellow men and their own manhood.

When Governor Basse arrived in East Jersey, he appointed two of the leading and trusted citizens of Middletown, Capt. Andrew Bowne and Richard Hartshorne, members of his council. Lewis Morris of "Tintern Manor" was "left out in the cold." This was a severe blow to his pride and ambition. He was that kind of a man who would either "rule or ruin." His very signature, if handwriting is any indication of character, shows that he had a high opinion of himself. This slight, together with the appointment of his political opponents, Bowne and Hartshorne, to the council stirred up all the gall in his body. He became a bitter and bold opponent of Governor Basse. He now arraigns the proprietors in the severest manner, telling some very unpalatable truths, and alleging that "Nothing they say or do can be depended upon or believed." This Lewis Morris made more history in East Jersey between 1695 and 1746, than any other man during those years. He was certainly a remarkable man. To understand his character we must consider his sayings and doings, for there is much of both in our county and colonial records. We cannot understand the history of these times unless we understand Lewis Morris. He was a nephew of one Lewis Morris who had served as Captain of a troop of horse under Cromwell, the greatest Englishman that ever lived. After the Stuarts were restored he emigrated to the island of Barbadoes, and from there removed to New York in 1673. He or his brother Richard, then deceased, had acquired a large tract of land in what are now Shrewsbury and Atlantic townships. He started an iron foundry at Tinton Falls with bog ore. He left Monmouth in 1686 and died in 1691, on his plantation near Harlem, N. Y., afterwards called by his nephew, Lewis Morris, the "Manour of Morrisania." He was very fond of calling his wild lands "Manors." It gave him consequence, he doubtless thought, for a grand name goes a long way with people, who cannot distinguish between words and their real meanings underneath.

At a court held at Middletown village in September, 1686, Lewis Morris is arrested and brought before the court, on a charge made "on oath of a negro woman named Franck." The offence or crime is not stated. This omission, together with the fact that Morris did not stand any open trial, would indicate that it was a scandalous or disgraceful accusation. Instead of fighting it by evidence and trial, he procures a writ of habeas corpus from Governor Gawen Laurie, and removed the complaint to the next court of Common Right at Perth Amboy. I do not know what the records of this court show in October, 1686, but would not be surprised if it was quietly consigned to the "Tomb of the Capulets." A poor negro wench, doubtless a slave, could not follow up such a case against a man like Lewis Morris, however grievous her wrongs.

The next entry is at a court held at Middletown village March 22, 1687:

"Lewis Morris' commission as justice of the peace is read."

This appointment made him one of the associate judges of the Common Pleas and General Quarter Sessions of the peace, according to the laws of England.

From this time until 1746, or about 60 years, Lewis Morris was a very conspicuous man in political affairs of East Jersey. No man either in colonial or state history, had a longer political life or more bitter quarrels and antagonisms. He reached the highest position, when he became His Majesty's Governor of New Jersey. He died in 1746, while in office.

On page 73 of Book C of Deeds, Monmouth clerk's office, we find one Benjamin Hicks, who with others had been indicted for same offense, giving information against Lewis Morris and others for "running of races and playing at nyne pins on ye Sabbath Day." No action however, was taken against the newly fledged justice, but Hicks and his comrades were fined five shillings each for "racing and playing nyne pins on ye Sabbath."

In 1691 we find Lewis Morris sitting as one of the associate judges of the Monmouth courts, John Johnstone, a Scotchman, being president judge, and Capt. Samuel Leonard acting as prosecutor, or as then called "His Majesty's attorney."

In 1692 Morris was appointed by Governor Hamilton a member of the Council of New Jersey. This was an influential position and gave Morris access to, and influence with, the men who then ruled New Jersey. He seems to have ingratiated himself into the confidence of Hamilton and his Scotch supporters, for he soon became Hamilton's right-hand-man and trusted lieutenant. From this time onward he was one of Hamilton's most zealous and faithful partisans.

We now find a third Lewis Morris turning up as a justice of the peace in this county, and sitting along side of the other Lewis Morris in our county courts. He is described in the old records as "Lewis Morris of Passage Point," (afterwards known as Black Point.) I think these two men were cousins, but am not sure of it. At all events they were close and intimate friends. "Lewis Morris of Tintern Manor," as member of the council had sufficient influence to have his friends in Monmouth appointed to office.

The records of a court held at Middletown village, September 1694, show that Lewis Morris of Passage Point is indicted because "he, with several of his negroes did feloniously take away the hay of William Shattock." As usual there is no trial, for the indictment is removed by habeas corpus to the Court of Common Right. "Lewis Morris of Tintern Manor" entered into bond for "Lewis Morris of Passage Point." It does not appear that Shattock ever got back his hay or received any other satisfaction.

The grand jury of this court also present Lewis Morris of Tintern Manor "for fencing in the highway." Although present on the bench, the two Morrises and the other judges order that a summons issue for his appearance at next court. At the next court held at Middletown village March 27, 1695, we find both Lewis Morrises on the bench, as they were very punctual in their attendance. Lewis Morris of Passage Point is arraigned on an indictment "for striking Nicholas Sarah several blows." The Honorable Lewis Morris of Passage Point did then inform Honorable Lewis Morris of Tintern Manor and other justices "how matters stood," for so the record has it, and then without hearing Nicholas Sarah, or any evidence or trial, "the indictment was dismissed by the bench."

Thereupon the two Lewis Morrises "did desire to withdraw and go home, by reason of their families being sick." Which request was granted, and so they went out, mounted their horses and rode out of Middletown, doubtless laughing and joking on their way home to Shrewsbury, over the fruitless efforts of poor Nicholas Sarah to take the law of a "big Lewis Morris." At next court, Lewis Morris of Tintern Manor is again presented by the grand jury for "fencing in ye highway that goes to Freehold and Middletown." Although present on the bench, the court orders a summons issued for him to appear and answer at next court.

The fates at this time step in and relieve the people of Monmouth of one Lewis Morris, for "he of Passage Point was murdered by his negroes." The surviving Lewis Morris, however, proved himself an able bodied and robust Morris, and gave the Middletown people all the trouble and fighting they wanted. At next court in March, 1696, Thomas Gordon, a Scotchman, who professed to be a lawyer, is appointed prosecutor. He was one of Lewis Morris' political and perhaps personal friends. When the presentment against Lewis Morris for "fencing in the highway" was called up, Gordon coolly turned to the people present, and demanded a fee from some one, before he would try this indictment. As Gordon well knew, no individual would volunteer in such a case, or pay such a fee as he demanded. The records then go on to say "there was no one to prosecute the said Lewis Morris, so the presentment was quasht."

At a Court held at Shrewsbury in September, 1698, Lewis Morris is again presented for fencing in the highway between "Tinton and Swimming River bridge," but no action is taken by the court. The same presentment was made in September, 1699, and nothing done. During a part of this period from 1692 to 1699 Lewis Morris had considerable private civil litigation with several of the citizens of the county. Capt. Andrew Bowne and Richard Hartshorne were judges of the county part of this time, but they did not permit Morris to have his way in everything. They learned from their intercourse with him to distrust him, and he had but little influence with them after 1696.

Capt. Bowne and Richard Hartshorne were also judges of the Court of Common Right held at Perth Amboy in 1698-9. At a court of Common Right held at Perth Amboy May 11, 1698, Governor Jeremiah Basse, presiding and Capt. Bowne and Richard Hartshorne with four other judges also sitting on the bench. Lewis Morris came into court and insolently demanded by what authority they held court. The judges replied "By the King's authority." This Morris denied. The Court then ordered his arrest for open contempt.

Lewis Moris defied them to arrest him, and said "He would fain see who darst lay hold on him." Thereupon, a constable took hold of him but he resisted, and tried to draw his sword or hanger, as then called. *

The judges fined him £50 ($250) for "his denying the authority of the court and open contempt" and ordered him committed to prison until paid. The fine, I think, he paid, but it did not quiet but rather spurred him on to more insolent measures.

He, and his political allies, Thomas Gordon and George Willocks go through East Jersey, holding public meetings and denouncing in the severest manner Governor Basse and the Proprietors. They soon stir up the people to acts of violence. In May, 1699, the following warrant was issued to arrest Lewis Morris. †

"To the Sheriff of the county of Middlesex, his under sheriff or deputy, or either of them:

"Whereas we are informed that Lewis Morris of Tinton, in the county of Monmouth, and province aforesaid, Gent., did in April last at Perth Amboy in the said province, seditiously assemble with others and endeavor to subvert the laws of this province and did by malicious and reproachful words, asperge the governor of said province, contrary to the peace of our Soverign Lord the King, and the laws in such cases made and provided. These are therefore to will and require, and in His Majesty's name, strictly to charge and com-

---

* Vol. III, N. J. Arch., p. 476-7, 479 and 480-81.
† Vol. III, N. J. Arch., p. 481-82.

mand you, to take into your custody the said Lewis Morris, and him to convey to the jail of your county, and there safely to keep, until he shall give sufficient security in the sum of three hundred pounds ($1,500) for his appearance at the Court of Common Right to be held at Perth Amboy the second Tuesday of October next, then and there to answer the premises; and in meantime to be of good behavior towards His Majesty and all his liege people. Hereof fail not at your peril, and for so doing this shall be your warrant. Given under our hands and seals May 11, in the eleventh year of the reign of our Soverign Lord, William the Third of England, A. D. 1699, at Perth Amboy in province aforesaid.

        ANDREW BOWNE,
        JOHN ROYCE,
        RICHARD HARTSHORNE,
        THOMAS WARNE,
        SAMUEL DENNIS.

On the 12th of May, 1699, or the next day after the date of the above warrant, the grand jury of Middlesex county presented Lewis Morris, George Willocks, and Thomas Gordon for a breach of the laws of this province, according to that act, entitled, 'For the better maintaining of and upholding the authority of this province.'‡ By order of the grand inquest, Ephraim Andrews, Foreman."

Lewis Morris and George Willocks were both arrested under these proceedings, and locked up in the County jail of Middlesex, then at Woodbridge.

They were "in durance vile," however, not many hours, for on the night of May 13, 1699, between 2 o'clock and 4 o'clock, when people sleep the soundest, Isaac Whitehead, with many other "Malefactors and Disturbers of the King's Peace," as the indictment states, "did assemble with clubs, staves, and other weapons at Woodbridge, and did with a beam break down the door, and did seditiously break into the common jail and released two prisoners, Lewis Morris and George Willocks, imprisoned for high crimes and misdemeanors" and let them out and set them at liberty.§ This imprisonment and his deliverance in the night by a mob of his friends, did not cool Lewis Morris down, for only three days later, he and George Willocks write the following impudent letter to the judges of the Court of Common Right, who had signed the above warrant:—

To Capt. Andrew Bowne, Mr. John Royse, Mr. Thomas Warne, and company, etc.

Sirs, We are now able (God be thanked) to treat with you, any way you think fit. If you had valued either your own or the welfare of the government, your procedure had been more calm. Your day is not yet out, and it is in your power to follow the things that make for peace, and if you do not, at your door will lie the consequences. Our friends will not suffer us to be putt upon [imposed on]. Farewell.
        GEORGE WILLOCKS,
        LEWIS MORRIS.":
May 16 at one in the afternoon, 1699. ‖

Upon receipt of this defiant and threatening missive, the council called for a conference with the House of Representatives, for the Provincial Legislature then convened at Perth Amboy. Capt. Bowne presented the above letter which was read, and time asked to consider what should be done. Finally a committee of seven members was appointed by the Assembly to confer with the council.

This conference resulted in a recommendation, that an Act be passed "to suppress any insurrection." ¶ In mean time to avoid arrest, Lewis Morris and George Willocks had procured a sloop to lay off the shore at Perth Amboy. As soon as Willocks had delivered the letter he went on board of this vessel, where Lewis Morris awaited him. Then they sailed along in front of Amboy, in full view from the building where the Council and representatives were assembled, firing guns and making other defiant demonstrations, and so went off down the bay. It is no wonder that the Provincial law-makers recommended a bill to suppress insurrection. ¶¶ Soon after this Morris wrote the letter published on pages 491-86 Vol. III, N. J. Archives. On page 495 he writes "you were very hott in binding us to our good behaviour." This shows that it was addressed to Capt. Andrew Bowne and others of the Council, and after his arrest, for there is no date on the letter.

This letter is well worth reading, for it shows how abusive and personal Morris could be, and the stinging way he had of saying things. It is a fair specimen of his ability in vituperation when so disposed.

Public affairs were now in such confusion and disorder, that Governer Basse lost heart, and to get away from the threatening danger, made an excuse that he had important business in England, and so sailed away, throwing the whole burden of his broken and disjointed administration on the shoulders of quiet but honest and sturdy Andrew Bowne of Monmouth, who was appointed Deputy Governor. Capt.

---

‡ Vol. III, N. J. Arch. p. 481.
§ Vol. III, N. J. Arch., p. 480 and p. 486.
‖ Vol. III, N. J. Arch., p. 483.
¶ Vol. III N. J. Arch., p. 483-4-5.
¶¶ Vol. III N. J. Arch., p. 407.

Bowne assumed the duties, and with his strong common sense managed to get along, without any other open outbreaks of a serious nature.

Governor Basse left New Jersey for England in June, 1699, but before he got back, another sudden change occurred, which put him out of office, and once more put Lewis Morris on the top wave of political power in East Jersey. "Vae Victis," his opponents perhaps thought, when they learned of this upheaval in political matters.

Governor Basse must have reached England some time in the early part of August, 1699, or perhaps in the latter part of July, for it depended very much upon favorable winds.

He no doubt reported truly to the proprietors how disorder and anarchy reigned rampant in East Jersey, and that the "Unruly Scots," led by Lewis Morris, were the cause thereof. There must also by this time, have been plenty of written communications coming over from East Jersey, filled with conflicting accusations and complaints. The proprietors themselves were split up into factions and cliques. Thinking that Hamilton, from his previous experience and influence as governor, could calm the troubled political waters, part of the proprietors on the 19th of August, 1699, commissioned him governor of East Jersey. This commission lacked the provincial seal of East Jersey, and was without the signatures of many proprietors who opposed Hamilton. Neither did they get King William of England to approve Hamilton's appointment, as the laws of England required.

Nevertheless, with this illegal and defective commission, Andrew Hamilton sailed for America and arrived in New Jersey in December, 1699. With the aid of Lewis Morris, Thomas Gordon, George Willocks, and his other old political followers, he published his commission, and took charge of the government of New Jersey, before the people knew of these defects in his commission. He at once appointed Lewis Morris president of the council and Capt. Samuel Leonard of Monmouth likewise a member. Capt. Andrew Bowne was relegated to private life. Thus Lewis Morris ranked next to the governor and had more influence with him than any other man in the colony. He was in power and authority, and no doubt remembered his incarceration in the Woodbridge prison and his midnight escape.

He used his power mercilessly and "turned down" all the old officials in Monmouth, putting his old friends, principally from Shrewsbury township, in their places, for he could not be expected to select justices from "the most ignorant and wicked people on earth," and his political opponents, too.

He had Governor Hamilton appoint Gawen Drummond, a Scotchman, in place of James Bollen, the old county clerk. Dr. John Stewart, a resident of what is now Eatontown township, also a Scotchman, high sheriff in place of Daniel Hendrickson; Samuel Leonard and three other residents of Shrewsbury township were commissioned justices of the peace. They were all new officers, with the exception of Capt. Leonard, who was a practical politician of experience. The first court in Monmouth to meet after their appointment was on the fourth Tuesday of March ensuing, after Hamilton's arrival in December, 1699. In the meantime the people of Middletown had become well informed as to Hamilton's defective commission, and that he had not been approved by King William. It was still believed among the English settlers of Middletown, as has already been mentioned, that all Scotchmen were debarred by English law from holding offices over "true born Britons." Although this was a mistake, yet it was an honest belief, founded on their feelings and prejudices and on former instructions from the proprietors themselves. Now they beheld to their great indignation and astonishment, a whole horde of Scots placed over their heads for them to render obedience to.

Lewis Morris and other leaders of the Scotch party, had in Basse's administration set an example of defiance and violence, and they were considered capable of any lawless or desperate act to grasp power or accomplish their ambitious designs. For was it not proved by the written declarations of three honest Quakers of Shrewsbury township, that Lewis Morris had said openly in their presence at the house of Abraham Brown in that township, that he had taken an office from Governor Hamilton, and would enforce his authority or "spill the blood of any man who resisted him!" That he had no scruples of conscience like Quakers; that he "would go through with his office though the streets run with blood." *

These bloody and savage threats by the president of Hamilton's council were, of course, carried to the people of Middletown, and stirred up the belief that Hamilton and his party would stop

---
* Vol. III, N. J. Arch., p. 485.

at nothing to enforce their authority. It also aroused their anger and strengthened their determination not to submit to a Scotch usurper and his bogus officials, for so they regarded them. Under such hot indignation, intense excitement, and wild rumors, Daniel Hendrickson, John Ruckman, John Bray, Samuel Forman, Eleazer Cottrell and other Middletown citizens, were summoned to serve on the grand jury at the first court, where Lewis Morris and the newly appointed justices, were to sit. This court met at Middletown village, March 26, 1700, and held court in the second story of the block house, which stood on the knoll where the Episcopal church now stands. The stocks and whipping post stood in front, next to the six-rod road, which ran through Middletown village from west to east, as it does now, except that it has been greatly narrowed at the west end of the village. In Vol. II, N. J. Archives, pages 364-5-6, appears what purports to be a true copy of the minutes of this court. The compiler has made an error of one year in the date.

The date is given as March 26, 1701, but according to the original minutes now in the Monmouth county clerk's office, which anyone can see, who will look, the true date is March 26, 1700.

This mistake in the archives throws confusion on the order of events and is an inexcusable one. The compilers might have known from the language of the record itself, that there was an error in the date. The first two lines state that "the Commissions of the Justices were read." This was only done when newly appointed justices took their seats for the first time on the bench. There were no newspapers or printing presses, and the only way of giving public notice was by oral announcements to the people. Besides the records of the court held March 25th, 1701, which is published on the preceding page, and which the compiler must have read, states that all the justices were made prisoners and kept under strict guard from the 25th to the 29th of March, 1701. How then could a court have been held while they were captives, or how could they have ordered their captors fined and taken into custody? Accuracy and truth are the first and last requisites in historical records, and such a mistake made in a record now on file in the Monmouth clerk's office, right under the nose of the compiler, throws doubt on the accuracy of the whole work. It may be said that the mistake was in the certified copy, sent by Morris to England, but if this was so, a note should have been made of this error in the archives.

The minutes of the court of general quarter sessions of the peace, now (1899) in Monmouth clerk's office, show that this court was held at Middletown village March 26, 1700.

None of the citizens or residents of Middletown township are represented on the bench. They are all from Shrewsbury township appointed by Hamilton, subsequent to December, 1699.

CAPT. SAMUEL LEONARD,
President.
JEDEDIAH ALLEN,
SAMUEL DENNIS,
ANTHONY PINTARD,
Justices.

After court opened, the new justices' commissions are read. Then the panel of grand jurors are called by Dr. John Stewart, the high sheriff.

Eleazer Cottrell is first called, and he refuses to serve as grand juror, because the justices have no legal authority to hold court, being appointed by a usurping Scotchman. That Hamilton was not approved by the King of England and had no right to commission them. The court answered this objection by ordering "the sheriff to take Cottrell into custody" for open contempt. Then Richard Salter, an Englishman, who professed to be a lawyer, arose and protested against the arrest of Cottrell. He denied the legal right of the men then on the bench to hold court, that it was a bogus court created by a usurper and a Scotchman, who was debarred by statute law of England from holding office over "free born Englishmen." The justices shut up Salter by ordering the sheriff to arrest him; and so his stream of eloquence ceased to flow.

Then James Bollen, the old clerk, was called on to deliver up the records and papers of the clerk's office to the new clerk, Gawen Drummond. Bollen flatly refused to do so, because of the serious questions about the legality of their appointment, and whether they were a lawful court, but still will give them up, so that they may go on with the business, if the justices will give him an indemnity bond in the sum of £10,000 ($50,000) so that he may not suffer financially, if it turns out that they are only sham justices under a usurping governor. Capt. Leonard and his associates appear now to be in a quandary. They do not know what to do. Without grand jurors and the court records, no legal business can be transacted. To gain time and consult as to the best course, court is adjourned for two hours. Lewis Morris is not present on the bench, but he may have been within convenient distance for consultation and to direct his men. It is quite likely he was with them at their two hours' consultation, or sent in his opinion as to what should be done. At the expiration of the two hours, the justices again open court, although Lewis Morris puts in no appearance on the bench. They have made up their minds as to their proper policy or course of action. They order Cottrell and Salter discharged from Sheriff Stewart's custody. They knew if they committed them to jail, that it was in Middletown village and in the enemy's camp, and that they would at once be released. Neither did they dare order the sheriff to take them to another place, as they saw from the temper of the people, that it would be resisted by force, as did happen later. Therefore to gain time and avoid actual violence, they release the two men, but order Cottrell fined £5 and Salter £15 (he being a lawyer who should know better), and that the sheriff should make their fines by seizure and sale of their personal property, and to have the money in the court to be held at Shrewsbury on the fourth Tuesday in September next.

They also fine Daniel Hendrickson, John Bray, John Wilson, Jr., Moses Lippet, and other Middletown men, for refusing to serve as grand jurors, or, as the record has it "contempt and misbehavior before this court" in the sum of forty shillings each ($10.00) and order the sheriff to levy on their goods and sell them, and have the fines before next court in September Finding that the people will not recognize them as a court, and that no business can be done, they adjourn court, mount their horses and ride over to their homes in Shrewsbury township. There must have been an interesting conference at Morris' house in Tinton Falls that evening, about the "bad and wicked people of Middletown."

The attempt of Sheriff Stewart to collect the fines from Salter, John Bray and others, led to resistance, and then other warrants of arrest were issued by the Morris justices. The sheriff and his deputy, Henry Leonard, in attempting to serve them and capture Salter and Bray, was set upon July 17, 1700, and badly beaten by Salter, Jacob Van Doren, Arie (Adrian) Bennett and others, as has already been detailed.

At the next court in Shrewsbury in September, 1700, following the above incidents, we find Lewis Morris sitting as presiding judge and the others already named, sitting as his associates on the bench.

Arie (Adrian) Bennett is brought before the court to answer an indictment for assault and battery on the High Sheriff and Henry Leonard. Bennett admitted that he was present when they "beat and wounded the sheriff and cracked their swords" but that he "did not assist with his own hands.

The court orders him committed to the sheriff's custody, until he gives security in £100, to appear at the next court. Another court is held in Shrewsbury by Morris and his justices on the 17th of October, 1700. It seems to have been one of Morris' special courts. John Tilton is committed to sheriff's custody for signing a seditious paper.

Thomas Gordon, the Scotch lawyer, is present, and he informed the court that he had some money for Cornelius Compton of Middletown, "one of those rioters and fellons" who refused to be arrested and brought before the court. The court orders Gordon "not to pay over this money until Compton was cleared by law." As this never occurred Gordon must still have the money. Joseph Clark is also committed to common gaol for one month, or pay a fine of 20 shillings, for refusing to assist the justices of the peace to "apprehend certain rioters."

Garrett Boels is also committed to gaol, unless he gives security in £20 for his appearance at next court to be held at Middletown on the fourth Tuesday of March next, and all this because Boels put his mark or cross to a "seditious paper."

Thomas Webly, "for contemptuous and reproachful words in court" and otherwise misbehaving himself in the presence of the justices, is ordered to pay a fine of five shillings immediately, for the use of the poor, or be put in the stocks for two hours. Mr. Webly preferred to pay the five shillings at once. Here it would be interesting to know when and how Thomas Gordon paid the money to the "poor." It perhaps got mixed up with "Compton's money."

Then comes High Sheriff Stewart, with another sad and unhappy complaint about the bad men over in Middletown. He tells the court that Garrett Wall, James Bollen and Arie (Adrian) Bennett, whom the court had committed to his custody on September 24th last, had forcibly escaped from, run away and stayed away, so that he was unable to obey the orders of the honorable court, and have their bodies before the court of the Common Right at Perth Amboy. Whereupon the sheriff is again ordered to have them before the court at Middletown on March 25th next.

The high sheriff also reported more perverse and ugly conduct on the part of the Middletown people. That the fines imposed on Richard Salter, Daniel Hendrickson, John Bray and others by the court on the 26th of March, 1700, for their "contempt and misbehavior," before the faces of the court, he, as high sheriff, had been unable to collect. The court again ordered him to make the said fines out of their respective goods and chattels, and have the money before the next court. No jury is called and no other business is done except as above.

Morris and his friends had full and sufficient warning and notice, that the Middletown people would not submit to and obey the courts as then constituted. When Hamilton and Morris with their little army of 50 armed men marched through Middletown village the preceding July, they had been resolutely met by 100 or more determined men, who meant fight, if a single blow had been struck. They, therefore, knew what was likely to happen and what did happen at the next court at Middletown.† To make a diversion they got a man named Butterworth to admit that he was a pirate, and had been one of Kidd's crew, and bound him over to appear at the court in Middletown on March 25, 1701. I should be glad to know the names of his bondsmen, if any. It was what in modern slang is called a "set up job." They wanted to raise a new issue which would receive favor in England. They knew the deficient and illegal nature of Hamilton's commission, and that they had no chance in those questions. It would only hasten the day when the right of government would be taken from them and vested in the English crown. This they wanted to avoid. These records were framed under the supervision of Morris, Hamilton or Gordon, some time after the occurrence. The records of the court of March 25, 1701, could not have been written up in the minutes until after expiration of their four days'

imprisonment, so that they had plenty of time to set out the facts about "the self-confessed pirate."

The following is a true copy of the record of this court, which made so much talk and excitement in New Jersey, and among the Proprietors in England, and which brought public matters to a conclusion so far as any further attempts to coerce and drive the people of Middletown township.

March 25, 1701.
Monmouth, ss.

At a court of sessions held for the county of Monmouth at Middletown, in the county aforesaid and province of New Jersey:

Being present:

COL. ANDREW HAMILTON,
Governor.
LEWIS MORRIS,
SAMUEL LEONARD,
Esquires of the Governor's Council.
JEDIDIAH ALLEN,
SAMUEL DENNIS,
Justices.

The court being opened, one Moses Butterworth, who was accused of piracy, and had confessed that he had sailed with Capt. Kidd, in his last voyage, when he came from the East Indies and went into Boston with him. He was bound over to appear at this court, that he might be examined and disposed of according to his majesty's orders. The said Butterworth was called and made his appearance. When the court was examining him, one Samuel Willett, an Innholder, said that the "governor and justices had no authority to hold court, and that they would break it up."

He accordingly went down stairs to a company of men, then in arms, and sent up a drummer, one Thomas Johnson, into the court, who beat upon his drum. Several of the Company came up with their arms and clubs, which together with the drum continually beating, made such a noise (notwithstanding open proclamation made to be silent and keep the king's peace) that the court could not examine the prisoner at the bar. And when there were (as the court judged) betwixt 30 and 40 men with their arms and some with clubs, two persons, viz. Benjamin Borden and Richard Borden, attempted to rescue the prisoner at the bar, and did take hold of him by the arms and about the middle and forced him from the bar.‡

The constable and under sheriff, by the command of the court, apprehended the said Bordens upon which several of the persons in the court room assaulted the constable and under sheriff, (the drum still beating and the people thronging up stairs with their arms) and rescued the two Bordens. Upon which the justices and king's attorney of the province, after commanding the king's peace to be kept; and no heed being given thereto, drew their swords and endeavored to retake the prisoner, and apprehend some of the persons concerned

---

†See letter of July 30, 1700, N. J. Arch., Vol. II, p. 329-31, threatening arrest of Morris and Hamilton.

‡The pirate seemed very unwilling to be rescued but had to be dragged out from the protection of the court!

in the rescue, but were resisted and assaulted themselves, and the examination of the prisoner torn to pieces. In the scuffle both Richard Borden and Benjamin Borden were wounded. But the endeavors of the court were not effectual in retaking the prisoner. He was rescued, carried off and made his escape.§ And the people, viz: Capt. Saftie Grover, Richard Borden, Benjamin Borden, Obadiah Holmes, Obadiah Bowne, Nicholas Stevens, George Cook, Benjamin Cook, Richard Osborne, Samuel Willett, Joseph West, Garrett Boulles, (Boels), Garrett Wall, James Bollen, Samuel Forman, William Winter, Jonathan Stout, James Stout, William Hendricks, John Bray, William Smith, Gershom Mott, Abner Heughs, George Allen, John Cox, John Vaughn, Elisha Lawrence, Zebulon Clayton, James Grover, Jr., Richard Davis, Jeremiah Everington, Joseph Ashton, with others to the number of about 100, did traitorously seize the governor, the justices, the king's attorney, and the under sheriff and the clerk of the court, and kept them under guard, close prisoners, from Tuesday the 25th of March 'till Saturday, following, being the 29th of the same month, and then released them.

GAWEN DRUMMOND, Clerk.

The above record contains names of the progenitors of many of the most reputable families in our county and state, and elsewhere in the United States, in this year 1899. They are here represented in a court record, as being guilty of rank rebellion for the mere purpose of enabling a strange pirate to escape. We never hear of this man afterwards, nor is there any previous mention of him, nor are his bondsmen ever called upon to pay, because of his departing from the court without leave. After serving the purpose of Lewis Morris' juggling, he vanishes like a ghost.

Governor Hamilton and his council send a complaint of this outbreak at Middletown to King William, above their own signatures.

This complaint is dated in May, 1701, and directed to "The King's Most Excellent Majesty. The humble petitions of the governor and council of your majesty's province of East New Jersey."

The following extract relates to the Middletown affair:

"Upon the 25th of March last, at a Court of Sessions held in the usual place at Middletown, in the county of Monmouth, and province aforesaid, where was present your Petitioners, Hamilton, in conjunction with Your Majesty's justices, to take the examination of a certain pirate belonging to Kidd's crew named Moses Butterworth, pursuant to Your Majesty's strict commands. While the pirate

§It does not appear that this pirate tried to escape or made any resistance. He seems to have been a good and docile "pirate," who stuck to the court until forcibly dragged away.

was under examination, those Libertines on purpose to hinder the court's proceeding in that affair, sent in one of their number to beat a drum, and others of them rushed in to rescue the pirate, and accordingly carried him from the bar. To hinder the rescue and suppress the rioters Your Majesty's justices, believing it their duty to assist the sheriff and constables in the execution of their offices, (in which one of the rescuers was wounded) were surrounded by the rioters in great numbers, having (appearingly), on purpose appointed the same day to be a training day, on which the court was to sit, and their destruction by them most insolently threatened (which had been most certainly executed, had the wounded died on the spot), and was confined by them four days, 'till they thought him past hazard to the great dishonor of Your Majesty in the abuse of your ministers."

ANDREW HAMILTON,
SAMUEL DENNIS,
JOHN BISHOP,
SAMUEL HALE,
BENJAMIN GRIFFITH,
WILLIAM SANDFORD.‖"

Finding that neither the power of the governor nor of the county court, grand jury, or sheriff, nor of the armed posse which Hamilton and Morris had headed and marched over to Middletown village in July, 1700, could frighten or cowe the people into submission—that any further efforts in this direction meant a bloody fight, Lewis Morris, instead of "spilling his blood," concluded like Basse, to sail for England and stir up the government there, to use the army and navy of England against the wicked men of Middletown, who rescued pirates from the officers of the law and arrested and imprisoned honorable representatives of His Majesty, while sitting in a solemn court of justice. Terribly bad people, Lewis Morris said, lived over in Middletown, and so he has put them on record, which has come down through two centuries to this day. Morris accordingly sailed for England, some time in May or June, 1701, for we find him in London the following August. The only account of his career in England, oustide of his own writings, which I have seen, is that contained in a letter dated November 28th, 1701, written by William Dockwra of London, one of the leaders of the English proprietors, to Capt. Andrew Bowne. This letter is in Dockwra's own handwriting. The original letter is now in possession of William S. Crawford, son of the late James G. Crawford of Holmdel township. A copy of this letter is also published in "Old Times in Old Monmouth," pages 283-4.

He speaks in this letter of Lewis Morris as "their Champion Goliath, L. M.," and that they have "boasted incredibly of their bringing in Colonel Hamilton again over your heads in East Jersey."

Dockwra further writes, that they have fully informed King William of the true situation of affairs, and that Hamilton will be rejected. He adds that "we, that have said less, have struck the mark and done more to rid you of a Scotch yoak." He says that "the surrender of the proprietory government of New Jersey to the English Crown will take place or occur in about two months," and concluding writes "I shall be pleased with the exchange for an English gentleman to govern an English colony."

The following petition was sent to William of Orange, the King, signed by John Ruckman, Arie Bennett, Jacob VanDorn, Garret Wall, Andrew Bowne, Daniel Hendrickson, Samuel Forman, John Bray and many others of the residents of Middletown township. Their names will all be found on pages 325 to 328, Vol. II, N. J. Arch. This petition shows partially their side of the case for the consideration of the government of England.

"To the King's Most Excellent Majesty:

The remonstrance and humble petition of Your Majesty's loyal subjects, inhabiting in your Majesty's Province of East New Jersey in America, humbly showeth,

That whereas Your Majesty's humble Petitioners did remove and settle themselves in the said Province of East New Jersey; and by virtue of a license from Hon. Col. Richard Nicholls, Governor of said province under his then Royal Highness, the Duke of York, to purchase lands of the Native Pagans, did according to said license purchase lands of the said natives at their own proper costs and charges. And whereas since, his said Royal Highness did sell and transfer all his right and interest in the said province of East New Jersey to certain proprietors; by whose license several others of Your Majesty's loyal subjects have since also purchased lands at their own proper costs and charges of the native Pagans of the same place; whereby they humbly conceive they have acquired and gained a right and property to the said lands so purchased. Yet notwithstanding, your Majesty's loyal subjects are molested, disturbed and dispossessed of their said lands by the said proprietors or their agents, who, under pretense and color of having bought the government with the soil, have distrained from, and ejected several persons, for and under pretence of quitt rent and Lord's rent, whereby Your Majesty's liege subjects have been sued and put to great trouble and charges, and have been compelled to answer to vexatious actions, and after they have defended their own rights, and obtained judgment in their favor, could not have their charges, as, according to law, they ought to have but have been forced to sit down under the loss of several hundreds of pounds, sustained by their unjust molestations. And further, notwithstanding, your majesty's liege subjects have purchased their lands at their own proper costs and charges, by virtue of the aforesaid licenses; yet the said proprietors, governors or agents, without any pretended process of law, have given and granted the greater part of said lands by patent to several of the said proprietors and others, as to them seemed fit.

And notwithstanding their pretence to government, yet they left us, from the latter part of June, 1689, to the latter part of August, 1692, without any government, and that too in time of actual war, so that had the enemy made a descent upon us, we were without any military officers to command or give directions, in order to our defence, or magistrates to put laws in execution. And during the whole time, the said proprietors have governed this, your majesty's province, they have never taken care to preserve or defend us, from the Native Pagans, or other enemies, by sending or providing any arms, ammunition or stores, but have rather provoked and incensed the said natives to make war upon us, by surveying and patenting their lands contrary to their liking, without purchasing the same from them, or making any satisfaction in consideration thereof. And, sometimes when the said natives have sold and disposed of their lands, as to them seemed meet, they, the said proprietors, have disposed of the same to others, or else forced them who had the property in it to purchase it of them, upon their own terms, which the said natives have highly resented, and often complained of and (may justly be feared) wait only for an opportunity to revenge it upon the inhabitants of this your majesty's province.

And further, to manifest the illegal and arbitrary proceedings of the said proprietors in contempt of Your Majesty's laws, and against their own knowledge signified in a letter by them (to the council here in East Jersey), wherein they say as followeth: "We have been obliged against our inclinations to dismiss Col. Hamilton from the government, because of a late act of parliament, disabling all Scotchmen to serve in places of public trust or profit. And obliging all proprietors of Colonies to present their respective governors to the king for his approbation. So we have appointed our friend, Jeremiah Basse, to succeed Col. Hamilton in government, whom we have also presented to the king, and is by him owned and approved of."

Notwithstanding which letter they have superseded the said Jeremiah Basse (whom they wrote was approved by Your Majesty) and have commissioned the said Col. Hamilton again without Your Majesty's royal approbation, although removed before, by them; as a person disabled by law. Who now by virtue of their, the said proprietors, commission only, would impose himself upon us as governor. And when in government, before superseded by the aforesaid Basse, was by them continued about a year, after the 25th of March, (1697), without taking the oath enjoined by law. And does now presume to exercise government, not having legally taken the said oath or having Your Majesty's royal approbation.

The said proprietors of East New Jersey have also in contempt of Your Majesty's known laws, commissioned a native of Scotland to be secretary and attorney general of this Your Majesty's province, (being both places of the greatest trust, next to the governor). And one of the same nation to be clerk of the Supreme court of this Your Majesty's province, which may be of ill consequence in relation to the act of trade and navigation, and to the great hinderance of Your Majesty's loyal subjects, (the power of government being chiefly in the hands of natives of Scotland) from informing against any illegal or fraudulent trading by Scotchmen or others in this province.

We, Your Majesty's loyal subjects, laboring under these and many other grieveances and oppressions by the proprietors of this Your Majesty's province of East New Jersey, do in most humble manner, lay ourselves before Your Majesty (the fountain of justice) humbly imploring your majesty will be graciously pleased according to your princely wisdom, to take into consideration our evil circumstances, under the present proprietors, (if the right of Government is invested in them) and that Your Majesty will be graciously pleased to give your royal orders to said Proprietors, that with Your Majesty's royal approbation, they commission for governor a fit person, qualified according to Law, who as an indifferent judge may decide the controversies arising between the proprietors and the inhabitants of this Your Majesty's province. And settle all the differences which at present they labor under. And Your Majesty's petitioners as in duty bound shall ever pray, etc."

Then follows signatures of over 200 citizens, many of them residents in the old township of Middletown. Here we have an explanation of some of the causes which induced the people of Middletown to resist Hamilton and Morris, set forth in their own words. It is very different from the cause given by Morris and Hamilton in the court record of March 25th, 1701. These men had some common sense, and from their conduct in other matters, were influenced by righteous principles, yet Morris would make the government in England believe, that they made themselves criminally amenable to law, solely to rescue a strange pirate.

The government by the proprietors was an ill-constructed and inconsistent one, just what we might expect to emanate from such scoundrels and tyrants as the reigning Stuarts, who never did anything right, except by mistake.

Even the proprietory title to the soil has caused trouble and great loss to the people of this state from the time it began, until within the memory of the present generation, when they sold lands covered by Shark River for a mere song, and clouded the titles of many valuable tracts of real estate on the coast of Monmouth county. The Legislative investigation of the East Jersey proprietors in 1881-2 shows how greedy and unscrupulous their methods were. ¶

Suppose the proprietors now had control of the state government, and the appointment of judges, as in 1700, what chance would the people have in the courts to vindicate their rights. This circumstance or consideration alone will show the justice of the resistance made by our fore-fathers to their one-sided government and administration of the law. Many of the proprietors were speculators in real estate and actuated wholly by mercenary motives. Government, law, justice, as well as title to the soil, were so many investments, out of which money was to be made. Like the railroad and other corporations of today, they controlled government to squeeze the hard cash out of the people.

The breaking up of the court at Middletown held by a usurping governor and his bogus justices, was the right thing to do at the right time. Richard Salter, Samuel Forman, John Bray, Daniel Hendrickson, Jacob VanDorn and the others, deserve the praise and gratitude of posterity for their stern and persistent resistance. It destroyed the government of these wrangling and contending factions, and relieved the people from much injustice and wrong. Is it any wonder that the pioneer settlers of Middletown issued the "first Declaration of Independence" and recorded it in their township book against the unfair and monstrous government by the proprietors? Such a name as we simple creatures "never heard of before," they write down in their records.

¶See report of committee on modern doings of the N. J. proprietors among New Jersey legislative documents of 1882.

JAN GYSBERTSEN METRN AND HIS FAMILY.

Kreijn, son of Jan Gysbertsen Metrn, as he spelled and wrote his name, was born in Bommel, in the Netherlands, March 10, 1650. When a boy of 13 years, or in 1663, he came over with his father to New Amsterdam. Although the father wrote his name as spelled above, yet in old records of Kings county, L. I., and on the records of the First Dutch church of Monmouth and in our county clerk's office, the name is spelled VanMetra, VanMetere, VanMetteren, and in several other ways. Jan Guysbertsen, the father, seems to have been better off financially than most of the Holland emigrants. We find him comfortably settled at New Utrecht, L. I., and one of the magistrates of that town in 1673. He was a deacon in the Dutch church in 1683. It has been thought by some writers that he was of the same family as Jacob VanMeteren of Antwerp, who caused the first complete edition of the Bible to be printed in the English language. This book was printed at Zurich in 1536, and was a great and expensive work. It is thought that VanMeteren made the translations himself, but employed an English scholar named Miles Coverdale to supervise the printing, in order to guard against errors in the translation. Through VanMeteren the English people had access to the Scriptures in their native tongue. They have, however, never exhibited any gratitude, and gave VanMeteren but scant credit for this costly and beneficial work.

Kreijn Janse VanMater is mentioned as a resident of New Utrecht, and among those who took the oath of allegiance to the English government in 1687; the length of his residence in America is then stated as 24 years.* In a census of Kings county taken in 1698, his name is spelled "Cryn Jansen" and he still resides at New Utrecht and has a family of four children.†

There is a tradition in the VanMater family, that "Jan Guysbertsen Metrn," the father, refused to take the oath of allegiance in 1687, and soon after went back to his native land. That he had urged his son very strongly to accompany him, but that he refused, on account of his great horror of sea sickness, having suffered intensely on his first voyage over. I think, however, that his great love for blue-eyed, flaxen-haired and pretty Nelly VanCleaf was stronger than his love for the motherland. He had married at New Utrecht, September 9, 1683, Neeltje (Eleanor), daughter of Jan VanCleef and a resident of the same town.

Jan VanCleef came from Holland in 1653 and settled at New Utrecht in 1659. His wife was Engeltje, a daughter of Laurens Pietersen. Neeltje, or Nelly, was born at New Utrecht January 1, 1663, the very year her future husband was tossing on the waters of the Atlantic ocean. She had a brother Benjamin, baptized in the Dutch church at New Utrecht in November, 1683. He married Hendrika VanSutphen and removed to Monmouth county. He and his wife are communicants in the First Dutch church of Monmouth in 1711 and 1719, but her name is spelled on the records as "Hank Sutphin."

Kreijn VanMater and Neeltje VanCleef, his wife, are named among the first members and organizers of the Dutch church of Monmouth. His name is first entered on the church records as "Kriin Jansen," and in 1716 when Elder as "Kriin VanMetra." He purchased a large tract of land in what are now (1899) Holmdel and Atlantic townships. His first dwelling, a log cabin, was erected on the farm where William Jones now resides in Atlantic township. The old family burying ground is on this farm, and in it many of the past generations of the VanMaters are interred. This farm is but a small part of the original tract. Kreijn died March 10, 1720, and his wife January 1, 1747. Both are buried side by side in this graveyard, with tombstones giving their names and dates of death. His age is stated about 75 years and her age about 84 years. Nelly, his widow, survived him 27 years and was faithful to his memory. She is said to have been a very handsome and attractive woman, and had several offers of marriage, but none of them would she accept. She never tired of talking about Kreijn and of telling what he said and

---
* Vol. I, O'Call. Doc. Hist. of N. Y., p. 660-1.
† Vol. III, O'Call. Doc. Hist. of N. Y., p. 135-6.

did, for in all the world there was no such man, she thought. An English visitor on one occasion thoughtlessly remarked in her presence that "Kreijn" was a "queer, harsh name." "Nodings queer," exclaimed the old lady in her broken English, which became more so when she was excited, "Kreijn von goodt name, gooter as effer vas. Just like de singing of de birdts, ven der sprink veather comes, and der coldt vinter go avay." So she ever dwelt fondly on the husband of her youth until the summons came for her. She died in peace with a smile on her lips, for at last she would meet her Kreijn in the "land of the leal," never again to part. The old générations of the VanMaters were noted for their faithful attachments to wife, children and kinsmen. They labored and planned, as their wills show, to provide comfortable homes and maintain and guard against misfortune, those near to them by ties of blood.

Kreijn Janse VanMater and Neeltje VanCleef had the following children:

Jan, b. April 26, 1687, died young.
John, b. April 17, 1688, at New Utrecht, L. I.; m. October 17, 1718, Ida, daughter of Ryck Hendrickse VanSuydam; d. January 10, 1761, in Monmouth county. He was a communicant in our Dutch church in 1713, and his wife in 1731. ‡
Ydtje, (Ida) b. August 24, 1691, m. Jan, a son of Adrian Bennett and Barbery, his wife. Communicants in Dutch church in 1731. She died September 13, 1774. They had the following and perhaps other children: (In all baptisms hereafter spoken of in these articles, if no church is named it is to be understood that the dates are taken from the records of the First Dutch church of Monmouth). A child unnamed, bap. January 14, 1724; Krynjans, bap. February 27, 1726; Neeltje, b. November 29, 1728; m. June 28, 1750, John, youngest son of Jan Schanck and Sara Couwenhoven, his wife, of Pleasant Valley, and died June 1, 1810. I er husband, John Schanck, was born June 22, 1722; d. December 24, 1808. Their children have been mentioned in a former article on the Schencks.
Gysbert, (Gilbert) b. February 24, 1694; m. Maijke, (Micha) daughter of Daniel Hendrickson and Kaatje VanDyke, his wife. He was

a communicant in our Dutch church in 1721, and she in 1740, when her sister, Francyntje, wife of Tunis DeNeis, (Denise) also joined the church. Gilbert VanMater owned and lived on the farm where Gideon C. MacDowell now resides near Old Scots burying ground in the township of Marlboro, but formerly a part of Freehold township. § I do not know where he died or where he is buried.
Engeltje, (Angelina) b. September 30, 1696, m. John Anderson.
Benjamin, b. January 22, 1702; m. Elizabeth, daughter of Jacob Laen (Lane) and Elizabeth Barkalow, his wife. Both were members of Dutch church in 1737. He died July 21, 1775, aged 73 years, 5 months and 29 days, according to inscriptions on his tombstone in the VanMater cemetery.
Cornelia, b. May 24, 1704; m. Hans (John) VanCleef.
Syrenus, (Cyrenius) b. August 28, 1706, m. Abigail, daughter of Auke Lefferts and Maria TenEyck, his wife. Abigail was born March 15, 1708; d. August 25, 1785, aged 77 years, 5 months and 10 days. Cyrenius VanMater died December 28, 1787, and is buried by the side of his wife in the VanMater graveyard. His age on the tombstone is given as 80 years, 4 months.
Joseph, b. in Monmouth county February 5; bap. Aug. 13, 1710; m. December 1, 1734, Sarah, daughter of Roelof Schanck and Geesie or Ghesye Hendrickson, his wife. Sarah Schanck was born May 22, 1715, and died, according to inscription on her tombstone in the VanMater cemetery, September 1, 1748, aged 33 years, 3 months and 9 days. Her husband rests by her side and his headstone states that he died October 15, 1792, aged 82 years, 8 months and 10 days. Joseph VanMater and Sarah Schanck, his wife, became members of the Dutch church in 1737, and were said to have been active and zealous in church work, and lived consistent lives. Their children and grandchildren always spoke of them with affection and reverence.

The following is a certified copy of Kreijn Janse VanMater's will as filed

‡ In Book H of Deeds, p. 211, etc., Monmouth clerk's office, is recorded a conveyance from Ryk Hendrickse Suydam of Flatlands, Kings county, Island of Nassau, to John VanMeeteren (VanMater) of Middletown township, for a tract of land in Middletown township "bounded west by Dominicus Vanderveer, east by Auken Leffertsen, south by Swimming River, and north by heirs of Quryn VanMeeteren, (Kreijn VanMater), and known as No. 4, containing 152 acres and thirteen fiftysixths parts of an acre, being the seventh part of a tract said Suydam with others bought of Col. Lewis Morris.

§ Book H of Deeds, p. 41, etc., contains record of a deed from Charles Hubs to Guysbert VanMetra and Benjamin VanMetra of Middletown township, dated April 19, 1727, consideration £365 for a tract of 148½ acres in Freehold township: bounded southerly by VanCleef's land, northerly by lands formerly Thomas Combs, northerly and easterly by other lands of said Hubs. In same book p. 127, etc., is a deed from Isaac Forman and Elizabeth, his wife, of Freehold township, to "Benjamin VanMatre and Syrenus VanMatre," dated April 4, 1730, consideration £900, for 250 acres in Freehold township: bounded southerly by Burlington road, east by lands formerly of Aaron Forman, west and north by lands formerly Robert Barclay's; and three other tracts adjacent to above. In Book I of Deeds, p. 35, etc., Benjamin VanMatre and Cyrenus VanMatre convey to this Gilbert VanMater by deed dated September 1, 1735, for consideration of £535, one-half part of a tract of land in Middletown township on which said Gilbert VanMater then resided, being the lands above mentioned conveyed to them by Isaac Forman and wife.

in the office of the Secretary of State at Trenton. It was not proved until March 21, 1729, or nine years after his decease, although Benjamin VanCleef, the testator's brother-in-law, and one of the executors swore to it May 25, 1720. This was not sufficient in law to admit to probate. The law of New Jersey, then as now, required the oath of a subscribing witness, that it was executed by the testator according to the requirements of the statute in such cases made and provided.

I Kryne VanMatre of Middletown In the County of Monmouth and Eastern Division of the province of New Jersey, Yeoman, This Six & Twentyeth Day of April In the fifth Year of the Reign of our Soveraigne Lord George over Great Brittain, &c, King, Anno dom, One Thousand Seven Hundred and Nineteen, Being in good and perfect health and of a Sound Mind and disposing Memory, (praised be the Lord for the same) Doe Make and Declare this to be my Last Will and Testament, in Manner and forme as followeth, viz: First and principally I Recommend my Soul to Almighty God that gave it, and my Body to the earth from whence it was taken, to be Buryed in such Decent and Christian like manner, as to my executors hereafter named shall seem Meet and Convenient; and as touching such Wordly Goods, as the Lord In his Infinite and Rich Mercy (far beyond my Deserts) hath been pleased to bestow upon Me, I Give and dispose of the same as followeth

My Will is that all my Just Debts be Well and truly paid and satisfied within some convenient time after my Decease, Out of my Personal Estate by my Executors hereinafter named.

My Will is that my Son John VanMatre shall have and keep that Fifty one pounds which I formerly paid to Rak Hendrickse for and towards a plantation for my said Son John, without being accountable to my Executors for the same or any part thereof.

My will is that at the time of the Marriage of my Daughter Yda she shall have two Cows and fifteen pounds, and my daughter Angeltje to have at the time of her marriage two Cows and fifteen pounds, and My Daughter Cornelia to have at the time of her Marriage two Cows and fifteen pounds to be delivered to them out of my personal Estate by my Executors.

I Give and Bequeath to my loving Wife Neeltje VanMatre, the use of my plantation, and the Use of the Remainder of my personal Estate, for and during the time that she shall remain my Widow; and after her decease or Remarriage My Will is, that the personal Estate that she has the use of, be Equally divided Amongst all my Chilldren, Namely John, Yda, Ghilbert, Angeltje, Benjamin, Cornelia, Sirynus, and Joseph.

I Give and Devise my whole Real Estate whatsoever and wheresoever, after the Death or Remarriage of my wife, which shall first happen, to my fowr Sons Namely Ghilbert VanMatre, Benjamin VanMatre, Sirynus VanMatre and Joseph VanMatre, as followeth, viz: My Will is that if my Son Ghilbert shall within the Space of Three Years Next after the Decease or Remarriage of my Wife, pay unto my daughter Yda or her heirs, the Sum of Seventy-five pounds, that then I give and devise One full and Equal fourth part of my real estate to him my said Son Ghilbert, his Heirs and Assignes forever, and if my Son Benjamin, shall, within the space of Three Years Next after the decease or Remarriage of my Wife, pay unto my Daughter Angeltye, or her Heirs the Sum of Seventy-five pounds, then I Give and Devise One full and Equal fourth part of my Real Estate to him, my said Son Benjamin, his Heirs and Assignes forever, And if my Son Sirinus shall live to the age of Twenty One Years, and shall within three years after the Decease or Remarriage of my Wife, or at the Age of Twenty-One Years, which shall last happen, pay to my Son John or his Heirs the Sum of Seventy five pounds, then I give and Devise One full and equal fourth part of my Real Estate to him my said Son Sirinus his Heirs and Assignes forever, And if my Son Joseph shall live to the Age of Twenty One Years And shall within Three Years after the Decease or Remarriage of my Wife or at the Age of Twenty One Years which shall last happen, pay to my daughter Cornelia or her Heirs, the Sum of Seventy five pounds then I Give and Devise the Remaining fourth part of my Real Estate to him my said Son Joseph, his Heirs and Assignes forever, And My Will is that if Either of the said fowr Sons Depart this Life before he Attain the Age of Twenty One Years, or leave Issue of his Body, that then that fowrth part of my Estate be equally divided between the Remaining Three, they paying that sum to the person that the party deceased was to pay. And My Will is and I do hereby give power to my Executors hereafter named, to divide my Lands in Fowr Equall parts or Lottments to my said fowr Sons.

And Lastly I doe hereby Revoke and Disannull all wills by me formerly made declaring this Only to be my last Will and Testament, And doe Nominate Make and Appoint my two friends and Brothers in Law Benjamin VanCleave and Philip Folcoertson* to be the Executors of this my Last Will and Testament, to see the same Executed. In Testimony whereof I have hereunto set my hand and seal the Day and Year first above written.

Signed Sealed and published by the above named Kryne VanMatre as his Last Will and Testament in the presence of

JACOBUS SWOT (or SMOK),
HENDRICK SMOCK,
JOHN LAWRENCE,
THOMAS LAWRENCE,
WILLM. LAWRENCE, Junr.

Memorandum: yt on ye 21st day of March, 1729, William Lawrence, Junr., and Hendrick Smock two of ye Subscribing Evidences to ye Above instrument come before me John Barclay, Surrogate, who upon their Oath Deposed that they saw the Above Kryn Janssen VanMeteren signe seale & declare ye same to be his Last Will and Testament, and that at ye same time he was of sound mind to ye best of

---

*Written "Volkertz" or "Volckertsen," on old records of New Utrecht, L. I.

each of their knowledge & that they also saw ye other Evidences subscribe their names In presence of ye Testator. Sworne ye day & year above sd before Me John Barclay, Surrogate.

Memorandome: yt on ye 25th day of May, 1729, Benjamin VanCleve one of ye Executors In the within mentioned Last Will & Testament of Kyahn VanMatre, Decd, Personally Appeared before John Barclay, Surrogate, Authorized & Appoynted to take ye Probate of Last Wills & Testaments was Duely sworne to the Execution thereof. Sworn ye day & yeare Above Written before Me

JOHN BARCLAY, Surg't.

John VanMater, the eldest son of Kreijn Janse by his wife Eyke (Ida) Suydam, had eleven children:

1.—Cryn Jans, b. September 28, 1718; m. about 1750, Marya, daughter of Guysbert Sutphen and Geertrury VanPelt, his wife. Cryn-jans VanMater d. in 1766. They had the following children:
John, bapt. August 19, 1753; m. Elizabeth Hance or Hons.
Engeltje, bapt. March 31, 1755.
Guysbert, bapt. July 31, 1757; married a Widow Clayton.
Anne, b. 1759, died young.
Isaac, bapt. November 2, 1760.
Neeltje, bapt. February 2, 1766.
2.—Ryck (Richard) b. April 16, 1720; m. Micah or Martha Osbourne, and had the following children:
Eyda, (Ida) bapt. June 9, 1751, at Presbyterian church of Freehold. On pages 132-3 of Symmes History of Old Tennent church, date of baptisms of several of Ryck's children are given. Mr. Tennent, the pastor, has entered on the records that Ryck VanMater stated the reason for coming to him, instead of going to the Dutch Dominie was "that his wife could not speak Dutch." This was true, for his wife belonged to the English family of Osbournes who have resided at Manasquan for several generations. Besides Eyda he had the following children baptized by the Presbyterian minister, viz:
Jannetje, (Jane) bapt. April 15, 1753.
John, bapt. August 24, 1755; m. Sarah Hendrickson.
Catharine and Mary (twins) bapt. June 22, 1758.
William, bapt. June 22, 1760.
Eleanor or Nelly, bapt. Feb. 13, 1763; m. Jacob Schenck.

I am under the impression that one or more of their children became owners of a tract of land on the south side of Wreck Pond in the present township of Wall, but then Shrewsbury. I am, however, in possession of no facts to prove this. The son William, baptized June 22, 1760, married Martha Ward. His will is recorded in Book C of Wills, p. 136, Monmouth Surrogate's office. It was dated March 28, 1828, and proved August 31, 1829.

3.—Gilbert, b. January 14, 1722, bap. Feb. 4 following, and died unmarried.

4.—Jannetje, b. October 29, 1724; m. Aart, son of Guysbert Sutphen and Geertrury VanPelt, his wife. He was bap. April 13, 1718.
This couple had the following children baptized:
Guisbert, bap. August 20, 1743; Jan, November 3, 1745; Geertje, February 14, 1748.
5.—Neeltje, bap. August 14, 1728; m. John VanLieu, (no other knowledge).
6.—Marya, b. January 7, 1731; m. first, Peter Lefferts, second, John Bennett. By Peter Lefferts she had
Maria, bap. August 3, 1760; m. Barnes J. Smock; d. January 27, 1832, aged 71 years, 10 months, according to her tombstone in the Lefferts and Logan graveyard on the old Garret Schanck farm near Vanderburg in Atlantic township. Her husband, known as Capt. Barnes J. Smock of the Monmouth militia during the greater part of our Revolutionary war, and at its close as Col. Smock, was born January 29, 1756; d. January 30, 1834, aged 78 years and 1 day, according to the inscription on his tombstone, is buried by her side.†
Krinjans, bap. February 14, 1762.
John, buried in Lefferts and Logan graveyard. Tombstone gives date of death Nov. 8, 1836, aged 74 years, 11 mo., 20 d. His wife, Zilpha, is buried by his side.
Lefferts, I think he is the Leffert Lefferts who owned and resided on a farm in Upper Freehold township during the middle part of the last century.
Engeltje, b. March 31, 1755.
7.—Eyda (Ida) b. February 12, 1733; bap. March 14 following; m. Benjamin, son of Jan Derrickse Sutphen and Engeltje Bennett, his wife. He was bap. November 14, 1758.
8.—John b. February 7, 1735; died young.
9.—Cornelia or Catharine, b. July 4, 1737; m. Stoffle (Christopher) Logan, and d. January 19, 1806; buried in Lefferts and Logan yard. Her husband's tombstone gives date of his death November 11, 1823; age 89 y, 3 mos, 13 d. They had the following children:
Sarah, b. April 14, 1760; m. John L. Bennett; buried in Lefferts Logan graveyard. Tombstone gives date of death March 6, 1833, age 72 y, 10 mo, 22 d. Her husband died November 27, 1843, aged 86 y, 7 m, 27 d., according to his tombstone.
Eyda, b. 1760, died young.
Eyda, b. —— ——, and perhaps others.
10.—Cornelius, bap. August 14, 1739.
11.—Geertje, bap. November 27, 1734; m. about 1764, Aart VanDerbilt, and had the following children baptized:
Hendrick, January 20, 1765.
Ida, August 16, 1767.
Aaron, June 16, 1776.
Jeremiah and Joseph, (twins), Dec. 16, 1788.

The descendants of John VanMater and Ida Suydam, his wife, seem to have removed from Monmouth county, so far as there are any male descendants now (1899) bearing the VanMater name. I am unable to state when they removed or where they settled. Besides, many of their descendants who emigrated to other parts of New Jersey and other states, adopted different ways of spelling their surnames, as VanMeter, VanMarter, VanMeteren, VanMetere, etc.

† Colonel Barnes J. Smock's will is recorded in Book C of Wills, p. 340, etc., Monmouth Surrogate's office. It is dated October 17, 1832, proved February 10, 1834. He describes himself as a resident of Middletown township. He gives Philip Tunison, son of his sister Rebecca, $200. To children of his sister, Eleanor Longstreet, $300. To Catherine Wilburt and Phoebe Stephen, children of his sister, Sarah Smock, $200. To John Lefferts, brother of his deceased wife, $500; to children of his sister, Phoebe Longstreet, $500. The residue of his estate is given absolutely to the celebrated lawyer of that day in New Jersey, Garret D. Wall, who is also made sole executor. During the war Col. Smock had been taken prisoner by some of the Monmouth Tories and incarcerated in the Sugar House, where he suffered great hardships and indignities at the hands of the infamous Cunningham. He was once taken out to be executed, but by the intercession of Col. Elisha Lawrence, who commanded a battalion of the American Loyalists and who had been sheriff of Monmouth under the King, and who knew Smock, he was reprieved. He never forgot or forgave these insults. He was a man of gigantic size, with very long legs, and was nicknamed "Leggy Barnes," on this account. He had a fierce temper which flashed out like fire. With him it was a word and a blow and the blow often came first. The Tories and such as sympathized with them he hated with a bitter hatred, and on the slightest provocation would assault them with great violence. Our court records for many years after the Revolutionary war show many indictments against him for assault and battery. He was generally defended by Garret D. Wall, who either cleared him or got him off with a moderate fine. In gratitude for these services he made this lawyer his residuary legatee and devisee, for he had no children. There are many stories told of his daring and adventures. He is said to have met his death in trying to drive for a wager close along the high bluff on the south side of the Shrewsbury river about opposite the Globe Hotel in Red Bank. That a portion of the sod near the edge of the bluff had been undermined by a late storm, and when the wheel of his carriage struck there it caved, and threw carriage and horses from the top of the bluff to the beach below. Strange to say neither his horses nor his negro driver were hurt, but he had his neck broken. Such was the end of one of the most reckless, stubborn and fiercest of the Monmouth officers in the Revolution. He was as strong in his friendships as he was bitter in his enmities. He owned and resided on the farm next to the Charles Lloyd farm, in the present township of Holmdel, owned and occupied by Joseph I. VanMater until recently. The Charles Lloyd farm was owned and occupied by Barnes Smock of the Artillery Company, and his son Barnes lived on the adjoining farm where the children of John I. Crawford now reside. Col. Barnes J. Smock owned a horse called Paoli. He thought more of this horse than of anything else in the world. Many stories are told of the intelligence and affection displayed by this animal for his master. In some of the accounts of the fatal accident at Red Bank, it is said he was riding Paoli, and was not in a carriage. I do not know which is the correct version.

GILBERT VAN MATER, HIS DESCENDANTS, AND HIS WILL.

Gilbert VanMater, second son of Kreijn Janse by Micha Hendrickson, his wife, had the following children:

Cyrenius, baptized December 15, 1725; married Mary Heard.

Daniel, b. January 23, 1728, m. December 29, 1754, Mary, daughter of Rulif Corneliuse Covenhoven and Sarah Voorhees, his wife. She was born July 16, bap. August 26, 1737; d. November 8, 1767, and interred in VanMater graveyard; her age is stated on the tombstone as 30 years, 3 months and 11 days. Daniel died in London, England, October 8, 1786, and according to tradition in the VanMater family was honored by interment in Westminster Abbey.

John, bap. August 23, 1731; m. Elizabeth Carroll, Carle or Kerle.

Neeltje, (Eleanor) b. in 1733; m. February 22, 1775, Edmund Bainbridge.*

* Edmund or Edmond Bainbridge with John Anderson (clerk) and two others, were indicted for a riot in 1747. [Vol. VII, N. J. Arch. page 455.] The coincidence of names, for above Edmund Bainbridge's wife was a niece of John Anderson who married her father's sister, indicates the same family. Edmund Bainbridge and Simon Wyckoff headed a crowd of men who knocked down the sheriff of Middlesex county, and broke open the jail at Amboy to release John Bainbridge, Jr., on the 17th of July, 1747. See the letter of Sheriff Deare, and the affidavit of particulars on pages 463 to 471, Vol. VII, N. J. Arch. Also charge of Judge Neville to the grand jury, page 456. Idem.—Also letter of Robert H. Morris, page 471. Idem.—This Morris was then Chief Justice of New Jersey, and had been lifted to this high position by his father, Lewis Morris, Governor of New Jersey. The artfulness and craft shown in this letter mark him as a true chip of the old block. His father, Lewis Morris, died in 1746, in the midst of popular tumults and disorders similar to those which occurred at the beginning of his political career in 1699-1700, and caused by similar selfish exactions and ruthless measures of the Proprietors. I am in doubt as to what relationship if any, existed between this Edmund Bainbridge who married Eleanor VanMater and the Edmund who was implicated in this outbreak of 1747. John Anderson married Angelina VanMater prior to 1747.

Hendrick, or Harry, bap. September 11, 1737, went to England with his brother Daniel, after the Revolutionary war, and was in England at the time of his brother's death. Since then nothing was ever heard of him so far as I can learn.

Joseph, bap. September 30, 1739, m. Catharine, daughter of James Kearney of Chinqueroras, as the region about Keyport was then called. She was b. July 26, 1752, and died May 10, 1807, aged 54 years, 9 months and 20 days, and is buried by her second husband, Rulif VanMater, in the VanMater cemetery.

Catharine, bap. February 20, 1742; m. October 7, 1788, Stephen Jones.

The following is a copy of the will of Gilbert VanMater, father of the above seven children:

Will of Guysbert (Gilbert) VanMater.

In the name of God, Amen. I Gisbert VanMater of Freehold, in the County of Monmouth and the Eastern division of the Province of New Jersey, being weak in body but of sound, disposing mind, and memory; considering the uncertainty of this life, do make this to be my Last Will and Testament. In manner following:

And first recommending my Soul into the hands of Almighty God, who gave it; into whose Kingdom notwithstanding my own unworthiness, I hope to be received through the merits and intercession of my blessed Savior, and Redeemer, Jesus Christ. My body I will to be buried at the discretion of my Executors hereinafter named.

And as touching such temporal estate wherewith it has pleased God to bless me in this life, I will, devise and dispose of the same in the following manner, and form:

First I will that all my just debts be duly and truly paid in some convenient time after my decease, by my three youngest sons, John, Hendrick and Joseph.

Item. I have already given to my two eldest sons, Cyrenius and Daniel VanMater, a plantation I formerly owned at the Scotch Meeting House, and to my eldest son Cyrenius, a negro wench—Nann—and my long gun for his birthright, and other goods and chattels; and to my son Daniel his negro Frank and other goods and chattels. I have already given my two eldest sons what I intend to give them. Secondly I give, devise and bequeath to my three youngest sons, John, Hendrick and Joseph, all my real estate, lands, and meadows whatsoever, and rights of lands which I am now seized and possessed of, interested in or entitled to, and to their heirs, executors, administrators, and assigns forever. To each an equal third in quantity, and in quality, to be divided by my executors hereinafter named. If my above named three sons or either of them, choses, it to be upon themselves, after the above named debts are paid or before, if my executors think fitt and proper.

Item. I give, devise and bequeath to my eldest daughter Nelly, my negro wench Matt, and her child Sally, and a horse and saddle and three cows, and fifty pounds in money, at eight shillings per ounce, for her outset, if she marry within the term of six years. If she should not in six years, then at the expiration of six years to be paid to her out of my estate, the aforesaid fifty pounds and three cows.

Item. My will is that my son John shall pay to my daughter Nelly the sum of fifty pounds money as aforesaid for part of her legacy, on or before six years after my death.

Item. My will is that my son Hendrick shall pay to my daughter Nelly the sum of fifty pounds, money as aforesaid, for part of her legacy on or before seven years after my decease.

Item. My will is that my son Joseph shall pay to my daughter Nelly the sum of fifty pounds, money as aforesaid, for the last part of her legacy on or before the term of eight years after my decease.

Item. I give and bequeath to my youngest daughter, Catharine, my negro wench Maryann and horse and saddle, and, when she marries, three cows and fity pounds in money as aforesaid for her outset; but if she shall not marry within the term of six years then the fifty pounds and three cows to be paid to her out of my estate.

Item. It is my will that my son John shall pay to my daughter Catharine, the sum of fifty pounds money aforesaid, on or before the term of nine years after my decease, for part of her legacy.

Item. It is my will that my son Hendrick shall pay to my daughter Catharine the sum of fifty pounds money aforesaid, before nine years after my decease, for part of her legacy.

Item. It is my will that my son Joseph shall pay to my daughter Catharine the sum of fifty pounds money as aforesaid, on or before the term of ten years after my decease for the last part of her legacy.

I mean in the whole, to be paid to my daughters two hundred pounds in cash each, as before described already.

Item. In case either of my daughters should lose their negro wenches, which I have given them, either Matt or Maryann (but not Sally) then I give either Pegg or Betty, as they shall see cause to chose, or both if they should die, they said Matt and Maryann. That is before my said daughters should marry, or either of them; but if married and then die, then no other in their stead or after the expiration of six years.

Item. I give, devise and bequeath the remaining part of my negroes to my youngest three sons, John, Hendrick and Joseph, to be equally divided amongst them, as my executors shall see fitt, excepting them already given.

Item. I give devise and bequeath all my household goods within doors, equally to be divided amongst my three youngest sons and two daughters, to be divided in six years after my decease equally.

Item. I give devise and bequeath the remaining part of my stock, goods and chattels, and all my farmer utensils, cattle, horses, sheep, and hogs, excepting what before I have given, to my three sons, John, Hendrick and Joseph, to be equally divided amongst them at the discretion of my executors.

Item. It is my will that if my executors should think my daughters should not be well used by my sons or either of them, to be in their power to board them at their discretion at such place and places as they shall see cause, out of my estate, until they marry or until their legacies become due.

Item. My will is that, if either, of my daughters should die without issue of their body, then the other to be heir.

Item. My will is if either of my sons die without issue of their body, the others of my sons to be their heirs and the said lands to fall to them living.

And lastly I do hereby nominate, constitute and appoint my two eldest sons, Cyrenius and Daniel VanMater, both of the County of Monmouth aforesaid, to be executors of this My Last Will and Testament, hereby revoking all former wills by me in anywise heretofore made, and declaring this to be my Last Will and Testament. In witness whereof I have hereunto put my hand and seal the —— day of October in the year 1758.

GISBERT VANMATER. (L. S.)

The copy is in possession of Mrs. Margaret Fick, wife of ex-sheriff Fick of New Brunswick, Middlesex county, N. J. She was a daughter of Joseph VanMater and Margaret Rapelje, his wife, born July 6, 1860, and granddaughter of Holmes VanMater and Micha, his wife, (daughter of Gilbert VanMater, grandson of above testator, who resided on Long Island.)

I do not know whether the will was admitted to probate, but presume it was, or else the devisees and legatees therein named were, VanMater like, governed by their father's wishes without regard to any legal compulsion. For the court records of Monmouth county show that the VanMaters have seldom engaged in litigation, either among themselves over family settlements, or with their neighbors. I do not know of any divorce or criminal suits among the past generation of the family. They have minded their own business and let others alone. Neither have they courted popularity for the sake of office or honors, but if anything have been retiring and modest in their claims and assumptions. They have as honorable record as any family in the county, considering their numbers and the long time they have resided in Monmouth.

Cyrenius, the eldest son named in the above will, was a miller and farmer. By his wife, Meary Heard, he had the following children:

John H., born (there is no record, he may have died young).

Gilbert, born ——, died single in 1807. Leaves a will recorded in Book A of Wills, p. 194, Surrogate's office of Monmouth. It is dated May 6 and proved May 12, 1807.

William, born Nov. 27, 1772, married December 24, 1797, Mary, daughter of Garret Hendrickson and his second wife, Lena VanLiew, and died May 9, 1844. Mary Hendrickson, his wife, was baptized May 2, 1779.

Mary, baptized, ——, died unmarried in 1813, leaves will dated April 19, 1808, proved Sept. 25, 1813, recorded in book A of wills, p. 662, Monmouth Surrogate's office. She describes herself as the daughter of Cyrenius VanMater, a miller. She mentions Cyrenius, son of her brother William VanMater, and Mary, daughter of her sister Micha, wife of Samuel Tilton. She devises all her property in fee to Cyrenius Tilton, son of her sister Micha. John W. Holmes and Micha Tilton are appointed executors.

Maykee (Micha) born ——, married Samuel Tilton.

Phoebe, born December 21, 1773, married January 20, 1791, Hendrick, son of Garret Hendrickson and Catharine Denise, his wife, died, March 12, 1836. †

Phoebe VanMater and Hendrick Hendrickson, aforesaid, had the following children:

Mary or Polly, bap. Oct. 30, 1791.
Garrett, bap. Oct. 13, 1793, d. March 6, 1800.
William Heard, b. Sept. 22, 1795, d. Aug. 9, 1855, buried in homestead yard aforesaid.
Eleanor, b. Dec. 7, 1797, d. June 22, 1806.
Garrett, b. Feb. 21, 1800, d. June 3, 1866, m. Angelina, daughter of Wynant Bennett of Long Island, who was born July 13, 1813, d. Sept. 24, 1876. Both buried in Long Island.
Cyrenius, b. Mar. 30, 1802, m. Sept. 18, 1823, Ida, daughter of Joseph VanMater and Ida Hendricksen, his wife, d. May 17, 1870, buried on homestead farm at Holland aforesaid.
Denyse, b. July 4, 1804.
Elinor, b. May 11, 1806.
Catharine, born—no record.

William VanMater, born November 27, 1772, by his wife, Mary Hendrickson, had the following children:

Cyrenius, b. July 1, 1798; m. Elinor Eendrickson; d. Dec. 18, 1882.
Rulif, b. ——, who went West and settled there.
Gilbert, b. July 10, 1802; m. Sarah Taylor; d. Feb. 6, 1881.
Garret, b. ——, m. Harriet Hopping; d. at Chapel Hill in 1879, leaving two children,

† A marriage license was granted to Garrett Hendrickson, (son of Hendrick Hendrickson and Neeltje Garretse Schanck, his wife) and Catharine (daughter of Tunis Denise and Francyntje Hendrickson, his wife) December 8, 1755. Garrett Hendrickson died December 18, 1801, aged 67 years, 10 months and 10 days, according to his tombstone in the Hendrickson burying ground on farm of late Senator W. H. Eendrickson at Holland in Holmdel township. His wife, Catherine Denise, is interred by his side. She was born May 8, 1732, baptized June 4th following, and died September 8, 1771, aged 39 years, 4 months. Hendrick, their son, and Phoebe VanMater, his wife, are also buried in this graveyard. Hendrick died June 6, 1837, aged 72 years, 10 months and 7 days. Phoebe, his wife, died Mar. 12, 1836, aged 62 years, 2 months and 2 days.

John H. and Mary. John H. VanMater is now a practicing physician of good standing at Atlantic Highlands. Garret VanMater left a will and codicil. The last was dated Dec. 13, 1878; proved Sept. 6, 1879; recorded in book M of wills, p. 494, Monmouth Surrogate's office.

Elinor, b. 1815.
Catharine, b. ——; m. William Story.

Daniel, second son of Gilbert VanMater, and Micha Hendrickson, married Mary Conover aforesaid, and had the following children:

Tryntje, (Catharine) b. Ap. 5, 1756; m. Aug. 14, 1774, Henry Disbrow and had three sons and one daughter Mary, who married Rev. Henry Polhemus. One of his sons, John H. Disbrow, married Sarah VanMater, his cousin.

Sarah, b. Aug. 13, 1759; m. Benjamin VanMater July 12, 1778, d. Sept. 5, 1840; buried in VanMater yard by her husband.

Gilbert, b. June 7, 1762; m. Margaret Sprague, widow of a Rapelye on Long Island. He removed to Brooklyn and lived on Long Island until his death, July 6, 1832. He had six daughters and two sons. One of his daughters, Sarah, b. Aug. 15, 1793, m. her cousin, John Henry Disbrow, above mentioned. Another daughter, Micha, b. Aug. 21, 1795, m. Holmes, son of Chrineyonce VanMater and Huldah Holmes, his wife. Holmes VanMater resided on the Academy farm in the village of Holmdel and was famous for his fast and thoroughbred horses.

Micha, b. Jan. 20, 1764, m. first Daniel Polhemus who died Jan. 29, 1820, aged 57 years, and married second George Clark.

Nelly, b. July 20, 1766, d. in infancy.

Jan or John, third son of Gilbert VanMater and Micha Hendrickson, married Elizabeth Carrol, Carle or Kerle, and had at least two daughters.

The fifth son of Gilbert VanMater and Micha Hendrickson was Joseph, who married Catharine Kearney, or Karney, as they spelled it. The descendants of this couple became known as the "Kearny VanMaters," and were noted for the marked difference in their characters, from the past generations of the family, and from the descendants of the other branches. They had the following children:

Rulif, bap. July 16, 1775,—no other record.

Joseph Kearney, b.——; m. Sept. 10, 1794, Ida Hendrickson, daughter of Garrett Hendrickson and Lena VanLieu, his seoond wife. He owned and resided on a farm west of Colts Neck and on the south side of the turnpike to Freehold, nearly opposite the Thomas Ryall farm, formerly known as the Stoutenburg farm.

There were other children, but I have no record of them.

Joseph K. VanMater, by his wife, Ida Hendrickson, had the following children:

Ida, b. May, 1795, m. Sept. 18, 1823, Cyrenius Hendrickson of Pleasant Valley, and were the parents of the late Henry D. Hendrickson, so well known to the present generation of people in this county, and of Catharine, wife of the late Joseph L. Tunis, who owned and resided on a farm near Wickatunk and died a few years ago.

James Kearny, b. Nov. 11, 1807, m. Elizabeth VanMater and died childless on Nov. 25, 1850. His will is dated March 24, 1849; proved Dec. 12, 1850, and recorded in Book F of Wills, p. 44. He leaves all his personal and real property equally to his three sisters, Ida, wife of Cyrenius Hendrickson, Ann K. VanMater and Elizabeth, wife of Joseph Probasco.

Ann K., b. May 11, 1815, m. Benjamin Vanderveer.

Elizabeth, b. Feb. 1, 1820, m. Joseph Probasco and had the following children by him: James K., Robert, Johanna, Hulda, Mary Jane, Hendrick and Cyrenius.

DANIEL AND HENDRICK VAN MATER WHO JOINED THE KING'S ARMY.

Daniel and Hendrick, two of the sons of Gilbert VanMater and Micha Hendrickson, and named in his said will, enlisted at the beginning of the Revolutionary war in the first battalion of Skinner's brigade, commanded by Elisha Lawrence of Upper Freehold township, and who was the last colonial sheriff under King George III in Monmouth county. The majority of Americans who belonged to this command of Col. Lawrence's were doubtless natives of this county, which then included Ocean county. They were called the New Jersey Royal Volunteers, but were popularly known from the color of their uniforms as the "Greens," or "Skinner's Greens." Many of the men who thus joined the British army were conscientious and honorable men and carried on war in an open, soldier-like way. They were widely different from the Refugees at Sandy Hook, the Pine Robbers, and other desperadoes who took advantage of the unsettled times to plunder and murder. The people, however, who suffered from their depredations were not in any condition of mind to make a distinction between the Americans who sided with the British.

One of the sisters of these two VanMaters had married a Bainbridge who belonged to an intensely loyal family, and one of their brothers, Joseph, had married a Kearny, a family likewise strong on that side. They were also socially intimate with Col. Elisha Lawrence, the Ex-Sheriff, with Ex-Sheriff John Taylor of Middletown, and other old colonial officials who had sworn allegiance to the king of Great Britain. It was perhaps these social, family and political influences which carried them away from their Dutch kindred into the ranks of the enemy. The same extravagant promises of royal approbation, honors and reward, were doubtless made to them, as to other Americans by the British officials and agents to get them to enlist.

At the close of the Revolutionary war they found themselves stripped of all their property, their families broken up and scattered, and themselves exiled from their homes and friends. They went to England, I think, with Col. Elisha Lawrence, in order to get some recognition from the English government for their services and losses, for, according to Lawrence's affidavit hereinafter printed, he was in London at the same time, and it was evidently made to help Daniel VanMater with his claims against the government. This affidavit is otherwise historically important, because it shows that Colonel Lawrence, with part or all of his command, was in Monmouth as early as December, 1776, arresting prominent and active patriots. At this time the people were disorganized, with many non-committal among them. Lawrence seems to have met with no resistance in capturing the "rebels," as they were called. This, too, helps explain the letter written by Hendrick VanBrunt and others to Governor Livingston of New Jersey, printed on pages 261-3 of "New Jersey Revolutionary correspondence." This letter is dated September 15, 1780. In it they write that the captivity of some of them has lasted nearly four years. This would agree with the time Lawrence says he was in Monmouth county taking prisoners, viz., December, 1776. Among the Monmouth officers named in captivity in 1780, we find Major Hendrick VanBrunt, Col. Auke Wyckoff, Capt. Jonathan Holmes, Lieut. James Whitlock, Lieut. Tobias Polhemus, Capt. Jacob Covenhoven, Col. John Smock, Capt. Barnes Smock and Henry Smock. It seems that some of these men had languished in captivity nearly four years, and it may be that some of them were not exchanged or released until the war closed.

Daniel VanMater and his brother Hendrick, had all their hopes of government aid outside of grants of land in Canada, dashed to the ground. Like other American loyalists who had been seduced by the fine and extravagant promises the English are so prone to make, when they need help or favors, they found only coldness and ingratitude on the part of the high-caste Englishmen, misnamed "nobility," who acted and spoke for the government, and who really control the government of Great Britain for their class interests. The following extract from the proceedings of the British House of Commons on June 19, 1820, shows what help and reward they got, after sacrificing everything. Mr. Williams, one of the members, speaking of the claims of the American loyalists, said: "It is more than 30 years since these claims accrued. Three-fourths of the claimants are dead, and many of them died of broken hearts." Mr. Lockhart, another member, said, "The American Loyalists have never received any compensation for their losses."

Daniel VanMater died in London, England, October 8, 1786, without receiving any compensation except a grant of land in bleak Nova Scotia. I doubt also the truth of the tradition handed down among the VanMaters, that he was buried among the heroes and great men who lie in Westminster Abbey. I think he had lost and suffered enough for the English government, to entitle him to this honorable grave, but he bore a Dutch name, and was a stranger from over the seas, and why should they care to bury his poor corpse when he was no longer of any service to them? In the eyes of the so-called "nobility" or the Brahmin caste of England, he was no better than a dead dog who had fetched and carried for them in his lifetime.

The following papers which belonged to him were probably sent to his children by his brother, Hendrick VanMater, after his death:

[Addressed]
"General Burch, Commandant etc.,"
[Endorsed]
"Referred for inquiry to the police."
S. B.
[Below] "This matter is one that must be decided after troops are gone."
D. MATHEWS, Mayor.

The above endorsements are in the handwritings of Gen. Burch and Mayor Mathews of New York city.

"General Burch, Commandant of the City of New York, v. v.

The humble memorial of Daniel VanMater most respectfully showeth:

Whereas your humble memorialist hath a cousin in New Jersey, who was brought up in our family, Built a schooner for his own private use, and she was impressed in the Provincial service in order to carry the cannon and sick to Brunswick. The British took the said schooner and converted her to their own service, where she has remained until lately, and now is in the hands of Captain Nailler, by the name of Schooner Pool. Your humble memorialist claims the said schooner by a deed of gift from under the hand of his cousin Cornelius Covenhoven. Now your humble memorialist prays, as she never was condemned and made a prize to the British, that the General will grant an order that said Captain Nallier shall deliver up the said schooner to your humble memorialist, or show cause why he detains the said Schooner Pool in his possession. Your humble memorialist shall be in duty bound to ever pray

DANIEL VAN MATER.

May ye 20th, 1783. *

As this claim was returned to him, it appears, they did not or could not return his schooner. Soon after this he must have sailed for England to push his claims there. The following affidavit shows that he was in London in 1785:—

AFFIDAVIT OF COL. ELISHA LAWRENCE.

Elisha Lawrence maketh oath that he has known Mr. Daniel VanMater, late of Monmouth county, New Jersey, in North America, many years previous to the late rebellion in America. That Mr. VanMater has always shown the strongest attachment to his Majesty's Person and Government. That in December 1776, this Deponent was ordered into the said County of Monmouth. Mr. VanMater was very active in rendering every assistance to the Troops, and disarming and taking Rebels prisoners. That he with some others took Tunis Vanderveer, a Rebel Captain† of Militia and some Privates and brought them unto this Deponent. That this Deponent as Sheriff of the said County of Monmouth, sold to Mr. VanMater part of the farm he possessed at the commencement of the Rebellion, as will appear by the titles, and is well acquainted with the land, and thinks it was worth about that time at least £8.00 ($40.00) per acre, New York currency. This Deponent is also

---

* The English army evacuated New York in the month of November, 1783.

† This is a mistake about Tunis Vanderveer being a rebel captain. He was a sergeant, and lived where his great-great-grandson, David Arthur Vanderveer, now lives in Freehold township. He was a bold, resolute and active patriot. He was in the British prison of New York at the same time Garrett Wyckoff was there. They were released at the same time and came home together, as they were quite near neighbors.

well acquainted with Thomas Leonard and John Longstreet, Esqrs. Thinks them to be good judges of land and particularly acquainted with Mr. VanMater's land, and from their characters, thinks that the greatest credibility may be given to their testimony. And further saith that Mr. VanMater was esteemed an Honest Man, as far as this Deponent Knoweth. As to the value of Mr. VanMater's movable estate the Deponent cannot pretend to say. He Knew he had many Negro Slaves and a considerable stock on his farm of all kinds, and in particular it was a general received opinion that Mr. VanMater's horses were some of the best in the country.

COL. ELISHA LAWRENCE.

London, March 2nd, 1785.

[Endorsed] Copy of Col. Elisha Lawrence's deposition.

In a letter from Cyrenius VanMater to his brother, Daniel VanMater, dated March 28, 1785, he speaks of the death of "Rike VanMater" about January 1, 1785. On the inside page is a letter addressed to Harry VanMater (Hendrick was his baptismal name). This is also signed "Your Affectionate Brother, Cyrenius VanMater." These letters are folded in the old fashioned way and addressed to

Mr. Daniel VanMater
in London, at Jacob Taylor's
Pimlico, near the Queen's Pallace No. 25.

This would show that Daniel and his youngest brother Henry or Hendrick, were both in England at that time. Another letter is dated at Brooklyn, February 17th, 1786, from Gilbert VanMater and addressed to Daniel VanMater, London. Gilbert heads the letter "Honored Father," and expressed a strong wish that he should return and live with his children. That the separation of so worthy a father "is much felt by your family in general and in particular by your affectionate son, Gilbert VanMater."

In another letter from the same son, dated "Hampstead South, May 26, 1785," he speaks of having returned to farming and is doing well. He begs to be excused from going to England on account of the expense and inconvenience. The letter is directed to "Mr. Daniel VanMater, at Pimlico, London."

In another letter from Gilbert, dated Brooklyn, October 11, 1786, he speaks of living in Brooklyn and in the same business as when his father left. He also speaks of the death of his grandfather, Conover, in New Jersey about two months before from a stroke of the palsy. The letter is addressed to

Daniel VanMater
to be left at the New York coffee house, London by favor of Capt. Townsend.

DANIEL, HENDRICK AND CHRINEYONCE VANMATER'S ESTATES CONFISCATED.—DEATH OF FENTON, THE PINE ROBBER.

In the clerk's office of Monmouth county, Book A of Executions, beginning in back part of book, is the record of 110 executions against Monmouth county land owners who joined the British army, or were detected going within their lines.

On page 11 of this book is an execution against Daniel VanMater, and on page 31 a similar one against his brother, Hendrick VanMater. Under these executions all their real estate was seized and sold to the highest bidders. The following is a true copy of the execution against Daniel VanMater. They all follow same form.

Monmouth County, ss.

The State of New Jersey to Samuel Forman, Joseph Lawrence, Kenneth Hankinson, and Jacob Wikoff, esqrs, Commissioners duly appointed for the said County, on the part and behalf of said State to take and dispose of, for the use and benefit of the same, the estates of certain Fugitives and offenders in the said County, or to any two or more of them, Greeting.

Whereas, lately, that is to say of the term of October, in the Year of Our Lord, seventeen hundred and seventy-nine, in the Court of Common Pleas held at Freehold in and for said county of Monmouth, before the Judges of the same Court, final judgment was had and entered in favor of the said State of New Jersey, pursuant to law, against Daniel VanMater, late of the Township of Freehold on an Inquisition found against the said Daniel VanMater for joining the Army of the King of Great Britain, and otherwise offending against the form of his allegiance to the said State, etc., and returnable to the said Court, as may fully appear of record. You are therefore commanded and enjoined to sell and dispose of all the estate, Real of what nature or kind soever, belonging to or lately belonging to the said Daniel VanMater, within the said County of Monmouth, according to the direction of "An Act for forfeiting to and vesting in the State of New Jersey, the real estate of certain 'Fugitives and Offenders' " made and passed the eleventh day of December, A. D. 1778.

Witness John Anderson, Esq., Judge of the said Court at Freehold af'd, the 22nd of January, A. D., 1779.
By the Court,
ANDERSON, C'l'k.

Recorded May 15, 1779.

On pages 76 and 99 of Book A of Executions are similar writs against Chrineyonce, son of Joseph VanMater, and Sarah Roelofse Schenck, his wife. The first seems to be for going within the British lines and the last for joining the King's army.

Chrineyonce, it is said, carried on the mill now known as Taylor's Mills, near the old VanMater homestead, in Atlantic township, but they were owned by his father Joseph, who did not die until 1792. He was also interested with his cousin, Daniel VanMater, in the ownership of several schooners, which carried hogshead staves, corn meal and flour to the West Indies, and brought back to Perth Amboy or New York, sugar, molasses, rum, wine and other tropical products. The fear of the loss of these vessels and their lucrative trade, may have influenced them in their political stand, thinking the English government must ultimately win.

The bold and out and out stand taken by these three VanMaters, named in above executions, for the English Crown, and because of their social standing, and the bitter feeling it aroused among their nearest relatives among the Covenhovens, Schencks, Van Dorns, Hendricksons and others, who lived all around them, and could not understand how a true Dutchman of republican antecedents, could take sides with the English King, their course was bitterly condemned. The impression prevails today among the people of Monmouth, that all the VanMaters were Royalists. This, however, is incorrect and not the fact. Like many other families, they were divided in their allegiance. There were more VanMaters who served faithfully on the American side than on the British, but as the VanMaters are not given to blowing their own trumpet, these patriots have been forgotten or overlooked.

For instance, Cornelius VanMater was a captain in the first regiment of Monmouth militia. Benjamin VanMater was a private in Capt. Barnes Smock's artillery company, Chrineyonce, son of Cyrenus VanMater and Abagail Lefferts, his wife, and Cyrenius, son of Benjamin VanMater and Elizabeth Lane, his wife, served in Capt. Waddel's company. It was through the instrumentality of William VanMater, born June 22, 1760, and a son of Richard VanMater, that the chief of the Pine Robbers was killed.

This was no less a person than Lewis Fenton, who for several years had headed those banditti, and perpetrated many robberies, murders, and other crimes. So daring and ferocious had been many of his atrocities, that he had become what in our day is called a "Holy Terror," to the people of Monmouth.

On page 351 of Barber & Howe's His. Coll. of N. J. is an account of the death of this Fenton. While generally correct, there are some errors in the details of this narrative, as I have heard the story.

It was not Burk, who helped Fenton rob and beat VanMater, but one DeBow, for Stephen Burk, alias Emmons, with "Zeke Williams" and "Stephen West" had been killed at Wreck Pond Inlet, by a party of militia under Capt. or Major Benjamin Dennis, in January, 1779, and Capt. Dennis had brought their corpses to Freehold for recognition, and to secure the reward offered by Governor Livingston. To avenge the death of these three men, Fenton waylaid Capt. Dennis in July, 1779, while traveling from Coryel's Ferry to his home in Shrewsbury, and brutally murdered him. Thomas Burk, alias Emmons, had been hung at Freehold in the summer of 1778.

In August, following the murder of Capt. Dennis, Fenton and his gang murdered two aged people, Thomas Farr and his wife, in their own home, not far from the Yellow Meeting House in Upper Freehold township. Wainright, a tax collector, was also found murdered about this time on the south side of the Manasquan river. This was also laid to the Fenton gang.

So great was the terror caused by his ferocity, cruelty, and daring, that Governor Livingston about this time, offered a reward of £500 ($2,500) for Fenton, and smaller sums for his abettors and followers.

This large reward is evidence of the dread he inspired, and how difficult it was to induce anyone to hunt him down in his pine lairs and swamps. It seems from concurrent testimony that he was a desperate and dangerous man, quick and active as a panther in his movements, cunning and deep in his plans, with a coolness and nerve no danger could shake. Masterful and cruel in his disposition, he exacted unquestioning obedience from the half savage denizens of the pine woods, whom he dominated and led.

On the 23rd of September, 1779, William VanMater, a lad of some 18 years of age, had been sent by his father on an errand to Longstreet's Mills, in the vicinity of what is now Our House Tavern. He rode there on horseback early in the morning. When within a mile or two of what is now Our House Tavern, but then a dense pine woods, his bridle was suddenly grabbed by John Fenton, a brother of Lewis, who was hidden behind a big pine tree close to the roadside. Lewis Fenton and DeBow then came out of the woods partially intoxicated. They pulled Van Mater off his horse and began to search his pockets, while John Fenton unbuckled and took the saddle off the horse. Finding no money on his person, DeBow began to strike and kick him, and finally knocked him down. Then, picking up his musket which had a bayonet affixed, he made a vicious lunge at his throat, as he lay on the ground. VanMater threw up his arm to fend off the thrust, and the bayonet pierced the fleshy part of his arm. At this moment a wagon with five or six men in it, was seen coming up the road from the direction of the Shark River salt works. The miscreants at once left their victim and retreated into the woods, John Fenton taking the saddle with him.

VanMater, who was young and active, at once sprang up, leaped on his horse and rode off bareback on a run. After going nearly a mile he stopped, tore off a strip from his shirt and bound up the wound in his arm. It then occurred to him that he had heard that Lee's rangers or light dragoons, were stationed at Freehold to protect the people. Smarting under the indignities to which he had been subjected, he at once resolved to ride there, and lodge his complaint against the robbers. This he at once did, running his horse all the way to Freehold. He fell in with a sergeant of the rangers to whom he told his story. This man had heard of Governor Livingston's $2,500 reward for Fenton, dead or alive. He at once went to Major Lee and obtained permission to take three of the soldiers and go after Fenton.

A large farm wagon with horses was procured, two barrels were set in front, and a lot of hay was placed in the body. The three soldiers with loaded and cocked muskets by their sides, were ordered to lie down behind the barrels, and were covered over with the hay, so that they could not be seen, and were instructed that when they heard the sergeant strike his foot against the barrel, they were to rise up and shoot any person, whom the sergeant had his pistol pointed at. Two bottles filled with applejack were also procured, one the sergeant placed in his pocket; the other he gave to VanMater to carry. He also took off his uniform and dressed himself in an old suit borrowed from a farmer. A board was placed across the two barrels, and, with two loaded pistols under his coat, the sergeant took his seat by VanMater on this board. The whole rig resembled the usual teams or wagons of the farmers going after salt to the Shark River salt works. VanMater was directed to drive to the place where the robbers had attacked him. They reached the spot early in the afternoon but found no one there.

The sergeant then ordered VanMater to drive on a slow walk down the road leading to the Shark River salt works. This he did, and when they had gone about two miles, a hoarse call came from the woods to "Halt." Out strode the robber chief, a cocked rifle in one hand and a big horse pistol in the other, and another in his belt. He was still under the influence of liquor and more reckless than usual. Addressing VanMater with a vile oath, said "After the licking you got, how dare you show your rabbit face around here?" Then, noticing the barrels, he asked "Have you got any rum in them bar'ls?" "I have got some in a bottle," replied VanMater. "Hand it out dam quick, then," commanded Fenton, "or I'll blow your head off." The young man passed the bottle to him; he put his pistol back in his belt, let the butt of his rifle drop to the ground, and seizing the bottle, raised it to his mouth. As the rum gurgled down his throat, the sergeant gave the signal, and fired his pistol at the broad breast of the desperado, who was only three or four feet from him. The ball struck him and he turned half around, letting the bottle fall, and made an effort to raise his rifle. At this moment the three soldiers, who had risen, fired, blowing off the top of his head. A few seconds later, the report of a gun was heard off in the woods. Thinking it was a signal, and that the gang might attack them from the thickets, they threw the corpse of the robber into the wagon and started back on a run towards the Court House.

They reached there without any molestation; and great was the rejoicing when the news of Fenton's death went over the county. I suppose Governor Livingston paid the $2,500 reward to these soldiers for killing Fenton. There ought to be records in the State House at Trenton to show this and who they were. It would be interesting to know their names.

At all events William VanMater did more for the people of Monmouth when he effected the slaying of this arch fiend of the pines than his three cousins ever did for the Royal sde. The many stories told generation after generation about the three VanMaters who joined the army of King George, and fought against their own kinsmen, has also added to the popular belief, that the whole family were the worst kind of Tories.

Such tales grow and are exaggerated each generation. Great injustice and wrong has in this way been done to the VanMaters, who, as a rule, have been conscientious and honorable men, and have contributed much by their industry and ability, to the agricultural progress of Monmouth county, particularly in introducing blooded and fast horses and other stock.

As a great writer has said:

"Rashly, nor oft-times truly, doth man pass judgment on his brother;
For he seeth not the springs of the heart, nor heareth the reasons of the mind.
And the World is not wiser than of old, when justice was meted by the sword.
When the spear avenged the wrong, and the lot decided the right.

When the footsteps of blinded innocence were tracked by burning ploughshares
And the still condemning water delivered up the wizard to the stake;
For we wait, like the sage of Salamis, to see what the end will be,
Fixing the right or the wrong, by the issues of failure or success.

Judge not of things by their events; neither of character by providence;
And count not a man more evil, because he is more unfortunate
For the blessing of a little covenant, lie not in the sunshine of prosperity,
But pain and chastisement, the rather show the wise Father's love."

Now I have seen an account, coming from the patriotic side, of a raid into Monmouth county, by a part of the brigade under Cortland Sknner. The three VanMaters served under him and were probably in this raid. This account says: "It is acknowledged in their favor that they behaved remarkably well to the persons of our people." There was a wide difference between these regular troops under reputable officers, and the whale boatmen from Long Island, the mongrel crew from the Refugee camp on Sandy Hook, and the bandits of the pines.

This story is given as an item of news fresh from Monmouth county, in the issue of the New Jersey Gazette of June 27, 1781. (See files of this newspaper in the State Library):

"On Thursday last a body of 1,000 men, New Levies, British, and foreign troops, under command of Cortland Skinner, made an incursion into Monmouth county. They arrived at Pleasant Valley about 11 o'clock a. m. The militia by this time were beginning to collect, and a pretty severe skirmishing was kept up the remainder of the day, in which our people behaved with great spirit.

"They began their retreat about sundown, and made no halt till they got to Garrett's Hill, where they continued during the night. During the night one of our gallant officers made a descent upon them and rescued a number of stolen sheep.

"The next day they embarked again. They have taken off 40 cattle, 60 sheep, with loss of one man killed, and a number deserted. Their loss in wounded is unknown.

"Loss on our side, 1 killed, 3 or 4 wounded.

"They burned two houses, but it is acknowledged in their favor that they behaved remarkably well to the persons of our people. By their coming out in such force it was expected their aim was to have penetrated further into the county. To prevent which the militia of the neighboring counties were called upon, and it was truly surprising to see with what spirit and alacrity they flew to arms, and were crowding down from every quarter to the assistance of their brethren on this occasion, when accounts of the hasty retreat of the enemy, rendered their further services unnecessary."

This was evidently a foraging party after beef and mutton from Staten Island or New York city, but it was a very strong force for our militia of Middletown township to fight, and compel them to retreat.

ESCAPES OF DANIEL AND CHRINEYONCE VANMATER, ROYALISTS.—THE PINE ROBBERS OF MONMOUTH.

There are also two stories told of Daniel and Chrineyonce VanMater, repeated generation after generation, during the long winter evenings around the firesides in many of our farm houses; and these tales have added to the belief that all the VanMaters were devoted Royalists. As has already been stated, Daniel and his brother Hendrick (Harry), were born and raised on the farm, near the Old Scots burying ground, only it included more of the adjacent lands. These and other lands belonging to them were confiscated and sold under the executions aforesaid. After serving in the New Jersey Royal Volunteers, or "Greens," a year or two, Daniel became very anxious to see his sister Catharine, who was then unmarried and kept things together at the homestead. He accordingly came over from Staten Island one night in the fall of 1778, and managed to reach his old home undetected. Next day one of the young negroes thoughtlessly mentioned to a patriotic neighbor that "Mars Dan'l was home." This news flew all over, and along in the afternoon a party of light horsemen surrounded the house and captured Daniel VanMater. He was allowed to mount one of his horses, and surrounded by armed horsemen, was escorted to Freehold to be lodged in jail. They reached the court house about dusk, and rode into the yard which was in front, and then inclosed by a stout and high board fence. A sentinel was placed at the gate while they awaited the coming of the sheriff, who happened to be away. Thinking that their prisoner, who still sat on his horse, was entirely safe within this yard, they paid but little attention to him. VanMater gradually walked his horse over close to the court house, so that the whole width of the yard was between him and the front fence. It was now quite dark, when VanMater suddenly started his horse on a dead run for the front fence, which is said to have been fully six feet high. His

JOSEPH C. VAN MATER

Son of Chrineyonce VanMater and Eleanor VanMater, who freed 100 negro slaves.

horse, accustomed to the fox chases of those days, leaped like a deer, and went over that fence like a bird. It was a wonderful jump, and done so quickly in the gloom of evening, that before the light horsemen could recover from their astonishment, the rapid beat of his horse's hoofs was heard on a dead run going down the road, and his wild whoop of triumph sounded through the darkness. They knew it was hopeless to follow him on his blooded horse, and so VanMater escaped, and was never afterwards seen in Monmouth county. The whole county rung with his daring jump and escape, and the story has been told over and over down to this day.

Another well authenticated story is told of Chrineyonce VanMater, who is said to have carried on the mills at the place now known as Taylor's Mills, in Atlantic township. He had a slave called Tommy, who was very faithful and of whom he thought a great deal, and made careful provision for his comfortable maintenance in his old age.

A small party of militia was sent to arrest him, but Tommy saw them before they reached the house, and gave him warning when the party was about a quarter of a mile away.

Chrineyonce at once mounted one of his best horses, and started down the road which led to the Refugee camp on Sandy Hook. Among the militia was a resident of Colts Neck, and a bitter personal enemy of Chrineyonce. He was mounted on a very fine and fast horse, and armed with a sabre and pistols.

As soon as the militiamen discovered that their "bird had flown," they started in pursuit, for VanMater was not over a quarter of a mile ahead of them. When they reached Ogbourn's corner without gaining on him they all gave up the chase, except the Colts Neck man, who swore he would have him or his corpse. Brandishing his sabre and striking his horse now and then with the flat side, he kept right on in VanMater's track, for he intended to cut him down or shoot him. They passed through Middletown village like a flash, but when VanMater began to mount the high hill, which lies east of the intersection of the Red Bank road with the road from Middletown to the Highlands, he discovered that his horse was showing signs of distress. Chrineyonce was a large, heavy man, resembling physically his maternal grandfather, and was noted for his great bodily strength, but his great weight was telling on his horse. When he reached the top of the hill and looked back, he saw his pursuer was now gaining on him, and not over 500 yards behind him, flourishing his sabre and showing in every move his deadly purpose. Just as Chrineyonce passed over the crest of the hill, he met a boy on a fine horse with a bag of meal in front, coming towards him. Riding close up to him he caught him by the collar, and lifted him off of the horse, at the same time tossing off the bag of meal. He at once changed horses and went on a run towards Sandy Hook. When the Colts Neck man reached the top of the hill and saw VanMater skimming away on a fresh horse, he swore many bitter oaths, but gave up the chase. Chrineyonce reached Sandy Hook, and from there went to New York and joined Col. Lawrence's battalion of the New Jersey Royal Volunteers, and for this the second execution on page 99, Book A of Executions, in clerk's office, was perhaps issued against him. His father, however, in his will, made provision that Chrineyonce's children should have what he left, if there was any likelihood of confiscation. This last execution was not recorded until February 4, 1784.

Gilbert VanMater seems also to have been on the patriotic side. The following news item appears in the June 14, 1780, number of the New Jersey Gazette, then printed and published at Trenton, N. J.

Extract from a letter from Monmouth Co. of June 12:

"Ty, with his party of about 20 Blacks and Whites last Friday afternoon, took and carried off Prisoners, Capt. Barnes Smock and Gilbert VanMater, at the same time spiked up the iron four pounder at Capt. Smock's house, but took no ammunition. Two of the artillery horses and two of Capt. Smock's horses were taken off. The above mentioned Ty is a negro who bears the title of Colonel, and commands a motly crew at Sandy Hook."

Although this is a brief notice, it involves quite a long explanation in order to understand it. Tye, who was a mulatto, and a runaway slave, was acquainted with all the bypaths and woods in this part of Monmouth. He had led his men through the woods, and by unfrequented paths, and had taken Capt. Smock by surprise. The spiking of the cannon was to disable the gun and prevent an alarm.

It has often been asked, why the Sandy Hook Marauders and the Pine Robbers passed by the rich and fertile farms around Shrewsbury and Eatontown villages, so much nearer to them, and went to a more distant region like

Colts Neck and Pleasant Valley.

The reason was that this was the very heart of Monmouth county, where the most active and resolute patriots lived. Around Shrewsbury they were lukewarm, to say the least. This Pleasant Valley region was known among the Tories of Monmouth as the "Hornets' Nest," a name given at a later date to the Democracy of the old township of Middletown. Capt. Barnes Smock lived on the farms where Charles Lloyd lived, and the one now owned by the children of John J. Crawford, deceased, lying on the north side of Hop Brook and west of the road from Holmdel village to the bridge over this stream. This last farm was afterwards owned and occupied by his son Barnes.

In Stryker's book, "Officers and Men of New Jersey in the Revolutionary War," he is described as Capt. Barnes Smock of an artillery company. The other Barnes Smock was captain of a light horse company. The last Barnes Smock was often called "Leggy" Barnes on account of his long legs, for he was a man of great size. They were both designated as captains during the Revolution. On the tombstone of the last Capt. Barnes Smock in Lefferts-Logan graveyard, his name is inscribed "Col. Barnes J. Smock."

The residence of Capt. Smock near Hop Brook was the rallying place for the Middletown patriots to meet. A circle of about four miles drawn around, with Capt. Smock's dwelling as the center, would take in the greater part of the most active and zealous of the patriots in old Middletown township. This region was well called the "Hornets' Nest," for their stings meant death to the Tories. The four pounder was placed here, and used as a signal gun. On any ordinary day or night, the boom of this cannon could be heard for miles around. The Schancks, Hendricksons, VanDorns, Smocks, Hyres, Holmeses, and Covenhovens, through Pleasant Valley could hear it. The Hulsarts, (Hulses), VanKirks, Wyckoffs, DuBoises, VanCleafs, Covenhovens and Schancks who lived in the vicinity of old Brick Church could hear the report.

So the boom went westward among the Strykers, VanSicklens (Sickles), Wyckoffs, Voorheeses, VanDerveers and Conovers, living through what is now Marlboro township. It went roaring southward to the Scobeyville and Colts Neck neighborhoods, among the VanBrunts, VanDerveers, Lefferts, Bennetts, VanSutphens, Polhemuses, Conovers and VanSchoicks. The report of this four pounder was a notice to all, that the enemy was making a raid somewhere in Middletown township. Every man among the associated patriots seized his rifle or musket, swung his powder horn and bullet pouch over his shoulders and often barefooted and in his shirt sleeves would spring on his horse, and ride as fast as the horse could run, over to Capt. Smock's house. Therefore, even in the middle of the night, if a scout brought word to Capt. Smock that the enemy was landing from their boats at Matawan creek, Navesink, Shoal Harbor creek (now Port Monmouth), or on the Middletown side of the Shrewsbury river, the cannon was fired. In a few minutes, from all around, armed men would come, riding in on horseback, and at once a troop was formed to meet the coming raiders, sometimes by ambush, and sometimes by a wild tornado charge on horseback. This explains the swiftness with which the many raids of the enemy were met and repulsed, although the newspapers of that time do not report one-fourth of the fights, skirmishes, and raids through this part of Monmouth. The rich farms with their cattle, horses, sheep, hogs, and well stocked cellars, smokehouses and barns, constantly attracted the Refugees from Sandy Hook, foraging parties from Staten Island, the crews from the British transports and men of war in the Lower bay, who craved fresh provisions like chickens, milk, butter, etc., after their long voyage across the ocean, living on salt provisions. The spiking of this four pounder by Tye and his gang was a serious matter, and so was the kidnapping of Capt. Barnes Smock with Gilbert VanMater, who doubtless helped him load and discharge this cannon.

The people of this vicinity were well called "Hornets," and Col. Tye knew enough not to bring them about his ears, for he got safely back to Sandy Hook with his two prisoners and four horses. Only two or three years previous the people of this vicinity were slow moving, good natured, kind hearted farmers, as many of their descendants, who still live on these lands, are today. They had no military training, and knew nothing of war or camp life, but were men of peaceable lives and kindly deeds.

After three years of war had passed these quiet and hospitable farmers had become a stern faced, haggard band of desperate men. In that time many of them had fathers, brothers, or sons, who had starved to death in the British prisons of New York. Others, who had been exchanged, came home emaciated skeletons, and told horrible and ghastly tales of Cunningham's brutality, of slow, lingering death, with insults and cruelties superadded to embitter the dying hour. When they heard these things, they thought it was easier to die fighting, than to suffer death by inches amidst such horrors.

Others of them had seen a father, brother, or son suddenly shot down while at work in his field by a hidden assassin in an adjoining thicket. Others again had seen a father, while working near his home to provide for wife and children, suddenly shot down, and then bayonetted before the eyes of his horror-struck wife and terrified children. Others again had come home from the battles of Brandywine, Germantown, or other scenes of conflict, and found their wives and daughters dishonored and gibbering idiots, their stock gone, and often their houses and outbuildings burned to the ground.

While these outrages cannot be charged on the Regulars, British and Royal American troops under honorable officers, yet they can be on many of the whale-boatmen from Long Island, the Refugees on Sandy Hook, and the outlaws of the pines. These wrongs and sufferings had changed the quiet farmers of Pleasant Valley, into a band of fierce and desperate men to whom fighting became a joy, if he could only kill, and kill, and kill these demons who had wrecked his life. Col. Asher Holmes' regiment was made up principally of these farmers, and, at the battle of Germantown, they stood and held their ground after the regular troops had twice broke and run. *

---

* See letter from Col. Asher Holmes to his wife, written after the battle of Germantown, and published in Monmouth Democrat. Asher Holmes was a native of the old township of Middletown, and a farmer by occupation. He was the first sheriff of Monmouth county under our republic, a staunch patriot, a brave man, and a good officer, although he had no military education or training.

The following extracts are from entries in

This, too, after marching all day and the preceding night, and going into battle without rest or food. The militia of Somerset county, and Monmouth had come under the eyes of General Lafayette, and he remarked that "for coolness and bravery they exceeded all his expectations of the militia."

But it had required a baptism of fire, misery and wrong for three years, to stir up their quiet blood and easy nature, and bring them up to this pitch of savage desperation and wild fury. Gilbert VanMater and others of this name on the patriotic side had endured and suffered with the rest, and therefore, I contradict the current story, which has so long been told, that all the VanMaters were Royalists.

---

an old Bible, much dilapidated, mouse eaten, and torn, now in possession of Asher H. Holmes, his great grandson, who resides on the Tylee Schanck homested in Marlboro township:

"John Watson and Hope Taylor, joyned in Bonds of Holy Matrimony ye 15th of December, in the year of our Lord, 173 7-8." (1738).

Then follows births of three children by this marriage, but names are torn off. On the next page, (first entry):

"Asher Holmes and Sarah Watson were married on Thursday, 21st day of February, 1771."

Then follow births of several sons and daughters, and, finally:

"Asher Holmes departed this life June 20, 1808, aged 68 yrs., 4 mo., and 4 da. Sarah Holmes, widow of Asher Holmes, departed this life Sept. 11, 1830."

Then follow two entries, copied from some other records, as follows:

"Sarah Salter, daughter of Samuel Holmes, died January 14, 1757."

"Samuel Holmes departed this life February 20, 1760."

I understand that Col. Asher Holmes is buried in the yard of the Baptist church at Holmdel village, but I have never made a personal examination of this cemetery. Asher Holmes Conover, who owned and occupied a farm in the township of Freehold, about a mile and a half from Old Tennent church, and who died last spring, and his brother, Peter H. Conover, who also owns a farm in this same vicinity, are great grandsons of Col. Asher Holmes.

GARRETT VANMATER, HIS CHARACTERISTICS AND DISPOSITION.

There is another VanMater, heretofore named along with the descendants of Gilbert VanMater and Micha Hendrickson, his wife, who, I think, deserves particular notice. This was Garrett VanMater, the fourth son of William VanMater and Mary Hendrickson, his wife, born during the early part of the present century, and who died at his home on Chapel Hill, Middletown township, in 1879. He was well known to many people still (1899) living, and familiarly addressed and called Garry VanMater. In his youth, without any advantages of education, save such as could be had in the rough country schools of his boyhood days, he engaged in business at Hoboken, N. J. By steady and persistent industry and his natural good judgment, he amassed quite a fortune, according to his modest desires. Instead of spending all the years of his life in piling up dollars, he came back to his native county to enjoy country life, before age had impaired his strength and interest in the world. He purchased a tract of five acres, known as the Cornelius Mount property, on one of the lofty eminences of that range of hills called the Navesink Highlands, and commanding a magnificent view of Raritan Bay, from the cedars of Sandy Hook to the two Amboys at the mouth of Raritan river. Here, where he could see the mingled glories of earth and sea and sky at one glance, he took up his abode, and lived until the end came in 1879. Garrett VanMater was a domestic man and neglected no step which would promote the comfort and welfare of his wife and children. The careful provisions in his will to guard them from the misfortunes of life, testify to his care and foresight in this particular. He possessed a logical mind, with the hard, practical sense of the Hendricksons, his mother's people, and the sensitive nature and buoyant disposition of the VanMaters. His laugh was hearty, spontaneous and contagious. Any one who ever heard Garry laugh will remember it. He was fond of argument and reasoned well, for he was a natural debater "wayback from Debaterville." Although no scholar or bookman, he had gathered from actual experience and treasured up many facts. He was an observant man and understood human nature well. For the mere pleasure of argument, he would often take sides contrary to his real convictions. In these wordy tournaments he was very earnest and vehement, and a stranger hearing him, would think some of his opinions highly reprehensible. Garry made no distinction between the man in his shirt sleeves and the man who wore a clerical gown. They were all men in his eyes, with their sins, foibles and weaknesses, for he had no bump of veneration. As he was always plainly dressed and looked like a country farmer, people often misjudged him. Country ministers, or some young theologian, fresh from the artificial life and training of a sectarian seminary or college, would sometimes tackle Garry, upon hearing him make some heterodox remark, as he stood in a crowd on a platform awaiting a train, or in some other public place. Much to Garry's delight, he would call the plain, ignorant old farmer, as he thought, to book for such unorthodox opinions. Then the ball would open, much to the entertainment of the bystanders. The clerical champion would strike at Garry with his book knowledge, his cut and dried sectarian learning, and his ipse dixit on eternal damnation. Whereupon, Garry, with his ready wit, shrewd practical sense, and knowledge of the world would give it back, in his high pitched voice, in a way to make all the bystanders roar with laughter. After a few years Garry became known, and none of the ministers cared to tilt with him. They always had business somewhere else, when Garry wanted to argue with them. The young farmers of Middletown township, who attended the debates at Headden's Corner schoolhouse many years ago, will remember the zest and interest which Garry took in these wordy combats. Although a great deal older than any of them, he seemed a companion, for his heart was always young, and he liked young company. His high spirits, hearty laugh, and the vehemence with which he debated a question, made him the life and soul of this debating society. He served

Lonely grave of Michael Fields, by the side of the public road, near Vanderburg. He was killed in a skirmish with the British near this place on June 28, 1778. Col. Asher Holmes, with a part of his regiment, made an attack on the baggage train, but were repulsed with the loss of this man killed and several wounded. Four of the British soldiers and one drummer boy were killed in the attack. The division of the British army in charge of the baggage train began their march from Freehold at 3 o'clock A. M. on June 28, 1778, and by daylight must have been several miles on their road. Garret Smock, who participated in the attack, stated the above facts to R. C. Smock, his grandson.

Bridge over Hop Brook and mill pond on the road between Marlboro and Brick Church.

Photographed in the summer of 1900 by Mrs. L. H. S. Conover.

occasionally on the grand jury, and made a good juryman, for the "axe-grinders" could never hoodwink or deceive him. He loved justice and hated wrong, with all the deep intensity of his nature. Any abuse of even a dumb beast in his presence excited his anger, and he would then express himself in language more forcible than polite; for a spade with him was a spade, and nothing more. There was nothing theatrical, deceitful or subterranean about him. He carried his "heart on his sleeve," as the saying is. Although at times rough in his words, he was truthful and faithful to principle and friends. He was hospitable to those he liked, and nothing pleased him more than to have them visit his home. He had a very pleasant and comfortable home. The magnificent view from the rear piazza seemed to harmonize with his broad, liberal, and charitable ideas. For the eye could take in at a glance, not only the whole expanse of Raritan Bay, but the lofty hills of Staten Island on the northwest, the spires and steeples of New York rising beyond the grim forts at the Narrows, with the white beach and background of green pines of the Long Island shore, stretching away eastward until lost in the Atlantic ocean. Here, seated on his piazza, Garry VanMater passed many hours gazing at this pleasant and grand view. The great ocean steamers with their pennants of trailing smoke, the ships, schooners, and other vessels with their snowy canvas, coming in from distant lands, or going down to the great ocean, afforded inexhaustible subjects of thought and speculation to one of his observant and active mind. From the foot of the lofty eminence on which his dwelling stood, the land sloped gradually away to the bay shore, and lay like a picture beneath his eye. The well cultivated gardens, fields and farms, the comfortable farm houses nestling amidst orchards and vineyards, afforded a marked contrast to the blue water of the bay, and what looked like fairy land beyond. The dock at Port Monmouth, the steamboat lying by it, taking in the products of this region from a long train of farm wagons, made a scene of animation and life, and just distant enough to lend enchantment to the view. I often think the same ideas must have passed through Garry VanMater's mind, when he gazed on this beautiful and animated scenery, as those expressed by Steadman in "Alice of Monmouth:"

"Ladies in silks and laces,
  Lunching with lips agleam,
Know you aught of the places
  Yielding such fruit and cream?

South from your harbor-islands,
  Glisten the Monmouth hills;
There are the Ocean Highlands,
  Lowlands, meadows, and rills.

Berries in field and garden,
  Trees with their fruitage low,
Maidens (asking your pardon),
  Handsome as cities show.

Know you that night and morning,
  A beautiful water Fay,
Cover'd with strange adorning
  Crosses yon rippling bay?

Her sides are white and sparkling,
  She whistles to the shore;
Behind her hair is darkling,
  And the waters part before.

Lightly the waves she measures,
  Up to the wharves of the town,
There unloading her treasures,
  Lovingly puts them down.

Come with me, ladies; cluster
  Here on the western pier;
Look at her jewels' lustre,
  Changing with the changing year.

First of the months to woo her,
  June her strawberries flings
Over her garniture,
  Bringing her exquisite things.

Rifling her richest casket,
  Handing her everywhere
Garnets in crate and basket,
  Knowing she soon will wear

Blackberries, jet and lava,
  Raspberries, ruby and red;
Trinkets that August gave her
  Over her toilet spread.

After such gifts have faded,
  Then the peaches are seen,
Coral and ivory braided,
  Fit for an Indian queen.

And September will send her
  Proud of her wealth and bold,
Melons glowing in splendor,
  Emeralds set with gold.

So she glides to the Narrows,
  Where the forts are astir;
Her speed is a shining arrow's;
  Guns are silent for her.

So she glides to the ringing
  Bells of the belfried town,
Kissing the wharves and flinging
  All of her jewels down.

Whence she gathers her riches,
  Ladies, now would you see?
Leaving your city riches,
  Wander awhile with me."

DESCENDANTS OF BENJAMIN VANMATER AND ELIZABETH LANE, HIS WIFE.

Benjamin VanMater, * third surviving son of Kreijn VanMater, and Elizabeth Lane, his wife, their children and some of their descendants:

Neeltje (Eleanor) † b. Sept. 8, 1730; m. 1748, Garrett Janse Couwenhoven, and was his first wife as already mentioned. She died

---

* In book I of deeds, page 255, Monmouth county clerk's office, is record of a deed from John Hartshorne and Lucy, his wife, to Benjamin VanMater, dated March 4, 1761, (consideration $2,600) for a tract of 274 acres in Shrewsbury township, beginning on northerly side of Hockhockson branch of Falls River. Also, on page 252 of same book a deed from Thomas Lemming and Hannah, his wife, to Benjamin VanMater, dated August 3, 1770, for 40 acres in Shrewsbury township, bounded on Pine brook and 'Tintern brook in part. This deed is witnessed by Cyrenius VanMater, Benjamin Couwenhoven and Cornelius VanMater.

† An old Dutch Bible was brought by Neeltje VanMater into the Conover family when she was first wife of Garrett Couwenhoven. It has remained there ever since and is now in possession of John Lyall, son of the late Peter G. Conover. The following are exact copies of certain entries in this Bible:
"Crinjance VanMater, deyed 10 March, 1720."
"Jon Lyle 10 January 1761."
"My father Jacob Lain dyed 21 Nov. 1761."
"My daughter Elizabeth Bennett dyed 10 Aug. 1769."
"My son Jacob VanMater dyed April 20, 1775."
"Benjamin VanMater dyed July 21, 1775—73y. 5m. 29d."
"My grandson Cyrenius VanMater son of Cornelius VanMater, dyed July 30, 1775—4 years 25 days."
The following entries were evidently made by Garret Couwenhoven:
"William Sehanck b. March 3, 1789."
"Nelly is born 8 Sept. 1730."
"I married with Nelly VanMater in 1748."
"My daughter Jacoba is born 10 sept 1749."
"Benjamin b. 25 Jan. 1753."
"Catharine, b. 25 Dec. 1755."
"John, b. Sept. 1, 1766, dyed 28 Aug. 1775."
"Garrett B. 28 Sept. 1770."
The last five entries give us names and births of children of Garrett Couwenhoven by his first wife Neeltje (Nelly) VanMater. The eldest daughter Jacoba is said to have been designated by the last syllable of her name "Coba," or as the Dutch expressed it, Cobatje, pronounced in English, "Cobauchee."

---

prior to 1786, for about that time Garrett J. Couwenhoven married his second wife, Antje Schanck.

Jacob, b. March 12, 1732; m. Neeltje, daughter of Iendrick Hendrickson and Neeltje Garretse Schanck, his wife. She was bap. Sept. 30, 1740. Jacob VanMater died April 20, 1775, aged 43 yrs., 1 mo. and 8 days, according to his tombstone in VanMater graveyard. His widow was about 35 years of age at date of his death and may have married again.

Cyrenius, bap. July 29, 1737; m. first, Anne, daughter of Arie VanDorn and Antje Janse Schanck, his wife. She died June 1, 1765, aged 27 yrs. 3 mo., according to her headstone in VanMater graveyard; m. second, April 6, 1766, Cobatje or Cobauchee Couwenhoven.

Cornelius, bap. April 28, 1744; m. December 3, 1767, Sarah, daughter of Cyrenius VanMater and Abagail Lefferts, his wife. She was born October 3, 1748; bap. October 23 of same year, and died February 25, 1824, aged 75 yrs., 4 mos., 22 days according to tombstone in VanMater yard. Cornelius VanMater is buried by her side and date of his death given as March 30, 1797, aged 52 yrs., 1 mo., 16 days. He was captain of a company of Monmouth militia during the early part of the Revolutionary war.

Sarah VanMater, widow of Cornelius, made her will February 20, 1824, proved March 10, 1826; recorded in Book B of Wills, p. 386, etc., Monmouth Surrogate's office. She describes herself as the widow of Cornelius VanMater. She bequeaths to her grandniece, Eleanor Hendrickson, (daughter of John Hendrickson and Mary Lloyd, his wife, and granddaughter of Daniel Hendrickson and Eleanor VanMater, his wife,) and to Elizabeth Weathers and Anna Scott, widow of James Scott, all her wearing apparel to "be equally divided between the three by her friend, Jane Lefferts." She also directs her son-in-law and executor, Jacob B. VanMater, to give each of them $10 to purchase black clothes. All her silver spoons and plate and residue of her personal property is given to her son-in-law, Jacob B. VanMater, in fee, and he is made sole executor.

Elizabeth, b. September, 1748; m. November 9, 1762, William, son of Jan Bennett and Ida VanMater, his wife; died August 10 1769. They had a child named Ida bap. July 28, 1769.

Jacob VanMater by Neeltje Hendrickson, his wife, had the following children:

Benjamin, b. January 28, 1757; bap. May 15 following; m. July 12, 1778, Sarah, daughter of

Daniel VanMater; d. May 31, 1817, aged 60 yrs., 4 mos. and 8 days, according to inscription on his tombstone in VanMater yard. His wife is buried by his side and her tombstone states that she died September 5, 1840, aged 81 yrs., 23 days.
Neeltje, bap. Oct. 18, 1761; m. first, Conrad Lovefield; second, Jacob Holmes.
Elizabeth, bap. April 30, 1764; m. Daniel, son of Johannes Polhemus and Mary Van-Mater, his wife; d. October 23, 1813, aged 49 years.‡
Hendrick, bap. March 6, 1766; d. unmarried November 20, 1840, aged 74 yrs., 9 mos. and 14 days, according to his tombstone in Van-Mater yard. He left a will dated August 1, 1829; proved February 20, 1841; recorded in C of Wills, p. 322, Monmouth Surrogate's office. He gives his nephew Henry, son of his brother Benjamin, six silver spoons and an eight day clock and all his wearing apparel. Residue of his property to be divided in six equal shares. Two shares to his nephew Daniel, two shares to his nephew Henry, one share to each of his nieces, Maria and Eleanor, daughters of his brother, Benjamin, "Not doubting," he says in the will, "but what they will contribute a support to their aged mother, for whom I ever entertained the most unfeigned respect and friendship, and also their two brothers, Jacob and Gilbert, who have exercised towards me innumerable acts of kindness, but whose misfortunes may require assistance and protection of my legatees." Daniel and Henry, his two nephews, are appointed executors.
The will is witnessed by James Nevius, Joseph H. VanMater and Catharine Nevius.

Cyrenius, second son of Benjamin VanMater and Elizabeth Lane, his wife, by Anna VanDorn, his first wife, had two sons:

Benjamin, bap. June 27, 1762; m. Sept. 11, 1787, Elizabeth, daughter of Cornelius Van-Mater and Sarah VanMater, his wife. She was baptised Oct. 9, 1768; d. March 16, 1795, aged 26 yrs., 6 mos. and 16 days, according to her tombstone in VanMater yard. Benjamin VanMater d. March 14, 1825.
Arie, (generally called and known as Aaron) bap. April 30, 1764; m. April 7, 1785, Mary, daughter of Albert Polhemus and Altje (Alchy) VanMater, his wife, and died Sept. 2, 1835, leaving only one daughter, Anne, bap. Dec. 20, 1785, who m. Joseph H. VanMater, the famous horseman of Monmouth county.

By his second wife, Cobatje Couwenhoven, he had the following children:

William, bap. May 10, 1767; m. Jan. 4,

---

‡ Daniel Polhemus died June 22, 1831, aged 71 years, according to his tombstone in Polhemus burying ground at Scobeyville, Monmouth county. He had the following children by his wife, Elizabeth VanMater: Jacob, b. June 28, 1795; Abbie, b. Dec. 19, 1797; m. William Schanck. John, b. Jan. 17, 1801; d. young. John, b. May 7, 1803, and Daniel, b. July 26, 1806.

1792, Ida Bennett, § and died about 1800, leaving two children, a son and daughter. His widow married for her second husband, James Smith.
Agnes, b. 1769; m. Jacob Smith.
Jacob, bap. May 19, 1772; m. Feb. 13, 1804, Mary Vanderveer.
Cornelius, bap. Sept. 5, 1773; m. June 18, 1797, Orpah Taylor.
Garrett, bap. Aug. 25, 1776; m. Betsey Lake.
Elizabeth, bap. May 10, 1778; m. John W. Bennett.
Mary, or Polly, bap. April 23, 1781; d. in infancy.
Nelly (Eleanor) bap. Sept. 9, 1781; m. William Wyckoff, and had following children, viz: John, b. Aug. 20, 1800; Mary, b. March 1, 1802; Garrett, b. Feb. 28, 1804; Cyrenius, b. Oct. 9, 1807; Charles, b. Aug. 23, 1809; and Sarah, b. Oct. 17, 1811.
Catharine, bap. Dec. 7, 1783; m. June 24, 1802, Matthias Golden.
Peter, bap. Oct. 15, 1786; m. Lavinia Beasley.
Sarah, bap. April 11, 1790; m. Joseph Lake.
John C., bap. April 5, 1793.
I do not know who this last son married.
Cyrenius VanMater, father of the above 14 children, made his will Oct. 13, 1800; proved Feb. 28, 1801, and recorded in Book A of Wills, p. 623, in Monmouth surrogate's office. He gives to his two sons, Benjamin and Arie (Aaron) by his first wife, Anne VanDorn, all the goods and chattels received from their mother and says that he gives them no more because they are well provided for by their mother's relatives.
He then gives to his second wife Cobatje, use of all his property during her widowhood. He then devises, subject to use of widow, to his two sons, Garrett and Peter, the farm he bought of Edmund Williams, formerly the John Tilton farm, to be equally divided be-

---

§ One of William VanMater's children was Elizabeth, or Betsy, born Feb. 16, 1794; m. Jan. 11, 1816, William Lake, son of Capt. John Lake of Colts Neck. Soon after this marriage, he removed to Freehold where he lived. Here he had one son, William Henry, b. Oct. 19, 1817. He then moved to New York City, where he followed his trade as a carpenter until about 1833, when he came back and took up his residence at Morrisville in this county. While in New York he had two sons born. John Bennett about 1824 and Joseph T., b. Sept. 26, 1830. His eldest son, William Henry, followed the sea and physically was as fine a specimen of the American sailor as ever trod the deck of a ship. He, however, contracted hasty consumption, which carried him off in the morn of his manhood. He is buried in the yard of the old White Meeting House in Holmdel township. The second son, John Bennett, was drowned while shad fishing in the North River. Joseph T. Lake, the youngest son, has resided in Freehold nearly all his life and is still (1899) living. He served during the war of the Rebellion as Captain of Company E, 29th Regt. N. J. Vols., and came home with the respect and good will of all of his men, for he looked after them like a father.

tween them.

He bequeaths to Chrineyonce ‖ and Elizabeth, children of his deceased son William Van-Mater, and to Sally Ann and Cyrenius Smith, children of his deceased daughter Agnes, who married Jacob Smith, $500 to be equally divided between them when they become of age.

All residue of his estate he devises to his seven children, Jacob, Cornelius, Elizabeth Bennett, Eleanor Wyckoff, Catharine Van-Mater, Sarah VanMater and John C. Van-Mater, after their mother's use has ended, share and share alike. His son Cornelius, and his friend Tylee Williams, are appointed executors.

Cornelius, third son of Benjamin Van Mater and Elizabeth Lane, his wife, married Sarah VanMater, and had the following children:

Elizabeth, b. Aug. 30, 1768; bap. Oct. 9, following; m. Sept. 11, 1787, Benjamin Van-Mater; d. March 16, 1795.
Cyrenius, bap. Sept. 15, 1771; d. when a boy.
Abagail, bap. May 14, 1780; m. Dec. 22, 1800, Jacob B. VanMater; died Aug. 25, 1802.

Benjamin, eldest son of Jacob Van-Mater and Nelly Hendrickson, married Sarah VanMater and had the following children:

Jacob B., b. Feb. 13, 1779; bap. April 4, following; m. Abagail VanMater, Dec. 22, 1800; d. Dec. 2, 1836, aged 57 yrs., 9 mo., and 9 days, and is buried in VanMater yard. His wife, Abagail, is interred by his side and her age given as 22 yrs., 10 mo.
Daniel, b. March 3, 1782; bap. June 20, following; d. May 10, 1852.

‖ This son of William VanMater, Chrineyonce, enlisted as a soldier in the war of 1812, and, while at Trenton, N. J., awaiting orders, was taken with a fever which proved fatal. He died unmarried. His sister, Elizabeth or Betsey, married William Lake, as stated above.

Gilbert, b. Dec. 18, 1787; bap. March 23, 1788; d. May 11, 1850.
Maria, b. Feb. 15, 1790; bap. May 2 following; d. unmarried May 18, 1867.
Henry, b. October 8, 1791; bap. Dec. 11, following; d. June 6, 1841. He married Catharine S. Bennett.
Eleanor, b. Oct. 20, 1793; bap. Oct. 21, (same year) d. single May 27, 1862.

It would puzzle one to define the relationship of the above six children, or state the exact relation of each to the other.

Benjamin, eldest son of Cyrenius Van Mater by his first wife, Anne VanDorn, married as already stated, Elizabeth, daughter of Cornelius VanMater and Sarah VanMater, his wife, and had the following children:

John, b. Nov. 11, 1800; m. Jane, daughter of William I. Conover (who resided in what is now Manalapan township) and d. Sept. 16, 1868, on his farm at Colts Neck which lay on the south side of the turnpike. He had the following children, viz: John, who m. Mary E., daughter of Hon. William P. Forman, who for many years was one of the lay judges of the Monmouth county courts and who resided in Millstone township on the farm now owned by his son, Hon. Peter Forman. John C. Van-Mater served as collector of Atlantic township many years and died only recently.
Benjamin, who married Ann Eliza Sherman; William, who married Kate Stillwell, and Eliza, who married Foster VanKirk of Mercer county.
Eliza Ann, b. June 30, 1804; m. March 9, 1824, Hon. Thomas G. Haight of Colts Neck, and d. about 1881. They were the parents of Hon. John T. Haight, who was collector of Monmouth county several years and elected clerk of the county after a memorable struggle at the primaries and ballot box. I e died in office greatly mourned by his numerous friends.
Cornelius, b. Dec. 13, 1807; d. young.
Jacob, b. Oct. 11, 1811; d. young.

DESCENDANTS OF CYRENIUS VAN MATER AND ABAGAIL LEFFERTS, HIS WIFE.

Cyrenius VanMater, fourth surviving son of Kreijn VanMater, and Abagail Lefferts, or Leffertse, his wife, had the following children:

Chrynjans (Chrineyonce), bap. March 20, 1730; m. his cousin Eleanor, daughter of Joseph VanMater and Sarah Roelofse Schanck, his wife; d. Sept. 11, 1785, aged 54 yrs., 9 mos., 17 days, according to his tombstone in the VanMater burying ground.
Mary, b. March 7, 1733; m. Nov. 16, 1758, Johannes (son of Daniel Polhemus and Margaret Albertse Couwenhoven, his wife). He was born Oct. 28, 1733; d. March 24, 1820. His wife Mary VanMater, d. Sept. 27, 1809. Both are interred in Polhemus cemetery at Scobeyville, N. J. They had the following children: Daniel, b. April 17, 1760; m. Elizabeth VanMater; d. June 22, 1831. His wife died Oct. 23, 1813, aged 49 years. Both are interred in the Polhemus yard.*
Abigail, b. May 3, 1762; m. Cornelius Suydam; d. June 7, 1801, aged 39 years; buried in above yard. I do not know where her husband is buried.
Margaret, b. March 11, 1766; m. Nov. 20, 1793, Chrineyonce Schanck of Pleasant Valley, mentioned in a former article.
Mary, b. June 16, 1768; m. Jacob Suydam.
Cyrenius, died young.
Neeltje, died young.
John, b. July 20, 1776; d. unmarried Nov. 26, 1814, aged 38 yrs., 4 mos. 6 days.
Eleanor, b. August 4, 1735; bap. Aug. 17, same year; m. according to marriage license dated Nov. 14, 1758, and on file in office of the secretary of state at Trenton, Daniel, son of John Hendrickson and Annetje (Jacobse) Couwenhoven. Daniel was born July 3, 1735, and d. Nov. 17, 1809. He and his wife are both buried in family burying ground on the farm which he owned, and which is still (1899) in ownership of his descendant, situated on south side of street at eastern end of Middletown village, next to so-called Presbyterian graveyard. This burying ground is near and in plain sight from the dwelling house on this farm.

In the above marriage license, Daniel Hendrickson is put down as a resident of Middlesex county. He was then holding some clerkship at Perth Amboy, at that time the seat of government of East Jersey. They had the following children:

Anne, b. Feb. 14, 1761; bap. April 26 same year; m. Charles DuBois, and died June 26, 1798. Her husband was born Feb. 25, 1757; d. Sept. 8, 1804, at Middletown village. Both are buried in the above family cemetery.
Cyrenius, b. May 3, 1766; d. young.
John, b. June 13, 1773; m. Nov. 27, 1793, Mary, daughter of John Lloyd and Sarah Cou-

---

* The Polhemus family burying ground is on the old homestead at Scobeyville, in Atlantic township, Monmouth county, N. J. The following inscriptions were taken from the tombstones in the fall of 1898 by Mrs. Lydia H. S. Conover:
Daniel J. Polhemus, d. Sept. 26, 1763, aged 57 yrs.
Margaret Couwenhoven, wife of Daniel J. Polhemus, died June 17, 1780, aged 70 yrs.
John Polhemus, son of Daniel and Margaret Polhemus, d. March 24, 1820, aged 89 yrs.
Mary, his wife, (daughter of Cyrenius VanMater and Abigail Lefferts) d. Sept. 27, 1809, aged 76 yrs.
John Polhemus, Jr., son of John and Mary, d. Nov. 26, 1814, aged 38 yrs., 4 mo., 6 days.
Tobias Polhemus, son of Daniel and Margaret Polhemus, d. Aug. 24, 1826, aged 82 yrs.
Mary, his wife, (daughter of Garrett Garretse Schanck and Jannetje Williamse Couwenhoven) d. July 17, 1826, aged 69 yrs.
Daniel T. Polhemus, d. Oct. 1, 1826.
Catharine Couwenhoven, (his first wife, daughter of Cornelius Couwenhoven and Mary Hendrickson) d. June 20, 1797.
Sarah VanDyke, second wife Daniel T. Polhemus, d. Feb. 7, 1857, aged 88 yrs.
Daniel J. Polhemus, d. June 22, 1831, aged 71 yrs.
Elizabeth VanMater, wife of Daniel J. Polhemus, d. Oct. 23, 1813, aged 49 yrs.
Alkey VanMater (widow of Albert Polhemus and wife of William Bennett) d. Oct. 24, 1804, aged 64 yrs.
Daniel A. Polhemus, d. Jan. 29, 1820, aged 57 yrs. Micha Clarke, his wife——.
Abigail Suidam, wife of Cornelius Suidam

(and daughter of John Polhemus and Mary VanMater) d. June 7, 1801, aged 39 yrs.
Hannah Polhemus (daughter of Daniel Polhemus and Margaret Couwenhoven) d. Oct. 29, 1792, aged 54 yrs.
Aukey Lefferts, d. Nov. 26, 1769, aged 92 yrs.
Mary TenEyck, his wife, d. Sept. 1, 1732, aged 55 yrs.
Benjamin Lefferts, d. July 28, 1785, aged 62 yrs.
Mary Lefferts, d. June 28, 1800, aged 94 yrs.
Colonel Auke Wikoff, d. April 16, 1820, aged 72 yrs.
The tenant of the last grave was one of the brave and trusted leaders of our Revolutionary sires. He was Lieut. Col. of 3rd Regt., Monmouth militia, and a stern, unyielding enemy of caste and royalty, as embodied in and perpetuated by the government of Great Britain. The Wyckoffs of Monmouth county were all sterling patriots and several of them rendered valuable services to the people in this war.

wenhoven, his wife; died in Jan. 1807, leaving one daughter, Eleanor, and three sons, Daniel J., Charles J., and John Lloyd, surviving.

Anne Hendrickson and Charles DuBois, her husband, left one daughter, Eleanor and two sons, Daniel H. DuBois and Peter DuBois, surviving them. The two sons both died in early manhood unmarried, and are buried by their parents in above yard. Eleanor DuBois, the only surviving child aforesaid, was b. Aug. 19, 1792; m. Jan. 12, 1812, William H., son of Capt. Hendrick Hendrickson, who owned the old Hendrickson homestead at Holland, in Holmdel township, and d. Sept. 25, 1879, aged 87 yrs., 1 mo., 6 days. She was the mother of Hon. William Henry Hendrickson, one of the honored citizens of this county, who recently died on the old homestead at Holland, which he owned and occupied all his life. Daniel Hendrickson, the husband of Eleanor VanMater and maternal great grandfather of the late Hon. William H. Hendrickson, made his will Aug. 4, 1809. It was proved Dec. 29 of same year and is on record in Monmouth surrogate's office in Book B of Wills, p. 316. In this will he speaks of the farm on which he then lived, and the one allotted to his son John Lloyd, as called the "Stout farm." He gives to his widow, Eleanor VanMater, and to Mary Lloyd, the widow of his deceased son John, use of all his property so long as they remain unmarried. He charges them with care, maintenance and education of his three grandsons, Daniel, John Lloyd and Charles, who he states are now living with him. At death of the two widows, all his real estate was to be equally divided between his said three grandsons, sons of John Hendrickson, deceased. He gives legacies to Eleanor, the daughter of his son John, and to the children of his daughter Anne DuBois. Tylee Williams, Joseph Taylor and Mary Lloyd, widow of John Hendrickson, are appointed executors. Daniel Hendrickson, his son John, and son-in-law, Charles DuBois, owned together a tract of about 20 acres near central part of Middletown village, on north side of the street. By Book O of Deeds, page 739, Monmouth deed dated July 3, 1804, recorded in clerk's office, Daniel Hendrickson conveys to his son John, certain lands on north side of Middletown street, and between lands of Edward Taylor and Jacob Covenhoven's lands. The last premises were afterwards known as the Murray homestead, and owned by George Crawford Murray, son of William W. Murray. The corner of Charles DuBois' lot is called for as one of the monuments in this deed, and also as a monument fixing the north line of the Middletown street. The DuBois lot was afterwards owned by John Casler, who for many years carried on the blacksmith business in Middletown village. His shop stood on the opposite side of the street from this lot on which his residence stood.

Daniel J. Hendrickson, the son of John and grandson of Daniel Hendrickson, received as his share of his grandfather's estate, a farm at the eastern end of Middletown village on north side of street, and about opposite to his brother, John Lloyd Hendrickson's farm on the south side. It is now in possession of the Morfords. It passed out of the ownership of Daniel J. Hendrickson prior to his death. He died Dec. 24, 1845, aged 48 years, 11 months, according to inscription on his tombstone in Episcopal churchyard of Middletown village. Charles J. Hendrickson was well known to the present (1899) generation, as an honorable man and a good citizen. He died only a few years ago at his residence on his farm, lying on north side of the street through Middletown village. For particular details of his life see biography and picture in Ellis' history of Monmouth county.

John Lloyd Hendrickson, m. Dec. 16, 1822, Adeline, daughter of George Crawford by his second wife, Eleanor Schanck, and d. Sept. 25, 1845, at his residence on the homestead farm aforesaid. He left one son George Crawford, and one daughter Mary L., surviving him. The son died unmarried on the homestead where he was born and had always lived, Oct. 12, 1875, aged 46 yrs., 6 mo., 4 days, and is interred in family plot on this farm. A brief but truthful sketch of his life and character, accompanied by a steel engraving which hardly does him justice, for he had a strong, intelligent face with regular well marked features, can be seen in Ellis' history. When he passed away he left a good name as an upright man, considerate and charitable to the poor, and helpful and obliging to his neighbors. He wronged no man; but dealt truly and fairly with all, so that no reproach rests upon his memory, although he never made any profession.

Altje (Alice) fourth child of Cyrenius VanMater and Abigail Lefferts, bap. Oct. 7, 1737; m. first Albert, son of Daniel Polhemus and Margaret Albertse Couwenhoven, his wife; m. second, William Bennett, who was then a widower, having first married Elizabeth, daughter of Benjamin VanMater and Elizabeth Lane. Altje VanMater d. Oct. 24, 1804. She had the following children by her second husband, William Bennett, viz: Elizabeth, b. June, 1773; John, b. Dec. 1774; Albert, b. July 1776; and Cyrenius, b. Aug. 1779.

The fifth child of Cyrenius VanMater and Abigail Lefferts was Sarah, b. Oct. 3; bap. Oct. 23, 1748; m. Dec. 3, 1767, Cornelius, son of Benjamin VanMater and Elizabeth Lane and d. Feb. 25, 1824, aged 75 yrs., 4 mo., 22 days, buried by her husband in VanMater yard. Her will, recorded in B. of Wills, p. 386, Monmouth surrogate's office, and the names of her children, have been heretofore given.

Chrynjans (Chrineyonce) the only son of Cyrenius VanMater and Abigail Lefferts, by his wife Eleanor VanMater, had two children, viz:

Joseph C., b——; m. Feb. 28, 1803, Catharine, daughter of his cousin Chrineyonce VanMater and Huldah Holmes, his wife. She was born Jan. 9, 1784; d. Jan. 20, 1804. She was a bride for only one year, and Joseph C. VanMater never married again. This is the Joseph VanMater about whom so many stories are told, as to the ownership of land, stock and negro slaves. He was called "Big Joe VanMater" on account of his size, and to distinguish him from others of the same name.

Abigail, b. May 7, 1775; died in infancy.

Joseph C. VanMater lived at what is now called the Phalanx, in Atlantic township, and owned an extensive tract of good farming land running from the vicinity of Tinton Falls on over to the lands owned by his maternal grandfather, Joseph VanMater, in the vicinity of Holmdel and Colts Neck. He also owned nearly one hundred adult negro slaves. Joseph C. VanMater executed his will January 20, 1825. It was proved before Peter C. Vanderhoef, surrogate of Monmouth county, Dec. 31, 1832, by oaths of Gilbert B. VanMater and Henry VanMater, two of the subscribing witnesses. Daniel T. Polhemus was the third witness to this will. It is recorded in Book C of Wills, pp. 300-3.

He gives to Joseph, son of Holmes VanMater, "my silver tankard." To Joseph I. Holmes, son of Daniel Holmes, $50 to buy a silver tankard. He gives to Mary Lloyd, Rhoda Holmes and Eleanor Croes, all his mother's wearing apparel, and to Eleanor Croes a chest of drawers belonging to his mother, Eleanor VanMater. He bequeaths to Sally Thompson $100. To John Bennett, son of "my uncle William Bennett," £100 ($500). To Albert Bennett and his brother Cyrenius Bennett each £100 ($500). To Charles and Catharine, children of William and Mary Lloyd, £1,400 ($7,000) to be paid to them when they arrive at age. To Rhoda Holmes, daughter of his uncle Chrineyonce VanMater, £1,400 ($7,000). To Louisa VanMater £1,400 ($7,000).

To children of Benjamin Cooper and Sarah VanMater, his wife, £1,400 ($7,000). To children of Rev. John Croes, Jr., and Eleanor VanMater, his wife, £1,400 ($7,000). To Elize Jane VanMater £1,400 ($7,000). He wills and orders that "all his black people" be set free, both male and female. "It is my will," he says, "that all those under 40 years be regularly manumitted by my executors before they have their freedom, and all the black children born free be given up to their parents." He adds "It is my will if any of the black people of my family or that have belonged to the family, become a charge upon my estate, the expense shall be equally borne by my legatees, (except Mr. Thompson, John, Albert and Cyrenius Bennett). I devise to my two brothers-in-law, Joseph H. VanMater and Holmes VanMater, the farm whereon I live, called the homestead farm, also the VanBrunt farm, together with all the remainder of my real and personal property, in fee, to be equally divided between them."

Joseph H. VanMater, Holmes VanMater and Daniel Holmes are appointed executors to administer the estate.

Joseph C. VanMater lived and died on the homestead at what is now called the Phalanx. He owned nearly 100 adult negroes not affected by the new law. He speaks of them in his will as the "black people of my family." He never married after losing his young bride of a year, but lived there among his colored people, whom he treated with great kindness. Like the other VanMaters, "Big Joe", never made merchandise of his black people, and by his will orders the freedom of them all, numbering nearly 100 adults, whom he could have sold, if so disposed. They were probably worth, at this time in the Southern markets over $30,000. Unlike many modern abolitionists, who take out their views in cheap talk or speeches "Big Joe" without any talk or fuss, frees them all at a great pecuniary loss, at a time when anti-slavery sentiments had made no great headway.

A story has been current for some two generations, among the farmers of Holmdel and Atlantic townships, that "Big Joe" VanMater, childless and wifeless, wanted to own an even 100 adult slaves, but although he made many efforts, yet when he reached this number, some accident or fatality would happen, which would cut down his "human chattels" to ninety and nine. As it was, he had more than he knew what to do with. After his death they were all set free, as directed by his will. Many of them by years of dependance for food, clothing and shelter on their easy going, good-natured master, were like children, unable to take care of themselves. Neither were they content with a new place of abode. They clung to their old home. It is said that after "Big Joe's" death the road from what is now the Phalanx to Colts Neck, was black with these newly freed negroes, and they wandered back and forth, perplexed and bewildered with the great change. For it was hard to find another home, where the "black people" would be treated as part of the family, and where there was another man, like lonely, but good-natured and generous-hearted "Big Joe" VanMater. Many of them sought homes and shelter from Joseph H. and Holmes VanMater, the devisees and legatees of the deceased. For in his will he strictly charges them to take care of the "black people of my family" and "those which had belonged to the family." This brought upon these two men, all the helpless and indigent ones of this estate, as well as those of their grandfather and father. There are people now living, who remember Joseph H. VanMater when he drove over to church at Holmdel on Sundays. Not only his immediate family, but crowded in with the whites, in a big carryall, would be all the colored people who wished to go to church. This burden of the negroes, together with heavy legacies charged in the will of "Big Joe" made a heavy financial load for his devisees to carry. For the land brought in no income except as farmed and the profits were then small.

THE LONG AND INTERESTING WILL OF JOSEPH VAN MATER.

Joseph VanMater, the fifth and youngest son of Kreijn Janse, and Sarah Roelofse Schanck, his wife, had the following children:

Eleanor, or Neeltje, b. Oct. 4, 1735; bap. June 20, 1736; m. her cousin Chrineyonce, son of Cyrenius VanMater and Abigail Lefferts, as already mentioned.

Ruloff, (named for his maternal grandfather) b. March 2, 1738, bap. April 23 ensuing; m. Catharine Kearney, then the widow of Joseph VanMater, as set forth in a former article. She was the daughter of James Kearney of Chinqueroras, as the region about Keyport was then called. Ruloff VanMater d. Dec. 10, 1817, aged 79 yrs 9 mo., 8 days, according to inscription on his tombstone in VanMater yard. His wife is interred by his side, and her headstone informs us, she died May 10, 1807, aged 54 yrs., 9 mo., 20 days. The above couple had only two children, both daughters, viz: Sarah, who married Benjamin Cooper, and Eleanor, who was married Oct. 13, 1812, to Rev. John Croes, Jr., by Rev. John Croes, Sr., then rector of Christ church at New Brunswick, N. J. In Book I of Deeds, p. 214 Monmouth clerk's office, is record of a deed dated July 23, 1787, consideration £820 4-5 current money of New York, from Catharine VanMater, wife of Ruloff VanMater, Jacob Tice, and Anna his wife, James Holmes, and Margaret his wife, Henry Chappe, and Sarah his wife, legatees of James Kearney, late of Middletown township, to Ruloff VanMater. They quit claim and convey to him four-fifths of a tract of land in Middletown township, lying at a place called Brown's Point, beginning at the very point, thence up Matawan Creek 32 chains to Whingson Creek, etc. After particular description by chains and links, comes this general description. A tract of 520½ acres bounded northeasterly by the Bay, northwesterly by Matawan Creek, and Wingson Creek, easterly by Luparticong Creek and brook, and southerly by lands lately the property of James Kearney, deceased. The witnesses are Gilbert VanMater, Joseph Throckmorton and Cyrenius VanMater (miller). The conveyance by a wife directly to her husband, as in this deed, is considered illegal and void by the artificial rules of law. The courts have solemnly adjudged that a man and wife are one person in law, and therefore cannot make a contract with each other. This, too, in face of the experience of mankind that the marital relation is formed and continued by mutual agreement or contract to give and take, to bear and forbear.

The third child of Joseph VanMater and Sarah Roelofse Schanck, Cyrenius, was b. Aug. 1740; bap. Sept. 21, following, and d. Dec. 23, 1745, aged 5 yrs., 5 mo., according to his tombstone in VanMater cemetery.

Catharine, b. March 15, 1743; bap. May 6 following and d. unmarried Aug. 27, 1763, aged 20 yrs., 5 mo., 12 days, as we are informed by her headstone in family burying ground.

Chrineyonce, b. Jan. 23, 1747; m. about 1772 Huldah, daughter of Obadiah Holmes and Catharine Remsen, his wife, and d. March 24, 1803, aged 56 yrs., 2 mo., 1 day, as stated on his headstone.

Cyrenius, b. Dec. 23, 1750; d. in infancy.

Only three of the above six children survived to grow up and marry, viz: Eleanor, Ruloff and Chrineyonce. These are the three mentioned in the will of Black Roeloff Schanck, as the three children of his daughter, Sarah VanMater.

Joseph VanMater, the father of the above children, lived on and farmed the old homestead, where Kreijn Janse first settled. The family graveyard is on these premises, and reserved forever for that purpose, by the will of this Joseph VanMater. The following is a true copy of the will of Joseph VanMater and codicil, as same are recorded in the office of the surrogate of Monmouth county:

JOSEPH VAN MATER'S WILL.

In the name of God, Amen; I, Joseph Vanmater of the township of Middletown, in the county of Monmouth and State of New Jersey, being of a sound disposing mind and memory, thanks be given to Almighty God, therefore duly considering the mortality of my body, and knowing it is appointed for man once to die, do make and ordain this my last Will and Testament, in manner and form following, that is to say, principally and first of all, I give and recommend my soul into the hands of God, &c., and as for my body I recommend it to the earth, to be buried in a christian like and decent manner at the discretion of my executors hereinafter named, &c., and as touching such wordly estate wherewith it hath pleased God to bless me with in this life, I give, devise and dispose of the same in manner and form following:—My mind and will is, and I do hereby order all my just debts and funeral charges to be well and truly paid, in some convenient time after my decease by my executors hereinafter named.

Secondly.—I give and devise to my beloved son Ruloff Vanmater, all that piece or lot of wood saplin marked on three sides, on the land and meadow beginning at a small buttensouth side of Hop brook in the line that part me, the said Joseph Vanmater from my son Ruloff; thence northerly across the meadow along said Ruloff's line till it comes to a ditch, on the north side of said meadow; thence easterly down the ditch to a small oak saplin marked on three sides, standing on the bank of said ditch; thence southerly across the meadow, as the fence now stands, on the westerly side of a road, to the mouth of a gully on the southerly side of Hop brook; thence up said gully untill it comes opposite the middle of the bank, thence westerly along the middle of the bank to said Ruloff Vanmater's line; thence to the beginning; also I give and devise to my son Ruloff Vanmater, all that tract of land called the Barren lands, which was taken up between me the said Joseph Vanmater and Benjamin Vanmater, also one certain piece or lot of salt meadow lying on Shrewsbury River, which I bought with the plantation I purchased of Joseph Holmes, as also one equal half of my upland or stacking place at Little Neck, also all that tract or lot of land which I the said Joseph Vanmater bought of Joseph Holmes, adjoining land formerly Peter Tilton. Also that small lott of land lying to the Northward of my farm and said Ruloff's farm next to Obadiah Holmes, Beginning at a poplar tree standing in the line between me and my son Ruloff, marked on two sides with the letter (R), on the east side from thence, easterly about ten paces to a small run of water, thence northerly down that stream until it comes to Hop brook, thence westerly up said brook, untill it comes to said Ruloff's line, thence along his line to the beginning, I also give unto my son Ruloff, my negro man Herculus, my negro woman Deon and her two boys named Cesar and Jersey, and my negro woman Dine, also one silver tankard and six silver spoons now in his possession, as also the one half of my wearing apparell, I also give unto my son Ruloff the one equal half of my farming utensils, as also the one equal half of my stock of creatures of all kinds, I also give unto my son Ruloff the fruit of the westerly half of my orchard four years after my decease, from the first of September untill the middle of November yearly, I also give unto my son Ruloff the sum of Five hundred pounds procklamation, to be paid to my said son Ruloff as shall be herein after ordered and directed; all which devises or gifts are to my son Ruloff his heirs and assigns forever.

Thirdly.—I give and bequeath unto my son Crineyonce Vanmater his heirs and assigns forever, these following tracts of lands (to wit) all my farm or plantation whereon I now live, called my homestead farm, except such parts thereof as are devised to my son Ruloff, also all that lot of land whereon William Arnold lately lived, beginning at a tree marked (L M.) as may appear by a deed of sale under the hand and seal of John Taylor, formerly high sheriff, also I give unto my son Chrineyonce one certain lott or piece of salt meadow lying at Shrewsbury River, which I bought of Thomas Shepherd, as also the one equal half of my upland or stacking place at Little Neck, as also the residue or remainder of my lands wheresoever the same may lay not herein disposed off; also I give unto my son Crineyonce one silver Tankard and six silver spoons now in my possession, as also my negro man Tom, and my negro woman Hagar, and her two sons, Sam and Robbin and all the remainder of my negroes, that shall not be herein otherwise disposed of, I also give unto my son Crineyonce the one equal half of my wearing apparrell, also the one equal half of my farming utensils, together with the one equal half of my stock of creatures of all kinds; all heretofore of my real and personal estate and what may hereafter be given him, my said son Crineyonce, shall be subject to the following conditions (to wit), that my son Crineyonce do pay my son Ruloff's legacy of five hundred pounds, procklamation, two years after my decease, and also pay unto my daughter Nelly, the sum of five hundred pounds procklamation one year after my decease, both of which legacies to my son Ruloff and to my only daughter Nelley, is to be paid by my son Crineyonce in gold or silver, allowing dollars in payment of the above legacies at seven shillings and six pence each, they being of full weight; and if it should so happen that my son Crineyonce should bring in any account against my estate after my decease, then and in such case I do hereby order, the amount of such account to be taken out of that part of my estate herein devised to my said son Crineyonce, and in case any law of this State or of the United States or any impediment whatever, should prevent my son Crineyonce Vanmater from holding or enjoying the aforesaid devises or gifts then it is my will and I do give and devise all the lands and moveables to him devised to the children of my said son Crineyonce Vanmater, to be divided by him in such proportion among his children, as he my said son thinks proper, under the same restriction as it is given and devised to my said son which devises or gifts is to them and each of them, their heirs and assigns forever, provided he my said son cannot hold and enjoy the same, nor enter into the peacable possession thereof at any time before the children shall arrive to the age of twenty-one, then the gifts and devises to remain good to the children, their heirs and assigns forever; but in case my son Crineyonce can hold and enjoy the same at any time before the children arrives to the age of twenty-one, and no law to prevent him from the same, then its my will that every of the devises and bequests given to my son Crineyonce, remain good to him his heirs and assigns forever.

Item—I give unto my daughter Nellie Vanmater and to her heirs and assigns, all my household furniture not heretofore disposed off, also all my linen cut up or not cut up, also one silver tankard and six silver spoons now in her possession, as also my negro woman called Roseatt and the said Roseatt's female children, and all her grandchildren, I also give unto my only daughter Nellie, the sum of Five hundred pounds proclamation money, to be paid her one year after my decease, by my said son Crineyonce as above enjoyned him; I also give unto my three children Ruloff, Nelley and Chrineyonce, all my bonds, bills noats and book debts and all other of my moveable or personal estate, not herein already disposed off, to be equally divided between them or each of their respective heirs or assigns; but if my son Crineyonce cannot hold and enjoy his bequests or gifts by means of any hindrance whatever, then it is my will and I do give the same to the children of my son Crineyonce, to be disposed off by him to his children as before directed, to them their heirs and assigns forever; Also it is my Will and I do allott and set apart and give one chain square of land where there is now our family's burying place, to remain forever for the family of the Vanmaters to bury their dead and for no other use whatever.

And Lastly, I do hereby nominate constitute and appoint my only daughter Nelly Vanmater, my son Ruloff Vanmater, Hendrick Hendrickson, Esq., and William Crawford,* Executors of

---

* William Crawford, one of the executors named in Joseph VanMater's will, was the paternal grandfather of the late James G. Crawford of Holmdel township, who was the father of Ann, who married Joseph H. Holmes, as mentioned hereafter.

William Crawford was a son of George Crawford and is named in his will probated at Perth Amboy May 10, 1745, and now on record in the Secretary of State's office at Trenton.

The above testator was not the son of John Crawford, the pioneer settler of this name, as has been heretofore supposed. This fact is established beyond any doubt, by a deed dated Feb. 29, 1723, from George Crawford to Nicholas Stillwell, conveying six acres, and recorded in Book H of Deeds, page 86, Monmouth county clerk's office. It is stated in this deed that this six acres is a part of a tract granted to John Crawford, the grandfather of said grantor, by patent dated Dec. 3, 1687, from the Proprietors. This patent is recorded in Book B, page 211, in office of the Secretary of State of New Jersey.

In Book A of Deeds, page 36, Monmouth clerk's office, is record of a deed dated Aug. 3, 1691, from John Crafford, Sr., to John Crafford, Jr., conveying in consideration of father-

this my last Will and Testament, ratifying this and no other.

In Witness Whereof I the said Joseph Vanmater have hereto set my hand and seal this twenty-fifth day of September in the year of our Lord one thousand seven hundred and ninety. Signed sealed published, pronounced and declared by the said Joseph Vanmater to be his last Will and testament in the presence off

JOSEPH VANMATER [L. S.]
CYRENIUS B. VANMATER,
BARNES SMOCK,
WILLIAM VANMATER.

Be it known unto all men by these presents, that I, Joseph Vanmater of Middletown in the County of Monmouth and State of New Jersey Yoeman, have made and declared this my last will and Testament in writing, bearing date the Twenty-fifth day of September in the year of our Lord one thousand seven hundred and ninety, I the said Joseph Vanmater do by these presents contained in this Codicil, confirm and ratify my said will only that part I intend to alter, I give and bequeath unto my son Ruloff the sum of Five hundred pounds now in his possession, in lieu of a legacy of the five hundred pounds, ordered to be paid him my said son Ruloff by my son Crineyonce. I give unto my said son Crineyonce all my farming utensils, and stock of creatures of all kinds.

Thirdly.—I give unto my only daughter Nelley VanMater, all my notes, bills, bonds and cash, except the five hundred pounds given to my son Ruloff, all which devises and gifts are to them and each of them, and to each of their heirs and assigns, And whereas Hendrick Hendrickson, Esq., is nominated and appointed an executor in my last Will and Testament, I do hereby make null and void all his power as an executor to my last will and Testament, on any pretense whatever. And my will and meaning is that this Codicil or sjedule be esteemed and adjudged to be part

---

ly affection, 280 acres of land in the township of Middletown.

The name Crawford is spelled in Books A, B, and C of Deeds, Monmouth clerk's office, Crafford, Crawfford, and other ways. This John Crawford, Jr., is named as a grand juryman in year 1693 in the minutes of the Monmouth courts. This would show he was then at least 21 years of age.

In Book C of Deeds, pages 111-12 is record of a deed dated May 8, 1691, from Sadler to Jobs. John Crawford and George Crawford appear as subscribing witnesses to its execution. They, together with Gideon Crawford, were sons of John Crawford, Sr., the pioneer settler. This George is said to have migrated to and settled in one of the southern counties of New Jersey, or in one of the eastern counties of Pennsylvania.

The John Crawford, Jr., to whom the real estate was conveyed by his father, according to tradition, married the daughter of Henry or Moses Lippet, and besides his eldest son George, had Richard, William, Samuel, John and Andrew. Several of these sons removed to other parts of New Jersey and Pennsylvania and there settled, according to family traditions.

and parcell of my said will and Testament, and all things contained and mentioned therein be faithfully performed, in as full and ample manner in every respect as if the same were so declared and set down in my said will.

In witness whereof, I the said Joseph Vanmater have hereunto set my hand and seal the Seventeenth day of July in the year of our Lord one thousand seven hundred and ninety two.

Sealed and delivered in presence of
JOSEPH VAN MATER (L. S.)
DANIEL SCHENCK,
JOSEPH VAN MATER,
    his
JOHN X WOLLEY,
    mark

Probated in Monmouth County Surrogate's Office January 20, 1821, and recorded in Book B of Wills, page 221, etc.

Joseph VanMater and Sarah Schanck, his wife, were both members of the First Dutch Church of Monmouth, and were particular to have all their children baptized, as records of the church now show. They were very regular and punctual in performance of all church duties. Their descendants have very generally followed their example down to this day. A number of the deacons and elders will be found among the different generations of this branch of the VanMater family.

This line, too, have been noted for their modest, unobtrusive manners, courteous address and peaceable dispositions.

They have avoided strife and litigation, and made very little business for our courts and lawyers. Neither have they pushed themselves forward for offices, honors and other political emoluments, but have pursued the honored and quiet occupation of farmers and asked favors from no man.

To this branch of the VanMaters our county is largely indebted for the blooded stock of race horses, for which Monmouth became celebrated during the first half of the present century. The VanMaters of the older generations were born lovers of thoroughbred horses. They seemed to possess an intuitive judgment about the good or bad qualities of a horse. They had a natural talent or ability to manage and train these animals so as to develop their best qualities. Their introduction of blooded and thoroughbred stock and successful training of race horses like "Monmouth—Eclipse," "Horn-blower," and others, whose names and pictures at one time were all over the United States, led many of the Monmouth farmers to engage in the business of raising blooded horses for sale or racing. Customers for blooded stock, and sporting or racing men came to Monmouth from all over the country, for no place at one time stood higher than Monmouth county for good horses.

Fifty years ago it was a very common remark for strangers visiting Monmouth county to make, that the people here "thought nothing and talked of nothing but trotting horses, races, and horse trading."

Chrineyonce VanMater and Huldah Holmes, his wife, their children and some of their descendants are as follows:

Sarah, b. March 17, 1773, d. unmarried Jan. 4, 1819.

Joseph H., b. Nov. 13, 1775; m. Sept. 28, 1808, Anne, the only child of Aaron (Arie) VanMater and Mary Albertse Polhemus, his wife; d. Oct. 10, 1860, and is buried in yard of "Old White Meeting House," which lies on north side of road from Holmdel village to Middletown, a little distant northeast from residence of Dr. Henry G. Cook. This is the "Joe H. Vanmater," famous in his day for thoroughbred and fast race horses. At one time his name was one to conjure with among the people of this county. He was a tall, well proportioned man, affable and courteous in his manners and very liberal and generous in his disposition. He and his brother Holmes, are the devisees in the will of their brother-in-law and cousin "Big Joe" VanMater. These lands, together with what came to them from their grandfather, Joseph VanMater, and their father Chrineyonce, made them the owners of one of the most extensive tracts of good farming lands, which could be found in Monmouth county. It extended almost continuously from Holmdel village over to Tinton Falls.

Catharine, b. Jan. 9, 1784; m. Feb. 28, 1803, Joseph C. VanMater (Big Joe as called) already mentioned. She died Jan. 26, 1804, childless and a bride of less than a year.

Mary, b. Sept. 13, 1786; m. William Lloyd; d. Feb. 10, 1869, leaving two children, Charles S. Lloyd, b. 1813; m. Emma, daughter of John W. Holmes, and Deborah, his wife, d. Feb. 18, 1881. He was a well known citizen and a leading farmer in Holmdel township. His sister, Catharine Lloyd, m. Aaron, son of Hendrick Longstreet and Mary Holmes, his wife.

Holmes, b. Aug. 20, 1789; m. Micha, daughter of Gilbert VanMater and Margaret Sprague (widow Rapelje) his wife, of Long Island. She was born Aug. 21, 1795. Holmes VanMater is interred by his brother, Joseph H., in yard of "White Meeting House."

Rhoda, b. Feb. 14, 1792; m. Nov. 15, 1813, Daniel, son of John S. Holmes. John S. Holmes d. Aug. 15, 1821, on the farm he owned in Pleasant Valley and the same farm on which his grandson, Joseph F. Holmes, lived and died. He is buried in family burying ground on this farm. Daniel, his son, was born Dec. 27, 1792—lived, died and was buried on this farm.

Schanck, b. June 1795; d. single June 20, 1812.

Daniel Holmes was elected sheriff of Monmouth county in 1828, and a member of the council of New Jersey in 1832. He was a very popular and influential man in the Democratic party of that time. A likeness of him and his son, Joseph H., with biographical sketches appear in Ellis History of Monmouth county. Rhoda VanMater, his wife, died June 20, 1838.

Only one son of Daniel Holmes and Rhoda VanMater, his wife, lived to grow up. This was Joseph H. Holmes, born July 28, 1824; married September 19, 1848, Ann, daughter of James G. Crawford of Crawford's Corner in Holmdel township; died November 28, 1892, and is buried on the homestead. His wife, Ann Crawford, was born September 1, 1821, and died June 6, 1894.

Joseph H. VanMater and Ann VanMater, his wife, had the following children, all born on the original VanMater homestead, now occupied by William Jones:

Huldah Holmes, b. Sept. 14, 1810; d. Feb. 1812.
Huldah Holmes, b. Oct. 15, 1812; d. single Feb. 27, 1868.
Aaron S., b. Aug. 17, 1814; m. Sept. 28, 1843, Ann, daughter of Peter R. Smock and Catharine Hendrickson, his wife.
William C., b. Oct. 20, 1816; d. Feb. 4, 1817.
William P., b. March 6, 1818; d. 1822.
Joseph C., b. Nov. 18, 1821; d. 1822.
Mary Polhemus, b. Feb. 14, 1822, and is still (1899) living. Mary Polhemus VanMater has always been active in church work, and for many years taught a class of girls in the Holmdel Dutch Reformed church. Many matrons now residing in Holmdel township are indebted to Miss Mary VanMater, not only for religious instruction, but the example of her gentle and refined manners has exerted a good influence.
Eliza Ann, b. Jan. 9, 1824; d. June 30, 1840.
Joseph I., b. July 20, 1825; m. Eliza M., daughter of Daniel Ayres of Brooklyn Heights, L. I.

Joseph I. VanMater, like many others of this branch, has been a zealous member of the Holmdel Dutch church, serving both as deacon and elder.

Holmes VanMater owned and resided at one time on one of the best farms in Monmouth county. At least it was so considered, and was known as the Academy farm. It embraced more land than it does now. By Micha VanMater, his wife, he had the following children:

Joseph H., b. Nov. 23, 1818; m. Margaret, daughter of Paul Rapelje and Catharine VanMater, his wife, (daughter of Gilbert VanMater and Margaret Sprague, his wife.)
This Joseph H. VanMater owned and resided on the farm now occupied by Edward Smith on the south side of the turnpike from Freehold to Englishtown, about three-quarters of a mile east of the latter place. He was a quiet, but pleasant and obliging man. His old neighbors in this vicinity still cherish his memory, and speak of him as a kindly neighbor and a good and charitable man. He died May 13, 1874.
Gilbert H., b. June 12, 1820; m. Sarah, daughter of John W. Holmes and Deborah, his wife. Gilbert L. VanMater, too, was a faithful adherent to the church of his fathers, and in his unobtrusive and modest way tried to live a Christian life. He removed a number of years ago from Monmouth county to a plantation in the state of Virginia, where he is still (1899) living and highly respected for his gentlemanly manners and honorable conduct. Prior to the Civil War he operated a large grist mill, known as the VanMater, or Red Mills, at Holmdel. The pond covered the meadow which lies in front of the Dr. Cook property, while the dam was where the public road crosses this meadow and the stream. The road then was laid over this dam and a bridge spanned the flood gates. These mills accidentally caught fire and were entirely destroyed. They were at the time full of wheat and other grain and wholly uninsured. It entailed a heavy loss on Mr. VanMater.
Catharine, b. Feb. 2, 1822; m. Jesse A. Dennis. They were the parents of Holmes VanMater Dennis, who now owns and resides on the Smock farm, near East Freehold.
Daniel H., b. Feb. 25, 1824; m. Frances L. Dennis.
Daniel H. VanMater represented Monmouth county in the New Jersey Assembly in 1869-70. He now resides on his farm which lies just west of Marlboro village. Like his forefathers he is a staunch and thorough supporter of the old Dutch church, wherein he has served as deacon and elder. Hon. Daniel H. VanMater has one son and three daughters.
William H., b. Nov. 5, 1828; d. young.
Augustus, b. June 28, 1830; m. M. E. Rapplije.
Margaret, b. Oct. 15, 1832.
Charles S., b. April 20, 1835; m. Anne Kirby.
Huldah, b. April 17, 1837.

Joseph H. VanMater and Margaret Rappelje, his wife, had the following children:

Elizabeth, b. Sept. 1841; m. a Mr. Gorselin of Long Island.
Catharine, b. Aug. 19, 1843; m. W. C. Jefferts.
Holmes, b. July 20, 1845.
Jacob, b. Feb. 17, 1847.
Paul, b. Aug. 29, 1849; m. Lou Kirby of Imlaystown, N. J.
John Henry D., b. July 11, 1851; m. Eliza, daughter of Daniel P. Schanck and Mary Conover, his second wife, and now (1899) owns and resides on the old VanCleef farm near Wickatunk station, in Marlboro township.
Joseph H., b. Aug. 27, 1852; m. a Miss Johnson of Spotswood, Middlesex county.
Gilbert and Augustus, twins, b. March 5, 1855. Gilbert d. young.
Gilbert, b. Oct. 20, 1858.
Margaret, b. July 6, 1860; m. ex-Sheriff Fick of New Brunswick, N. J.
William, b. May 16, 1867.

THE HULSES OR HULSEHARTS OF MONMOUTH AND OCEAN COUNTIES.

The men and women bearing above names are very numerous in Monmouth and Ocean counties. They are all descendants of "Benjamin Holsaert" and "Annetie Luyster" his wife, as their names are spelled on the records of the Dutch church of Monmouth, where they became communicants in 1717.

A writer on the early migration of the Dutch from Long Island to Somerset county, N. J., says that Benjamin Holsaert settled there. This is a mistake, originating from the fact that the people of Kings county, L. I., in those times spoke of their relatives and friends who had migrated to New Jersey as "gone to the Raritans."

The territory south of Raritan Bay as well as that through which the Raritan river flows went with them under this one name. In this generation Raritan is the name of one locality in Somerset and one township in Monmouth. Sloops carried the early settlers with their goods and stock from the Brooklyn shore of the East river down the upper bay, through the Narrows into Raritan Bay, until they reached the south end of Staten Island; here the settlers going to Middlesex or Somerset counties sailed up the Raritan river, while those coming to Monmouth continued on the same course landing up Matawan or Waycake creeks. In the family records kept in some of the old homesteads in Kings county, they were often put down as removed to the "Raratons." Modern writers on family genealogies have seen these entries, and jumped at the conclusion that "Raritan" was the same region or place it is now. Some persons who settled in Monmouth, like Derrick Barkalow and Benjamin Holsaert, are said to have settled along the Raritan river in Somerset county.

An agreement and deed recorded in Book E of deeds, p. 340, etc., Monmouth clerk's office, shows beyond any doubt, that Benjamin Hulse, (to us the modern name), first settled in Monmouth. A Mark Salem and Cornelius Salem of Freehold township purchased together a tract of 230 acres in same township (now Marlboro), generally described as said deed as bounded "E. by 'Hopp Brook,' W. by Gravel Brook, N. by Thomas Hart's land and S. by unappropriated lands." Cornelius Salem by deed dated June 5th, 1718, conveyed his individual half of said tract to "Benjamin Holsaert," described in said deed as a cordwainer by trade, and a resident of New Utrecht, Kings county, L. I. By this agreement said tract is equally divided, the southermost half to be the separate property of Holsaert, and the northermost half to belong to Mark Salem.

This name has been spelled in several different ways. Persons who write their names today "Hulse" had parents who wrote the name "Hulshart." Among the many marriages of this family recorded in Books A and B of marriages in our county clerk's office, the following have been selected to show this fact:

Samuel Hulshart to Mary Emmons, August 11, 1796.
Tunis Hulshart to Margaret Covenhoven, January 5, 1797.
John Hulse, son of William, to Elizabeth Harvey, daughter of William Harvey, June 15, 1805.
William Hulse was married to Sarah Forman, April 18, 1799, by Rev. John Woodhull, D.D.
Ezra Havens was married to Mahala Hulse, both of Howell township, May 3, 1814, by John Cooper, V.D.M.
Hendrick Hulst,* widower, was married to

---

* "Our county records show that this name was sometimes spelled Hulst and Hulz. The following entry from minutes No. 6 of Monmouth Sessions, 1775-1788, shows one of these ways:

OCTOBER TERM, 1778.
Before
  John Longstreet, Esq.,
  Joseph Lawrence, Esq.,
  Peter Forman, Esq.,
  Denise Denise, Esq.,
        Judges.
John Hulst, Appellant, ads. The State. Appeal from a Militia fine, £18.15 under the substitution.

It appearing that the Appellant when called, was employed at a salt works which boils at least 1000 gallons of salt water for the purpose of making salt, and as the Legislature of the State of New Jersey passed an act the 11th day of December, 1777, for the exempting one man from Military Duty for every 500 gallons of salt water boiled as aforesaid, and a substitute hired in his stead. Ordered that said fine of eighteen pounds and fifteen shillings be remitted and entirely set aside."

Margaret Yetman, widow, by Rev. Benjamin DuBois.

Sidney Hulshart was married to Ann Bennett, both of Freehold township Feb. 24, 1820.

Thomas Hulshart was married to Anndoshe Hulshart April 23, 1824, by John D. Barkalow, elder of the Independent Methodist church.

Stephen Hulshart to Jane Matthews, Dec. 29, 1829.

Joseph G. Hulshart, Esq., was married January 19, 1832, to Agnes M. Ely Bennett, by John D. Barkalow, elder, etc.

The last couple were the parents of John W. Hulse, Esq., one of the justices of the peace of the township and police justice of the town of Freehold. Justice Hulse has abbreviated his name to the first syllable of his father's surname, and many others have done the same. John W. Hulse enlisted as a private when a lad of eighteen years, and served as a Union soldier until the close of the Civil War. He has served one term as justice of Freehold township, and gave such satisfaction by his fair and impartial decisions that he was elected to his second term without opposition. In his physical appearance he is a fair type of the old generations of this family and also seems to have their usual mental traits. For the Hulsharts have ever been a plain and unpretentions people, without those meddlesome propensities, overweening self-conceit and insatiable curiosity which make the descendants of certain people such unmitigated nuisances to their neighbors. Justice Hulse has in his possession a letter dated August 16, 1830, written and signed by "John Holsart" as he spells his name, who is also one of this family.

It is addressed to "John Barcalow," then overseer of the poor of Freehold township, and the grandfather of Wicoff Barkalow, the present overseer of poor of this township. He signs himself in this letter as a justice of the peace of Middletown township. The letter is well written and words correctly spelled. This man lived and died on his farm which lay about a mile west of Colts Neck. This part of Middletown was taken off when Atlantic township was formed. He married Mary, daughter of Tobias Polhemus of Upper Freehold township, and was one of our soldiers in the Revolutionary war, and was with Col. Asher Holmes at the battle of Germantown. He died December 6, 1846, aged 87 years, 6 months, 27 days, according to the inscription on his tombstone in yard of Marlboro Brick church. His wife, Mary Polhemus, died February 13, 1851, aged 84 years, 10 months, 3 days. Their unmarried daughter, "Maria P. Holsairt," as name is spelled on headstone, is interred by them. She was born December 24, 1792, and died August 12, 1883.

John Holsart's will is recorded in Book E of Wills, page 173, Monmouth Surrogate's office. He gives his wife Mary, and his daughter Maria, full possession of his lands, stock and household goods as long as they live together and his widow remains unmarried. All his weaving apparatus he gives to his son-in-law, Elias Sickles, his watch to his grandson, John Holsart Sickles, but if he dies under age, then to his brother, DeWitt Sickles. He directs 150 acres to be run off so as to take in all the buildings on his homestead farm and devises it in fee to his daughter Mariah. The remainder of his lands is to be equally divided between his daughter Mariah, and his daughter Hannah, wife of Elias Sickles. He provides for his colored man Jack and orders that he shall be maintained on the homestead out of his estate. His daughter Mariah, and "trusty friend" John Statesir, are appointed executors. Henry D. Polhemus, J. M. Hartshorne, and R. S. Hendrickson are the witnesses. The will is dated June 27, 1838, and proved January 27, 1847.

'Squire Holsart had another daughter not named in this will, Eleanor. She married Daniel, son of Daniel Barkalow and Annetje Luyster, his wife, and they removed to and settled in Western New York or Ohio.

Elias Sickles, who married Hannah Holsart, and named in above will, resided near the village of Marlboro and was a deacon in 1830 and elder in 1844 of the Dutch church. He is a descendant of the "VanSiclin" or "VanSikkele," family who settled in the vicinity of Gravesend, L. I. The name on the old records of Monmouth Dutch church is spelled in the latter way; see page 87 of Wells' Memorial Address at Brick church.

Elias Sickles by Hannah Holsart, his wife, had eight children. One of his daughters, Willempe, married Peter Antonides, who has always lived and carried on a blacksmith business at East Freehold, where his father, Peter Antonides,† and grandfather, John Antonides, also lived and carried on same business.

He was born November 12, 1818, and

---

†Peter Antonides is buried in old graveyard near East Freehold, called erroneously the Wyckoff burying ground. His tombstone states he died Dec. 6, 1828, aged 53 yrs. 5 m. 16 d. Mary Lloyd, his wife, died March 3, 1836, aged 56 yrs. 11 m. 26 d.

JOHN W. HULSE,
Justice of the Peace of Freehold Township,
N. J.

WICOFF BARKALOW,
Overseer of the Poor of Freehold Township,
N. J.

JOHN R. LONGSTREET,
Son of Gilbert Longstreet, of Upper Freehold
Township, Monmouth County, N. J.

MARY MIERS,
Wife of John R. Longstreet, and Granddaughter of Garret Conover and Alice Hendrickson, his wife.

was a son of Peter Antonides and Mary Lloyd, his wife. She was a daughter of David Lloyd. Mr. Peter Antonides, although now over four score years, is as straight and erect as a flag staff, supple and quick and able to shoe a horse and do other blacksmith work as well as any other young man in this county. One of his uncles, Vincent, or Vincentius Antonides, removed to and settled in Ohio during the early part of this century. It is said he has raised a large family there.

The grandson, John H. Sickles, named in Squire Holsart's will, and to whom the watch is given, is still living. He was a Union soldier in the war of the rebellion and very strong in his devotion to the Union cause, hating rebels or rebel sympathizers with all his heart. He is still a bachelor, for like a celebrated judge of Monmouth county used to remark, he believes a "man is never satisfied until he gets as bad off as possible, as is the case when married." So he has escaped the marriage noose and rejoices in single blessedness. He is Dutch clear through on both sides, and sometimes remarks that not a drop of mongrel or English blood beats in his heart.

The Hulsharts have generally followed agricultural or kindred pursuits and have been as a rule good citizens.

THE AUMACKS OR AUMOCKS OF MONMOUTH AND OCEAN COUNTIES.

The name of "Teunis Amak" and Lena Laen (Lane), his wife, appear as members of the Monmouth Dutch church in 1723, while his brother, "Stephen Aumack" and Jannetie Janse, his wife, are entered on the church records five years later. *

Abraham Emans † (Emmons), a resident of Freehold township, conveys to Hendrick Hendrickson and Jaques Denys (Denise) of New Utrecht, L. I., by deed dated May 1, 1719, ninety-six and a half acres of land in Freehold township, bounded east by Bartlett Brook, west by lands of Thomas Cooper, south by lands of Samuel Dennis and north by lands formerly William Scott's. This tract is described as beginning at William Layton's, formerly John Scott's corner. ‡ The grantor and grantees named in this deed, all join in a deed dated May 5, 1730, conveying this same land to Stephen Aumack. Emans joins in order to cure a defect in the former deed. "Theuny Amack" and "Peter Jansen," as they spell their names, are witnesses to this second deed.§ Solomon Deboogh (Debow) by deed dated March 11, 1739, conveys a tract of 100 acres in Freehold township to "Theunis Amack" who is described as a weaver, and resident of Monmouth county. Bartlet Brook and Long Brook are mentioned as part of the boundaries of this tract.‖

"Thunis Amack" is named among the grand jurors impannelled by Sheriff Bernardus Verbryck at April term, 1735, and Stephen Amack among the grand jurors impannelled by Sheriff James Stevenson at April term, 1744. ¶

In Book H of Deeds, page 275, is the record of a public Highway laid out on June 14, 1740, by the surveyors of the highways. "Theunis Amack's" lands and "Stephen Amack's" mill are named in this return. They also make "void" (vacate) a 2-rod road laid through the Amack's, Tunis Denis (Denise), Gilbert VanMater, Judah Williams, Thomas Borden, and Nathan Tilton's lands. This record shows that the two Aumack brothers lived near each other on this new road, and that Stephen Aumack operated a grist mill. Teunis Aumack married Lena, a daughter of Jacob Thysen Laen (Lane) and Elizabeth Barkalow, his wife, and had the following children baptized:

Jannetje, Nov. 24, 1723.
Child unnamed, August 8, 1725.
Elizabeth, August 5, 1733.
Afhie, August 17, 1735.
Jan, April 15, 1738.
Mathys, August 2, 1742.

---

*Wells' Memorial Address at Brick Church, page 87.

†Abraham Emans and Hendrick Emans, who settled at Six Mile Run, Somerset county, N. J., in 1703, were sons of Andrews Emans, who came to America in 1661 and settled at Gravesend, L. I. This name in Monmouth county is now spelled Emmons. Margaret, wife of above Abraham Emans, was a member of the Monmouth Dutch church in 1713. See Wells' Memorial Address, page 85.

‡Book G of Deeds, page 61, etc., Monmouth records.

§Book H of Deeds, page 114, Monmouth records.

‖Book H of Deeds, page 237, Monmouth records.

¶Minutes of Monmouth courts, 1735-1744.

Teunis and Stephen Aumack were born at Flatlands, L. I., and were the sons of Theunis Janse VanAmach, of that place. He is named among the citizens who took the oath of allegiance in 1687, and he is then put down as having been 14 years in America.** The name is there spelled as VanAmach. I do not know how many children he had. The name was first spelled in Monmouth "Amak" and "Amack."

In Book A of Marriages, page 59, is record of a marriage, where the parties were both of this family, and it shows how unsettled they were a century ago in the spelling of this name.

"Teunis Aumack to Mary Aamach, Nov. 26, 1801," is the way it is entered. According to tradition Theunis Janse VanAmach was a marine on one of Admiral Cornelius Evertsen's or Jacob Binckes' ships, when they compelled the English to haul down their flag over New York in 1673. The red, white and blue of the Netherlands Republic waved over New York and New Jersey for about a year. VanAmach, then a young man, during this occupation, became attached to the daughter of a Dutch settler who lived in Brooklyn. Either his term of enlistment expired, or he was discharged, for when the fleet sailed away, he remained and became a resident of Flatlands, where he raised a family. He is therefore the progenitor of all the Aumacks and Aumocks in Monmouth and Ocean counties.

This family can therefore look back to one of the Dutchmen who wrested the New Netherlands from the English in 1673, and helped fight in the memorable war of that year, as their progenitor. This conquest of the New Netherlands was not a secret, treacherous attack, without a declaration of war, but a fair conquest after announced hostilities. England and France with the German Provinces of Munster and Cologne, had combined in an alliance to wipe out the Republic of Holland from the map of Europe. It is true, there was a party in England opposed to this alliance and war, but they were made up principally of the old Republicans and Roundheads, who had followed Cromwell. They knew King Charles II was a papist at heart, and this alliance was really a blow at the Protestant religion, and to restore the Roman Hierarchy to its old power over the world. Charles II had attacked and seized the Dutch colony of New York in 1664, in order to provoke the States General into a declaration of war against England. Such an attack must cause war as a child might know. This in England would be represented as a defensive war, and so, the Protestant party would be compelled, nolens volens, to stand up for their country.

As Charles II and his secret instigator, Louis XIV expected and intended, this capture of the Dutch colony in America, together with an attack on their African trading posts at about the same time, and the seizure of Dutch merchant ships, compelled the States General to declare war against England. The successes of the Dutch admirals at sea, together with other troubles, led the English Parliament to interfere with the purposes of their King. A hollow peace was patched up, but the English puppet of the French monarch, held to the same resolution to destroy if possible, the Holland Republic. It became necessary, however, to educate public opinion, and inflame the passions of the English people, in order to overcome the opposition of the Protestant leaders. Pamphlets and other writings were circulated, filled with the most outrageous accusations against the Dutch.

A roorbach was circulated through England that Admiral VanTromp, as they called him, after defeating the English fleet in the late war, had hoisted a broom at his masthead and cruised up and down the English coast, to show that he had swept the English ships from the seas.

This canard was well calculated to arouse the patriotism and wrath of the English masses, and make them support any alliance, even with the Turks, to punish such insolence. There was no one in England to contradict this lie, so it run its full course, and aroused the English people to bitter anger and fury against the Dutch. Admiral Tromp was a brave, bluff sailor, without the bravado of the French or the cant and hypocrisy of the English. He was no more likely to perpetrate such a puerile, fantastic and idiotic act, than General Grant was to stick a peacock feather in his hat, and strut around with it, after the surrender at Appomattox. Nevertheless, every charge against the Dutch was believed without any question. No one ever asked how it was possible to see a little broom, fastened high up among the ropes and sails of a ship's mast, two or three miles off at sea from the English coast. Like the story of the Dutch drinking intoxicating liquors before going into action, it was a lie cut out of the whole

---

**Vol. I, O'Call. Doc. Hist. of N. Y., p. 661.

cloth. At that time and for many generations after, it was the custom of the English navy to serve out grog to their sailors before going into action. It was supposed to give them courage, yet in this, as in many other things, they charged all their vices on the Dutch, while they arrogated all the virtues to themselves.

It would have been far more in accordance with the truth, to have labelled it Cockney or British courage, instead of Dutch. Not only were such roorbachs industriously circulated, but plays were written and acted in the theatres of England, showing the Dutch up in the most odious light.

Even the famous John Dryden devoted his talents to composing such a play, which was acted to crowded houses, and excited the fury and hatred of the lower classes, so that private citizens of Holland were mobbed in the streets of London. This play was written and acted long before the open alliance between France and England was consummated, yet there are several passages in it which point to it, and show that Dryden was either conversant with the plans of the king, or else wrote the play under particular instructions. Straws, it is said, show which way the wind blows, and this play coming from a man like John Dryden, shows that it was one of the methods used to educate public opinion, and shut the mouths of the Protestant or peace party. This play, called Amboyna, met with great success. The theatres were crowded to overflowing by the people, and it seemed to move them as much as the play of Uncle Tom's Cabin influenced the people of the North, prior to the election of Abraham Lincoln. A strong appeal to the feelings will often move the masses more strongly than the best argument addressed to their reason. The copy of "Amboyna" which I have, was printed in London, England, during the latter part of the 17th century. It begins with a personal address to the "Right Honorable Lord Clifford of Chudleigh," who appears to have been high treasurer of England and one of Dryden's patrons. As a specimen of fulsome flattery, and snobbish sycophancy it is unequalled.

Dryden says that this play was "contrived and written" in a month, and ends up his adulations with these words:—

"I pretend not by it (the play) to make any manner of return for your favors; and that I only give you a new occasion for exercising your goodness to me, in pardoning the failings and imperfections of, My Lord, Your Lordship's most humble, most obliged, and most obedient servant.

JOHN DRYDEN."

Then comes what he calls a prologue to Amboyna in verse as follows:—

"As needy Gallants in the Scriv'ners' hands,
Court the rich knave that gripes their mortgag'd lands,
The first fat buck of all the Season's sent,
And keeper takes no fee in compliment;
The Dotage of some Englishmen is such.
To fawn on those who ruin them—the Dutch.
They shall have all, rather than make a war
With those, who of the same religion are.
The Streights, the Guiney Trade, the Herrings too;
Nay to keep Friendship, they shall pickle you.
Some are resolved not to find out the cheat,
But cuckold-like, loves him who does the feat:
What injuries so'ever upon us fall,
Yet still, the same religion answers all:
Religion wheedled you to Civil War,
Drew English blood, and Dutchmen's now would spare:
Be gull'd no longer, for you'll find it true,
They have no more Religion, faith—than you:
Interest's the God they worship in their State,
And you, I take it, have not much of that.
Well, monarchies may own Religious name,
But States are Atheists in their very frame,
They share a sin, and such proportions fall
That like a stink, 'tis nothing to 'em all.
How they love England, you shall see this day:
No map shows Holland truer than our Play:
View then their falsehoods, rapine, cruelty;
And think what once they were, they still would be;
But hope not either language, plot, or art,
'Twas writ in haste but with an English heart;
And let's, hope, wit in Dutchman would be
As much improper as would honesty."

The play is entitled "Amboyna, or the Cruelties of the Dutch to the English Merchants." The scene opens at Amboyna, with a dialogue between the Dutch Governor and his fiscal, in which they congratulate each other, in damaging the English East India company to an immense amount, and then settling for a trifling sum. The fiscal then proposes to carry out a "Plot" against the English, which he has contrived. The substance of it is, to cut all their throats and seize their wealth.

The history of England during this century is full of charges and counter charges, of plots and conspiracies. As it was a favorite accusation among themselves it became very easy to make it against foreign people.

An English captain named Towerson, in the employ of the English East India company, and an English merchant are next brought on the stage. The English merchant and the Dutch fiscal engage in the following dialogue. The English merchant thus speaks of the Hollanders:

English Merchant—"Not being gentlemen, you have stolen the arms of the best families in Europe, and wanting a name, you make bold with the first of Divine attributes, and call'd yourselves the 'High and Mighty;' though, let me tell you, that besides the blasphemy, the title is ridiculous, for 'High' is no more proper for the Netherlands, than 'Might' is, for seven little rascally Provinces, no bigger in all than a Shire in England. But for my main theme, your ingratitude to England. We have set you up and you undermind our Power and Circumvent our trade."

Dutch Fiscal—"Yes, and good reason, if our interest requires it; besides you give one of the names of the 'Almighty' to your high men in England, by calling them Lords, and so make the vulgar people worship them, as Deities or Human Gods."

English Merchant—"That leads me to your religion, which is made up of interest; at home ye tolerate all worships in them who can pay for it, and abroad you were latterly so civil to the Emperor of Pegu (Peru) as to offer sacrifices to his idols."

Dutch Fiscal—"Yes, this is all true, and you English were such precise fools as to refuse it."

English Merchant—"For frugality, we confess we cannot compare with you. Our English merchants live like noblemen, while you gentlemen, if you have any, live like Boors. You are the mill horses of Mankind; a pickled herring is all your riches. You have good title to cheat all Europe, for you cozen your own backs and bellies."

Dutch Fiscal—"Yes, this is all true."

English Merchant—"Your liberties are a greater cheat than any of the rest. You are ten times more taxed than any people in Christendom. You flatter our Kings and ruin their subjects."

Dutch Fiscal—"You English are so honest, that we Dutch can easily fool you in name of our Protestant religion."

English Merchant—"I prophesy the day will come, when some English king will see through your hypocricies and frauds and protect the honest and true-hearted English, against the rascalities of the Dutch, and resume the fisheries of the seas, and the riches of the East Indies."

Some light scenes and dialogues are next introduced to relieve the gravity of the play. Then an English woman, pale, weak, and in tattered garments, appears on the stage. She tells a horrible story, how she and her husband had been on an English ship, and by treachery certain Hollanders had murdered the English crew and plundered the ship. That she and her husband had escaped in a small boat, and after terrible suffering her husband died, but she was rescued by a noble English captain. Then follow scenes in which great outrages are perpetrated by a son of the Dutch Governor, and the English Captain, Towerson, fights with and kills him in a fair duel. The Dutch Governor and his fiscal then arranged a treacherous plot against the English. They falsely accuse them of trying to capture the Dutch fort, and put them to horrible tortures to elicit a confession. Scene opens and shows the English tortured in the most fiendish manner by fire and water, while the Dutchmen joke and laugh at their sufferings. The Governor remarks, as they burn the English merchant, that he will light his pipe just where the "wyck" is fed with English fat; that "the tobacco tastes divinely after being so fired."

After torture, the English captain is put to death, and the play closes with a scene in which the Dutch are feasting and making merry over a division of the wealth of the murdered English. Then follows an "Epilogue" as Dryden calls it, as follows:

To one well-born, th' affront is worse and more,
When he's abus'd and baffled by a Boor:
With an ill-grace the Dutch their mischiefs do,
They've both ill nature and ill manners too.
Well may they boast themselves an ancient nation,
For they were bred 'ere manners were in fashion:
And their new Commonwealth has set 'em free
Only from honor and civility.
Venetians do not more uncouthly ride
Than did their Lubber State mankind bestride.
Their sway became 'em with as ill a mien,
As their own paunches swell above their chin;
Yet is their empire no true growth but humor,
And only two kings touch can cure the tumour.††
As Cato did his Afric fruits display;
So we before your eyes their Indies lay,
All loyal English will like him conclude
Let Cæsar live and Carthage be subdued.

This is a clear and plain effort to educate public opinion in England, so that an alliance with France against Holland would be popular among the English masses. This play is well contrived to stir up their anger and pride, and was intended for that very purpose. It fell in with the policy and purposes of Charles II, and we can see why Dryden was a favorite of the court and patronized by the high officials.

This play was written and acted in the theatres of London several years before the alliance between England and France against Holland was consummated by an aggressive movement against the Republic.

---

††The two Kings refer to an alliance between England and France.

EFFORTS OF FRANCE AND ENGLAND TO CRUSH HOLLAND REPUBLIC.

Louis XIV of France was one of the most astute and able of the kings of Europe. His zeal and devotion to the Roman Hierarchy is proved by the banishment of half a million of his protestant subjects from France. These refugees were known as French Huguenots. As Macaulay, Dickens, and other truthful historians of England have shown, Charles II was a mere puppet of this champion of Rome. Behind both stood the priests, dictating and urging a union which would restore, as they thought, the church to its old authority and power in the world. Their object was to crush the Protestant Republic of Holland. They were not only heretics but republicans, setting a bad example to Christendom. Their great prosperity and wealth also excited jealousy and alarm. This Republic so near the territory of France and England was a continual menace to the existence of monarchies. If people without a king could prosper so, what necessity was there for royalty and an aristocratic or Brahmin caste, to uphold it. Kingcraft and priestcraft were therefore in hearty agreement to wreck this upstart Republic. These "seven rascally little provinces," as Dryden put it, "not as big as an English shire." The two great monarchies of France and England could easily wipe Holland off the map of Europe, everybody thought. The two Catholic Bishops of the German Provinces of Munster and Cologne also joined this alliance with England and France to destroy Holland. This fact alone would show that behind this alliance of nations stood the Roman Hierarchy. Our American historian, Bancroft, thus describes this great and most eventful contest:—

"Charles II had begun hostilities as a pirate, and Louis XIV did not disguise his purpose of conquest.

"With armies amounting to 200,000 men, to which Holland could oppose no more than 20,000, the French monarch invaded the Republic. Within a month Holland was exposed to the same desperate dangers she had encountered a century before, while the English fleet, hovering off the coast, endeavored to land English troops into the heart of the wealthiest of the provinces. Ruin was imminent and had come but for the public virtues.

"The annals of the human race record but few instances where moral force has so successfully defied every disparity of force, and repelled such desperate odds by invincible heroism.

"At sea, where greatly superior numbers were on the side of the allied fleets of France and England, the untiring courage of the Dutch would not consent to be defeated. On land the dikes were broken up and the country drowned. The son of Grotius, concealing his anger, at ignominious proposals of the French, protracted the negotiations till the rising waters could form a wide and impassable moat around the cities. At Groningen, men, women and children worked on the fortifications. Fear was not permitted to the women. William of Orange (afterwards King of England), was advised by Arlington, one of the great Virginian proprietors, to seek advancement and gain for himself, by yielding to England; 'My country,' calmly replied the young man, 'trusts in me. I will not sacrifice it to my interests, but if needs be, die with it in the last ditch.'"

The landing of the British troops in Holland could only be prevented by three naval engagements. The veteran DeRuyter and the younger VanTromp, a son of the old Admiral, had been bitter enemies. The latter had been disgraced on the charge of the former. June 7, 1673, at the battle of Soulsbay, where the Dutch with 52 ships of the line engaged an enemy with 80, DeRuyter was successful in his first manoeuvers, while the extraordinary ardor of VanTromp, plunged him headlong into danger and he could not recover. The frank and true hearted DeRuyter checked himself in his career of victory, and turned to the relief of his rival. "Oh, there comes grandfather to the rescue!" shouted VanTromp in ecstasy. "I will never desert him, as long as I breathe." The issue of the battle was uncertain. June 14, seven days later, a second battle was fought, and the advantage was with the Dutch. About three weeks after the Dutch captured New York, August 2, 1673, the last and most terrible conflict took place near Helder. The enthusiasm of the Dutch mariners dared almost infinite deeds of valor.

The noise of the artillery boomed along the low coast of Holland. The churches on the shore and the dikes were thronged with people, praying to the God of Battles to give victory to the right cause and their country. The contest raged and exhausted, and was again renewed with unexampled fury. Victory was with DeRuyter and Van-Tromp. The British fleet retreated and was pursued. This defeat caused the English Parliament to refuse Charles II further supplies. This led to peace with England, although war went on with France. At one time affairs seemed so hopeless, with the great French army in the heart of the country, and the mighty allied fleet on the coast it was resolved with inflexible Dutch resolution, to defend the country to the last, and, if all failed, to take to their ships, and sail to some other part of the world, and there found a new country and so preserve the liberties of which Europe was unworthy.

About a month after the defeat of the allied fleets, or between the 7th and 13th of September, 1673, Capt. Knyff and Lieut. Snell with a company of Dutch mariners from one of Admiral Evertsen's ships which lay in the North River before New York, came over in a sloop to Monmouth county, landed at Waycake creek, and marched up to Middletown village and administered the oath of allegiance to the States General of Holland to the citizens there and then went to Shrewsbury and did the same. The people with exception of a dozen or so who were absent, took the oath of allegiance. So our people of Monmouth were a part of the little Netherland Republic and entitled to some share of the glory which belonged to their mother country at this time. If this alliance had succeeded in crushing Holland, there would have been no Stadtholder with his Dutch army to land at Torbay, and deliver the Protestants of England from the tyranny of James II. The great revolution of 1688 would never have occurred. James II, backed by the subtle brain and strong arm of Louis XIV would perhaps have crushed protestantism in England, as completely as Louis XIV had done in France by revoking the Edict of Nantes.

For after the failure of Monmouth's rebellion, the spirit of the English people seemed crushed. The savage and brutal punishments inflicted by Jeffrey and Kirke hardly called forth a whimper of protest, so abject was the terror and fear they inspired with the gibbet, hot pitch and dismembered corpses hung up at nearly every cross road in England.

This victory of the Dutch made the deliverance of the English by William of Orange possible. The hand of Providence was never more signally displayed in the history of states and nations than in the defeat of these powerful nations by "seven little rascally provinces, all told no bigger than an English shire," to use Dryden's expression. It was a year big with future events in the history of Christendom and the world, as subsequent results show.

The sacrifices, services, and patriotism of William of Orange * in this war wth England, France and the two German provinces, together with those of his great grandfather, Willam the Silent in the Spanish war, have made their names venerated in Holland, as Washington's is in America.

The descendants of the Dutch in the United States claim all three as their worthy trio of heroes, and worthy of each other to stand in eternal union and glory. For all three, one as much as the other, they feel a veneration and gratitude which words cannot express. The following song, so popular in Holland, gives but a feeble echo of what is in the hearts of all who prize justice, independence and liberty for "the Frisians shall be free as long as the winds of heaven blow!"

We leven in Nederland vrij en blij,† hoezee!
Wars zijn we van elke dwingelandij, hoezee!
Vervloekt zij eeuwig het vreemde juk,
Op vrijheid, rrijheid zijn we tuk,
    VIVAT ORANJE, HOEZEE!

Oranje maakte ons vrij en groot, hoezee!
Oranje was altijd een vriend in den nood, hoezee!
Oranjeklant lijn we dus op en top!
Oranje boven, Oranje voorop!
    VIVAT ORANJE, HOEZEE!

Oranje blijv, Nederlands toeverlaat, hoezee!
Alleen met Oranje ons Nederland staat hoezee!
Lang leve Oranje! met Rood Wit en Blaauw!
Oranje, we zweren U houw en trouw!
    VIVAT ORANJE, HOEZEE!

---

†Vrij en Blij means Free and Happy.
*Bishop Burnet thus describes William of Orange:
"I had occasion to know him well, having observed him very carefully in a course of 16 years.
"He believed in the truths of the Christian religion very firmly, and expressed a horror of atheism and blasphemy.
"He was constant in his private prayers and in reading the Scriptures.

"His indifference to the form of church government and his being zealous for toleration, together with his cold behavior towards the clergy, gave them generally an ill opinion of him. He loved the Dutch, and was much beloved among them; but the ill returns he met from the English nation, their jealousies of him, and their perverseness towards him, had soured his mind, and had in a great measure alienated him from them, which he did not take care enough to conceal, though he saw the ill effect this had upon his business.

"Watching over the court of France, and bestirring himself against their practices was the prevailing passion of his whole life. I considered him a person raised up by God to resist the power of France and the progress of tyranny and persecution.

"The series of five Princes of Orange that was now ended in him was the noblest succession of heroes we find in any history. And the 30 years from 1672 to his death in which he acted so great a part, carry in them so many amazing steps of a glorious and distinguishing Providence that in the words of David he may be called 'The man of God's right hand whom he made strong for himself.' He received, however, in his life time little else than calumnies, abuse and ingratitude from the nation he served so well. He once remarked to Lord Halifax, when speaking of the treatment he had received from the two great parties of England, that all the difference he knew between them was 'the Tories would cut throat in the morning and the Whigs in the afternoon.' Subsequent generations and posterity in England have acknowledged his great services and abilities, but in a grudging spirit and without any heartiness, as though jealous of the contrast between their native born monarchs and this Dutchman from over the sea. Macaulay, who is of Scotch ancestry, has done him justice but even he thus describes him: 'His manners, (when King of England) were altogether Dutch. Even his countrymen thought him blunt. To foreigners he often seemed churlish. In his intercourse with the world he appeared ignorant or negligent of those arts which double the value of a favor and take away the sting of a refusal.'"

THE BARKALOW FAMILY.

After the New Netherlands were seized in 1664 by the English Government the public records were kept in the English language. Many of the scriveners who wrote legal papers like wills, deeds, etc., were ignorant of the Dutch language, so they spelled and wrote Holland names, like the Indians, from sound. They also made many surnames from the Dutch custom of calling a person by his christian name followed by his father's christian name, with z, s, se, or sen, affixed. Thus if Derrick Barkalow had a son named Pieter, he would be called Peter Derricks, or Dericksen. If the latter had a son Jan, he would be known as Jan Pietersen, or Pieterz. If he called his son Hendrick; he would be designated as Hendrick Jans, or Jansen. The English conveyancers would often write these names according to above custom in deeds and other legal documents, which went on permanent record. In two or three generations such names would become fixed and unchangable, according to the English custom, to identify persons and families and keep land titles straight. This is the reason why several family surnames have originated from one Dutch progenitor. It often makes it very difficult and in some cases impossible, to trace family connections, especially if they frequently changed their residence and neglected to keep a family record or have their children baptized. For this reason it is now difficult to trace the Barkalow family. This name, too, in changing from the Dutch to the English language, has been spelled in many different ways, as VanBerculo, VanBurkalow, Borckelloo, Berkelue, etc.

The original emigrant from Holland was William Janse Barkelo. He came to America at an early date, and settled permanently at Flatbush, Long Island, where he raised a family of several girls and boys. Among the list of persons taking the oath of allegiance to the English government in 1687, and published on page 661, vol. 1, O'Callaghan's Documentary History of New York, we find the name of William Williamsen Borcklo, who is put down as born in America, and a resident at that date of Flatlands. Also, Jan Williamsen Borcklo, also a native and then resding at Gravesend, L. I. Elizabeth Barkalow, who married Jacob Thysen Laen (Lane), and whose name is found among the original members of the Monmouth Dutch church in 1709, is supposed to be one of his daughters. One of his younger sons, Conradt, settled in Somerset county of this state as early as 1714, and is the ancestor of the "Barcalows" there, as they generally spell their names. I have, however, an original receipt in my possession given 130 years ago, which is signed by "Daniel Barricklo." It is his genuine signature and shows another of the many ways the name has been spelled. The following is a true copy: "1770, April 25, then received from Cornelius Ten-Broeck the sum of seventeen pounds, light money, being in full for a yoke of oxen, I say, received by me. Daniel Barricklo." Another son of the first emigrant who was born at Flatbush, Long Island, and learned the weaver's trade was Derrick. He married on Long Island, September 11, 1709, Janetje VanArsdalen, and soon after removed to Monmouth county, for both of them are named as members of the Dutch church here in 1711. He seems to have been among the active workers in this church, and was made an elder in 1739. He died in 1744 before all his children had arrived at age. The minutes of the Monmouth courts show that he was on the grand jury in January term of 1735, and several times afterwards. His name is here spelled "Derk Barkelo."

In Book E of Deeds, page 336, etc., Monmouth clerk's office, is record of a deed from Thomas Foreman and Mary, his wife, of Freehold township, to "Derrick Barcalow" of same township, dated April 15, 1719, conveying in fee 90 acres in same township. It is generally described as bounded on the north by the Burlington road, south and west by John Oakerson's lands, and east by two ditches and a run of water. Passequenecke brook is also mentioned in this description. It was part of a tract conveyed to Thomas Foreman by deed from John Oakerson dated May 1, 1710.

Jacob Laen and John Sutven (Sutphen) are the witnesses.

The records of the Monmouth Dutch church show that Derrick Barkalow and Jane VanArsdalen, his wife, had the following children baptized:

Alke (Aeltje) Oct. 1, 1710; m. Jan, son of Jan Pieterse Wyckoff and Neeltje Williamse Couwenhoven, his wife.

Elizabeth, bapt. May 11, 1712; m. about 1735, Ryck Suydam. Her name is entered on church records as a communicant in 1740, as follows: "Elizabeth Borckloo, wife of Reik Zedam." She had the following children baptized: Elizabeth, Dec. 20, 1736; Ryke, Sept. 10, 1738, and Jannetje, May 24, 1741.

Wilm (William) bapt. Jan. 16, 1714; m. Dec. 2, 1737, Aeltje, daughter of Aert (Arthur) Williamson* and Annetje Couwenhoven, his wife. Only two of their children were baptized: Jannetje Sept. 4, 1738, and Aert, Aug. 10, 1740. Soon after this last date he removed to Upper Freehold and settled on a tract of land there, where he lived until his death sometime in 1766. After removing to Upper Freehold he seems to have lost all connection with the church of his forefathers. The dis-

tance perhaps was the cause. His name appears as a landowner in Upper Freehold township in an assessment made in 1755, while his two brothers, Daniel and Cornelius, are named as freeholders the same year in Lower Freehold.

Cornelius, bapt. Nov. 17, 1717; m. Nov. 10, 1743, Jannetje, daughter of Stephen Aumack and Jannetje Janse, his wife. He purchased a large tract of land in the southern part of Freehold township. It lay on both sides of the present line between Freehold and Howell townships. It was partly bounded by Squan brook. Here he lived and died, but I do not know where he was buried. A number of his descendants have owned and lived on part of these lands down to the present day. He and his descendants drifted away from the Dutch church, because of the distance, I suppose. The last recorded connection with the church in which his father had been a zealous member and prominent officer was the baptism of a daughter named Jannetje, June 27, 1756. He had three sons baptized before, viz; Derk, April 16, 1745; Stephanus July 24, 1748, and Johannes March 24, 1751. His name appears as a grand juror at a court held at Freehold July 1781. He and his two sons, Stephen and John, were members of the league for protection and retaliation formed by the patriotic citizens of Monmouth during the dark and terrible days of the Revolution. See page 373 of Barber & Howe's Hist. Coll., of N. J. His son Stephen, is said to have been one of the most active and resolute of the men who served under Col. Asher Holmes. He was in the battle of Germantown and distinguished himself by his coolness and courage. This story was re-published by the late Edwin Salter on page 24 of Old Times in Old Monmouth, and is entitled "Jersey Blue at the Battle of Germantown. Barkalow of Old Monmouth." Stephen Barkalow must have prized his gun highly for in his will on record in the Monmouth Surrogate's office it is the first article mentioned. He bequeaths this gun and accouterments to Stephen, son of his son David.

Daniel, bapt. Jan. 1, 1720; m. Oct. 17, 1744, Annetje, daughter of Johannes Luyster and Lucretia Brower,† his wife, who was baptized April 8, 1725. Daniel Barkalow had only one of his children baptized. This was Jannetje, Dec. 29, 1745. I e died June 28, 1795, aged 74 ys., 6 mos., 12 d., according to his tombstone in the old graveyard at East Freehold.

Maria, bapt. Aug. 5, 1722; m. about 1743, first Abraham Sutven, (Sutphen); had two children baptized: Antje, May 6, 1744, and Jacob, June 17, 1749. Married second, Anthonius Holzart (Hulshart) about 1754, and had one child Jacques, bapt. Oct. 30, 1756.

Helena, bapt. Dec. 17, 1723; m. Isaac Voorhees, and had a child Derrick, bapt. June 22, 1755, who removed to Ohio, and was grandfather of Hon. Daniel Voorhees of Indiana, the famous orator known as the "Tall sycamore of the Wabash." Another son, David, born Dec. 4, 1757, removed to Somerset county, N. J.

Janeka (Jannetje) bapt. Jan. 21, 1727; m. about 1755, Isaac Sutvan, and had one child, Lea, bapt. May 16, 1756.

William, eldest son of Derrick, settled in what is now the township of

Upper Freehold, and had several sons and daughters, but I am unable to give the names of all of them.

Tobias Polhemus, a citizen of Upper Freehold, made his will November 26, 1780. It was proved January 22, 1781, and recorded at Trenton, N. J. He mentions his daughter Sarah as wife of "Ort" (Aert) Barkalow and a grandson named Tobias Barkalow. This Ort Barkalow I think, is the same person heretofore named as baptized August 10, 1740, as Aert (Arthur). In Book P of Deeds, p. 62, etc., Monmouth records, is record of a deed dated April 17, 1767, from Arthur (Aert) Barkalow to Richard (Derrick) Barkalow, his brother. Both are described as residents of Upper Freehold, and the lands conveyed are situate in that township, beginning at a stake 12 links from southwest corner of a plantation formerly belonging to Leffert Leffertson, deceased, and is bounded on one side by Doctor's creek. After a particular description by chains and links, the following general boundaries are given: 215 acres bounded southerly by lands of Richard James and Michael Mount; easterly by lands of Joseph Grover and Luke DeWitt, northerly by lands of Elisha Lawrence, and westerly by other lands of said Arthur Barkalow.

In Book Q of Deeds, p. 28, is recorded a deed dated April 1, 1805, from Ann Tapscott, (late Ann Barkalow) and James Tapscott, her husband, James Baird and Joseph James, executors of Richard (Derrick) Barcalow, deceased, of Upper Freehold, to Thomas Potts of same township. For a consideration of $13,129.80, a tract in that township is conveyed, and described as being a part of a larger tract conveyed to William Barcalow, deceased, by deed dated April 3d, 1764, from the heirs of Leffert Leffertson,‡ deceased. It is therein stated that William Barcalow had died intestate, and the lands described in this deed to Potts, descended to his son Arthur as an heir-at-law. That Arthur Barcalow had paid certain sums to his brothers and sisters, and also by deed dated April 17, 1767, (deed aforesaid in Book P, p. 62, etc.), quit claimed to his brother Richard (Derrick) the tract now conveyed to Potts. The said Richard Barcalow by his will dated March 14, 1803, directed his executors to sell this tract containing 218.83 acres.

Ann Tapscott, the widow of said Richard but now wife of James Tapscott joins in the deed with executors to relinquish her thirds or dower right. In Book M of Deeds, p. 283, etc., Monmouth records, is a deed showing that Arthur Barcalow on April 2, 1801, conveyed those lands which he inherited from his father, to Jacob Couwenhoven of Lower Freehold. It describes these lands as beginning at southwest corner of Derrick (Richard) Barcalow's lands, and containing 220 acres, and the said grantor was then residing on this property. The Jacob Couwenhoven named in the deed was well known throughout Monmouth county as "Farmer Jacob." His will was proved Nov. 15, 1825, and recorded at Freehold in Book B of Wills, p. 466, etc. He devised his property equally to his two sons, Hendrick and Garret, who were his only children. He and his wife, Mary Schanck, are buried in Schanck-Couwenhoven cemetery, Pleasant Valley. Garret, his younger son, married Alice, daughter of Tobias Hendrickson§ and Rebecca Coward his wife, and removed to Upper Freehold township. He perhaps resided on this farm which Arthur Barcalow sold to his father.

Garret Couwenhoven's will was proved January 14, 1832, and recorded at Freehold in Book C of Wills, p. 247. His sons-in law, James Ivins and Thomas Meirs are named as executors. He and his wife are interred in yard of "Old Yellow Meeting House" known in early days as "the Crosswicks Baptist Church." His headstone gives date of his death as Dec. 21, 1831, aged 56 yrs., 7 m., 1 d. Alice Hendrickson his wife, is buried by him. She died August 20, 1855, aged 80 yrs., 5 m., 7 d. Their son Jacob, who died when 28 years old, and their daughter Catharine, wife of William Meirs who died when 20, are interred near them.

William Barcalow, the first settler of the name in Upper Freehold, purchased those lands which descended to his children from Joseph Aplin, William Miller, and the heirs at law of Leffert Lefferson. The above is all the knowledge I have of the "Barcalows" who have lived in that part of Monmouth county.

---

*In Book E of Deeds, p. 334, etc., Monmouth clerk's office, is a record of a deed from John Lawrence and Rachel his wife, of Freehold township, to "Aert (Arthur) Williamson of Flatlands in Kings county, on the island of Nassau," dated January 3, 1718, for 370 acres in Freehold township, and described as the most part of a tract called "Cooper's Neck," and beginning at a corner of land formerly Governor Laurie's, and bounded S. W. partly by lands of Nicholas Lake and partly by lands formerly Isaac Bryans; S. E. by the "brook that parts it from Colts Neck;" E. by lands of Peter Nevins (Nevius), and N. E. by unsurveyed lands. "Derick Barkeloo," William Lawrence, Jr., and Ruleph Schenck are witnesses. William Lawrence, Jr., seems to have done considerable conveyancing for the people at that time and later. His spelling of Dutch names in deeds and wills, etc., had much to do with making several surnames from one. His spelling went on the public records, and in the course of time became a guide or precedent for later generations.

Aert Williamson and Annetje his wife became communicants in the Dutch church of Monmouth in 1717.

†The following inscriptions were taken by Mrs. Lydia H. S. Conover in June, 1899, from headstones in the family burying ground of the Luysters at Holland, in Holmdel township:

Johannis Luyster, [son of Cornelius Luyster and Sarah Catharine Nevius, his wife] d. Jan. 29, 1756, aged 64 y, 10 m, 7 d.

Lucretia Brower [wife of above and daughter of John Brower] d. Apr. 12, 1771, aged 83 y, 4 m. Johannis Luyster was born at Flatbush, L. I., March 22, 1691; m. Lucretia Brower April 10, 1716. His grandfather, Peter Cornelius Luyster, imigrated from Holland in 1656 and settled at Flatbush, L. I.

Sarah Luyster [daughter of above and wife of Ryck Suydam] d. Sept. 7, 1764, aged 47 y, 5 m.

Johannis Luyster, Jr., [son of Johannis Luyster and Lucretia Brower above] d. Sept. 7, 1766, aged 43 y, 3 m, 13 d.

Lucretia Luyster [daughter of Johannis Luyster and Lucretia Brower] d. Mar. 26, 1792, aged 65 y, 6 m, 26 d.

Cornelius Luyster [son of Johannis and Lucretia Luyster aforesaid] d. Oct. 7, 1792, aged 71 y, 9 m, 24 d.

Arinthia Couwenhoven [daughter of William Couwenhoven and Arinthia Bennett, his wife and first wife of Cornelius Luyster aforesaid] d. Apr. 16, 1769, aged 46 y, 1 m, 2 d.

Margaret VanDerbelt [daughter of Aris Janse Vanderbilt and Jannetje Cornelise Couwenhoven and second wife of Cornelius Luyster aforesaid], d. Nov. 24, 1816, aged 85 y. 10 days.

Sarah Vanderbilt d. May 19, 1812, aged 75 y, 3 m, 16 d.

Peter Luyster [son of Johannis Luyster and Lucretia Brower, aforesaid] d. Feb. 12, 1810, aged 90 y, 9 m, 7 d.

Anne Luyster, [wife of Peter Luyster aforesaid] d. Nov. 23, 1799, aged 73 y, 10 m, 15 d.

Lucretia, [daughter of Peter and Anne Luyster aforesaid] d. Dec. 29, 1838, aged 78 y, 4 m. 16 d.

John P. Luyster d. Sept. 11, 1848, aged 84 y, 9 m., 12 d.

Anne Couwenhoven b. Sept. 18, 1764, daughter of Matthias and Williampe Couwenhoven], wife of John P. Luyster, d. Nov. 6, 1853, aged 88 y., 1 m. 18 d.

Anne Luyster d. Nov. 1, 1862, aged 69 y., 3 m. 20 d.

Willempe Luyster b. Aug. 7, 1791, [daughter of John P. Luyster and Anne Couwenhoven his wife], d. Dec. 12, 1875, aged 84 y., 5 m. 3 d.

Jane Luyster d. Sept. 12, 1862, aged 60 y., 5 m. 28 d.

Sarah Luyster, b. July 12, 1795, [daughter of John P. Luyster and Anne Couwenhoven, his wife], m. May 8, 1816, William D. Hendrickson; d. Oct. 15, 1821, aged 26 y., 3 m. 3 d.

William D. Hendrickson [son of Daniel Hendrickson and Elizabeth Stephenson, his wife] d. Jan. 14, 1823, aged 30 y, 2 m, 15 d.

Peter Luyster, b. June 18, 1806, [son of John P. Luyster and Annie Couwenhoven, his wife] d. Dec. 1, 1875, aged 68 y, 8 m.

Miranda Suydam [wife of said Peter Luyster] d. Oct. 24, 1855, aged 47 y, 6 m, 24 d.

Sarah Luyster [daughter of Peter Luyster and Miranda Suydam, his wife] d. May 22, 1850, aged 19 y, 6 m, 21 d.

John P. Luyster [son of Peter Luyster and Miranda Suydam, his wife] d. Mar. 26, 1858, aged 17 y, 10 m.

John C. Luyster [son of Cornelius Luyster] d. Oct. 28, 1847, aged 75 y, 11 m, 21 d.

Catharine [wife of John C. Luyster aforesaid] d. Nov. 18, 1864, aged 77 y, 11 m, 26 d.

John Brower, d. Feb. 2, 1800, aged 36 y, 2 m, 27 d.

Hendrick Brower, d. Feb. 12, 1802, aged 67 y.

Abigail Hunt, d. Jan. 14, 1827, aged 81 y, 11 m, 11 d.

Garret Brower, d. Apr. 28, 1826, aged 34 y, 2 m, 15 d.

Lucretia Luyster [daughter of John P. Luyster] consort of Garret Brower d. Feb. 26, 1874, aged 76 y, 6 m.

Anne Snyder, d. March 9, 1816, aged 39 y, 5 m, 22 d.

Ailette Snyder, d. Sept. 13, 1815, aged 36 y, 3 m, 6 d.

Catharine Snyder, d. March 21, 1859, aged 62 y.

Christopher Snyder, d. March 30, 1797, aged 50 y, 5 m, 17 d.

Sarah Luyster, d. Oct. 7, 1835, aged 77 y, 5 m, 27 d.

Jacob H. Aumack d. April 6, 1861, aged 78 y, 9 m, 2 d.

Francinkey, wife of Jacob H. Aumack, d. Feb. 21, 1832, aged 39 y, 11 m, 5 d.

Eleanor Stephenson d. Feb. 24, 1847, aged 55 y.

‡Leffert Leffertson was a son of Auke Lefferts and Mary TenEyck, his wife. Baptized October 14, 1711,. married Jannetje, daughter of Aert Williamson, and died on his farm in Upper Freehold township, August 4, 1755. His daughter Mary married Tobias, son of Johannes Polhemus and Annetje TenEyck, his wife. His son, Auckey Leffertson, married Sarah, daughter of Garret Garretse Schenck and Jannetje Covenhoven, his wife. This last couple are buried in yard of Brick church, Marlboro. Tobias Polhemus of Upper Freehold, made his will November 26, 1780, proved January 22, 1781, recorded at Trenton. Mentions sons John, Nathaniel and Joseph; grandson John, son of his son Daniel; son Leffert or Lefferts; daughter Sarah, wife of Ort Barkalow; Tobias Barkalow, grandson; daughters Hannah, Catherine, Jane and Mary; sons Tobias, Benjamin and Arthur.

§Tobias Hendrickson was a son of Guisbert (Gilbert) Hendrickson and Elizabeth Polhemus his wife, of Upper Freehold township. Elizabeth Polhemus was baptized August 13, 1710, and was a daughter of Johannes Polhemus and Annetje TenEyck, his wife. Tobias had been named for his maternal grandfather, Tobias TenEyck of Brooklyn, L. I.

Tobias Hendrickson and Rebeka Coward, his wife, lived and died on a farm in Upper Freehold, and are buried in yard of "Old Yel-

EARLY DUTCH SETTLERS OF MONMOUTH. 109

low Meeting House," known in old times as the "Crosswicks Baptist church." It was organized in 1766 by certificate from the Baptist congregation of Middletown.

Joseph Holmes, Jonathan Holmes and 39 other members of Middletown Baptist church residing in and about Crosswicks, desire to organize a church there and are authorized to constitute a church and are dismissed from this congregation of which they are members in full communion. Signed at Middletown, April 5, 1766. Part for whole:
JAMES PEW,
JOHN CHASEY,
GEORGE TAYLOR,
RICHARD CRAWFORD,
ABEL MORGAN,
JAMES MOTT,
GARRET WALL,
OBADIAH HOLMES,
THOMAS GROVER,
EDWARD TAYLOR.

Inscriptions on tombstone of Tobias Hendrickson gives date of death May 25, 1811, aged 70 yrs, 11 mos, 2 d. His wife died June 6, 1815, aged 72 yrs, 7 mos, 10 d. Two of their sons are also buried here, viz: Samuel and Gilbert.

Samuel Hendrickson died March 13, 1813, aged 44 yrs, 1 m, 3 d. His wife, Alckey, died March 2, 1828, aged 58 yrs, 1 m, 17 d.

Gilbert Hendrickson died February 21, 1837, aged 72 yrs, 6 mos, 13 d. His wife Allis (Alice) died January 23, 1852, aged 84 yrs, 2 m.

Gilbert, a son of the last couple, married Alchey (Aeltje) Conover, a sister of the well known Samuel Conover, twice sheriff of Monmouth county. He owned and died on the farm near Sutphen's Corner in Freehold township, now owned and occupied by his youngest son Gilbert Hendrickson, one of the leading and well known farmers of Freehold township.

RECORDS OF DANIEL AND CORNELIUS BARKALOW, SONS OF DERRICK.

The other two sons of Derrick, viz: Daniel and Cornelius, lived and died in Freehold township. Daniel left a will recorded in secretary of state's office at Trenton. In Book P of deeds, p. 640, etc., is record of a deed dated April 10, 1806, from Nicholas Barcalow, and Jane his wife, and Daniel Barcalow, both of Freehold township, to Catharine Throckmorton, widow, of Middletown Point, (now Matawan), conveying 4 62-100 acres in Freehold township. It is noted in this conveyance the grantors get title to this land under will of their father, Daniel Barcalow, dated February 11, 1791, and also as heirs-at law of their brother, Derrick Barcalow, deceased.

It therefore appears from this deed that Daniel Barcalow and Annetje Luyster his wife, had three sons, Derrick, Nicholas and Daniel.

Derrick is buried by his father in the old cemetery near East Freehold. His tombstone states that he died July 28, 1801, aged 23, y. 10 m. 17d.

Nicholas Barcalow was married January 14, 1806, to Jane Williamson by Zenas Conger, an elder of the Independent Methodist church, according to entry in Book A of marriages in Monmouth county clerk's office. I do not find any mention of his name after the year 1806, and therefore presume that he had removed from this county.

Daniel the remaining son, married Eleanor, daughter of Squire John Holsart and Mary Polhemus his wife, and removed to Western New York or Ohio, and there settled. I do not know of any descendants of these three sons now living in this county.

Cornelius, the third son of Derrick Barkalow, the first settler of this name, had three sons, Derrick, Stephen and John, who were baptized in the Dutch church as already mentioned. All the Barkalows now (1900), residing in Freehold, Atlantic and Howell townships are descendants of either Derrick or Stephen. I cannot learn anything of the youngest brother, John.

Derrick lived and died on lands which came to him from his father, in the southern part of Freehold township. He was a weaver by trade and seems to have carried on that business. After his death one of his sons, John D., commonly known as "Preacher Barkalow," carried it on until about 1835 or 1840. His book of accounts is still in existence, and it may interest some people to learn what were the usual charges for weaving. I have copied two entries from his book as follows:

1825 March 31. Derrick Barkalow, Sr.,
  To John D. Barkalow,   Dr
To weaving 10½ yds. cotton and wool at
 10 cents yer yd, $1.00
1829 Nov. 15, Henry Barkalow
  To John D. Barkalow,   Dr
To weaving 15½ yds. all wool at 1 shilling per yd, $1.93¾

This account book shows by the

charges that John D. Barkalow carried on several trades or occupations. There are charges for making and mending boots and shoes, cutting and making clothing for men, selling dry goods and groceries, meats, grain and vegetables besides doing day's work in hay and harvest, making cider, chopping cord wood and other work. John D. Barkalow seems to have been what they call a "jack of all trades."

A great many of the Barkalows seem to have dealt with him, and the following names appear on his account books: 1816-17, John Barkalow, Sr., Cornelius D. Barkalow and Derrick C. Barkalow; 1818-19, Cornelius S. Barkalow, Peter Barkalow, John Barkalow, Sr., John J. Barkalow, Daniel Barkalow and Matthias Barkalow. Between 1820 and 1830, Cornelius D. Barkalow, Stephen Barkalow, John S. Barkalow, Henry Barkalow, Matthias Barkalow, and Derrick Barkalow, Sr.

John D. Barkalow seems to have lived and carried on these various occupations in the dwelling house where his son-in-law, William B. Hulse now (1900) lives in Freehold township.

The account book from which above items and names were taken began August 14, 1816, and on the first page of this book, in the handwriting of John D. Barkalow, is the following motto: "Deal justly with all, speak evil of none."

Derrick, eldest son of Cornelius Barkalow and Jane Aumack his wife, was baptized in the Dutch church April 7, 1745; married March 28, 1775, Sarah daughter of Matthias Couwenhoven* and Williampe Couwenhoven his wife, of Middletown township. She was born

---

*Matthias (sometimes called Martin or Martenus) Couwenhoven, was youngest child of Jacob Couwenhoven and Sarah Schanck, his wife. He is buried by his parents in Couwenhoven burying ground, situate on that part of Golden farm which lays on south side of the old highway from Middletown village to Ogbourn's corner, called in early times "Plain Dealing" road. The following inscriptions were taken by Mrs. Lydia H. S. Conover, May 22, 1899, from all the tombstones on the Conover side.

Jacob Couwenhoven (son of William Garretse Couwenhoven and Jane Montfort his wife), d. June 4, 1744, aged 65 y, 4 m, 6 d.

Sarah, (wife of above and daughter of Roelof Martense Schanck and Annetje Pieterse Wyckoff, his wife) died November 1, 1727, aged 41 y, 9 m, 3 d.

Matthias Couwenhoven, (son of above) died October 22, 1765, aged 40 yrs, 7 m, 18 d. Williampe, his wife, does not appear to be buried here. She was then about 38 years old, and may have married again.

Arinthea, (first wife of Jacob Janse Cou-

April 12, 1751, and was the firstborn child of Matthias Couwenhoven and Williampe his wife. Williampe was daughter and only surviving child of William Cornelise Couwenhoven by his first wife Jannetje Wyckoff, a daughter of Peter Wyckoff and Willemptje Schenck his wife, who are named among the organizing members of the Monmouth Dutch church in 1709. Jannetje Wyckoff died June 22, 1743, and is buried by her father in Schanck-Couwenhoven cemetery. Her husband married March 17, 1744, for his second wife Antje, daughter of Ex-Sheriff Daniel Hendrickson, and then the widow of his cousin William Jacobse Couwenhoven, and had two children by her, viz: Cornelius, baptized April 7, 1746, and Catherine, baptized April 16, 1749, Derrick Barkalow and Sarah Couwenhoven his wife lived on the farm in the southern part of Freehold township, which came to him from his father. He devised part of these lands to his son, John D., who lived and died there. One of his daughters, Alice, married William B. Hulse, September 27, 1852, and she and her husband now (1900) reside on and own this farm. Mrs. William B. Hulse has in her possession an old Dutch book printed at Amsterdam, Hol-

wenhoven and daughter of Jacob Jacobse Couwenhoven and Margaret Couwenhoven, his wife), died May 4, 1780, aged 33 yrs, 8 m, 23 d.

Eleanor, (second wife of above Jacob and daughter of John Smock and Elizabeth Janse Couwenhoven, his wife), died April 26, 1788, aged 31 yrs, 5 m, 28 d.

Jacob Janse Couwenhoven owned and ran VanDorn mills near Holmdel village, and married for his third wife Eleanor or Nelly Schenck.

If he and his last wife are interred here there are no stones to mark their graves.

Jane Couwenhoven, (first wife of Matthias W. Conover, and daughter of Cornelius Roelofse Couwenhoven and Jane Teunise Denise, his wife), died December 12, 1820, aged 40 yrs, 9 m, 6 d.

Matthias W. Conover and his second wife, Anne Schenck, are buried in yard of Dutch church at Middletown village.

Sarah Tice, wife of John Tice, died October 28, 1771, aged 58 yrs.

Catharine Tice, wife of John Tice, died November 24, 1785, aged 37 yrs, 2 m, 13 d.

Sarah, relict of John Nivison, died November 2, 1837, aged 80 yrs.

Jacob Couwenhoven (son of Jacob Jacobse Couwenhoven and Margaret Couwenhoven, his wife), died January 31, 1774, aged 31 yrs, 3 m, 7 d.

Sarah Sedam (wife of above), died March 31, 1806, aged 57 yrs, 4 m, 28 d.

William Couwenhoven, (son of above) died March 29, 1778, aged 3 yrs, 8 m, 2 d.

A number of persons have been buried here without any monument to mark their graves.

land, in 1710, which once belonged to Sarah Couwenhoven, the wife of Derrick Barkalow. It contains the New Testament, Psalms of David set to music, and the Heidleberg catechism. It is finely bound in morocco, and at one time was ornamented with silver clasps and a ring. This silver, however has been removed by some vandal who thought the old silver worth more than the book. The name "Jannatie Wyckoff" is written on the front page, showing that it once belonged to her and was perhaps a wedding present from her parents, when she married William Couwenhoven. The following family records appear in this book:

Jannatie Wyckoff is born January 20, 1702.
William Kouenhoven is ge-boren in het Jaer 1600, July 20.

He has inadvertently written 1600 for 1700, as the new century had just begun, and he had not become accustomed to 1700.

William Kouenhoven married Jannetie Wyckoff July 2, 1722.

Then follows births of their children

Cornelius Kouenhoven born November 4, 1723.
Williamtee Kouenhoven born July 24, 1727.

Cornelius evidently died in infancy as he gave this name to a son by his second wife. Williamtee was doubtless named for her maternal grandmother Williamptje Schenck, but they have been "stuck" on the spelling of this name as you or I might easily be.

The Dutch Testament must have been given to Williampe, the only surviving child, when she was old enough to appreciate her mother's Bible. She was about 17 years old when her father married his second wife. Her marriage license in secretary of state's office is dated July 27, 1749, as follows: Matthias Couwenhoven to Williamtee Couwenhoven." After her marriage she has taken this book to her new home on the Middletown hills. She has made only one entry in it, that of the birth of her first born child as follows:

April 12, 1751, my daughter Sarah was born.

This was the daughter who married Derrick Barkalow, and she has taken the book to her new home on the edge of our Southern pines, where it has remained to this day.

Sarah Couwenhoven, wife of Derrick Barkalow, must have been a woman of strong religious convictions, for she seems to have impressed two of her sons, Matthias and John D. with sincere and hearty belief in the Scriptures, and zealous devotion to christianity. Both of these sons made many sacrifices and labored all their lives to teach and promulgate the gospel. Through her the Couwenhoven name of Matthias has been brought into the Barkalow family.

CHILDREN OF DERRICK BARKALOW AND THEIR DESCENDANTS.

Derrick Barkalow lived and died on the lands in Freehold township which came to him from his father Cornelius. Only two of his sons were baptized in the Dutch church, viz: Cornelius, his eldest son, June 2, 1781, and Matthias, June 24, 1787. Lucretia was his firstborn child. She married first, one Stephen Wills, July 25, 1790. Was married to Thomas Stricklin, her second husband, February 28, 1799, by Rev. Benjamin DuBois. He states in church record of this marriage that she was the widow of one, Wills.

Besides above three children he had two other sons, John D. and Peter. They are all named in order of their ages in his will dated May 12, 1827, proved May 15, 1828, and recorded at Freehold in Book C of Wills, p. 66, etc. He provides first for his wife Sarah. Gives to his daughter LucretiaStrickland, for life, that part of his land lying south of the line of John Barkalow, Sr., bounded on east by lands of Stephen Barkalow, deceased, on south by a ditch and on west by Wadell's line. At her death these lands were to be equally divided among her children in fee.

He next devises to his eldest son Cornelius, another piece of his lands for life with fee to his children equally, except Derrick C., who is to have "onehalf of an acre at northwest corner of Readle's woodland, and nothing else."

This son was known as Cornelius D., to distinguish him from Cornelius S., son of Stephen, Cornelius J., who was probably a son of John Barkalow, Sr., and Cornelius C., then a boy of about sixteen years, and a son of Cornelius S.

Next follow devises of other portions of his real estate to his sons Matthias, John D. and Peter. They are each given a life interest with fee to their respective children, share and share alike. Thomas Strickland, his son-in-law, and his four sons are appointed executors. James VanNote, Cornelius J. Barkalow and Thomas Coward are the subscribing witnesses.

Cornelius D., the eldest son, married October 6, 1800, Mary Harbert or Herbert, and lived and died on the lands left to him by his father. He is said to have been buried in the old Baptist cemetery* on the outskirts of Freehold town, but no monument marks his grave. He left three sons as follows: First, Derrick C., who married April 12, 1825, Deborah Francis, and lived and died on the homestead in Freehold township, leaving three sons and one daughter. James Barkalow, the present active and obliging janitor of the Monmouth court house is one of his sons; Hugh and Conover Barkalow are the other two.

Second, Matthias C., who was married November 5, 1835, to Elizabeth or Bessie Emmons by John D. Barkalow, an elder of the Independent Methodist church. He left two sons and three daughters surviving him, viz: Cornelius M., who was also married by Elder John D. Barkalow, February 5, 1860, to Deborah Chambers, and carried on his trade as carpenter in the town of Freehold until his death. He served as a soldier in the civil war, and was an obliging neighbor and a good citizen. Garret, the second son of Matthias C., married Rebecca Miller, and is still residing in Freehold township. His three daughters were: Mary Eliza, who married Matthias, a son of Elder John D. Barkalow; Kate, who married William Jones and removed to Ohio; and Ann, who married James Errickson.

Third, Henry, married Eleanor, daughter of John Errickson, and had only one child born August 23, 1835, and named James J. He married Roxanna, a daughter of John Garrets of New Egypt, Ocean county, and has always resided in the town of Freehold. For many years he carried on the undertaking business in Freehold, and became well known throughout Monmouth county. He is still in this year 1900, active, alert, and as fond of a practical joke or a little fun as ever, in spite of the sad and solemn occupation of his life. I am indebted to him for part of this family history.

Matthias, the second son of Derrick

---

* The Baptist cemetery was the site of the first "meeting house" or church erected by the Baptists in Freehold township.

The Burlington Path as called by the first settlers, and later the Mount Holly road, followed the old Indian path from South Jersey. It passed through Freehold on same course as Main street does now from Dutch Lane road until you reach the corner opposite the Presbyterian stone church or about where the house erected by Alfred Walters stands. Here the old highway curved easterly and passed between the "old Quay house" now occupied by William M. Moreau and this cemetery. Just beyond this old house the road curved back to present lines of the Smithburg turnpike and ran as present road to West Freehold. About here too, where the road curved westerly, and quite near the house the road forked; the easterly branch running off to "Richmonds Mills," or what is now the village of Blue Ball. The "Quay house," so called, was erected prior to the Revolution, and at the battle of Monmouth was occupied by a number of British officers.

The peculiar appearance of the house arises from the fact that when erected it faced squarely the old Burlington path, and what is now the rear was then the front. The Baptist church faced the Blue Ball road. The congregation was composed principally of farmers, who came from the country for five or six miles around.

As soon as the church was built the people began to bury their dead in the adjacent yard. This church was finally torn down or removed, and a new edifice erected on the lot where the present church stands in the town of Freehold. While walking with a friend through this cemetery one Sunday in summer, and examining the inscriptions, I thought of those Sundays when the people from "far and near" gathered here for worship, and the following verses occurred to me as very descriptive of the great change:

"Thou hast been torn down, old church!
 Thou hast forever passed away,
And all around this lonely yard
 The mossy tombstones lay.
The worshippers are scattered now
 Who knelt before thy shrine,
And silence reigns where anthems rose
 In days of 'Auld Lang Syne.'

"And sadly sighs the wandering wind
 Where oft in years gone by
Prayer rose from many hearts to Him,
 The Highest of the High.
The sun that shone upon their path,
 Now gilds their lonely graves;
The zephyrs which once fanned their brows
 The grass above them waves.

"O! could we call the many back
 Who'd gathered here in vain,
Who've careless roamed where we do now,
 Who'll never meet again,
How would our very souls be stirred
 To meet the earnest gaze
Of the lovely and the beautiful,
 The light of other days."

Thos P Bartkalew

Barkalow and Sarah Couwenhoven, his wife, was married September 18, 1808, to Elizabeth Jeffrey, by Zenas Conger, an elder of the Independent Methodist church. He resided on a farm in Wall township and raised his family there. When quite young he became interested in the religious organization called the Independent Methodist church, and was appointed as elder. He was very active and zealous in preaching and trying to spread the tenets of this sect. Through his efforts and those of another elder named John Saplin Newman, a meeting house or chapel was erected at what is now Glendola, and services held there every Sunday. He also was instrumental in getting another small house of worship built near Our House Tavern in Howell township, and another just west of Colts Neck. He also compiled and had printed and bound at his own expense a hymn book of 272 pages, containing 297 hymns, some of which were composed by him. The copy which I saw was well but plainly bound in leather and fairly printed on good paper. This book must have cost Matthias Barkalow much labor, time and money. The last two hymns in this book are of his own composition and acrostics, giving his own name and that of his wife. The following is a true copy of the one which spells his name by taking the first letter of each line:

HYMN NO. 296.   C. M.

ACROSTIC.

My Saviour, my Almighty friend,
    Attend my humble cries;
Thy succor and salvation send
    To aid me to the skies.

Hear all my cries for Zion's peace,
    In power thy word attend,
A blessing send to all that pray
    Salvation to the end.

Break ev'ry bar through which I groan,
    And full deliverance send;
Ransom'd from all malignant foes,
    Kept safe unto the end.

And may my pilgrimage below,
    Like conquering Zion end,
O'er-coming all, through faith, may I,
    With all the holy stand.

Whether this hymn was given out to any congregation to sing, I am unable to say.

John D. Barkalow, the third son of Derrick and Sarah Couwenhoven, his wife, was born October 5, 1789, married March 2, 1814, Elizabeth, a daughter of Gilbert Hendrickson† and Allis (Alice) Wyckoff, his wife, of Upper Freehold township. His wife was born October 29, 1793, and died January 11, 1848. He died December 31, 1876. They are both buried in the Baptist cemetery. Close to his grave is a cedar tree, so near that the branches extend over his grave. It is the only cedar in this burying ground. I thought it an appropriate and emblematic monument of this man's life. It should be allowed to remain as a living memorial of "Preacher Barkalow" as he was called, who spent his life and means in trying to do good in his unpretentious and homely way to the people residing through our Southern pines. He had no artificial education or training so as to wind adroitly through the difficulties of life, pleasing all and offending no one. He had no diplomacy to manage public opinion. No adventitious aids such as vestments,

---

† Gilbert Hendrickson was a son of Tobias Hendrickson and Rebecca Coward his wife, of Upper Freehold township. He is named in Tobias' will recorded in Book A of Wills, page 430, at Freehold. Gilbert Hendrickson lived and died on his farm in Upper Freehold and is buried in yard of old Yellow Meeting house, as heretofore mentioned. His will was proved March 4, 1837, and recorded in Book D of Wills, p. 60, etc. William Barcalow, Wesley Wilbur and Daniel Barcalow are the witnesses. He mentions his wife "Allis" (Alice) and ten children, among whom are Elizabeth, wife of John D. Barkalow, and Gilbert.

His son Gilbert married December 26, 1821, Alchey (Alice) a daughter of Richard Conover and a sister of the well known Samuel Conover, twice sheriff of Monmouth county. He bought and resided on a farm near Sutphen's Corner in Freehold township, now owned and occupied by his youngest son, Gilbert Hendrickson. He had three other sons, viz: Rulif S., James Conover and Richard Conover, who are now deceased. His daughter Alice was the first wife of Tunis Denise, one of our leading and well known farmers of Freehold township. Gilbert Hendrickson died on the farm where his son Gilbert now, (1900), lives, January 31, 1847, aged 48 yrs., 10 mos., 28 d., and is buried in old Baptist cemetery. His wife rests by him. She died October 27, 1880, aged 78 yrs, 4 mos, 28 d. She was the second child of Richard Conover, who owned and lived on the farm adjacent to the farm on which her son Gilbert now lives. James Conover was the eldest. Aaron, his third child, married Francyntje Conover. Eliza, the fourth, married Joseph Hornor, who carried on the wheelwright business at West Freehold many years ago. Samuel, the fifth, was the popular "Sheriff Sam" of Monmouth county who hung Donnelly. William R., the sixth child, lived and died on the homestead now owned and occupied by his two sons, Miliard and Frank. Richard, the youngest, married a Miss VanNote, and lived and died on his farm at Burnt Tavern (now Ely).

ceremonies, choirs and beautiful architecture to impress the popular mind. He officiated at funerals, married people and preached, without salary or reward save such gifts as gratitude might evoke. He talked to the people in a plain, unlettered way, as men talked in everyday business. He could tell no pathetic or amusing anecdotes or play the actor in the pulpit, so as to draw a crowd. He simply told the plain truth as he read it in his Bible, and would "add no more."

He frequently held what were called "wood meetings," where his words and manner were as unconventional and natural as the forest around him. On Sundays even when very old he would often walk six or ten miles to preach at some out of the way place in the pines. The people to this day remember and often talk about "Preacher Barkalow," for so he was generally called.

He was Overseer of the Poor in Freehold township from 1830 to 1840. He was then elected justice of the peace for this township. His commission as justice is dated October 30, 1843, and signed by Governor Daniel Haines.

His dockets are in existence and show that he had not over six or seven contested cases during his five years' term. Nearly all the cases are marked settled, and his total fees in each case was about 75 cents. Also as elder of the Independent Methodist church he kept a careful record of all marriages, funerals and baptisms, beginning in 1812 and ending in 1873, when he was over fourscore years of age. His books show 286 funerals attended, and 191 couples married. The last entry is very feeble and tremulous. Only part of these marriages are recorded in the clerk's office, for in many cases no money was left to pay the clerk's fee for recording. The only record, therefore, of many marriages is that in his book, now in possession of his son-in-law, William B. Hulse.

One of his sons named Wicoff, (Wyckoff, the surname of his wife's mother) married Elizabeth, a daughter of James Vannote, and died when a young man, leaving one child also named Wicoff, who was born April 17, 1839. He is the well known overseer of the poor of Freehold township. As will be seen from this genealogy he is of unmixed Dutch blood on both sides clear back to the first settler from Holland on Long Island. In his personal appearance he shows all the physical characteristics of the Hollander. He stands six feet in his stockings, and weighs over 200 pounds. Like his grandfather, the preacher, he has given careful attention to the poor of this township who have come under his charge, doing for them in many instances what a father would do for a child. This consideration, kindness and attention which he has shown to these unfortunates have given him the reputation of being one of the best overseers that Freehold ever had.

The fourth and youngest son of Derrick Barkalow and Sarah Couwenhoven was Peter. He married August 30, 1818, Abigail Longstreet, and lived and died in township of Freehold.

Matthias and John D. Barkalow were both elders of the Independent Methodist church. I am not familiar with the purpose or history of this sect. In the preface to his hymn book Matthias Barkalow laments "immoderate attachment to particular opinions or modes of worship or ceremonies, instead of doing justice, loving mercy, and speaking the plain truth." "That harmony among professing christians can only come from having in their hearts a sincere love for God. This will make them resemble God in trying to do good to their fellow men." In closing, he says, "The day is fast approaching when Jesus will make all the different denominations one." "Then the children of God will be a mighty host against the workers of darkness."

Several letters are in existence from Elder Samuel Stanton of Mt. Pleasant, Wayne county, Pa., Elder Samuel Croaker and others to Matthias Barkalow, giving an account of general meetings in Pennsylvania, Genesee county, N. Y., and elsewhere.

The following circular was found among Elder Barkalow's papers. In it they speak for themselves, and as it was part of the history of those days now forgotten, I think it should be published just as spelled and punctuated:

CIRCULAR LETTER.

Dearly Beloved Brethren:

We, the members of the Methodist Independent or Free Brethern Church, as instituted in the state of New Jersey, being assembled in general meeting or yearly conference, agreeable to previous appointment, Do feel it our duty to lay something before you to incourage you to stand fast in the glorious Gospel Freedom, and not be entangled in any yoke of bondage either spiritual or temporal; for whom the Son makes free is free indeed, and, consequently, constitute a part of the Lord's heritage, who are baptized into one body and made to drink into one spirit. Shurely, dear Brethern, it is not the will of our God, who has begot us again to a lively hope in Christ Jesus thro' sanctification of his spirit and belief of the truth, that we should feel the iron arm of oppression from any who, though assuming to themselves spurious titles through an overbalance of power in their own hands, seperate from the body of the people whom they represent; which power, when vested in the hands of one or more individuals, is seldom relinquished for the benefit of community, which ever render those under such representatives in danger of Ministerial oppression and drowns the idea that al men are brethern, or that God out of one flesh and blood hath made all nations. Surely, dear brethern, if this superiority, one over another, accompanied with men's traditions confounds the pure language of the GOSPEL OF CHRIST and keeps many of us who profess to be followers of the meek and lowly Jesus, at sword's point;—hence it is, we would ask the solemn question is it not high time to forbear building babels of party to rend the seamless coat of Jesus? But raise a standard against such corruptions as split and divide those whom the Lord hath united—for our Saviour has prayed that we might all be one as He and the Father is one. Hence it is, dear brethern, that everything which millitates against love and a general union amongst christians, must consequently spring out of the coruptions of the day in which we live: For scripture informs us that the multitude that believed were of one heart and one soul; hence it is that love to God and one another breathes the pure spirit of the Gospel and constrains the world to believe there is reality in the religion of Jesus. Hence it is, dear brethern, that we congratulate you on the glad news that light is now bursting forth in the different states, while many have taken a decided stand.

On the part of Gospel freedom and scripture holiness, praying for a reciprocation in preaching the word of God and the adminstration of the holy sacrament—we also learn by a pamphlet lately published in N. York that a decipline suited to an itinerancy will shortly appear which we can bid God speed out of love to souls and a desire for the universal spread of the Gospel of Christ in all the earth; hence we would praise God that they that are not against us are on our part and from the best information that we can gether our main object is one; namely: holiness of heart, a pure church and a consistant government. From this consideration we can see no just reason why the various branches of the church in these United States should not be brought together in one happy union, &c.

And now, dear brethern, in order that such a union should be brought about the conference have appointed our brother elder, Jesse Oakley, a missionary in behalf of this branch of the church of God; whose common residdence is when not traveling, in Broom street, city of New York, who in conjunction with brother R. Cuddy of the same place, are hereby impowered to form a union with any branch of the church of God at any time previous to the session of our next yearly conference meeting to be held, the Lord willing, on the 5th of October, 1821—at Long Branch in the township of Shrewsbury county of Monmouth state of New Jersey, at which time and place we solicit all those branches of the church who are now in union with us or that may at any time hereafter form a union with us or intimate a desire to form a union with us, to send delegates to represent them in the aforesaid conference.

N. B. our quarterly conference meetings will take place at the following times and places.

First at Long Branch on Saturday before first sabbath in January, 1821.

Second. At Colt's Neck on the Saturday before the first sabbath in April, 1821.

Third. At the Free Communion Chapel in Howell on Saturday before the first sabbath in July, 1821.

Temporary Quarterly meeting to be held when and where it may be most expedient to fill up the vacancies, &c.

Signed in behalf of the conference this 10th day of October in the year of our Lord 1820.

JESSE OAKLEY, Pres't.
MATTHIAS BARKALOW, Sec'y.

The second son of Cornelius Barkalow and Jannetje Aumack, was named for his maternal grandfather, Stephen Aumack, who was a miller by occupation. It is likely that he learned how to operate a grist mill when a boy in his grandfather's mill, for we find him engaged in this business through life. His mill was located on Squan brook, about where the Wyckoff mills are now situated in Howell township. They were formerly known as the "old Barkalow mills." Stephen Barkalow was born in April, was baptized July 24, 1748, and lived on his property near this mill. He married twice. The christian name of his first wife was Ann, who died July 16, 1799. His second wife was Margaret, who died April 2, 1854.

In Book P of deeds, p. 599, in the Monmouth County Clerk's office, is record of a deed dated March 9, 1805, from Stephen Barkalow and Margaret, his wife, of Howell township, to William Barkalow of the same township, which shows that he must have married again in a few years after his first wife's death. Stephen Barkalow was a soldier of the Revolution, and distinguished himself by his cool courage at the battle of Germantown where the Monmouth militia under Col. Asher Holmes was engaged. He died March 15, 1825, and is buried in the yard of Bethesda church, near Blue Ball. His will dated January 29, 1825, proved April 6th, 1825, is recorded in Book B, p. 433, etc., Surrogate's office of Monmouth county. Samuel Forman, John Hulsart and Jonathan Errickson are the witnesses.

His first bequest is to his grandson Stephen, son of his son David. He gives to him "his gun and all the accrutrements." This was the weapon he carried during the war and spoken of in the story republished by Edwin Salter in Old Times in Old Monmouth. He evidently prized it highly, in thus first naming it in that solemn hour when a man executes his will and realizes that he can take nothing out of this world except the good will of immortal minds.

He next mentions Mary Sagers and John Sagers, two of his grandchildren, and then ordered all his property sold and proceeds divided in eight equal shares, and gives one share to each of his children who are named, I presume, in order of their ages, as follows: John, William, Cornelius, Richard, David and Jane. One share to the three daughters of Hannah Sagers, so they have their mother's share between them, and one share to his grandson, John Sager, equally with his children. He also gives to his grandson Stephen, son of David Barkalow, his silver knee and shoebuckles. From the fact of possessing such ornaments he must have taken some pride in his personal appearance. His sons William and Cornelius, and his grandson John Sagers, are appointed executors.

John, his eldest son, removed to New York city, where he lived until his death, September 15, 1854. I am informed that one of his daughters named Margaret was married in this county October 11, 1828, to Robert Havens, by John Saplin Newman, an elder of the Independent Methodist church. This, however, may be a mistake. William, the second son, learned the business of a miller in his father's mill. When a young man he was either employed in or rented the grist mill lying east of Colts Neck, and in that part of Atlantic township which was taken off of Shrewsbury township. They were formerly known as the "Jake Probasco Mills" to distinguish them from the first Probasco mills, which are located west of Colts Neck. During the present generation they have been known as the Snyder and Mulinbrink mills. While living here he married a daughter of Thomas Parker, who resided near Smithburg, in Freehold township. He was the father of Charles Parker, sheriff of Monmouth county, and grandfather of Joel Parker, twice governor of New Jersey. Rev. John Woodhull, D.D., married them and he has thus entered it on record in Monmouth county clerk's office in Book A of marriages: "William Barkalow of Shrewsbury township, to Lydia Parker of Freehold township, February 1, 1798."

William Barkalow died August 16, 1849, aged 77 years, 7 months, 28 days, according to his headstone in the yard of the old Baptist cemetery at Freehold. His name is here given as William S. Barkalow. His wife is interred by him and the date of her death given as October 4, 1834, aged 61 yrs, 10 mos, 8 d. They had three children to grow up and marry, two daughters and one son, viz:

Ann, the eldest married Job Emmons, who owned and lived on the farm in the township of Freehold which lies between the farm now owned by Nathan J. Conover and the farms of Koert and Elisha Schanck, sons of Henry Schanck, deceased. This old Emmons farm was considered one of the best farms in Freehold township.

Amy, the second daughter, married Daniel D. Denise. She was his second wife.

Thomas Parker, the only son, was born near Colts Neck March 21, 1811; married, November 3, 1830, Ann, daughter of John Woolley of Long Branch, (born November 9, 1808, died October 1st, 1891.) Thomas P. Barkalow died August 11, 1872, and was buried in Maplewood cemetery at Freehold. He left four children, of whom more hereafter.

Cornelius S., third son of Stephen Barkalow, was born February 22, 1774, married August 11, 1799, Jedidah Errickson, (born July 8, 1780, died May 6, 1860), and died February 8, 1842; buried in Bethesda church yard. He lived and died on the farm now, (1900) owned and occupied by Wilson Hendrickson in Howell township, about a mile south of Buckshootem bridge. In Book O of Deeds, page 974, Monmouth County Clerk's office, is record of a deed from this Cornelius Barkalow and Jedidah, his wife, of Howell township, to his brother Richard Barkalow, of the same township, dated September 29, 1804, and conveys one equal undivided third part of a tract of 30 72-100 acres in same township. It is described as beginning at a sapling on the north side of Polly Pod brook; and where Polly Pod brook and Haystack brook empty into Meteteecunk river, is called for in the boundaries. Cornelius S. Barkalow and Jedidah Errickson, his wife, had the following children:

Hannah Stout, born April 1, 1801, died May 22, 1803.

Hannah, born September 22, 1804; married January 19, 1826, to Jesse Cowdrick by James M. Challis, pastor of Upper Freehold Baptist church; died July 20, 1871. Jesse Cowdrick died May 21, 1857, aged 57 yrs, 7 mos, 27 d. This couple had thirteen children, of whom only one, the wife of Brittain C. Cook, who keeps the well known hostelry at Toms River, is now living. Among their children was Cornelius, born October 8, 1826, and was associated with Brittain C. Cook in keeping this hotel. John B., born December 17, 1828, and David, born January 13, 1831.

Cornelius C., born August 24, 1812, married first March 29, 1837, Catharine, daughter of John Errickson; married second, January 4, 1863, Angeletty Clayton, a widow, and daughter of William Bennett. Cornelius C. Barkalow is now, 1900, in his eighty-eighth year, but in full possession of all his mental faculties. I am indebted to him for this information about his near relatives. The dates he furnished me from two family Bibles in his possession. He now, 1900, lives on the old Havens farm near Blue Ball, which he bought a number of years ago. Prior to this he lived on the old homestead of his father mentioned above, and now occupied by Wilson Hendrickson. Cornelius C. Barkalow by his first wife, Catharine Errickson, had three sons, but no children by his last wife.

Silas, born May 16, 1839; married and settled at Jackson, in the State of Michigan. He is still living and it is said has accumulated a very large fortune.

Cornelius S., named for his grandfather, was born February 8, 1842, and now deceased.

John E, the youngest son, now residing at Blue Ball.

Cornelius S., the second son, deserves more than a passing notice. Like his great grandfather, Stephen Barkalow, who distinguished himself at the battle of Germantown, so this descendant, by his cool courage and activity distinguished himself in several battles during the late civil war. He enlisted in Company A, 14th Regiment New Jersey Volunteers, when he was about 21 years old. It will be seen from the Barkalow genealogy, he was almost of unmixed Dutch blood, for the Erricksons, although of Swedish origin, are nevertheless a kindred race to the Hollanders. In his physical appearance he bore a general resemblance to his cousin, Wicoff Barkalow. Standing full six feet in height, with broad, square shoulders, and deep chested, with a natural military carriage, he attracted attention wherever he went. He was made first sergeant July 31, 1862, of Company A, then commanded by Austin H. Patterson; was promoted to first lieutenancy September 10, 1864, and captain of Company I, December 1 of the same year. Brevetted Major for gallant and meritorious services before Petersburg April 2, 1865, to date from April 2 of that year. See pages 663, 668 and 1712, Record of Officers and Men of New Jersey in the Civil War, 1861-1865. Brought up on a Monmouth county farm with only such education as our country schools could give, yet he made as gallant and heroic an officer as any ever turned out by West Point. Naturally good natured and kind of temper, with a jovial, fun loving spirit, he at the same time was very considerate of the feelings of others and always ready to extend a helping hand to those in trouble or need. Those traits made him one of the most popular men in the 14th regiment. His rapid promotion was due to his zealous discharge of duty and his cool courageous conduct in battle.

At the battle of Monocacy in Maryland, July 9, 1864, he was shot through the body just below the heart, and left unconscious on the field as our men fell back before the Confederates. Then occurred an incident well worthy of remembrance, for it shows that gratitude and chivalry sometimes flourished in rebel hearts as among the knights of old. That even in the wild frenzy of battle where men seek to slay, that influenced by gratitude they can turn from slaughter and try to save life instead of destroying it. I have this account from Colonel Austin H. Patterson and John H. Hurley, both of whom are still living, and both had personal knowledge of the facts.

After the battle of Antietam Captain A. H. Patterson with part of his company was detailed to conduct some rebel prisoners to Fort Delaware and deliver them to the officer in charge. Cornelius S. Barkalow was one of the non-commissioned officers selected for this duty. These prisoners were taken by railroad to the city of Baltimore, and from there transported in a steamboat to this fort. Captain Patterson stated to me that these rebel prisoners were in most wretched condition from want of food, exposure, and from vermin. Some of them too were suffering from malarial fever and so emaciated that they looked like living skeletons. Others, wretched and despondent, had made no effort to relieve their persons from vermin, and had holes eaten in their necks and backs. While on the cars they could do nothing for them, but at Baltimore Sergeant Barkalow managed in some way to have suitable provisions, with some medicines and delicacies, and clean shirts sent to the steamboat on which they were to embark. On their passage Barkalow went among them in his frank and friendly way distributing provisions to those who could eat, and medicines and delicacies to the sick, and clean shirts to all. When the Confederates were delivered at Fort Delaware they all shook hands with our men and expressed great thanks for the kindness shown. Now at the battle of Monocacy it happened that among the Confederates was an officer who had been among those prisoners and had been exchanged. He at once recognized Barkalow as he lay unconscious on the battlefield. He ordered a private to go for a rebel surgeon whom he knew and who was near at hand. The surgeon came at once and was requested by the rebel officer to examine Barkalow. This he did and found that the ball had passed through his body just beneath his heart, and that he was bleeding internally. A silk handkerchief was torn in strips and one of these strips passed through this wound so as to cause the blood to run out. He was treated with the greatest care and it was this which saved his life. Other wounded soldiers lay around, but Barkalow was the only one who received treatment from the rebels and it was due to his generous and kind attention to those rebel prisoners. The following affidavit also gives the facts:

STATE OF NEW JERSEY, } ss.
County of Monmouth.

John H. Hurley, being duly sworn, on his oath saith that he was a private in Company A, 14th N. J. Vols. That he was in battle of Monocacy on the 9th of July, 1864. That he was wounded by a rebel sharpshooter so badly that he could not walk and was left on the battlefield as the soldiers fell back. That Cornelius S. Barkalow, then an orderly sergeant, was also wounded in same fight. That a ball passed through his body just below his heart and he lay near this deponent. That as this deponent lay there a force of the Confederate soldiers came up, who, or some of whom, recognized said Cornelius S. Barkalow, as said Barkalow had before that time shared part of his rations with some rebel prisoners who were half starved. That said rebels saw condition of said Barkalow, that unless he bled externally he would die. That some of them went to said Barkalow and passed a silk handkerchief through the wound and caused it to bleed externally, which deponent thinks saved his life. That said rebels treated him with great consideration and pains, but did nothing for this deponent. That they left said Barkalow and this deponent there and we were taken off by our people afterwards. This deponent further saith that said Barkalow was one of the best and bravest of the under officers of said regiment. That he was always full of fun and jokes and did all he could to make his men comfortable and to see to their wants. That everybody in the regiment liked him and respected him.

JOHN H. HURLEY.

Sworn and subscribed before me this 16th day of May, 1899.

JOHN W. HULSE, Justice of the Peace.

The testimony of above soldier is that of every man in this regiment. He recovered from this wound but before it was entirely healed he was back with his regiment and served until war closed, when he came back to his father's farm. He died from blood poisoning, caused by what was thought a trifling wound in his foot. His death occurred only three weeks after his marriage. He was buried in the yard of the old Bethesda church, near Blue

Ball, and his grave there will always be honored by the people of Monmouth county. His name will always be remembered and cherished. If the flowers, strewn each Decoration Day on his grave, had the faculty of speech they could truly say:

"Blossoms there are for day of troth,
And blushing bride array;
Blossoms to make for trembling feet,
A rosy marriage way.

Daisies that star the early fields
For chubby hands to hold,
And buttercups which God has sent
To be the babies' gold.

But we, a higher fate is ours;
Ordained from bud to bloom,
To lie amidst the green, young grass,
Above a soldier's tomb.

And when upon his quiet grave,
With love and tears we're laid,
And music swells from martial bands,
He heard when on parade.

And when the tattered flags are raised
He fought and died to keep,
We feel a stir, through tangled growth,
A thrill from hearts that sleep.

And when the dew falls silently,
With throbbing drums gone by,
We are on guard, we flowers, and proud,
Upon his grave, to die."

The fourth son of Cornelius S. Barkalow and Jedidah Errickson, his wife, was John C., born February 16, 1820, married Mary Irwin, a sister of the well known squire, Levi G. Irwin, who died a few years ago. John C. Barkalow died at his residence in the village of Colts Neck, June 28, 1892. His will was proved July 19, 1892, and recorded at Freehold in Book V of Wills, page 372, etc. His wife and one son, William, survives him and still reside at Colts Neck.

Richard, (Derrick) fourth son of Stephen Barkalow, married February 14, 1807, Margaret, a daughter of Alexander Low, a prominent citizen of Freehold at that time. Richard Barkalow and Margaret Low, his wife, were the parents of two sons, William D. and Alexander L., and two daughters, Mary Ann and Cornelia, who died unmarried. The two sons lived together in a house on the right hand side of the Blue Ball turnpike on the outskirts of Freehold town and were strongly attached to each other, but not in any demonstrative way.

William D. died unmarried, but his brother married Rebecca A., widow of William Emmons and died leaving one son, William F., surviving him. The two brothers, as many people now living will remember, were plain, prudent, and reliable men, just what they appeared to be without cant, quack or pretentions.

David, the fifth and youngest son of Stephen Barkalow, was born December 22, 1780; married March 2, 1805, Mary Borden, (born April 6, 1785, died April 25, 1862) and removed to Wayne county, N. Y., where he raised a family and died there April 27, 1864. It was to Stephen, son of this David, that the famous gun was bequeathed.

I have but little information about Jane, the daughter of Stephen Barkalow, and who is named in his will. Cornelius C. Barkalow informed me that she married one Stoffel (Christopher) Probasco and removed with her husband to the state of Ohio and there settled. Neither do I know anything of the Sagers family in which the daughter Hannah married.

Thomas P. Barkalow, the only surviving son of William S. Barkalow and Lydia Parker, his wife, seems to have learned the miller's business in his father's mill at Colts Neck. Soon after his marriage to Ann Woolley he purchased and moved to a farm near the village of Toms River. He also bought the mill which his grandfather Stephen, owned on Squan brook, now known as Wyckoff's mills. After residing on the farm at Toms River a number of years he removed to Forked River in Ocean county, and became associated with his cousin, Stout Parker, in the business of building schooners for the coasting trade and in shipping cord wood to the New York and other markets. In 1858 he bought at Sheriff's sale the famous old hostelry in Freehold known as the Union hotel. Prior to and during the war of independence it was called the "White Hall Tavern." John Longstreet, a zealous loyalist, owned and conducted this tavern when the war began. He was active in raising a company for the battalion of Jerseymen which Sheriff Elisha Lawrence commanded in Skinner's brigade, and was made a captain or lieutenant in the British army. If this old part of the Union hotel could have spoken many interesting and exciting tales could have been told of those days which tried men's souls. Our county records show that on an inquisition taken June 9, 1778, John Longstreet was found guilty of joining the king's army. Judgment was entered and execution issued directing seizure and sale of his real estate. The

White Hall tavern was purchased at this sale by Major Elisha Walton. The deed to him is dated June 10, 1779, and recorded in Book R of Deeds, page 558, etc., Monmouth county clerk's office.

From this time on down to 1834, when Barzillai, son of Daniel Hendrickson and Elizabeth Grover, his wife, became the owner and landlord, there were several different owners and landlords and the name was changed to the "Union Hotel." From 1844 to 1850 it was run by the well known Nathaniel S. Rue, who is still living at an advanced age in the township of Upper Freehold. About 1842 an addition was put up between the old building and South street which was used until 1856 for a general country store, but in that year it was made a part of the hotel by Sheriff Holmes Conover and John Vanderveer Carson, who were then the owners. The deed from Sheriff Samuel Conover to Thomas P. Barkalow was dated March 23, 1858, and is recorded in Book G 6 of Deeds, page 126, etc. Mr. Barkalow carried on the hotel business here until November 18, 1865, when he sold the property for $14,000. It then included all the land in the rear of the buildings along South street as far as the railroad track. This part of the property was covered with sheds, barns and stables. The entrance to this rear yard was about where the front of the brick store now stands from South street. September 11, 1886, the hotel was destroyed by fire which started in the adjoining building. The Belmont hotel now stands on the site of this old building.

Many changes in methods and customs of the old fashioned taverns have taken place since the day when Mr. Barkalow was the landlord. I now know of but one hostelry conducted in the old way and that is the one at Toms River of which the well known Brittain C. Cook is landlord.

When Mr. Barkalow moved to Freehold in 1858, he brought with him his wife and two daughters. He had the following children:

Lydia, born August 21, 1831; married George Cowperthwait, who came of the well known Quaker family of this name in West Jersey. Mr. Cowperthwait resided at Toms River and for many years conducted a general country store at that place.

William, born December 27, 1833, died young.

John Woolley, born February 12, 1835; married Mary Catherine Conover, at Forked River, N. J.

Elizabeth, born July 11, 1837, and still resides in the old home on Main street in Freehold, where her father and mother lived the last years of their lives.

Eleanor Laird, born March 20, 1840; married December 25, 1861, Joseph Stillwell Conover, who, prior to his death, was associated as a partner with Hon. George W. Shinn in a general country store at Freehold. Mr. Conover was a very affable and pleasant man and popular with the people. She married in 1875, Mr. Charles L. Holmes, and died April 25, 1900, leaving three children by her first and one by her second husband surviving.

During the period when Mr. Barkalow conducted the Union hotel there was but one railroad running from Freehold, that to Jamesburg. Stages ran to Toms River, Long Branch and Keyport. The sound of a bugle early in the morning and about sunset in the summer, announced the departure and arrival of the Keyport stage. The fare to New York city by stage and steamboat was fifty cents, or about half what it is today. During the first week of the regular terms of our county courts the Union hotel would be overcrowded with jurymen, witnesses, and persons with law business on hand. The overflow were lodged at various private houses about town but they all boarded at the hotel. Mr. Barkalow personally looked after the comfort of each guest and presided at the regular meals. He was a man of rotund, portly figure, broad, square shoulders and ruddy complexion. Of courteous address and dignified manners he was the very ideal of a landlord. The stirring times of the great rebellion began and ended during his occupation of this tavern.

The political excitement and discussions, enlistment of men and later the draft, the departure and arrival of officers and men from the front, news of battles, men killed or wounded, and the thousands of wild rumors gave unusual animation to the daily occurrences at such a public house. The first meeting of the citizens of Freehold to enlist men for the three months service under President Lincoln's call for 75,000 men was held in the room adjacent to the bar-room. The Freehold newspapers of that date give an account of this meeting and the names of the men who enlisted. One tall thin fellow enlisted that evening who wore a pair of new and heavy cowhide boots. Some one inquired what he got such boots for. He very earnestly replied "to stamp the bowels out of the d—— rebels." In the news of the first battle the report came back that this chap had hidden behind a big log. So the rebels never suffered any from those boots. During this period Mr. Richard Davis, generally called "Uncle Dick;" Mr. Thomas M. Vanderveer and his son, D. Augustus Vanderveer, Lewis Hoffman, Rev. Wilbur F. Neil, the young and popular rector of St. Peter's church, and several other bachelors and widowers boarded and lodged there.

The utmost harmony and good feeling prevailed among them for there were no "lady boarders." They all became warm friends of Mr. Barkalow and family. While there was no glitter, tinsel or pretensions, yet everything was substantial and comfortable and kept scrupulously clean and neat under the watchful supervision of Mrs. Barkalow and her daughters. Domestic affairs in a private home could not have moved along more quietly and orderly. In the fall and winter the bar-room was a kind of social club for the business and professional men of Freehold. Well supplied with cushioned seats along the whole side next to South street, and comfortable armed chairs with a great stove in the center of the bar-room, hardly an evening passed but what they were occupied. The war, politics, law suits, horse races and horse trades, interspersed with stories and anecdotes were the principal subjects of conversation. Governor Parker, Dr. John Vought, A. R. Throckmorton, Sheriff Sutphen, Sheriff Sam Conover, William V. Ward, Joseph D. Bedle, and many others of our leading citizens, dropped in nearly every evening. Their stay would be short or long, according to persons present and the subject discussed. A wonderful change in the social relations of Freehold has taken place since then. The adjacent room was used for public meetings, trials of justices court cases, auctions, etc. Mr. Barkalow was respected by everybody. Good natured, frank and consistent in his dealings, he had no enemies. Generous and kind hearted, he had many friends. I never heard a profane or vulgar word fall from his lips, nor any harsh criticism or condemnation of others behind their backs. In many solid qualities of heart and head Thomas P. Barkalow, the landlord of the Union hotel, had few equals and no superiors among the people of Freehold.

THE HENDRICKS OR HENDRICKSON FAMILY.

Daniel and Wilm Hendricks, as they wrote their names and were called among their own folks, were brothers and sons of Hendrick Hendricks by his first wife. They came from Flatbush, in Kings county, Long Island, to Monmouth county, about 1692 or 1693, and settled on a tract of land at what is now Holland in Holmdel township. This land has been in the continuous ownership and occupation of the descendants of Daniel Hendricks, the pioneer settler, down to the present year 1900, or over two centuries.

The late Hon. William Henry Hendrickson, who twice represented Monmouth in the New Jersey Senate, was born, lived, died and was buried on this homestead farm, as his father, grandfather, and great-grandfather, (who was the youngest son of the first settler) had been before him. I therefore take up Daniel Hendricks and his posterity before his brother William, because the latter has no descendants living in this vicinity.

We find Daniel Hendrickson first mentioned in Book C of Deeds, p. 78, in our county clerk's office. An agreement dated September 23, 1693, is here recorded between Daniel Hendrickson and "John Gibbonson" as name is spelled, of Flatbush, Kings county, L. I., of the one part, and William Whitlock of Middletown, Monmouth county, of the other part. It seems they had on September 22d, 1692, leased of Whitlock 104 acres of land, described as partly bounded by Mahoras brook, and they now agree to pay him £25 in yearly installments until whole is paid by 10th of March, 1697, and Whitlock agrees to convey it when whole sum is paid. Daniel Hendrickson conveyed 28 acres of this tract to Gybertsen or Guisbertsen as name is spelled, who with Ester his wife, by deed dated December 22d, 1701, conveys it to John Ruckman. This Guisbertsen was the progenitor of the Giberson family as name was afterwards spelled, and I think was really a VanPelt.

In Book I of Deeds, p. 166, Secretary of State's office, Trenton, N. J., is the record of a deed dated May 16, 1698, from John Whitlock and Mary his wife, late of Middletown township, but then of Freehold, to Daniel Hendrickson, conveying 104 acres for the consideration of £164. This land is described as situated at Strawberry Hill, now occupied by Daniel Hendrickson, bounded south by lands late of William Whitlock, east by lands of Thomas Whitlock, north by a small run coming from the hills, and west by another small brook; which 104 acres John Whitlock with other tracts of land got from the proprietors of East Jersey by patent dated January 20, 1676. Also another tract bounded northerly by James Wall's land, westerly by John Whitlock's land, southerly by land late William Whitlock, and east by Mahoras brook. Also 13 acres of salt meadow at Shoal Harbor, bounded north by the creek.

In this same Book I of Deeds, p. 184, etc., is record of a deed dated February 5, 1706, from Thomas Cooper of London, England, a merchant, to Obadiah Bowne, Garret Wall, Gershom Mott, James Hubbard, James Grover, James Cox, Joseph Cox, Richard Stout, Daniel Hendricks, Obadiah Holmes, William Lawrence, James Lawrence and Benjamin Lawrence, all of Middletown township, in Monmouth county. Cooper, for the consideration of £260 conveys to them one full equal half propriety, or 48th part of all lands taken up or to be taken up in the Eastern Division of the Province of New Jersey, excepting only 5,000 acres already taken up by said Cooper in right of first division, and 86 acres taken up in right of second division of said half propriety or 48th part of said Eastern Division of New Jersey, and which are already sold by said Thomas Cooper. He also conveys by this deed 600 acres of land at Barnegat, in what is now Ocean county.

On page 194, etc., of this same Book I of Deeds, is record of a deed from Obadiah Bowne and rest of grantors aforesaid except Daniel Hendricks, to said Daniel Hendricks, dated February 5, 1706. It recites that said grantors with said Daniel Hendricks, purchased of Thomas Cooper one-half propriety or 48th part of the undivided Eastern Division of New Jersey, and also 600 acres of land at Barnegat; and by this deed they convey to said Daniel Hendricks, his heirs and assigns, a tract of 141 acres and right to take up 184 acres more under the second and third divisions. They also convey to him 21 acres of land and marsh at Barnegat.

In this same Book I of Deeds, p. 376, is record of a deed dated December 7, 1709, from Richard Hartshorne and Margaret, his wife, to Daniel Hendrickson, John Schenck, Garret Schenck, Cornelius Couwenhoven, Peter Wyckoff, all of Middletown, in Monmouth county, conveying to them three tracts of land at a place called by the Indians "Conescunk." The first tract contains 200 acres and lays next to bay. The second tract contains 70 acres and is situate on west side of "Conescunk Neck." The third tract is made up of several pieces of meadow containing in all 50 acres.

Minutes of Monmouth county courts labelled No. 1, 1688-1721, show that Daniel Hendrickson was a grand juror at March term, 1699. He was again summoned to serve on grand jury March 26, 1700, when the new judges appointed by Governor Andrew Hamilton, took their seats for the first time. As has been already explained Daniel Hendrickson with many others of the Middletown people refused to serve or to recognize the authority of these judges. For this he was fined $10 and the sheriff was ordered to make the money by seizure and sale of his personal property. His brother, William Hendricks, is named among the men who broke up the court March 25, 1701, and held Governor Hamilton, the county judges and other officers prisoners for four days. The surrender by the Proprietors of the right of government to the English crown in 1702, brought about an entirely new condition of affairs, and settled for a time their old quarrels and animosities.

Daniel Hendrickson * was appointed

---

* Teuntje Thysa Laen VanPelt, the mother of Daniel Hendrickson's wife, came to America with her father and settled at New Utrecht, L. I. Her brother Guisbert married Jannetje Adraanse Lambersen, and removed to Monmouth county. He wrote his name or was known as "Gisbert Laen," and he and his wife were among the organizing members of the Dutch church in 1709. He had the following children:

Adraan, b.——, married Marytje Smak (Smock).

Janntje, b.——, died single.

Wilhelmyntje, bap. Sept. 16, 1677; married William Hendricks, the brother of Daniel Hendrickson. Her name appears as "Williampe" on records of Dutch church in 1709.

Mathys, bap. Aug. 23, 1679; died young.

Catalina, bap. April 24, 1681; married Elyas DeHart.

Matthys, bap. March 30, 1683; married Antje, daughter of Garret Schanck and Neeltje Voorhees his wife, of Pleasant Valley.

Cornelius, bap. April 3, 1685.

Mary, bap. March 3, 1689; married Ferdinand VanSiclen.

Joost (Joseph), died single and was blind.

Maikan or Moyka married Stoffle Longstreet and they were the parents of Stoffle Longstreet who settled in Upper Freehold township.

Tobias Hansen of Dover, in New Hampshire, conveyed to Gilbert Lane of New Utrecht, L. I., 200 acres in Shrewsbury township, by deed dated March 30, 1699, recorded in Book D of Deeds, p. 128, Monmouth county clerk's office. In Book E of Deeds, p. 344, etc., Gilbert Lane

Dwelling house on Hendrickson homestead at Holland, N. J. The original part was built by Daniel Hendrickson, the first settler, between 1700 and 1720; remodeled and enlarged by the late Hon. William H. Hendrickson.

one of the constables of Middletown township in 1704-5 and three years later sheriff of the county. He was the first Netherlander to hold this office. We also find him and his wife, and his brother William and wife among the organizing members of the Dutch church in 1709, and a few years later he was an Elder. He was also appointed captain of the militia of Middletown township.

Daniel Hendrickson married in Brooklyn Catherine, daughter of Jan Janse VanDyke and Teuntje Thyse Laen VanPelt, his wife. Daniel Hendrickson died in January, 1728, leaving his widow and 11 children surviving.

The following is a certified copy of his will recorded in Book No. 2 of Wills, p. 491, etc. The scrivener who wrote it was evidently ignorant of the Dutch language as he has given the English names for some of the children, while he has spelled others according to sound. Tryntje is Dutch for Catherine, but in writing the name of Daniel Hendrickson's wife he spells it "Taytye."

IN THE NAME OF GOD AMEN.—I Daniel Hendricks of Middletown in the county of Monmouth and Eastern Division of ye Province of New Jersey Gent. This Sixteenth day of November in the Year of our Lord one Thousand seven hundred & Twenty Seven, being very Sick & weak of Body but of a Sound Mind and Disposing Memory (Thanks be to God for ye Same & calling to mind ye uncertainty of this present Life knowing That it is appointed for all Men once to Dye) Do make & declare this to be my Last Will & Testament as followeth Vizt. first and principally I recommend my Soul to Almighty God that gave it and my Body to ye Earth from whence it was taken to be buryed at ye Discretion of my Executors herein after named and as Touching Such Wordly Goods and Estate as it hath

of Middletown township, conveyed to his son Matthias Lane, 460 acres which Alexander Innes had deeded to him April 28, 1709. Gilbert Lane made his will Nov. 7, 1720; proved May 27, 1727, and recorded at Trenton in Look B of Wills, p. 66, etc. Names his wife Jane, and all his children. Speaks of his daughter Willimea, who married William Hendrickson, as deceased, and also her husband as dead.

Gilbert Lane had a brother Peter, who settled in Monmouth, and was known as Peter Tysen. In Book E, p. 314, etc., Monmouth county records, is a deed dated October 6, 1709, from John Bowne to Peter Tysen and Derrick Tysen of New Utrecht, and John Tysen of Brooklyn, L. I., for 750 acres at Wiquetunk. This property was afterwards conveyed to Roelf Schanck. See page 313 "Old Times in Old Monmouth.".Some of this family removed to Bucks or Lancaster county, Pennsylvania, and retained the surname Tysen. Those who remained here spelled their names "Tice." The Lane, Tysen or Tice, Pietersen and Giberson surnames are all derived from a VanPelt progenitor.

Pleased Almighty God (far Beyond my Deserts) to bestow upon me I give Devise & Dispose of ye Same in Manner & form following Viz. IMPRIMIS my Will is that all my Just Debts be justly and truly payd by my Executors hereinafter named and for That end & purpose my Will is, and I do by These Presents give To my Three Executors, or in case of Death or Refusal to any two of Them full power to sell and Dispose of my Two Largest Lotts of Wood Land on Conescunk Neck & my Land at Barnegate & Right to Property, pt I give and Devise to my Son Hendrick the plantation on which he Dwells, formerly Benjamin Stouts, and the full halfe of all my Lotts of Meadow at Conescunk, on condition that he pay the Sum of Three hundred Pounds to my Seven Daughters in such Payments & at Such Times as hereafter expressed viz. That he pay to my daughter Catharine the Sum of thirty seven pounds Ten shillings at ye Time of her Marriage or ye Age of Twenty one Years which shall first happen & to my Daughter Jonayfye the sum of Thirty seven pounds Ten shillings at ye Time of her marriage or ye age of Twenty One years which shall first happen & ye Remaining Two hundred Twenty five pounds by equal parts to my Seven Daughters Namely Ghesye, (Geesie) Teuntye, (Teuntje) Maykije, Catharine, Anne Francis (Francyntje), & Janayfye (Jannetje), the first Payement to commence four Years after my Decease to my Eldest Daughter & so on yearly the Like Sum to ye Next oldest till ye Seven Daughters hath Received ye same. That Then I Give & Devise the si Lands and Meadows to my Son Hendrick Hendricks his heirs & Assigns for Ever, pt I give and Devise to my Son John the plantation whereon he Dwells that I purchased of Stephen Warne, on condition That he pays the sum of five hundred pounds to my Daughters as hereinafter expressed viz That he pay to my Daughter Anne ye Sum of Thirty Seven pounds Tenn Shillings at ye Time of her Marriage or ye age of Twenty one Years which shall first happen and ye Remaining Two hundred Sixty two pounds Tenn Shillings by equal parts to my Seven Daughters above named, the first payment To Commence Four Years after my Decease, to my Eldest Daughter, and so on Yearly the Like sum to ye Next oldest till ye Seven Daughters have received ye same. That then I Give & Devise the said Plantation to my Said Son John his Heirs & Assigns forever. pt. I give and Devise to my Son William ye Remaining half of My Salt Meadow Lotts at Conescunk & to him his heirs and Assigns forever and my Will is That the fee simple of the Three Hundred Acres of Land I Lately purchased from ye Executors of Obadiah Bowne Deced be settled & Confirmed to my said Son William his Heirs & Assigns forever on condition That he pay ye Sum of four Hundred pounds to my Daughters as herein After Expressed viz: That he pay to My Daughter Francis (Francyntje) the sum of Thirty Seven pounds Tenn Shillings at ye Time of her Marriage or the Age of Twenty One Years which shall first happen and ye Remaining three hundred Sixty-two pounds Ten Shillings by equal parts to my Seven Daughters Above named the first payment to commence Six Years after my Decease to my Eldest Daughter and so on Yearly the Like Sum to ye Next oldest till ye Seven Daughters have Received the Same. pt. I give and bequeath to my Loving Wife Tayte the use of my Homestead plantation & three parcels of Land more, the One I purchased of Jarat Wall, one of John Wall & a parcel adjoyning to Wallens Land, and my Salt Meadow at Shoal Harbor with the use of my Personal Estate for & During the Term of her Widowhood, if the Same continue Not Longer than That my Youngest Son Daniel Attain ye Age of Twenty One Years. If at That Time she be my widow unmarryd my Will is that ye Said Lands be Equally Devided between her and my Said Son Daniel During her Widowhood and at the Expiration thereof, I give and Devise all ye Lands and Meadow I have herein given her the use of to my Said Son Daniel His heirs & Assigns for Ever on condition that he Pay to my Seven Daughters the Sum of Three hundred & fifty Pounds VIZ fifty Pounds to my Eldest Daughter within One Year after he is of the age of twenty One Years and Lawfully possessed of the whole Plantation, and so Yearly fifty Pounds to ye Next Eldest till ye Seven Daughters have Received their fifty Pounds a Piece, and Personal Estate Equally to all my Children. pt. I give and Devise to my Nephew Daniel Hendricks a small Lott of Land I have in Amboy purchased of Stephen Warne VIZT TO Daniel Hendricks, the Son of my Brother William Hendricks his heirs and Assigns forever. pt. I give & Devise Two Small Parcels of Upland at Conescunk called ye Landing and Landing Lotts, Equally to my four Sons Namely Hendrick, John, William & Daniel and To their heirs & Assigns for ever as Tenants in common pt. and Lastly I do Nominate & appoint my son Hendrick Hendricks and my Sons in Law Rocleff Schank and Jonathan Holmes, Junr., † Executors of this my Last Will and Testament to see ye Same executed.

IN TESTIMONY whereof I have hereunto Sett my Hand & Seal the Day & Year first Above Written Signed Daniel Hendricks with a (Seal) SIGNED, SEALED and PUBLISHED by Daniel Hendricks as his Last Will & Testament in ye Presence of Cornelius Wyckof, Johannis Leiister (Luyster), Cornelius Dooren (Doorn), William Lawrence Junior.

WILLIAM BURNET, Esqr., Captain General & Governour in Chief of ye Provinces of New Jersey, New York and Territories thereon depending in America, and Vice Admiral of ye same &c, KNOW YE That in ye County of Monmouth in ye Province of New Jersey, The Twenty Ninth day of January one Thousand seven hundred & Twenty Seven, The Last Will and Testament of Daniel Hendricks Late of Middletown in ye County of Monmouth yeoman Deced, was proved before LAWRENCE SMYTH who is Thereunto by me authorized and appointed for That purpose, having while he Lived and at ye Time of his Death, Goods, Chattels & Credits in Divers places within This Province, by Means Whereof ye full Disposition of all & Singular ye Goods Chattels &

---

† See letter of Jonathan Holmes explaining this will on page 309 "Old Times in Old Monmouth." Jonathan Holmes was the eldest son of Obadiah Holmes and Alice Ashton, his wife. He was known as Jonathan Holmes, Jr., to distinguish him from his uncle, Jonathan Holmes, Sr., who is buried in old Topanemes graveyard.

Credits of ye said Deced, and ye Administration of Them, also ye hearing of Account, Calculation or Reckoning and the final Discharge and Dismission from ye Same unto me Solely, and not unto any Other Inferiour Judge are Manifestly known to belong, and the Administration of all & Singular ye Goods chattels & credits of ye said Deced, & his Last Will and Testament in any Manner of Ways Concerning was Granted unto, Hendrick Hendricks, Roeleff Schank & Jonathan Holmes, ye Executors In the sd Last will & Testament Named Chiefly of well & Truly Administring the same, and of making a True and perfect Inventory of all & Singular ye Goods Chattels and Credits of ye said Deced and Exhibiting ye same into ye Registry of ye Prerogative Court in ye Secretary's office at on or before ye Twentyeth day of June next Ensuing & of rendering a just & True Account when thereunto required.

IN TESTIMONY whereof I have caused ye PREROGATIVE SEAL of ye sd Province of New Jersey to be hereunto Affixed at Burlington in New Jersey Afd. ye 22d Day of February in ye First Year of our Reign
JAMES SMITH Secry.

Geesye, b. Oct. 9, 1696, at Flatbush, L. I.; m. 1714, Roelef, eldest son of Jan Schenck and Saartje Couwenhoven, his wife, of Pleasant Valley, in what is now Holmdel township. She died September 20, 1747, and was buried in Schenck-Couwenhoven cemetery. Her headstone is still in a state of good preservation, and gives her age 50 yrs. 11 mos. 11 d. Her husband is buried by her, and his age given as 73 yrs., 10 mos., 28 days. Roelef Schenck became a communicant in the Dutch church of Monmouth county in 1715, and his wife 32 years later or in 1747. Her brother, Daniel Hendrickson, and his wife, Catrina Couwenhoven, and her sister Jannetje, then the widow of Roelef Couwenhoven, joined the church at the same time. See page 87 of Wells' address at Brick church. Six of Daniel Hendrickson's daughters became members of this church, or all except Catharine. Geeyse Hendrickson and Roelef Schenck, her husband, had the following children:

Sarah, b. May 22, 1715; m. Dec. 1, 1734, Joseph VanMater, (b. Feb. 5, 1710, d. Oct. 15, 1792) and died Sept. 1, 1748, aged 33 y, 3 mos, 9 days, according to inscription on her headstone in family burying-ground on old VanMater homestead in Atlantic township. The names of her children have heretofore been published in genealogy of the VanMater family.

Katrinje, bap. March 19, 1717; died young.

Kalrya, (Catharine) bap. Dec. 21, 1718; m. first, Simon DeHart; second, Peter, son of Jacob Couwenhoven and Sarah Schenck, his wife. The marriage license of last couple is recorded in office

Front view of house erected by Hendrick Hendrickson on his farm in Pleasant Valley, N. J., between 1730 and 1750.

Photographed in 1900 by Mrs. L. H. S. Conover.

Rear view of house erected by Hendrick Hendrickson on farm in Pleasant Valley, N. J., between 1730 and 1750.

Photographed by Mrs. L. H. S. Conover in summer of 1900.

of the secretary of state at Trenton. It was granted July 27, 1749. The names of her six children by these two husbands appear on page 310 of "Old Times in Old Monmouth."

Jan, b. January 22, 1720; m. Nov. 26, 1741, Jaconmyntje, daughter of Cornelius Couwenhoven and Margaretta Schenck, his wife, of Pleasant Valley; died June 27, 1749, aged 29 y, 5 mos, 5 days, according to his headstone in Schenck-Couwenhoven cemetery. His wife is not buried by him. She may have married a second husband.

Daniel, bap. May 26, 1723; d. Sept. 20, 1747.

Neeltje (Eleanor), b. Sept. 10, 1724; m. Oct. 12, 1744, Garret, son of Jacob Couwenhoven and Saartje Schanck, his wife, (b. Nov. 5, 1716, d. Dec. 9, 1797), and died Nov. 25, 1800. She is buried by her husband on Conover homestead near Taylor's mills, Atlantic township. The names of her children have been heretofore given in the Couwenhoven genealogy.

Hendrick, b. July 29, 1731, married his cousin Catharine, daughter of Jonathan Holmes, Jr., and Teuntje Hendrickson his wife. Their marriage license was granted Feb. 28, 1749. He died on his farm near Brick church, Marlboro township, August 24, 1766, aged 35 yrs, 25 days, according to his headstone in Schenck-Couwenhoven yard. He left one son Rulef, and four daughters surviving. A strange coincidence attends Hendrick's will and his father's will. They have same subscribing witnesses, were proved same year, and are both recorded in Book I of Wills at Trenton, N. J.

Engeltje, bap. April 28, 1732, died young.

Teuntje, (Antonia) bap. in Brooklyn, April 9, 1699; m. 1715, Jonathan Holmes, Jr., eldest son of Obadiah Holmes and Alice Ashton, his wife. Teuntje was the first of the seven daughters of Daniel Hendrickson to join the Dutch church. This was in 1737. Her husband, Jonathan Holmes, Jr., was so called to distinguish him from his uncle, Jonathan Holmes, Sr., and Jonathan Holmes, minor.

Jonathan Holmes, Jr., made his will Sept. 6, 1766; it was proved Nov. 2, 1768, and recorded at Trenton in Book K of Wills, p. 264. The witnesses are Obadiah Holmes, Obadiah Holmes, Jr., and Asher Holmes. He describes himself as "I, Jonathan Holmes, Jr., of Freehold township." He devises all his real estate to his sons, William and James, (baptized Jacobus). He also mentions sons Jonathan, John, Daniel, Samuel, and children of his son Joseph, deceased. His daughters named in this will were Alice VanBrakle, Catherine Schenck, and Mary. Obadiah Holmes, the father of Jonathan Holmes, Jr., was the eldest son of Jonathan Holmes and Sarah Borden, his wife, and was born July 17, 1666, at Gravesend, on Long Island. They were probably staying with Capt. John Bowne who lived there, and who had married Lydia Holmes, a daughter of Rev. Obadiah. The settlement at Middletown in Monmouth county was being effected, and Jonathan Holmes, with his family, remained at Gravesend until his dwelling-house could be built and made ready for occupation. The next year, 1667, we find this Jonathan Holmes among the first officers elected in the township of Middletown.

Jonathan Holmes, whose name appears so prominently on our first records from 1667 to 1684, was born in 1637 in England, and came with his father to America in 1639. He was the firstborn and eldest son of a man famous in the annals of the Baptist church, and who was a zealous preacher of this faith at Newport, R. I., from 1652 to his death in 1682. Capt. John Bowne, who was the leading spirit of this colony from Gravesend to Monmouth, had married his daughter, and he doubtless lent him his name and influence to make this enterprise a success. His name appears on Nicolls patent of 1665 as one of the patentees, but he never removed here. Two of his sons, Jonathan and Obadiah, represented him and his interests. The latter, however, only remained a short time, for we find him residing on Staten Island and a Justice of the Peace there under Jacob Leisler. The troubles arising from his connection with this man led him to remove to Salem county, N. J., where he lived the rest of his life. Jonathan Holmes remained in Monmouth until 1684, and then returned to Rhode Island, where he remained until his death in 1713.

His will was proved Nov. 2nd of that year, and is recorded at Newport, R. I. He devised all his real estate in Monmouth county equally to his sons, Obadiah and Jonathan, who both settled, lived and died here. Obadiah married Alice Ashton, as already stated, and Jonathan Holmes, Jr., was his firstborn and eldest son. Jonathan Holmes, the first settler, was one of the trusted leaders, next to Capt. John Bowne, both in industrial, religious and civil matters of the early colonists. He was a deputy to the first general assembly which met at Elizabethtown in 1668. The next year he was dismissed for refusing to take the oath of allegiance to the Proprietors. Soon after Governor Carteret sent commissioners to the people of Monmouth demanding their submission and obedience to the Lords Proprietors as they grandiloquently called themselves. The people of Shrewsbury managed to evade committing themselves. The people of Middletown spoke out boldly and frankly, and their answer is recorded in full in the old Town Book of Middletown. It is well worth reading, as it is the first public declaration for popular rights against government by favoritism and caste put forth on this American continent. Tradition reports that Jonathan Holmes, who had been rejected as a deputy for refusing to take the oath of allegiance and fidelity to the Proprietors, framed this answer. Neither the proclamation of Charles I, King of England, ordering them to submit, nor this threat of Governor Cartaret that they would be punished as "mutineers" or rebels, seems to have intimidated them. It is a strong, honest and sensible declaration of their rights, and shows what a difference then, as ever since, has existed between the people of the two original townships.

Jonathan Holmes' son Obadiah, married in 1696 Alice, (b. 1671, d. 1716) daughter of James Ashton and Deliverance Throckmorton, his wife. Obadiah Holmes died April 3, 1745, leaving a will dated Dec. 24, 1744, proved April 17, 1745, and recorded at Trenton in "D" of Wills, p. 265, etc. He mentions Jonathan, Obadiah, James, Samuel, Joseph and John, six sons, and Deliverance, wife of Joseph Smith, and Mary, wife of James Mott, two daughters. He gives his homestead farm at "Ramnessin," on Hop Brook, in present township of Holmdel, to his son John, and his lands at Crosswicks, (now Upper Freehold) to his son Joseph, whose descendants have owned and resided on it to this day.

Our present chosen freeholder from Upper Freehold township, Joseph Holmes, now owns this homestead and is a lineal descendant of this son of Obadiah Holmes, to whom he devised these lands. Obadiah Holmes was sheriff of Monmouth in 1699, and one of the leaders of the people in breaking up Governor Hamilton's court at Middletown, March 26, 1701.

Obadiah's son Samuel, (b. April 17, 1704, d. Feb. 23, 1760), married Dec. 7, 1731, Huldah, daughter of Gershom Mott and Sarah Clayton, his wife, and lived and died on a farm called "Scotschester," in the present township of Marlboro. They were the parents of Asher Holmes, (b. Feb. 22, 1740, d. June 20, 1808) who was first sheriff of Monmouth county under our Republic. He was Colonel of our county militia and of state troops, and was engaged in the battles of Germantown, Princeton and Monmouth. He also represented Monmouth in the state council in 1786-88. The officers of our Monmouth militia during the Revolution were neither professional soldiers nor literary or learned men. They never made any efforts to perpetuate the memory of their deeds, and never claimed any particular credit for doing what they thought was their plain duty. Therefore, when we find any writing by them detailing the part they took in this memorable war, we should especially prize it. The following letter was written by Colonel Asher Holmes to his wife after the battle of Germantown, merely to assure her of his safety, and without any idea it would be treasured up and preserved for other generations.

Camp on the Mountain near Perkamie Creek, 29 miles west of Philadelphia,

Oct. 6, 1777:

DEAR SALLIE:

The day before yesterday there was a general engagement. The first part of the day was much in our favour. We drove the enemy for some miles. General Howe had given orders for his army to retreat over the Schuykill River; but the afterpart of the day was unfavorable to us; our line of battle was broken, and we were obliged to retreat.

The battle was near Germantown. This attack was made by different divisions in different quarters, nearly at the same time, but the morning being very foggy, was much against us, and the severe firing added to the thickness of the air, which prevented our seeing far, therefore a great disadvantage to us. The Jersey militia and the Red Coats * under General Forman, and the Maryland militia with some 'Listed troops under Gen. Smallwood, were on the left wing of the whole army. We drove the enemy, when we first made the attack, but by the thickness of the fog, the enemy got into our rear. Therefore had to change our front, and then retreated to a proper place.

Gen. McDougall's 'Listed men then

---

* Red Coats under Gen. Forman, were the Jersey Minute men, who wore red hunting coats, and in a fog or smoke of battle might easily be mistaken for the British who also wore red coats, and thus cause confusion.

formed to the left of us and Gen. Green's 'Listed men to the right of us, but they all gave way except the Monmouth Militia, and Gen. Forman's Red Coats stood firm, and advanced upon the British Red Coats, who were at least three times our number, to a fence where we made a stand. The fire was very severe and the enemy ran.

They brought a field-piece to fire on us with grapeshot, but our Monmouth men stood firm until their ammunition was nearly exhausted, and the enemy advancing around our right flank. Gen. Forman then ordered us to retreat, which we did in pretty good order until our Continental troops broke and ran the second time, and this running through our men broke them entirely. Our Jersey Brigade suffered very much by storming a strong stone house in Germantown, which first stopped our progress, and I believe was one great cause of breaking our line in that quarter.

I have seen Brother John Holmes, Capt. Mott, Capt. Burrows and Bostwick and most of our Monmouth officers. We are all well. Since the battle our army is in good spirits although our duty has been very severe. The night before the battle our men marched all night and had very little sleep the night after. Providence seems to have protected our Monmouth Militia in a particular manner, as we have lost very few, if any killed, and not many wounded, although the enemy was within 120 yards of us in the hottest of the fire, and their field piece firing on us with grapeshot a great part of the time. I have escaped without being hurt, although I was much exposed to the enemy's fire.

From your ever affectionate
ASHER HOLMES.
To Mrs. Sarah Holmes.

This letter is directed
"To Mrs. Sarah Holmes in Freehold forwarded by Mr. Logan."

Teuntje, the second child of Daniel Hendrickson, was an earnest and active member of the Dutch church, while her husband, Jonathan Holmes, like all his family, was a zealous believer in the tenets of the Baptist faith. The baptism by immersion was one of their most important doctrines. Neither did they believe in infant baptism. Teuntje Hendrickson must have been a woman of great resolution, for she had her children baptized in the Dutch church and taught the Heidelberg catechism. Her children are the only Holmeses whose names appear on the old records of the Monmouth Dutch church.

There must have been much talk and holding up of hands in amazement among the good brethren of the Baptist faith, that these descendants of the sturdy Rev. Obadiah Holmes should be sprinkled and not immersed. There must have been many earnest appeals made to their father against this woeful departure from the true faith. The only reply Jonathan Holmes, Jr., could make, I suppose, was "When a woman will, she will, and when she won't, she won't." Teuntje, however, was never able to bring her husband clear over, as Margaret Wyckoff had done with Jonathan Forman, but she turned her "Holmes" children into good "Dutchmen."

The records of our Dutch church show that Jonathan Holmes and Teuntje Hendrickson, his wife, had the following children baptized:

Obadiah, bapt. Oct. 28, 1716, died unmarried in 1752. The records in the office of the Secretary of State show that letters of administration on his estate was granted to his brother, Joseph Holmes, Jr., Oct. 17, 1752, Book B of Wills, p. 69.

Daniel, bapt. April 9, 1721, m. 1752, Leah, (b. 1736, d. March 15, 1813) daughter of James Bowne and Margaret Newbold, his wife. Both are buried in yard of Holmdel Baptist church.

Jonathan, bapt. July 19, 1722, married Sarah Potter in 1758, and was a merchant in New York city in 1752. He may have been the "Jonathan Holmes" called "Minor."

Joseph, b.——, m. June, 1752, Sarah, daughter of James Mott and Mary Holmes, his wife, and was engaged with James Mott, Jr., in mercantile business in New York city. He died in 1763. James Mott and James Mott, Jr., appointed administrator of Joseph Holmes, Sept. 22, 1763, Book H of Wills, p. 293, Secretary of State's office.

John, b.——; m. 1764, Catharine Brown, was associated with his brother Jonathan in business in New York city in 1752. In 1763 he resided at and operated a grist mill at Forked River in what is now Ocean county, but then part of Monmouth. During the Revolutionary war his dwelling was plundered by a party of refugees. He left three sons who married and had numerous descendants. Many of these followed the water and were captains of vessels in coasting trade.

Alice, bapt. March 30, 1730; m. 1749, John VanBrakle, d. May 19, 1796.

Catharine, b. May 11, 1731; d. May 12, 1796, aged 63 years, 1 day, according to the inscription on her headstone in Schenck-Couwenhoven yard, where she is buried by her first husband, Hendrick Schenck. She left a will, recorded at Trenton, N. J. She married first in 1749, Hendrick, son of Roelof Schenck and Geesey Hendrickson, his wife, who died August 24, 1766. She married second, John, son of Garret Schenck and Neeltje Voorhees, his wife. She was his third wife. He died Feb. 13, 1775, on his wife's farm near what is now

Bradevelt station, and was buried by his father and mother in Schenck-Couwenhoven yard. There were no children by the last marriage.
Mary.
James, bapt. Jacobus, May 1, 1737.
Samuel, bapt. July 8, 1739.
William, b.——, died in 1776. Letters of administration in his estate were granted to his brother, Daniel Holmes, Feb. 28, 1776. See Book M of Wills, p. 29, Secretary of State's office, Trenton.

Catharine Holmes, the seventh child of Jonathan Holmes, Jr., and Teuntje Hendrickson, his wife above mentioned, by her first husband, Hendrick Schenck, had seven children, of whom five lived to grow up, viz: one son, Ruliff, and four daughters, Mary, Eleanor, Catharine and Ann. Her youngest child, Ann, was born on her farm near what is now Bradevelt station, June 14, 1766, and married Jonathan Holmes, son of Samuel Holmes, and Mary Stout, his wife. Samuel Holmes (b. Oct. 4, 1726; d. Aug. 26, 1769) was a son of Jonathan Holmes, Sr., by Rebecca Throckmorton, his second wife. They are both buried in old Topanemus grave yard. This Jonathan Holmes, son of Samuel Holmes and Mary Stout, his wife, married Ann Schenck, as above stated, and died without children, Nov. 16, 1814. His will is dated January 6, 1810, proved Nov. 22, 1814, and recorded at Freehold in Book A of Wills, p. 685, etc.

He first orders that one-quarter of an acre of land on the farm where his brother, John S. Holmes, then lived, and "where the burying ground now is" shall be a burying place for the Holmes family. He then gives to his brother, John S. Holmes, the use of all his real estate, and at his death to go to his two sons, Daniel and John, or the survivors of them in fee simple. This is the same farm in Pleasant Valley where ex-Sheriff Daniel Holmes lived, and where his son, the late Joseph H. Holmes, lived and died. The Holmes family still own it.

Jonathan Holmes then made the following bequests: To his sister Lydia, wife of Garret Stillwell, $250; to the children of his sister Parmelia, wife of John Stillwell, $250; to his brother, Stout Holmes, $375. This brother married first Elizabeth Pintard, second Mary Ogbourns, widow of Samuel Bray. One of his daughters, Alice, married ex-Judge Joseph Murphy, and was the mother of Holmes W. Murphy, who served two terms as clerk of Monmouth county and represented this county in General Assembly during the years 1880-81. He was associated with the writer as partner in law business for several years.

Jonathan Holmes also gives by this will $375 to his sister Catharine, wife of Nathan Stout. To his brother, Samuel Holmes, he gives the interest yearly on $3,750 for life, and at his death to his son, Jonathan, if living. If dead, then $750 of principal to Samuel's two daughters, Mary and Catharine, and the remaining $3,000 to Daniel and John, sons of his brother, John S. Holmes. To Jonathan, son of his brother, Joseph Holmes, $500, and to Nelly, daughter of his brother Joseph, $125. To Joseph, son of David Crawford, $62.50, and to Joseph Covert, son of Daniel Covert, $62.50.

To Jonathan Holmes, son of his brother Samuel, his clock, sideboard, silver tankard, best horse he has, his fusee and implements belonging to it. Orders all legacies paid in gold or silver. Directs Daniel and John, the two nephews to whom he gives all his real estate, not to sell it, but keep same in Holmes family forever.

John S. Holmes named in this will married Sarah, daughter of Col. Daniel Hendrickson who commanded the Third Regiment of Monmouth militia during the Revolution, and was speaker of General Assembly of New Jersey in 1784. John S. Holmes also represented Monmouth county in General Assembly during years 1810-11 and 1813-14. His son Daniel married Rhoda VanMater, as has been mentioned in VanMater records. This Daniel Holmes was a member of the constitutional convention of 1844.

The following paper has the genuine signatures of John S. Holmes, Col. Asher Holmes, and others who have been mentioned in these articles. It also shows that they appreciated education and good schools and made an effort to have an academy or high school established in Holmdel:

"On condition that the acre of ground, this day sold by Obadiah Holmes unto us the undersubscribers, for erecting an academy; that if it should fail of success, then if its ever convenient to any other use, we engage to pay said Obadiah Holmes or his lawful representatives, the further sum of fifty pounds for said lot. This we engage in case that either us or our heirs shall convert it to any other purpose. Witness our hands this twenty-fourth day of December, seventeen hundred and ninety-three.
ASHER HOLMES,   BARNES SMOCK,
THOMAS LLOYD, DANIEL KETCHAM,
JOHN I. HOLMES, JOHN S. HOLMES,
BARNES H. SMOCK, CHRINEYONCE VanMATER, GARRET HENDRICKSON.
Witness present:
    HEN. HENDRICKSON,
    JARRET STILLWELL,
    WILLIAM BRITTON."

On Conditioned that the acre of Ground this day Sold by Obediah Holmes, unto us the undersubscribers, for erecting an Accademy, that it should fail of success, then if its ever converted to any other use we engage to pay said Obediah Holmes, or his lawful Representative, the further sum of Fifty pounds for said Lott, this we engage in case that either us or our heirs shall convert it to any other purpose, and Witness our hands this twenty fourth day of December Seventeen hundred and Ninety three

Witness Present
Attings Present
Hon Hendrick
Jarrat Stillwell
William Britten

Asher Holmes
Barnes Smock
Thomas Lloyd
Daniel ...
John I Holmes
John S Holmes
Garret Hendrickson
Barnes H. Smock

Old document executed December 24, 1793, showing signatures of Barnes Smock, Asher Holmes, Garret Hendrickson, Barnes H. Smock and others.

Garret Hendrickson, who has signed above, was Lieut. Garret Hendrickson in Capt. Wm. Schenck's company, and Barnes Smock commanded an artillery company during the revolution. Hendrick Hendrickson, who signs as witness, was one of the county judges and part of time presiding judge, as our court minutes from 1790 to 1800 show.

As the Holmes family has always been prominent in this county and have numerous relatives, there are many who will feel interested in the following extracts from a letter written by the Rev. Obadiah Holmes to his wife in 1675: "if she remains in the land of the living, after my departure" to use his own words. After speaking of the "comfort their children have been," he writes: "Wherefore make use of that he is pleased to let thee enjoy. I say make use of it to thy present comfort. Thou art but weak and aged, cease from thy labors and great toil and take a little rest and ease in thy old age. Live on what thou hast, for what the Lord hast given us, I freely have given thee, for thy life, to make thy life comfortable; wherefore see thou doeth it, so long as house, land and cattle remain. Make much of thyself, and at thy death, then what remains may be disposed according to my will. And now, my dear wife, whom I love as my own soul, I commit thee to the Lord, who hath been a gracious merciful God to us all our days. Not once doubting He will be gracious to thee in life or death, and will carry thee through this valley of tears, with his own supporting hand. Sorrow not at my departure, but rejoice in the Lord, and again I say rejoice in the Lord of our salvation. And in nothing be careful, but make thy requests to Him, who only is able to supply thy necessities and to help thee in time of need. Unto whom I commit thee for counsel, wisdom and strength, and to keep thee blameless to the coming of the Lord Jesus Christ, to whom be all glory, honor and praise, forever and ever. Fare Thee Well."

Extracts from a letter to all his children: After urging them to seek the kingdom of God and his righteousness, he says: "And now my son Joseph: Remember Joseph of Arimathea was a good man, and a disciple of Jesus, and was bold and went boldly and asked the body of Jesus and buried it."

"My son John: Remember what a loving and beloved disciple he was."

"My daughter Hope: Consider what a peace of God hope is, and court after that hope that will never be ashamed, but hath the hope of eternal life and salvation by Jesus Christ."

"My son Obadiah: Consider that Obadiah was a servant of the Lord and tender in spirit, and in a troublesome time hid the prophets by 60 in a cave."

"My son Samuel: Remember that Samuel was a chief prophet of the Lord, ready to hear his voice saying "Speak Lord, for thy servant heareth."

"My daughter Martha: Remember Martha, although she was cumbered with many things, yet she loved the Lord, and was beloved of him, for He loved Mary and Martha."

"My daughter Mary: Remember Mary chose the better part, that shall not be taken away, and did hearken to the Lord's instructions."

"My son Jonathan: Remember how faithful and loving he was to David, that servant of the Lord."

"My daughter Lidiah: Remember how Lidiah's heart was opened, her ear bowed, her spirit made willing to receive and obey the apostle in what the Lord required, and was baptized, and entertained and refreshed the servants of the Lord."

"Let your conversation in life be squared by the Scriptures, and they will direct you how to behave toward God and man. And next to loving and fearing the Lord, have you, a most dear and tender respect to your faithful, careful, tender hearted, loving, aged mother. Show your duty in all things. Love her with high and cheerful love and respect, and then make sure you love one another. Let it continue and increase. So you may be good examples to others. Visit one another as often as you can, and put one another in mind of the uncertainty of life, and what need there is to prepare for death. Take counsel one of another, and if one see cause to advise or reprove the other, hearken to it and take it well. Be ye content with your present condition and portion God giveth you, and make a good use of what you have, by making use of it to your comfort for meat, drink and apparel, it is the gift of God. And take care to live honestly, justly, quietly, with love and peace with all men, etc., and forget not to entertain strangers according to your ability, etc."

OBADIAH HULLMES.
The 17th day, 10th month, 1675."

Hendrick, the eldest son of the pioneer settler, was born in 1700; married 1725, Neeltje, daughter of Garret Schenck and Neeltje Voorhees, his wife, of Pleasant Valley, and died intestate February 21, 1753, aged fifty years, according to his headstone in the family burying ground on the old Hendrickson homestead at Holland in Holmdel township. His wife is not buried by him, as she married in 1761 Elias Golden and is probably buried by him on the Golden homestead. Administration on his estate, at request of the widow, was granted March 20, 1753, to his brothers, Daniel and William, and his brother-in-law, Garret Schenck. See Book F of Wills, page 107, Secretary of State's office at Trenton, N. J. He had the following children:

Tryntje, baptized April 3, 1726; died in infancy.

Daniel, born November 11, 1727; married in 1767, Mary Schenck, (see license in Secretary of State's office) and died without surviving children March 2nd, 1776, aged 48 years, 3 months, 21 days, according to his headstone inscription in homestead yard. His wife is not buried by him, which would indicate that she has married again. His will is recorded at Trenton in Book M of Wills, page 16-17. He describes himself as "Daniel Hendrickson, Jr., of Middletown township." He gives his wife Mary £1400, with household goods and a negro girl. All his real estate is devised in fee equally between his two brothers, Garret and Hendrick. He bequeaths £100 to his sister, Nelly VanMater, and the same amount to his sister, Mary Couwenhoven, and £20 to his sister Ann, with a negro man. To James Schenck, a cow and calf. This will is dated February 18, 1775, proved March 12, 1776. His two brothers, Garret and Hendrick, divide the lands so devised between them by quit claim deeds, recorded in Book I of Deeds, page 92, Monmouth county clerk's office.

Neeltje, baptized January 4, 1734; died young.

Garret, born January 22, 1734, died December 2, 1801, and is buried by his first two wives on the homestead. He married first, according to license granted, December 8, 1755, and on record at Trenton, his cousin, Catharine, daughter of Tunis Denise and Francyntje Hendrickson, his wife, (born May 8, 1732, died Sept. 8, 1771). Married second, Lena, or Helena, (born Sept. 26, 1753, died Jan. 1, 1785) daughter of Denise VanLieu, or VanLieuwen, and Ida Wyckoff, his wife. Married third, Nelly, daughter of Arie VanDoorn and Antje Janse Schenck, his wife, and then the widow of Hendrick Smock. She died February 11, 1834, aged 91 years, 10 months, 8 days, according to her headstone in Schenck-Couwenhoven cemetery. Garret Hendrickson lived and died in the old Dutch built farmhouse, still (1900) standing, on the farm where Cyrenius Hendrickson lived and died in Pleasant Valley, afterwards owned and occupied by his only son, Henry Denise Hendrickson, well known to our present generation of people in this county. Garret Hendrickson was a lieutenant in Capt. William Schenck's company of militia during the Revolutionary war and rendered good service to his country.

The following extract from the New Jersey Gazette of June 28, 1780, speaks of him, although by mistake his name is printed "Henderson" instead of Hendrickson. There was no officer by the name of Henderson in the Middletown militia. Thomas Henderson of Freehold, was a lieutenant-colonel and a physician, and is said to be the writer of those letters from Monmouth county published from time to time in this newspaper. Our county records show that a pension was granted to Garret Hendrickson and Walter Hier (Hyres) for wounds received in a skirmish on June 21, 1780. The United States government at a later date placed Garret Hendrickson on the pension roll for this same injury. "Letter from Monmouth county dated June 22, 1780. Yesterday morning a party of the enemy consisting of Tye with 30 Blacks, 26 Queen Rangers and 30 Refugee Tories landed at Conascung. They got between our scouts undiscovered, and went to James Mott's, Sr., and plundered his and several neighbors houses of almost everything, and carried off the following persons: James Mott, Sr., James Johnston, Joseph Dorsett, Joseph Pearce, William Blair, James Walling, Jr., John Walling, son of Thomas, Phillip Walling, James Wall, Matthew Griggs, several negroes and a great deal of stock; but all the negroes except one, and a great deal of stock were retaken by our people. Capt. Walling was slightly wounded and a Lieut. Henderson (Hendrickson) had his arm broken. Two privates supposed mortally and a third slightly wounded in a skirmish we had with them on their retreat. The enemy acknowledge loss of seven men, but we think it more considerable."

It appears that there was hand to hand fighting, for in an affidavit on record in the Monmouth clerk's office to support Hyres' claim for pension, it is stated "that he received a cutlass wound while boldly fighting." Doctor Barber and Doctor Thomas Henderson, (writer of these letters) certify that

Garret Hendrickson has lost almost entire use of his right arm from injuries received in this fight on June 21, 1780. See page 303 of Old' Times in Old Monmouth, although there is a typographical error here, for the month is printed January instead of June.

In this and several other raids the enemy landed at Conescunk. The reason of this was the depth of water at this place near the shore which enabled them to get off their boats at any stage of the tide. At other places the flats would be bare for a considerable distance or water too shallow to float their barges at low tide. Captain John Schenck is said to have led our forces and pressed close upon them until they embarked. So closely were they pressed that they abandoned nearly all the cattle, sheep and hogs they had taken, and all the negro slaves except one.

While their last boat was within musket shot from the beach an officer stood up in the stern of the boat and deliberately aimed and fired at Captain Schenck, who had come down to the water's edge. The bullet whistled close to his head. "They shoot as if they wanted to kill a body," said the grim farmer, "but two can play at this work." Then seizing a gun from one of his men he walked into the water up to his armpits and carefully aiming, fired at the man who still stood up in the stern of the boat. He was seen to fall back but how badly hurt was never learned.

Hendrick, the fifth child of Hendrick Hendrickson, and Neeltje Schenck, his wife, was born April 23, baptized June 5, 1737, and died October 11, 1811, according to his tombstone in family yard on homestead farm. He married first, according to license granted, March 7, 1757, Lydia, daughter of Ensign Elias Couwenhoven and Williamsee Wall, his wife, (born March 11, 1738; died March 16, 1805) married second, Helena Longstreet, October 18, 1806, according to marriage records in Monmouth clerk's office. I think she was a widow, and the daughter of Joseph Covenhoven and Hannah, his wife. She was born November 28, 1754, died October 3, 1820. Both wives are buried by him in homestead yard at Holland. By his first wife he had the following children, but none by his second wife.

Hendrick, born November 13, 1758, baptized February 18, 1759; died unmarried, November 8, 1803. He served in light horse company during Revolution and was also the schipper or boss of a crew of whaleboatmen, whose boats lay concealed in the ravines near Matawan creek and swamps near Waycake creek.

Williampe, born February 2, 1761; married first, November 9, 1778, Aaron Longstreet; second, Dr. Pitney, and died October 21, 1837.

Elias, baptized September 29, 1765; married Gitty, who died May 10, 1805, when only nineteen years old, according to headstone in homestead yard. He died childless July 28, 1805, aged 40 years, and is buried by her. He also served during the Revolution in light horse company.

Hendrick Hendrickson, the father of these three children, served as one of our county judges many years, and part of the time was presiding judge of the Monmouth courts; see Nos. 7, 8 and 9 of court minutes of Monmouth county. Denise Denise, Garret I. Covenhoven, John Covenhoven, Peter Schenck and Peter Wyckoff were associate judges with him part of this time. As a judge he was fair and impartial, with strong common sense. In addition to lands he inherited from his father, he got 200 acres under will of his brother Daniel. He also purchased of John Covenhoven 130 acres, and some years later 150 acres more, adjacent to his farm in Pleasant Valley. He also bought 37 acres of adjacent land from Garret Schenck, and so became the owner of some 600 acres of as good land as there was in Pleasant Valley. As his sons died childless, this large and valuable farm passed out of the Hendrickson name under his will dated July 12, 1811, proved November 28, 1811, recorded at Freehold in Book A of Wills, page 457, etc. He devised all his real estate to his grandson, John Longstreet, subject to the comfortable maintenance of his widow for life. This devise passed into the Longstreet family one of the finest and most productive farms in Pleasant Valley. He gives to his daughter, Williampe Pitney, interest on £342, then in hands of Aaron Pitney. He gives Anne Seabrook and Lydia Smock £600 each. To his grandson, Hendrick Longstreet, £5, to Aaron Schenck, son of Obadiah Schenck and Nelly Longstreet, £500. Hendrick Longstreet, his grandson, and friend Denise Hendrickson, are appointed executors.

The sixth child of Hendrick Hendrickson and Neeltje Schenck, his wife, was Mary, born December 6, 1740, married January 13, 1767, Cornelius (b. Feb. 11, 1746, d. Oct. 10, 1806), son of William Cornelise Couwenhoven and Annetje Hendrickson, his second wife. She died January 3, 1806, and is buried by her husband in Schanck-Couwenhoven cemetery.

Tryntje, (Catharine) bap. September 30, 1740; died young.

Neeltje, bap. September 30, 1740, married 1756, Jacob VanMeter (b. March 3, 1732, d. April 20, 1775), already mentioned in VanMater records.

Antje, bap. October 7, 1744, married David Hansen VanNostrandt, who was bap. September 18, 1737.

William, bap. December 18, 1748, died young.

Garret and Hendrick Hendrickson owned some of the best farming lands which could be found in Monmouth county. They were well stocked with cattle, sheep and swine. The hams and bacon made by them were of the best. In the fall an abundant supply of smoked meats, salted provisions, and other things to eat and drink, were laid away in cellar, smoke house and garret. This is the reason why so many raids were made through Pleasant Valley. The last of these expeditions occurred February 8, 1782. Forty refugees from Sandy Hook under command of a Lieutenant Steelman who belonged down in Cape May county, came up during the night and surrounded Garret Hendrickson and his brother Hendrick's houses before daylight. This was directly after a heavy snowstorm and I suppose these men on the Hook were in a state of starvation and ready for any desperate adventure to get provisions. They succeeded in taking Hendrick Hendrickson and his two sons, Hendrick and Elias, with all women folks and negro slaves, and Garret Hendrickson with his people, and John Covenhoven, his family and servants on adjacent farms, prisoners and placed them under close guard. A young man named William Thompson at Garret Hendrickson's house, managed in some way to escape undiscovered and hurried off to Captain John Schanck's home where he gave the alarm. They seized five woodsleds on these different farms. On two they fastened hay shelvings with boards nailed against the sides and on the bottom. On the other three they placed the bodies of farm wagons. Then they hitched two teams or four horses to each sled, for the snow lay deep and the roads were unbroken in many places. They put two barrels of apple whisky in one end of the hay shelvings and barrels of pork in the other, and between five live sheep. Barrels of flour, corn meal, potatoes, and all the poultry they could kill was placed on the other shelving. The other sleds were loaded with bacon, smoked meats, hams, corned beef, butter, and all other kinds of provisions they could lay their hands on. They also took clothing, blankets, and cooking utensils. Mrs. Garret Hendrickson's silk dress was taken and used to wrap up hams. After loading up with all kinds of plunder they started back for the Hook. In the meantime Captain Schanck was gathering his men and succeeded in getting thirty mounted men ready in about an hour after the Refugees had started. The deep snow and unbroken roads with the heavy loads made the progress of the Refugees slow. They were overtaken and a lively skirmish ensued in which three of them were wounded and twelve taken prisoners. The rest escaped. One of them cut a horse loose from among the teams and rode off. All the plunder was retaken. Our people lost one man killed. This was young Thompson who had given the alarm. On their return they were attacked unexpectedly by a detached party of Refugees consisting of sixteen men under command of Shore Stevenson. Captain Schanck at once ordered a charge before they could reload their guns. They at once threw down their arms and asked for quarter. In the confusion, however eight of the first prisoners got away, leaving only four who with Stevenson and his sixteen men made 21 prisoners.

Lieutenant Garret Hendrickson by Catharine Denise, his first wife, had the following children:

Hendrick, baptized March 20, 1757, died young.

Francyntje, baptized March 18, 1758; married William Forman. Both buried in yard of Old Tennent church. She died June 19, 1815, and her husband January 31, 1823, aged 71 years, 5 months, 5 days.

Denise, born November 12, 1761, died March 7, 1839. He married December 28, 1786, Anne, (born Nov. 15, 1766; died Aug. 6, 1858) daughter of John Schenck and Nelly Bennett, his wife, of Pleasant Valley. Both are buried on homestead farm at Holland.

Hendrick, born July 19, 1764; married January 20, 1791, Phoebe VanMater; died June 6, 1837. Both are buried on homestead farm at Holland. Names of their children have been heretofore given in VanMater genealogy.

Neeltje, baptized August 10, 1766; married John, son of Hendrick Brower and Abigeltje Hunt, his wife.

Catharine, born April 8, 1768; married September 18, 1794, Peter, son of Hendrick Brower and wife aforesaid. She died August 8, 1822, and is buried in homestead yard.

By his second wife, Helena VanLieu, he had the following children:

Ida, baptized March 19, 1775; married September 10, 1794, Joseph K. Van-Mater, already mentioned in VanMater records.

Daniel G., baptized June 1, 1776; married December 21, 1797, Sarah, daughter of Cornelius Albertse Couwenhoven and Mary Logan, his wife They removed to some other part of New Jersey.

Mary, baptized May 2, 1779; married December 24, 1797, William VanMater, whose children have been already named in VanMater articles.

Lydia, born October 9, 1781; married Stephen Crane and died May 4, 1851, aged 69 years, 6 months, 25 days, according to her headstone in homestead burying ground at Holland. Her husband is not buried by her; I do not know where he was.

Anne, baptized December 7, 1783; married October 3, 1799, Garret Terhune.

Denise Hendrickson and Anne Schenck, his wife, named above, had the following children:

Garret D., born July 7, 1787; died October 12, 1861. He married March 23, 1808, Jane, daughter of Capt. Hendrick Hendrickson and Francinke Covenhoven his wife. One of their daughters, Catharine, born April 20, 1815, married the late William Henry Sickles of Red Bank. Another daughter, Adaline, married John Vanderveer Carson, now (1900) residing in Freehold, and the parents of the Carson Brothers, who have so long carried on the butcher's business here.

Catharine, born October 8, 1801; married December 24, 1821, Peter R. Smock, and died September 9, 1890. Both are buried in Smock burying ground near Holmdel village on the farm where Peter R. Smock lived and died. They are the parents of ex-Sheriff Ruliff P. Smock, now a resident of Freehold.

John Schenck, born May 9, 1807, married Ellen Hyres.

John, the second son and fourth child of Daniel Hendrickson, the pioneer settler, was born about 1702; married about 1734, Annetje, (born in February 1708) daughter of Jacob Couwenhoven and Saartje Schenck, his wife. The parental homestead of these young people in a direct line over the meadows and hills were less than a mile apart. They had know each other from their earliest childhood. After his marriage John settled on a farm in county of Middlesex, which his father had pur-

chased of Stephen Warne and which he had given to him by will. Here the following children were born:

Daniel, born July 3, 1735; married in 1758 Eleanor VanMater (b. Aug. 4, 1735, d. Feb. 12, 1828). He died November 17, 1809, and is buried in family yard on farm of late George Crawford Hendrickson, his great grandson, at east end of Middletown village and still owned by this family. Names of his children have already been published in history of the VanMater family.

Jacob, baptised February 12, 1738; no other information. John Hendrickson died in 1740, and letters of administration of his estate were granted October 11, 1740, to his eldest brother Hendrick, to his brother-in-law William Couwenhoven, and Henry Disbrow, see Book C of Wills, page 335, secretary of state's office, Trenton, N. J. I do not know whether his widow survived him or not. She would have right of administration, but as she is not named, it would seem that she had died prior to her husband.

Maijke (Micha) the fifth child, married Geysbert VanMater (b. Feb. 24, 1694). Names of their children have been heretofore published in genealogy of the VanMaters.

Tryntje (Catharine) sixth child, is the only one who married and removed from this county and the only one of the seven daughters who did not join the church in this county. She married one Henry Dusberry or Dusenberry and removed to some other part of New Jersey or some other colony. She, however, while visiting her parents in Monmouth, had three of her children baptized in the Dutch church, viz:

Antje, baptised December 19, 1736. Her brother John Hendrickson and his wife, Annetje Couwenhoven, appear as sponsore on church records.

Anne, baptised December 24, 1738. Her brother, Hendrick Hendrickson and his wife, Neeltje Schenck, are sponsors.

William Hendrickson, baptised October 12, 1743. Her brother, William Hendrickson, and his wife, Mary Longstreet are sponsors. This is all the records given us of Catharine, where she lived and when and where she died is unknown.

William the third son of Daniel Hendrickson and Catharine VanDyke, was baptized, November 6, 1709, married about 1731, Mary or Maria (bapt. May 6, 1702) daughter of Stoffle Langstraat and Maicken or Moyka Laen his wife. His wife's name appears as a communicant on records of Dutch church in 1741 as "Maria Langstraet, wife of Wilm Hindrickson." They had the following

children:
Catharine, baptized August 8, 1732, maried Jacob, son of Rem Remsen of Brooklyn, N. Y. He was born in 1719, died 1784. Their marriage license in Secretary of State office at Trenton was granted, August 11, 1747. "Catharine Hendrickson of Monmouth County to Jacob Remsen, Sr., of New York." They have one child baptized in our church May 6, 1750, and named William His maternal grandparents were put down as sponsors.

Daniel, baptized December 25, 1736, married in 1756, Catharine (b. Jan'y 29, 1738,) daughter of Rutgers VanBrunt and Elizabeth Voorhes, his wife, of New Utrecht, L. I. This Daniel Hendrickson was a land surveyor and was very prominent during the war war for Independence as Colonel of the 3rd Regiment of the Monmouth militia. These two children are the only ones William Hendrickson and Maria Longstreet, his wife had. William Hendrickson died intestate in 1783, and the records in the Secretary of State's office show that letters of administration were granted to their son Daniel, October 27, 1783. I do not know where he or his wife are buried but would not be surprised if it was somewhere in the vicinity of Tinton Falls, as his son Daniel, then resided there. Colonel Daniel Hendrickson by Catharine VanBrunt, his wife, had the following children:

William, baptized July 31, 1757, died young.

Elizabeth, baptized July 16, 1758, married Richard McKnight, Captain of Monmouth militia during Revolution.

William, baptized January 11, 1761, died young.

Daniel, born 1763, married Elizabeth, daughter of Barzillai Grover and Theodosia, his wife, of Upper Freehold.

Mary, baptized March 17, 1765.

Sarah, born March 9, 1767, married John S. Holmes, (b. Nov. 29, 1762, d. Aug. 15, 1821) son of Samuel Holmes and Mary Stout, his wife.

Daniel Hendrickson and Nicholas VanBrunt represented Shrewsbury township in the Provincial Congress of New Jersey, in 1775. In minutes of Provincial Congress and of the Committee of Safety of New Jersey, for years 1775-6, his name is frequently mentioned. After the Revolution he represented Monmouth county four years in the General Assembly and in 1784 was Speaker of the House. I cannot find out where he is buried or date of his death. Like Captain Joshua Huddy, Captain Chadwick, and some others that served the people faithfully, the Republic has forgotten their graves.

In Book M of Deeds, pages 161-165 in Monmouth County Clerk's office is record of two deeds from Daniel Hendrickson of Shrewsbury township. Both deeds are dated April 30, 1791. One conveys to Cornelius Luyster of Middletown, ten acres of land, being part of the lands which William Hendrickson, late of the township of Middletown, died seized of and which said Daniel Hendrickson claims title in part as an heir-at-law of his father, William Hendrickson, aforesaid, and in part by a quit claim deed from Catharine Hendrickson, (Remsen) daughter of said William Hendrickson deceased, as one of his heirs at law. The ten acre tract is described as beginning at a maple tree on the west side of Mahoras brook, adjoining Luyster's land and the northeast corner of Daniel Hendrickson's cleared land.

The second deed conveys to Peter Luyster a tract of woodland containing 20 acres, which William Hendrickson died seized of, and goes on to set out Daniel's title as in first deed. This land is described as beginning at the corner of the ten acre tract conveyed to Cornelius Luyster, and runs along line of this lot to Mahoras brook, and along said brook, etc.

In Book L of Deeds, p. 97, etc., Monmouth county clerk's office, is record of a deed dated April 4, 1797, from Colonel Daniel Hendrickson of Shrewsbury township to Daniel Hendrickson, Jr.,† of Upper Freehold, and John S. Holmes of Middletown, in which it is set out that said Daniel Hendrickson, Sr., being justly indebted to several persons in the sum of £1,720 ($8,600), and the said Daniel Hendrickson, Jr., (his son) and John S. Holmes, (his son-in-law) being engaged jointly with him, said

---

†In Book M of Deeds, page 473, etc., Monmouth county clerk's office is record of a deed from Jacob Hendrickson and John Polhemus, executors of John Polhemus, deceased, to Garret Wyckoff of Upper Freehold, dated March 18, 1794, which sets out that John Polhemus, late of Upper Freehold, deceased, was seized of 213 68-100 acres in Upper Freehold, by deed from James Holmes dated May 1, 1762, and that said John Polhemus, by his will dated June 7, 1788, authorized and directed his executors to sell the land generally described as bounded westward by Daniel Hendrickson's land in part and in part by Joel Clayton, Timothy Hankins, and Amos Miller; easterly by said Garret Wyckoff's land, and northerly by John Britton's mill pond and brook below said pond. This deed is witnessed by Daniel Hendrickson, Jr., and Samuel Imlay, and it shows where Daniel Hendrickson, Jr., lived in Upper Freehold.

Daniel Hendrickson, Sr., for the payment of said sum, he thereby sells and conveys all his real estate to them to secure them for these liabilities, etc. In same Book L of Deeds, p. 100, etc., is record of another deed from Daniel Hendrickson, Sr., of Shrewsbury township, to Daniel Hendrickson, Jr., of Upper Freehold, John S. Holmes and John Holmes of Middletown township, Catharine Remsen, widow of Jacob Remsen of New York city, and Rutgers VanBrunt of Kings county, L. I. This deed dated April 5, 1797, sets out that Daniel Hendrickson, Sr., grantor, being justly indebted to Daniel Hendrickson, Jr., of Upper Freehold, *John S. Holmes and John Holmes of Middletown, Catharine Remsen and Rutgers VanBrunt of New York, does sell and convey them in settlement of said indebtedness all his real estate, consisting of several tracts of land at and near Tinton Falls in Shrewsbury township. Then follows description of these lands and statement: That the first two tracts at Tinton Falls, on which grist and saw mill stands, he claims title under a deed from Tunis Vanderveer dated May 10, 1773. The third tract by deed from John Morris dated May 25, 1783, and fourth tract by deed from Nicholas VanBrunt dated May 1, 1784.

Like many other officers of the Revolution he served his country at a sacrifice. The seven years of war and confusion ruined his business. The raids of the refugees of which he was a victim two or three times, caused him great loss. The depreciation of the continental currency had also depreciated the value of his real estate, and there was no sale for real estate except

---

* John S. Holmes left a will, proved August 25, 1821, recorded at Freehold in Book B, p. 257, etc. Provides for his wife Sarah. Gives $7,500 to each of his four daughters, together with his grist mill and carding machines, viz: Mary, who married Albert VanBrunt; Catharine, who married Daniel H. Ellis of Freehold; Emma, who married George Taylor of Freehold, and Eleanor, who married Charles Hasbrouck. All residue of his property, both real and personal, he gives to his two sons, Daniel and John H. in fee.

at a ruinous sacrifice. He was thus compelled to make this transfer of all his lands to these near relatives in order to prevent an entire loss under a forced or sheriff's sale.

Colonel Daniel Hendrickson died soon after this assignment, probably discouraged and broken hearted over his troubles and sorrows. When and where he died is unknown. Neither is his place of burial known. He lies in an unknown and unmarked grave. Such is the gratitude of a republic.

We find Daniel Hendrickson and Elizabeth, his wife, of Upper Freehold, and John S. Holmes and Sarah, his wife of Middletown, by deed dated August 9, 1799, recorded in Book M of Deeds, p. 98, etc., Monmouth clerk's office, conveying part of this real estate to Colonel Barnes Smock, viz: that tract at Tinton Falls on which grist and saw mill and other buildings stand with benefit of millpond and stream as far as Colonel Daniel Hendrickson's, dec'd, right extended. Also a tract of 12 50-100 acres near Tinton Falls, which tracts with other lands were sold by Lewis Morris Ashfield, Esq., to Jacob VanDerveer by deed dated May 5, 1762, and then sold at sheriff's sale January 28, 1772, to Tunis Vanderveer and by him sold to Col. Daniel Hendrickson by deed dated May 10, 1773, and by him to above grantors by deed dated April 5, 1797; also 96 65-100 acres on west side of the road from Tinton Falls to Middletown.

In Book N of Deeds, p. 184, etc., is record of a deed from Daniel Hendrickson and Elizabeth, his wife, of Upper Freehold, to John S. Holmes of Middletown, a merchant, conveying to him two tracts of land at Tinton Falls, which his father, Colonel Daniel Hendrickson, deceased, owned in his lifetime.

In Book O of Deeds, p. 109, etc, is record of a deed from Daniel Hendrickson and Elizabeth, his wife, of Upper Freehold, and John S. Holmes and Sarah, his wife, of Middletown, to Jacob Hubbard, dated April 25, 1800, conveying 19½ acres of land which Col. Daniel Hendrickson owned in his lifetime.

ACCOUNT OF A RAID OF TORY REFUGEES IN THE YEAR 1779.

The following account of a raid on Col. Daniel Hendrickson at Tinton Falls by a party of refugees is taken from files of the New Jersey Gazette now in our state library in Trenton:

"On June 9, 1779, a party of about 50 refugees landed in Monmouth and marched to Tinton Falls undiscovered, where they surprised and carried off Col. Daniel Hendrickson, Col. Wyckoff, Capt. Chadwick, Capt. McKnight with several privates of the militia, and drove off sheep and horned cattle. About thirty of our militia hastily collected and made some resistance, but were repulsed with loss of two men killed and ten wounded. Loss of enemy unknown."

Thomas Chadwick and Richard McKnight were both captains of the Monmouth militia and the latter was a son-in-law of Col. Daniel Hendrickson. Auke Hendrickson was a miller by occupation and a lieutenant in Captain Peter Wyckoff's company from Upper Freehold. At this time he was employed in Col. Hendrickson's grist mill at Tinton Falls. Col. Hendrickson had collected quite a magazine of powder, arms and other military stores at Tinton Falls for the use of our county troops. Besides he had ground a large quantity of flour and meal for use of the American army. It is said that he had borrowed from his relatives, Mrs. Catharine Remsen and his father-in-law, Van-Brunt, in New York, £1,000 ($5,000), which he had used in the purchase of these stores. The spies of the enemy had carried information to the refugees on Sandy Hook and hence this raid, which entailed great pecuniary loss to Col. Hendrickson.

The notorious James Moody in an account of his career, dictated by him and published in London, England, after the close of our Revolutionary War, gives his version of this raid.

He says that on June 10, 1779, he was at Sandy Hook and in command of sixteen men. There he asked a friend named Hutchinson, who had six men and some guides, to assist him on an expedition against the rebels in Monmouth county.

They started from Sandy Hook for Shrewsbury village and eluding the rebel guards reached a place called the Falls undiscovered, and surprised and made prisoners, one colonel, one lieutenant-colonel, one major, two captains and other persons of lesser note. They destroyed a considerable magazine of powder and arms. With their prisoners and such stores as they could carry or bring off, Hutchinson took charge of, while Moody and his men remained in the rear. They were pursued by double their numbers. Moody with his sixteen men made a stand and kept up such a sharp fire on the rebels as to hold them back, while Hutchinson moved on with the prisoners and plunder.

After Hutchinson had got a considerable distance ahead, Moody and his men would fall back. When they reached another good place they would make another stand, until in this way they reached Black Point (now Seabright). Here they transported their prisoners and plunder over the inlet. The rebels were reinforced by ten men and made a determined attack, in which Captain Chadwick and Lieutenant Auke Hendrickson were shot dead. Moody says there was something peculiarly shocking in the death of the rebel captain. He was shot through by Moody while with most bitter oaths and threats of vengeance, after having once missed fire he was again leveling his gun at him. That after three men were killed and a number of others lay wounded, the rebels raised a flag of truce and asked for cessation of hostilities to remove their dead and wounded. This was agreed to on condition that they were allowed to remove and take away all their plunder. Moody says their goods and stores taken were sold for £500 ($2,500) and the money all divided among the men who were with him in this raid.

Moody may have had only 16 men of his own and six of Hutchinson's when he started but he had at least fifty when he reached Tinton Falls before daylight. They found our men in bed and wholly unprepared. They threw a large quantity of powder in the mill pond and broke the guns. They seized all the horses and wagons they could find at Tinton Falls and vicinity and loaded them with a large quantity of stores, meal and flour from the mill, together with all the provisions and goods of value they could find. They drove off all the sheep and cattle on the farms around there, besides slaughtering several hogs, whose carcasses they took off in one of the wagons. They collected all this plunder and moved off down the road towards Shrewsbury village before our militia could gather. Then not over thirty men were in our force when they began their pursuit. They overtook the rear guards commanded by Moody in person somewhere in the vicinity of what is now Fair Haven. He, however, had all his prisoners stationed close by his men, so that our people could not fire, without endangering their lives as much as those of the refugees.

Thus holding back our force he allowed Hutchinson with his train of wagons, cattle and sheep to get well in advance. Then falling back, still with the prisoners as shields to his men, he slowly followed. In this way they reached Black Point. There our people had ten more men to join them, and made a sharp attack on their flank while they were getting their plunder over the inlet. In the confusion Captain Chadwick and Lieutenant Auke Hendrickson broke loose from the enemy and ran over to our men. Lieutenant Hendrickson was a man of fiery temper and Captain Chadwick also was very excitable and passionate under provocation. The tantalizing and unfair way in which they had been used and treated while prisoners, by Moody had exasperated both to the verge of insanity. As soon as Lieutenant Hendrickson reached our line he grabbed a musket which had been discharged, and at once turned and ran towards Moody with loud threats and imprecations for his cowardly usage. His gun, of course, missed fire and he was shot down by Moody. Captain Chadwick, who had also turned on them, was killed at the same time by some of the other refugees.

Some ten of our men were also wounded which made any further effort useless. A flag of truce was raised and Moody agreed to allow the removal of our dead and wounded provided they were permitted to carry off all their plunder. Like Captain Joshua Huddy, Captain Dennis, Lieutenant Whitlock, and many other patriots of our Revolution, who gave up their lives for American independence, Captain Chadwick and Lieutenant Auke Hendrickson lie in unknown and unmarked graves. Surely this is a reproach and a shame to the people of Monmouth county.

Daniel Hendrickson, son of Col. Daniel Hendrickson and Catharine VanBrunt, his wife, married Elizabeth, daughter of Barzillai Grover. He resided in Upper Freehold township and carried on a grist mill located on Doctor's Creek in that township. I think this mill was at Red Valley, although I may be mistaken as to that. They had the following children:

William, born June 2, 1782, married and removed to one of the western states.

Barzillai, born February 19, 1784, married Elizabeth Horsefull. He owned and conducted the Union hotel at Freehold during the thirties of last century.

Daniel, born May 19, 1786, died unmarried. His will was proved September 18, 1862, and recorded in Book G of Wills, page 470 at Freehold. Makes a bequest to his sister Theodosia, wife of Forman Hendrickson, and if dead, to her daughter Eliza, wife of Jacob Ellis. He gives to George Imlay $100, and residue of his property to his nephews, Enoch Hendrickson and Richard M. Hendrickson.

Joseph, born March 14, 1788.

James G., born February 19, 1791, married March 3, 1813, Hannah Morris.

Samuel, born July 26, 1793, married Phoebe Mount.

Theodosia, born November 2, 1795, married Forman, son of Jacob Hendrickson and Elizabeth Mount, his wife.

Richard Howell, born November 2, 1795, married Lyde Perrine.

Katharine, born June 29, 1797, married Peter Imlay.

John B., born January 26, 1799, married Parmilla Grover.

Enoch, born April 7, 1802, married Achsah Parker.

Pierson, born July 31, 1803, married August 7, 1823, Sarah VanDorn. This last son resided many years at Tinton Falls, where he carried on a country store.

Elizabeth Hendrickson, the mother of these ten boys and two girls, made her will January 27, 1843, proved December 6, 1851, recorded at Freehold in Book F of Wills, page 107, etc.

CHILDREN OF DANIEL HENDRICKSON AND CATHARINE VANDYKE, HIS WIFE.

Annetje, (Ann) the eighth child of above named parents, was baptized December 30, 1711, married 1732, William, son of Jacob Couwenhoven and Saartje Schenck, his wife. Their names appear as communicants on records of the Dutch church in 1741 as follows: "Wilm Couwenhoven and Antje Hendrikze, his wife."
They had three children, viz:

Saartje (Sarah) born in 1733, married Jacob, (born 1730) son of William Wyckoff and Agnes VanDorn, his wife. Their license was granted January 7, 1754. She died August 25, 1796, and her husband March 5, 1812, according to their headstones in Tennent church yard.
Daniel, baptized March 30, 1737, married August 23, 1757, Helena, daughter of George Taylor, and died December 26, 1808, according to inscription on his tombstone in Lippet and Taylor burying ground on the old Daniel J. Hendrickson farm, now owned by the Morfords at east end of Middletown village. An old Bible with name of "Rebecca Covenhoven" written on front leaf, as owner, contains the following family record:
"Daniel Covenhoven, born January 27, 1737. Helena Covenhoven, his wife, was born February 10, 1737, married August 23, 1757.
Anne Covenhoven, their daughter, was born July 9, 1758, about nine o'clock in the forenoon.
Rebecka Covenhoven, born. March 27, 1761, about five o'clock in the afternoon.
William Covenhoven, born April 7, 1763, about five o'clock in the morning.
George Covenhoven, born December 13, 1767, about three o'clock in the afternoon.
Daniel G. Conover and Sarah Ann Cooper were married December 16, 1818."
Jacob, third child, was baptized October 14, 1739; no other record.

William Conover, as name is now spelled, the father of above three children, died intestate in 1742. Letters of administration on his estate were granted October 17, 1742, to his widow, Ann, his brother Ruliph, and his brother-in-law, William Hendrickson. The widow, however, did not remain long in mourning for she married March 17, 1744, William Couwenhoven, (born July 20, 1700; died November 10, 1755) son of Cornelius Couwenhoven and Margaret Schenck, his wife, of Pleasant Valley. He, too, had lost his first wife, Jannetje Wyckoff and buried her by his father in the Schenck-Couwenhoven cemetery.
By this second marriage there were two children, a son and daughter, viz:
Cornelius, born February 11, baptized April 7, 1746; married January 13, 1767, Mary (born December 6, 1740, died January 3, 1860), daughter of Hendrick Hendrickson and Neeltje Schenck, his wife and heretofore mentioned. He died October 10, 1806, aged 60 years, 7 months, 27 days, according to his headstone in Schenck-Couwenhoven yard. His will is recorded in Book A of Wills at Freehold.
By Mary Hendrickson he had following four children:

Anne, baptized December 6, 1767; married October 13, 1785, Abram VanHorne.
Nelly, baptized February 24, 1771; married December 14, 1790, Cornelius VanHorne.
Lydia, baptized December 20, 1778; married January 22, 1807, Daniel Polhemus of Middlesex county, N. J.
William Hendrick, baptized June 2, 1782; died unmarried September 26, 1805, and is buried by his father, grandfather, and great-grandfather in Schenck-Couwenhoven yard.

Catharine, the only daughter, was baptized April 16, 1749; married January 15, 1767, Nicholas VanBrunt, son of Nicholas VanBrunt and Geesye Hendrickson, his wife, whose names appear as communicants in records of the Dutch church in 1731. This Geesye Hendrickson was a sister of Daniel and William Hendrickson, the pioneer settlers. Nicholas VanBrunt was Sheriff of Monmouth county in 1778. He removed all the prisoners in our county jail to Morris county before the British army reached Freehold in June, 1778. He and Colonel Daniel Hendrickson were deputies to the Provincial Congress of New Jersey from Shrewsbury township in 1775. He was an active and zealous patriot during the Revolution and a Captain in the militia.
By Catharine Couwenhoven, his wife, he had following children:

Cornelius, baptized July 23, 1769.
Nicholas, baptized August 4, 1771.
Antje, baptized May 8, 1774.
Mary, baptized June 25, 1775.
Hendrick, baptized April 5, 1778.
Daniel Covenhoven, baptized April 30, 1780; died young.
Sarah Wyckoff, baptized September 28, 1783.
Daniel Conover, baptized November 18, 1787.

Sheriff Nicholas VanBrunt, a few

years after the close of the Revolutionary War, sold his farm near Tinton Falls to Col. Daniel Hendrickson and removed with his family to Cherry Valley, New York, where he lived the rest of his life.

Francyntje, (Frances) the ninth child of Daniel Hendrickson and Catharine VanDyke, his wife, married 1731, Teunis (born June 15, 1704, died June 10, 1797), son of Denyse Denyse and Helen Cortelyou, his wife, of New Utrecht, L. I. She was his second wife, as he first married Catharine, a daughter of Hendrick VanDyke, by whom he had one daughter named Helena, born March 14, 1728; married April 17, 1759, Samuel Forman (born November 13, 1713; baptized February 13, 1714; died January 18, 1792), a son of Jonathan Forman and Margaret Wyckoff, his wife. She died January 20, 1789, and is buried by her husband in old burying ground at Mt. Pleasant or Freneau station.

Teunis Denyse married for his third wife, December 2, 1779, Rachel, daughter of Garret Schenck and Neeltje Voorhees, his wife, and the widow of Geisbert Longstreet and Jacob VanDorn. It was the third venture of both in the lottery of matrimony. History not only repeats itself with nations, but with individuals, for we have today in Monmouth county a lineal descendant of Teunis Denise, who not only bears the same name, but has been married three times and whose second wife was also a Hendrickson.

Tunis Denyse made his will April 2, 1792, proved January 16, 1798, and recorded in Book 37 of Wills, page 350 at Trenton, N. J. His son Daniel and son-in-law, John Forman, are named as executors. His sons-in-law were among the most influential and prominent of the patriots during the revolution.

Francyntje Hendrickson and Tunis Denyse, her husband, had the following children:

Tryntje, (Catharine) born May 8, 1732; died September 8, 1771, married Garret Hendrickson, (born January 22, 1734; died December 2, 1801) who has already been mentioned in a former article.

Eleanor, baptized May 26, 1734; married John Forman, (born 1731, died 1811) son of Samuel Forman and Mary, his wife. Their license was granted May 2, 1752. John Forman served as one of our county judges. She died in 1796.

Anna, born June 16, 1736; married June 16, 1757, David Forman, (born October 1, 1733; died March 30, 1812) son of Jonathan Forman and Margaret Wyckoff, his wife. Their license was granted June 9, 1757, according to records in secretary of state's office. She died September 9, 1798, and is buried in Tennent church yard. David Forman was Brigadier General of our Monmouth militia during the Revolution and one of the most energetic and active of the patriotic leaders. On account of his swarthy complexion he was called Black David Forman.

Nuis or Denyse baptized January 4, 1738, died young.

Jannetje (Jane) born August 19, baptized October 2, 1740, married Cornelius R., (born July 29, baptized September 14, 1740, died July 12, 1796) son of Roelof Cornelius Couwenhoven and Sarah Voorhees, his wife. Their license was granted December 5, 1758. She died March 26, 1799, and is buried by her husband in Schenck-Couwenhoven yard. This couple had ten children, three boys and seven daughters, who all married well. *

Fammetje (Phoebe) born August 11, baptized September 4, 1743; married October 19, 1765, Rev. Benjamin DuBois, the famous pastor for over 50 years of the Monmouth Dutch church. He was born March 30, 1739, and died August 12, 1727. She died January 7, 1839, and is buried by her husband in yard of Marlboro Dutch church.

Denyse, baptized December 22, 1745; married April 17, 1768, Margaret, daughter of Richard and Sara Francis, who died April 18, 1770, aged 22 years, 10 months, 24 days, according to her headstone in Topanemus burying ground where she is interred by her parents. He married for his second wife Catharine, daughter of Garret Garretse Schenck and Jannetje Williamse Couwenhoven, his wife. She was baptized September 5, 1756. Denyse Denyse was a major of our militia and also a judge in our county courts during and subsequent to the Revolution.

Daniel, baptized May 15, 1748, married first April 18, 1771, Jane Schenck, who was born in 1754; married second, Mary Stillwell. Bur-

---

* Marriages of the ten children of Cornelius R. Couwenhoven and Jane Denise, his wife, from records of the Dutch church.

Francinke, to Hendrick Hendrickson, May 13, 1781.

Teunis to Hannah VanBrockle, March 19, 1783.

Sarah, to Robert Ashton, June 21, 1783.

Mary, to Samuel Forman, March 12, 1789.

Rulif, to Sarah Vanderveer, January 12, 1789.

Catherine, to John Vanderveer, April 7, 1791.

Margaret, to Teunis Hobburt (Hubbard) January 5, 1797.

Eleanor, to Caleb Stillwell, December 10, 1797.

Jane, to Matthias or Martin Covenhoven, March 10, 1804. She was his first wife and died December 12, 1820, aged 40 years, 9 months, 6 days.

Cornelius R., to Mary Stoutenburg, March 9, 1807.

Cornelius R. Covenhoven died April 11, 1817, aged 33 years, 11 months, 8 days. Mary Stoutenburg, his wife, died April 29, 1861, aged 74 years, 24 days. They were the parents of Holmes Conover, who married Caroline, daughter of James G. Crawford, and died May 22, 1860, aged 52 years, 4 months, 13 days. He was sheriff of Monmouth county. His wife died August 28, 1843, aged 24 years. Buried in Schenck-Couwenhoven cemetery, but afterward removed to Holmdel cemetery.

ied in old yard near East Freehold.

Mary, born July 9, 1750; married July 31, 1767, John Schenck, the famous leader of our militia during the Revolution. He was born August 28, 1745, and died August 28, 1834, on the farm in Pleasant Valley where his grandson, David Schenck, now resides. She died July 15, 1829. Both were first buried in Schenck and Couwenhoven yard, but with many others have been since removed, or rather what little was left of their bodies has been removed and their tombstones set up in the Holmdel cemetery.

John Schenck, who married this youngest daughter, was next to Gen. David Forman, his brother-in-law, one of the most active and daring of the officers of our county militia. So troublesome was he that the enemy offered a reward of fifty guineas for his capture or death.

An attempt to capture the notorious tory, mayor of New York city, David Matthews, by some Monmouth men led by John Schenck and William Marriner, was perhaps the primary cause of this offer. This was a very bold move and failed of success through the absence of Mayor Matthews from home that night. He had been accidentally detained in New York city.

The kidnapping of prominent patriots in Monmouth by raiding bands of refugees was of frequent occurrence, and their treatment as prisoners of the harshest kind. It is said that Cunningham often boasted when in liquor, that he had used up more rebels by starvation and neglect than the whole British army had killed by their bullets and bayonets. At all events reprisals or retaliations of some kind were the only means left to compel decent treatment and exchange of prisoners. Accordingly it was resolved to capture David Matthews and two or three other prominent loyalists who resided at Flatbush, L. I., and within the lines of the British army. John Schenck had a number of relatives living in the vicinity of Flatbush, and when a boy had often visited them and so became well acquainted with the country and roads. Marriner presented this plan to the council of safety who sanctioned it.

Nearly every neighborhood through which a large stream or creek flowed into Raritan river, and from Cheesequake creek to Compton's creek along the Bayshore had its association of men to own and man what was called a whaleboat. Raritan Bay was wholly commanded by the guns of the British men of war so our people were obliged to hide their boats up in some swamp or ravine. The large barges or gun boats were kept well up Raritan river. The usual crew of a whaleboat on the patriot side was fifteen men, of whom one steered and gave commands while the others rowed. Picked men of great physical strength and endurance were selected. The least sign of cowardice on part of a man led to his instant dismissal from the crew. They were trained to row without noise and could propel the boat at the rate of twelve miles an hour. Each man was armed with a cutlass and pistols, and the boat supplied with a few pikes and hooks on long poles, a few grappling irons, lanterns and heavy blankets.

These boats were about thirty feet in length with flat bottoms to float in shoal water, wide in the centre with high sides to carry big loads, and pointed on both ends. They were called whaleboats, but altogether different from the small boats used in the whale fishery. They were built of cedar or some other light wood so that they could be lifted from the water and carried over land by the crew and concealed in some swamp or ravine up in the woods. These boats were originally built to carry on a secret traffic with the enemy and smuggle goods back and forth. A whale boat loaded with butter, eggs, poultry and other farm truck, in summer, and hay, grain, firewood, etc., in winter, slipping out of the inlets, or rivers on our coast were safe from capture on the ocean or bay unless intercepted by the whale-boats of the patriots. Coming back with the specie or other valuable goods after trading with the enemy, they were valuable prizes to our people when captured. Transports loaded with munitions of war and other supplies for the British army in occupation of New York were constantly coming and going out of Raritan Bay. A constant demand existed for fresh provisions on part of the people within the British lines and there was a constant traffic to supply this demand.

An association of men existed through this region back of Middletown Point, as Matawan was then called, who had two whale-boats hid in the ravines southeast of the village. These men were seen by John Schenck and agreed to help him and Marriner in their raid. The first cloudy or dark night was agreed on. This happened the second Saturday in June, 1778. Eleven of the regular crew met Marriner and Schenck at Brown's Point late in the afternoon. The boat was taken from its hiding place and launched in the Creek a little after sunset. The sky was overcast with clouds and there was every indi-

EARLY DUTCH SETTLERS OF MONMOUTH. 141

cation of an easterly storm. They rowed directly across to Staten Island, and guided by the lights which shone out from the houses on land skirted the shore until they reached the Narrows. Here they rowed across and landed some distance above what is now Fort Hamilton. Leaving two men in charge of the boat and guided by John Schenck they went over to Flatbush. They reached here about midnight and effected a noiseless entrance into the dwelling of Mayor Matthews. The women were placed in one room under guard, but the mayor was not at home. They took however, four of his negro slaves. At the next house they captured a Major Moncrieff and a Mr. Bache. With these two white men and four negroes they got back to their boat without exciting the least alarm. They rowed back and reached the mouth of Matawan creek with their six prisoners by daylight next morning. A newspaper of that day in speaking of this raid says they traveled over fifty miles between six o'clock Saturday night and six o'clock next morning and behaved with the greatest prudence and bravery. This spiriting away of prominent men at night from their homes within the British lines naturally aroused great alarm. No one felt safe or secure against capture and same treatment as they gave the American prisoners. Their fears made them more humane.

Following is the British account of the Flatbush raid from the journal of Lieut. Col. Stephen Kemble, published in N. Y. Hist. Collection for year 1883, Vol. 1, pages 151-2.

"Sunday, June 14, 1778. About 2 o'clock this morning, a party, said to be about 20 men, some armed, others not, with faces blacked, took off Major Moncreiffe and Mr. Bache. Attempted the Mayor, Mr. Matthews' house, but it being well fastened, and a shot being fired, which they apprehended might give the alarm, induced them to go off, with the two first mentioned gentlemen, supposed into Jersey, but at this time no certain account can be given. All else is quiet."

In this account the Mayor is left out as though he was home and his house fastened, but the truth is he was not at home, and if a shot had been fired it would have created an alarm as the British sentinels were posted all around for Flatbush was within their lines.

Jannetje, (Jane) the tenth child and youngest of the seven daughters of Daniel Hendrickson, was born and brought up on the homestead at Holmdel. She married Ruliph, (born March 1, 1712) a son of Jacob Couwenhoven and Saartje Schenck, his wife, their nearest neighbors. She had known him from her earliest recollections. They had played and romped together, sung Dutch nursery songs and followed the customs and usages which prevailed at that time among their own people. The same characteristics, manners and usages marked them as those described by Miss Gertrude Lefferts Vanderbilt in her book called "The Social History of Flatbush and the Manners and Customs of the Dutch in Kings County, L. I." They were the children of these Long Island people and were like them in all respects, for the "Dutch were not given to change but were stable in all their ways." It was not until the Revolutionary war tore up the foundations of society and government, that there was any great change in families and classes. Up to this time the Dutch language was generally used in family intercourse or the home life. There are a few persons now living, born and brought up in Pleasant Valley, Holmdel township, who can remember when children, of hearing and singing the words of the following Dutch nursery song which Miss Vanderbilt has published in her book:

Trip, a trop, a tronjes,
De Varkens in de boonjes,
De Koejes in de Klaver,
De paarden in de haver,
De eenjes in de waterplass,
So groot myn Kleine Claus-was."

These lullabies and a few words like "stoep," "blickey," "paas," "skipper" and "baas" (boss) are the last lingering echoes of the mother tongue once spoken by those old settlers in Monmouth who came from Kings county on Long Island.

There is a wide difference in the spirit and sentiment expressed in these lullabies of the Dutch, from those of the English, or Mother Goose melodies as called.

The former represented people and animals comfortable and contented, pleasant associations and memories, and cheerful and sunny prospects. Or they inculcated some lesson of industry, economy, faithfulness or other everyday virtue. Their saint Santa Claus was jolly and benevolent, always doing generous and kindly acts. But childhood and youthful days soon pass. On the 12th of August A. D. 1741, Jannetje Hendrickson married Ruliph Couwenhoven. Their marriage license is published in full on page 34 of Wells' Memorial Address at Brick Church. It was signed by Lewis Morris so prominent in the early history of Monmouth county, but at that time Governor of New Jersey. These licenses are all recorded in secretary of state's office at Trenton and in annexed note is a list from the records of all licenses issued to the Hendricksons and Hendricks in Monmouth county, between 1748 and 1772. Jannetje and Ruliph Couwenhoven her husband, had three children, viz:

Sarah, bapt. August 12, 1742, married in 1763 Benjamin (baptized October 10, 1742) son of Benjamin VanCleaf and Helina or Neeltje Couwenhoven, his wife.
Daniel, baptized January 15, 1744. No other knowledge.
Catrina, baptized Feb. 16, 1746, married February 28, 1765, David (baptized September 25, 1748) son of Tunis Vanderveer and Aeltje Garretse Schenck, his wife. This couple had a son Tunis, who married December 12, 1792, Margaret, a daughter of Rev. Benjamin DuBois.

Ruliph Couwenhoven died intestate in 1746. Letters of administration on his estate were granted same year to his brother, Peter Couvenhoven, and his brothers-in-law, William Hendrickson and Tunis Denise.

Jannetje, however, did not remain a widow long, for the next year, 1747, she married Peter, a son of Jan Schanck and Saartje Couwenhoven of Pleasant Valley. He had lost his first wife, Jannetje VanNostrand or Ostrandt and was ready for another. By Peter Schenck she had following children:

Roelef P., known as "Long Ruly" born December 27, 1748, baptized January 22, 1749, married Elizabeth Gordon (born December 8, 1757, died August 15, 1837) and died November 26, 1814. Both buried in Tennent church yard.
Jannetje, born June 1, bapt. July 28, 1751; married December 5, 1769, John Walter (born June 11, 1730, died October 11, 1775, according to his headstone in Schenck-Couwenhoven cemetery) and died January 6, 1774. A son of this couple named John Walter, is buried by them in above yard and his headstone gives date of his death October 13, 1837, aged 66 years and 11 months.
Antje, baptized September 30, 1753, married Garret Janse Couwenhoven. She was his second wife and died April 5, 1803, according to her headstone in yard of Marlboro Brick Church. Her children have been already named in Conover genealogy.
Leah, baptized November 9, 1755, married November 30, 1775, John, (baptized August 26, 1750) son of Benjamin VanCleaf and Neeltje or Helena Couwenhoven, his wife.
Francyntje, baptized March 7, 1762, married February 5, 1803, William Nicolas.
Neeltje, baptized June 17, 1759. No other record.

Hendrickson marriage licenses as recorded at Trenton, in office of Secretary of State between 1748 and 1772.

Elizabeth, Monmouth, John Vanderbilt, Staaten Island, 20 May 1754.
Catharine, Monmouth, Jacob Remsen, Sr., New York, 11 Aug. 1749.
Mary, Monmouth, Corn's Conover, Monmouth, 12 July 1767.
Neeltje, (widow) Monmouth, Elias Golden, Monmouth, 30 July 1761.
Abram, Kings Co., Anna van Kirk, Monmouth, 23 May 1759.
Albert, Monmouth, Johanna Mills, Monmouth, 3 Jan. 1755.
Coonradt, Monmouth, Mary English, Monmouth, 18 June 1759.
Cornelius, Monmouth, Mary Thorn, 28 Jan. 1767.
Daniel, Middlesex, Eleanor van Mater, Monmouth, 14 Nov. 1758.
Daniel, jr., Monmouth, Mary Schenck, Monmouth, 2 Sept. 1767.
Garret, Monmouth, Catharine Denice, Monmouth, 8 Dec. 1755.
Hendrick, Middletown, Sara Thomson, Middletown, 3 April 1751.
Hendrick, Monmouth, Ledy Conover, Monmouth, 7 March 1757.
Jacob, Monmouth, Elizabeth Mount, Monmouth, 2 May 1771.
Tobias, Rebecca Coward, 21 March 1762.
William, Charity Robinson, Monmouth, 21 Dec. 1756.
William, Monmouth, Mary Douglas, 22 April 1762.
William, Monmouth, Rachel Longstreet, 22 Feb. 1768.
Hendricks, Abraham, Monmouth, Mary Wykoff, Monmouth, 17 Dec. 1754.
Hendricks, Coonradt, Monmouth, Mercy Knott, 17 June 1763.
Hendricks, John, Monmouth, Phoebe Smith, 31 Oct. 1759.

Hendrickson marriages from records of Dutch church, prior to 1825:

Jannetje, to Roelof Covenhoven, Aug. 12, 1741.
Daniel, to Catherine Covenhoven, Dec. 22, 1743.
Ann, to William Covenhoven, March 17, 1744.
Mary, to Cornelius Covenhoven, Jan. 13, 1767.
Willimpe, to Aaron Longstreet, Nov. 9, 1778.
I endrick, to Francinke Covenhoven, May 13, 1781.
Cornelius, to Lydia Vanderbilt, March 24, 1785.
Catharine, to Cornelius VanDerhove, Nov. 29, 1785.
Denise, to Anne Schenck, March 24, 1786.
Hendrick, to Phoebe VanMater, Jan. 20, 1791.
John, to Mary Lloyd, Nov. 27, 1793.
Ida, to Joseph Kearney VanMater, Sept. 10, 1794.
Catharine, to Peter Brewer, Sept. 18, 1794;
William, to Elizabeth Vanderrype, Nov. 26, 1797.
Mary, to William VanMater, Dec. 24, 1797.
Catherine, to Jacobus Hubbert (Hubbard) May 2, 1798.
Anne, to Garret Terhune, Oct. 3, 1799.
Lydia, to Hendrick Brewer, March 16, 1802.

Garret D., to Jane Hendrickson, March 23, 1808.
William H., to Eleanor DuBois, Jan. 2, 1812.
Pierson, to Sarah VanDorn, Aug. 7, 1823.
Cyrenius, to Ida VanMater, Sept. 18, 1823.

Hendrickson marriages from Book A of marriages in Monmouth clerk's office:

Page 8—William, to Hannah Middleton, Feb. 7, 1796.
Page 35—Daniel, to Sarah Covenhoven, Dec. 21, 1797.
Page 40—Cornelius, to Catherine Reynolds, both of Freehold township, Sept. 26, 1799.
Page 45—William, to Eleanor Emmons, both of Freehold township, April 4, 1800.
Page 59—Cornelius, to Anne Smith (widow) April 11, 1802.
Page 59—Hendricks, John, to Christianna VanDeventer, Aug. 15, 1802.
Page 69—Hendrickson, Joseph, to Catherine Anderson, both of Freehold township, Nov. 20, 1803.
Page 96—Peter, to Catherine Cox, both of Upper Freehold township, Dec. 19, 1807.
Page 85—Hendrick, of Middletown, to Helenah Longstreet of Shrewsbury township, Oct. 18, 1806.
Page 88—Samuel, to Deborah Combs, Dec. 6, 1808.
Page 89—William, to Ruth Horsefull, June 3, 1804.
Page 148—Jacob, to Sarah Vanderveer, Feb. 18, 1810.
Page 148—Tobias, to Idah Conover, Feb. 10, 1813.
Page 160—James G., to Hannah Morris, March 3, 1813.
Page 161—Daniel, to Deborah Tilton, Jan. 12, 1813.
Page 209—William, to Sarah Luyster, May 8, 1816.
Page 215—Joseph, to Elizabeth Hendrickson, June 1, 1816.

Daniel, the eleventh and youngest child of the first Daniel, was born, lived, died and was buried on the homestead at Holland in the present township of Holmdel, which was devised to him by his father. He was born January 5, 1723, baptized May 5, 1723, married December 22, 1743, Catherine (born June 2, 1720, died May 5, 1810,) the youngest child of Cornelius Couwenhoven and Margaretta Schenck his wife, and died intestate June 24, 1788. The records in our secretary of state's office show that letters of administration on his estate were granted to his widow, July 31, 1788.

The headstones at their graves in the family burying ground on the old homestead, give their names, dates of death and respective ages. Their son Hendrick, grandson William H. and great-grandson, the late Hon. William Henry Hendrickson, who all lived and died on this farm, are interred in this same burying ground.

Daniel Hendrickson and his wife Catherine, with his eldest sister Geesye, and youngest sister Jannetje, joined the Dutch church of Monmouth together in 1747. From this time to his death Daniel Hendrickson was very zealous and active in church work. In his own home he conducted regularly family worship by reading the Scriptures and prayer, and when requested, at the houses of his neighbors. Sometimes when the regular minister was absent or sick he would conduct the services on Sunday from the pulpit. It is said that he could preach almost as good a sermon as the pastor himself. A sermon written by him and printed in the Dutch language was in the possession of the late Rev. Garret C. Schenck, whose first wife was his great-granddaughter. The Dutch settlers of Monmouth while not demonstrative, theatrical, or noisy in their religion or worship were nevertheless firm and practical believers in an everyday Providence.

"Trust in the Lord with all thine heart, and lean not unto thine own understanding," was a real conviction in their minds. Daniel Hendrickson voiced these convictions and sentiments so often, that he became known as "Dominie Dan'll Hendrickson" and was called "Dominie" to the day of his death. Those of his numerous descendants who have followed in his footsteps and who have lived and died on this fertile farm with its healthful surroundings, and beautiful scenery, and enjoyed the good will of their neighbors have good reason to say as "Dominie Daniel" did in his day:

"Except the Lord build the house, they labor in vain that build it; except the Lord keep the city, the watchman waketh but in vain."

"They that trust in the Lord, shall be as Mount Zion, which cannot be removed but abideth forever."

"The sun shall not smite thee by day, nor the moon by night."

"The Lord shall preserve thee from all evil, He shall preserve thy soul."

"The Lord shall preserve thy going out, and thy coming in from this time forth and even forever more."

Daniel Hendrickson by Catherine Couwenhoven his wife, had following children:

Daniel D., born October 29, baptized December 9, 1744; married Elizabeth (born June 21, 1763, died July 30, 1836,) a daughter of Daniel Stephenson or Stevenson, who owned the farm which lay adjacent to the Hendrickson homestead at Holland on the north, and being the same farm the late Hon. William B. Hendrickson lived and died on. Through this marriage he acquired the Stevenson farm for in the division of the real estate of his father no share was allotted to him. He probably had all the land he wanted and took his share in the personal property of his father. During the Revolutionary war he commanded a troop of light horsemen and rendered good service to the patriotic side. He has sometimes been confounded with his cousin, Colonel Daniel Hendrickson, who commanded the 3rd Regiment of Monmouth militia and resided at Tinton Falls. Like other officers of our militia he suffered great pecuniary loss through the neglect of his private business and devoting his time and means during the seven years' war to the American cause. He died November 23, 1836, and was over ninety-two years of age. He and his wife are buried on the farm where he lived. There are only four graves in this family burying ground which is near the residence of the late Hon. William B. Hendrickson, viz: these two and their son, Daniel D. and his wife, Catherine Bedle.

Daniel D. Hendrickson and Elizabeth Stevenson, his wife, had two sons, viz: Daniel D. and William D. The latter married May 8, 1816, Sarah, (born July 12, 1795, died October 15, 1821,) daughter of John P. Luyster and Anne Couwenhoven, his wife. He died January 14, 1823, aged 30 years, 2 months, 15 days, according to his tombstone in the Luyster family burying ground at Holland. His will is recorded at Freehold in B of Wills, p. 316, etc. He left surviving two children, both daughters; one of them named Anne Luyster, married James Madison Burrows, the other Elizabeth Stephenson, married Joel Stout. Daniel D., the other son, was born April 22, 1786, married Catherine, (born September 28, 1787, died January 12, 1859) daughter of Thomas Bedle, and died May 15, 1858, and was buried on the farm where he was born, lived and died. He was a Captain of a company of militia of Monmouth county, which during the war of 1812 was stationed at Sandy Hook, and was generally known or called by the people "Captain Daniel Hendrickson." He was also active in the erection of the Dutch church at Middletown village in 1836.

At the first meeting of those friendly to the erection of a Dutch church in Middletown village, held at the tavern of William Wilson in this village, February 25, 1836, he was appointed chairman of the committee to select and purchase a location for the church edifice. He was also on the committee to oversee the work. His will was made August 18, 1851, proved June 24, 1858, and recorded at Freehold in G of Wills, p. 133, etc. He gave the use of all his property to his widow for life and at her death he devised all his lands together with his personal property and "cider house and distillery" on the farm to his son, William B. Hendrickson. This devise is subject to payments of certain sums to his eight living daughters and the children of his daughter, Martha Winters, deceased, and children of his son, Daniel B. Hendrickson, deceased.

Captain Daniel D. Hendrickson by Catherine Bedle, his wife, had three sons and ten daughters. One of the sons and one daughter died young, the others grew up and married. Only one of this large family is now living, viz: Henrietta, who married Daniel, son of James Wilson, who now (1901) owns and occupies the Wilson homestead. Mrs. Henrietta Wilson is still living on this farm adjacent to the one where she was born and raised.

Daniel B., one of Captain Daniel's sons, was married and settled on a farm at Nut Swamp where he died when a young man, leaving one son, Joseph A. Hendrickson, who now (1901) owns and resides on this farm, and is one of the prominent and respected farmers of Middletown township.

William B., to whom the homestead was devised, was born February 10, 1830, married November 24, 1852, Catherine, daughter of Joseph S. Applegate, Esq. He represented Monmouth county in the Assembly in 1872-3 and was one of the influential citizens of Middletown township. A sketch of his life and a fair likeness can be seen in Ellis' History of Monmouth county. He died on the farm where he was born and always lived, a few years ago, leaving two children, a son and daughter. Cornelius, second son of Daniel Hendrickson and Catherine Couwenhoven, his wife, was born August 28, baptized October 11, 1747, married March 24, 1784, Lydia (baptized November 22, 1761, died October 22, 1822) daughter of Cornelius VanDerbilt and Margaretta Lamberson, his wife,* and died October 10, 1802. He and his wife are buried in family yard on the old Hendrickson homestead at Holland. He served during the Revolution in his brother's, Captain Daniel Hendrickson's troop of light horsemen and also under Colonel Asher Holmes. After his father's death in 1788, his share in real estate was arranged by deeds, from his sister Catherine and brothers Daniel D. and Hendrick. The principal tract deeded to him lay north of the present Daniel Wilson farm and east of Mahoras brook and extended well down toward Harmony school house.

His son, Daniel C., was born January 11, 1785, married January 12, 1813, to Deborah Tilton, by Rev. Benjamin Bennett, and died September 7, 1863. He is buried on the homestead farm at Holland. Cornelius also had two daughters, who were both baptized June 15, 1788, viz: first Margaret, who married, May 31, 1809, Daniel Herbert, died April 5, 1883. Daniel Herbert died October 6, 1836, aged 57 years, 3 months, 2 days. Both are buried in yard of Middletown Dutch church. Second Catherine, born January 8, 1788, married Murphy Tilton, died September 24, 1881, and is buried in family yard on homestead.

Daniel C. Hendrickson and Deborah Tilton had a son Cornelius, born April 17, 1814, married Mary, daughter of John G. Taylor and Elizabeth Couwenhoven, his wife. Also a son, Daniel T., born in 1822, married Deborah Ann Morris, and died March 26, 1857, aged 35 years, 1 month, 28 days, according to inscription on his headstone in yard of Middletown Dutch church.

The third child and only daughter of Daniel Hendrickson and Catherine Couwenhoven, his wife, was Catherine, born August 8, baptized September 30, 1753, and died unmarried on the homestead where she always lived, March 1st, 1835, aged 81 years, 6 months, 23 days, according to inscription on the headstone at her grave in the homestead burying ground. Her will recorded at Freehold in C of Wills, page 459, etc., is very voluminous for she remembers with some kind of gift nearly all her nephews and nieces. The fourth child of the second Daniel Hendrickson was Hendrick, born May 2, baptized June 12, 1758, married May 13, 1781, Francinke, (b. Nov. 18, 1763, d. March 26, 1845,) daughter of Cornelius R. Covenhoven and Jane Denise, his wife, who have been mentioned in a former article. Hendrick died December 1, 1840, aged 82 years, 6 months, 29 days, and is buried on the homestead where he always lived. William, the fifth and youngest child of the second Daniel Hendrickson, was baptized November 22, 1761, and died young and unmarried.

As the father of these children died intestate June 24, 1788, the three surviving sons and daughter by amicable arrangement among themselves divided the real estate.

In Book K of Deeds, page 56, etc., Monmouth Clerk's office, we find record of a deed executed August 6, 1789, from Daniel, Cornelius, and Hendrick Hendrickson, the three sons to their sister, Catherine Hendrickson. It is recited therein that the grantors and grantee are the only children and heirs-at-law of Daniel Hendrickson of Middletown township, who lately died intestate. That they have agreed among themselves as to shares of each in the real estate of their father and by this deed the three sons convey and quitclaim to their sister Catherine, her heirs and assigns forever, the following described lands and premises, situate in said township of Middletown. The tract first described begins at an apple tree standing at the southeast corner and beginning of a line settled by releases between Johannes Luyster and Daniel Hendrickson, dated April 11, 1745. Then follows a particular description by chains and links, and that it is the westermost part of the home tract "whereon said Daniel Hendrickson did live."

Then comes a general description of a tract containing 122 87-100 acres, bounded southerly in part by Luyster's land and in part by a branch of Mahoras brook and Colonel Daniel Hendrickson's land; westerly, in part by land formerly John Bowne's * esquire, de-

---

* Cornelius VanDerbilt was a son of Aris VanDerbilt and Jannetje Cornelise Couwenhoven, his wife. He died August 18, 1800, aged 69 years, 3 months, 7 days, according to inscription on his tombstone in yard of Middletown Dutch church.

* John Bowne was the eldest son of Obadiah Bowne and had one son Andrew, and two daughters, Lydia and Catherine. His daughter Catherine, married William, son of George Crawford. His son Andrew, died unmarried. I is will was proved January 13, 1776, and recorded in Book M of Wills, page 10, etc., at Trenton, N. J. He devised all his real estate to John and William Crawford, sons of his sister Catherine, subject to payment of £250 to their sister, Esther Crawford. Residue of his estate is left to John, William, and Esther Crawford, the three children of his sister, Catherine Crawford. William Crawford, Robert Hartshorne, and Garret Wall of Mount Pleasant, were appointed executors; will is witnessed by William Hendrickson, Richard Crawford and Safety Bowne. John and William Crawford divided the real estate so left, and John Crawford became owner of the part next to the Hendrickson homestead and which John Bowne had owned in his life time. John Crawford was the father of the late James G. Crawford of Crawford's Corner, Holmdel township.

ceased, now John Crawford's and in part by Colonel Daniel Hendrickson's land; northerly, by a brook coming from the hills and Humphrey Wall and John Stillwell's lands, and easterly by the east-most line named in this particular description first given. It is then stated that part of the said land was purchased of John Whitlock by Daniel Hendrickson, the elder, by deed dated May 16, 1698, and the other part by deed from Garret Wall, dated December 29, 1709. Four and one half acres of fresh meadow lying on the north side of a neck of woodland and conveyed by John Wall to Daniel Hendrickson the elder, by deed dated May 8, 1711, and two and two-fifths acres of salt meadow at Shoal Harbour, are also conveyed to Catherine Hendrickson by this deed.

Catherine Hendrickson, however, did not retain this land long, for on April 1st, 1800, by deed of that date and for the consideration of $2,000, she conveyed all the above premises to her brother, Hendrick Hendrickson. This deed is recorded at Freehold in L of deeds, p. 571, etc., and gave Hendrick the ownership of all the original homestead owned by the first Daniel and devised by him to his youngest son, Daniel. Hendrick Hendrickson by his will left all these lands to his grandson, the late Hon. William Henry Hendrickson, so well known to the present generation of our people in Monmouth county.

By deed dated August 26, 1789, recorded in same book K of deeds, page 67, etc., Daniel, Cornelius and Catherine Hendrickson convey and quitclaim to Hendrick Hendrickson the easternmost part of the homestead on which their deceased father lived. In particular description first given the "Southwest corner of a mill dam" and "the middle of the floodgate" are called for as monuments. Then follows a general description as 154 acres bounded southerly and easterly by Luyster's land and in part easterly by Mahoras brook; northerly in part by John Stillwell's line and a small brook coming from the hills, and in part by the lower edge of the upland bank on south side of the meadow on said brook; westerly, by the westermost line named in the particular description.

Six and four-fifths acres of salt meadow at Shoal Harbour was also conveyed, and then reference to chain of title same as in above deeds to Catherine. These two deeds were witnessed by William Crawford, John Covenhoven and Colonel Asher Holmes and were proved by affidavits of Colonel Asher Holmes before Hendrick Hendrickson, one of the judges of the Court of Common Pleas of Monmouth county on February 10, 1792.

In this same book K of deeds, page 71, etc, is a record of the deed from Daniel, Hendrick, and Catherine Hendrickson to Cornelius Hendrickson, dated August 26, 1789, with same witnesses and proof of execution before Judge Hendrick Hendrickson. Several tracts are conveyed by this deed. First a tract of 119 acres and in the particular description given, the "southwest corner of the milldam where it joins the uplands" and "middle of floodgates" were called for as monuments. Then follows a general description as 119 acres more or less, bounded easterly by lands of John Taylor, Esq., northerly by Aumack's now Edward Taylor, deceased, land, westerly in part and in part northerly, by lands formerly Daniel Stevenson's now in possession of Daniel Hendrickson, Junior, and in part by Mahoras brook as it now runs, which tract of land was deeded by John Taylor, Esq.,† to Daniel Hendrickson, deceased, by deed dated August 10, 1763, together with half part of grist mill built by said Daniel Hendrickson, and the right and privilege of digging, carting off earth for use in making, mending and repairing the mill dam from southwest of said milldam forever. Also a tract of 157 acres near "Whakake" and four and one-half acres of salt meadow on east side of "Whakake Creek." Half of 36 acres situate a mile south of "Sandy Hook" (Raritan) "Bay" and one and one-half miles southwest of Point Comfort; 50 acres on north side of public road from Middletown to Perth Amboy, and six and one-half acres of salt meadow at Shoal Harbour, are likewise conveyed to Cornelius Hendrickson by this deed. No share in his father's land is conveyed to Daniel who at this time owned and occupied the Stevenson farm. The father may have advanced money to him to purchase this land or he may have taken his share in personal property or in money.

†John Taylor, Esq. was appointed sheriff, first in 1751, and held office to 1754, when Robert Cummings succeeded him. He was again appointed sheriff of Monmouth county in 1757 for three years. At the breaking out of the Revolutionary war he was one of the judges of our county courts. He was also one of the Peace Commissioners appointed by Admiral Howe on the part of the British government. In 1792 he sold his farm at Middletown Village to George Crawford and a few years after removed to Perth Amboy where he died.

Hendrick Hendrickson by Francinke Couwenhoven, his wife, had the following children:
Catherine, baptized March 14, 1782, married May 23, 1803, Garret Lane, and resided with her husband at Piscataway, Middlesex county, N. J. She had the following children:

Hendrick Hendrickson, bap. June 3, 1807.
Eliza Jane, born Sept. 22, 1809.
William Hendrickson, } twins born Sept. 24, Garret Smock,   } 1811.
John, born April 21, 1814.

William H., born January 28, 1787, married January 12, 1812, Eleanor (b. Aug. 19, 1792, d. Sept. 25, 1879,) daughter of Charles DuBois and Anne Hendrickson, and already mentioned among the descendants of Daniel Hendrickson and Eleanor VanMater, his wife. William H. Hendrickson died February 9, 1831, and was buried on the homestead. He left a will proved before Peter C. Vanderhoef, Surrogate, April 2, 1831, and recorded in C of Wills, page 194, etc. As his father was living at this time he left no real estate, only personal property. He mentions in this will the gold watch which once belonged to his brother-in-law, Peter DuBois.

Jane, born March 6, 1792, married March 23, 1808, Garret D. Hendrickson, (b. July 7, 1787, d. Oct. 12, 1861) and died August 5, 1875. Both buried in family yard on homestead farm at Holland. Their children have been named in a former article.

Hendrick Hendrickson made his will December 9, 1834, proved December 21, 1840, and recorded at Freehold in D of Wills, page 310, etc. He provides for his widow, Francinke, and mentions his daughters, Catherine Lane, and Jane, wife of Garret D. Hendrickson. "The farm of 296 acres where I now live" with all stock, etc., on same, he devises in fee to his grandson, William Henry Hendrickson. The following clause also appears in his will: "I do hereby reserve one acre of land on the farm where I now live to be used as a burying ground for the Hendrickson family and their connections, which said graveyard is to include the present graveyard and as much land on each side of it as shall make said acre." A codicil is added August 1, 1836, in which he directs that the widow and children of his deceased son William, shall reside with him and no charge be made against them for maintenance. In his will he orders his grandson, William Henry to pay to his sisters, Sarah Ann, Francinke, and Mary, $2,000 each.

William Henry, son of Hendrick Hendrickson, married January 12, 1812, Eleanor DuBois, and had the following children:

William Henry, born June 3, 1813, married first, February 28, 1839, Elizabeth Woodward; married second, Mrs. Rebecca P. Fields, widow of Thomas Fields. He twice represented Monmouth county in New Jersey Senate and was one of the leading and respected citizens of Monmouth county. A very good likeness and full history of his life appears in Ellis' history of Monmouth county.

Sarah Ann, born April 14, 1816, married, October 21, 1834, Rev. Garret C. Schanck (b. September 14, 1806, d. September 17, 1888,) and died February 20, 1843. Both buried in yard of Marlboro Brick church.

Charles DuBois, born April 21, 1818, died October 31, 1834.

Francinke, born August 18, 1822, married March 4, 1840, George W. Cox, and died April 29, 1854. Buried by her husband in yard of Yellow Meeting House, Upper Freehold.

Mary, born October 1, 1825, married December 25, 1856, Henry Corlies, (born October 20, 1821, and son of Benjamin W. Corlies.) She died in August, 1898.

WILLIAM HENDRICKSON, OR WILM HENDRICKS, AS WRITTEN, BROTHER OF DANIEL.

Wilm Hendricks, as he wrote his name, was a brother of Daniel Hendrickson, the first settler at Holland, in the present township of Holmdel. I think Hendrick Hendricks, the father of Daniel and William, lived in Monmouth between 1694 and 1706. Our court minutes for this period show that one Hendrick Hendricks served on the grand jury and also on a coroner's jury, called to view a corpse thrown up by the sea on Sandy Hook beach. After above dates no Hendrick Hendricks is named on our public records as resident of this county until Daniel's eldest son arrived at age. Hendrick Hendricks was a widower and married again about 1706, Helen Cortelyou, the widow of Nicholas VanBrunt and of Dionyse Denyse. After this marriage it is said that he lived with his wife on lands at New Utrecht, L. I., which her father, Jacques Cortelyou, had devised to her.

William Hendricks is first mentioned in our county records as one of the persons who broke up Governor Hamilton's and Lewis Morris' court at Middletown village, March 25, 1701, as has been already related. In Book I of Deeds, page 219, Secretary of State's office, is record of an agreement between William Hendricks and Jarret Wall of Middletown, Monmouth county, dated June 17, 1703, fixing division line between their lands. The beginning of the line is fixed at mouth of William Hendricks' ditch on west side of Mahoras brook and to run due west from this point to west side of Hendrickson land. On page 152 of court minutes of Monmouth under date of December 6, 1709, William Hendrickson with others appears before the court as a committee from Dutch church to present Joseph Morgan as their pastor. He is also mentioned in these same minutes in record of two public highways laid out by the commissioners. The first under date of September 27, 1705, of a highway from Middletown to the county line towards Amboy. "William Hendricks mill" is named as on line of this road. In the return of another road laid out April 2, 1706, the beginning is at "William Hendricks' mill" and running thence "direct to Cocowders' brook, where Walter Wall's path went over, and then to Ruckman's path which goes to Waykake." This road return is published in full on page 266-7, Old Times in Old Monmouth.

Some forty years ago the remains of an old dam, extending about half across the meadow, could be seen a few hundred feet south of the dwelling house where Joseph Dorsett lived until his death, and where George Dorsett, his father, had lived before him. The track of the New York and Long Branch railroad run a little distance north of this place. The banks on both sides of the Mahoras meadow south of this old dam are quite high. The east bank curves around to the west so as to make a natural dam half the width of the meadow. The Mahoras brook which flows north along the west bank of the meadow makes a turn opposite the remains of this old dam and for a short distance flows westerly and then turns northerly along the farm of the late Hon. William B. Hendrickson. It only needs a short dam across this narrow neck of the meadow to unite the east and west banks, and so dam up the waters of Mahoras brook. In the division deeds, between the children of the second Daniel Hendrickson executed in 1789 and heretofore mentioned, this dam and floodgates are referred to as monuments in the description.

The fact that the deceased father had erected a mill and conveyance of half of same to the son Cornelius, is mentioned in the deed to him. I think that here is the site of the first grist mill erected in Monmouth county. The old Town Book of Middletown township contains records of the contract between the first settlers in 1668 and one Robert Jones, of New York, to put up and operate a grist mill. It was to be built at a place called by the Indians "Choncis Sepus." The early settlers had oxen and a few horses, and were obliged to select a place on some stream with sufficient water to run a mill. Mahoras brook is the only stream near the village of Middletown with sufficient water for this purpose. The banks on each side at this place favored the construction of a short dam. The hills were then covered with dense forests and beneath were vines and underbrush, so that the storm water was held from running off rapidly. All the

Justice of the New Jersey Supreme Court, appointed in 1901.

EARLY DUTCH SETTLERS OF MONMOUTH. 149

streams carried a greater volume of water and the meadow or lowlands had not been filled up or raised by the washings from the banks and hillsides after they were cleared and plowed.

The Mahoras brook drains an extensive region and during heavy storms an immense amount of water flows down from the hills. Robert Jones erected a mill at this place in 1669, for on May 24, 1670, town lot No. 33 is transferred to him, which indicates that he must have completed his part of the contract. He did not, however, operate it long, for soon after we find James Grover in possession of the mill and running it. I think Daniel Hendricks purchased the property of Whitlock and Wall on account of the close proximity of this mill. He was a man of more than ordinary intelligence and energy for we find him a constable and then sheriff in less than fifteen years after he settled. This, too, among strange people of a different race and language. It was doubtless his ownership of the adjacent lands which enabled him to secure this mill site for his brother William. At all events this same family held it from 1705 until the close of the century, as the deeds of 1789 inform us. A miller and blacksmith were two of the most important men in a new settlement. A great demand existed in early times, as the settlements were pushed to west and south, for men understanding these trades.

William Hendricks married Willimptje, (baptized at Flatbush, L. I., September 16, 1677,) a daughter of Guisbert Thys Laen VanPelt and Jannetje Adrianse Lambersen, his wife, who are named among the organizing members of the Monmouth Dutch church in 1709. His name, however, on church records is entered "Gisbert Laen" for the VanPelt was dropped. At a later date the name was spelled "Lane," which surname has been retained by his descendants to this day. One of his daughters, "Moika" (Micha) married Stoffel Dircksen Longstraat of Flatlands, L. I., who also removed to Monmouth county, and were the parents of Stoffel Longstreet (baptized December 25, 1713, died 1784) who was the first settler of this name in Upper Freehold township and lived there until his death. William Hendricks died in April or May of 1711, before any of his children had arrived at age. His will is dated April 2 and proved June 14 of the year 1711, and recorded at Trenton, N. J., in Book I of Wills, page 326, etc. Cornelius Doorn (VanDorn), William Brudenseck and Barnes Lambersen are the subscribing witnesses. His brother Daniel Hendrickson, and friends, Peter Wyckoff and Stoffle Longstreet are named as executors. He does not mention his wife, Willimpe, and I therefore infer that she had died prior to this time (1711). He mentions Guisbert (Gilbert) as his eldest son and gives him four shillings extra on this account. He gives his youngest son Daniel, £20 more than the others. This is the nephew Daniel Hendrickson also mentions in his will, giving him a small lot of land at Perth Amboy which he purchased of Stephen Warne.

William Hendricks also speaks in his will of his daughters, but does not name them or any other sons except Gilbert and Daniel. He states, however, that all his children are minors. Gilbert Lane, his father-in-law, in his will dated Nov. 7, 1720, proved May 17, 1727, and recorded at Trenton in Book B of wills, p. 66, etc., speaks of his grand-children "born of my daughter Williamea Hendrickson, late deceased, formerly the wife of William Hendrickson, likewise deceased, and gives them their mother's share in his estate. These orphan children of William Hendricks and Williamptji Lane, his wife, who were all under age in 1711 were: Guisbert, Geesye, Hans (John), Jannetje (Jane), Hendrick and Daniel. As their father ran a grist mill on Mahoras brook, it is likely that these boys all learned the business of a miller, for we find some of them or their children following this business at a later date in other parts of New Jersey. I do not now know of any descendents of these four sons residing in the old township of Middletown. They all removed to other parts of this county or state and to Bucks and Lancaster counties in Pennsylvania. Some retained the name of "Hendricks" and others the "Hendrickson" surname.

Guisbert, the eldest son, married about 1728, Elizabeth (bapt. Aug. 13, 1710,) daughter of Johannes Polhemus and Annetje TenEyck, his wife, who have been heretofore mentioned. She was a sister of Tobias and Johannes Polhemus, who also settled in Upper Freehold township probably soon after Guisbert Hendrickson settled in that vicinity. This part of Monmouth together with adjacent territory in what was then Burlington and Middlesex counties, went under general name of Crosswicks, now confined in one small village.

Nottingham township was then in Burlington county. Part of this township was taken off of Burlington and called Hamilton township when Mercer county was formed in 1838. I think Gilbert Hendrickson settled in this part of Burlington, but now Mercer county, somewheres near Yardville. He devised this plantation or farm to his youngest son, David Hendrickson, who I believe lived and died on it. I should not be surprised to learn that Gilbert Hendrickson operated a grist mill in the vicinity of his farm. This however is a conjecture. As his father helped organize the Dutch church in 1709, so Gilbert helped the first Presbyterian church at Allentown. As will be seen from his will he remembers this church with the gift of £10 or fifty dollars, which was a considerable sum in those days. Gilbert Hendrickson, like his father, read his Dutch Bible and accepted its teachings when he read therein.

"Who is among you that feareth the Lord, that obeyeth the voice of his servant, that walketh in darkness and hath no light? Let him trust in the name of the Lord, and stay upon his God."

"I, even I am he that comforteth you; who art thou, that thou shouldst be afraid of a man that shall die, and the son of man which shall be made as grass?"

"And forgettest the Lord, thy maker, that hath stretched forth the heavens and laid the foundations of the earth?"

"Fear thou not, for I am with thee: be not dismayed; for I am thy God. I will strengthen thee; yea I will help thee; yea I will uphold thee with the right hand of my righteousness."

He believed in the word of God and trusting in the "righteousness" of God, and not his own goodness, he passed away from this earth in March or April of 1777, leaving his wife surviving and seven stalwart sons. He mentions no daughter in his will, but a granddaughter, Margaret Emley. He therefore may have had a daughter who married an Emley and died prior to date of this will. His descendants are numerous and will be interested in his will where he speaks for himself.

The will and inventory of Guisbert Hendrickson:—In the name of God, amen, I Gisebert Hendrickson of the township in the county of Burlington in the Western Division of the Province of New Jersey, being weak in body but of Sound Mind and Memory Blessed be God, do this Eleventh day of November, in the year of Our Lord one thousand seven hundred and Seventy-Six I do make and publish this my last Will and Testament in manner and as followeth that is to say FIRST I give and Bequeath unto my beloved Wife Elizabeth the sum of fifteen pounds Yearly during her natural Life and to have any one of the rooms in the house where I now live that she shall Choose with every necessary thereunto belonging with the use of one Negro Wench with all other necessaries of life found her as long as she shall remain my Widow, and it is my will that all the Estate that my Wife shall have at her death shall be equally divided between my six sons hereafter mentioned or the Survivors of them.

ITEM I give and bequeath unto my Son William the sum of One hundred pounds Besides his Equal part with the Rest of my Sons that is to say with himself & John & Daniel & Tobias and Cornelius & Jacob and it is my desire that he may be Contented with the proportion of my Estate with what he already had.

ITEM I give and Bequeath unto my son David all the Plantation whereon I now dwell which I purchased by Sundry Surveyes now adjoining together to him his Heirs and Assigns for ever together with four horses three cows twelve sheep Waggon plows Harrows Gears He paying to my Six Sons above named three hundred pounds in three Years after my Decease and fifteen pounds Yearly unto my Widow as above said during her Natural Life and make such provisions for her as is Bequeathed her in this Will.

ITEM it is my will and do Bequeath to Margaret Emley my Granddaughter one hundred pounds four years after my decease to be paid by my Son David.

ITEM It is my Will and I do Order that that Lot of Land lying at the North East Corner of the Plantation formerly Abraham Tilton's lying upon Doctor's Creek to be sold by my Executors And the Money arising from the sale thereof to be Equally Divided amongst my Six Sons above mentioned to them their heirs and Assigns for ever.

ITEM it is my will & I do Order that if either of my said sons should die without issue that his part and portion herein bequeathed him shall be equally divided amongst the Survivors that have Issue to them their heirs and Assigns for ever.

ITEM it is my Will and I do order that all my Moveable Estate be sold Except what is already Bequeathed in this Will and after all my just debts and funeral Charges are paid that then the Overplush be Equally Divided amongst my Six Sons above mentioned that is William, John, Daniel, Tobias, Cornelius, & Jacob all as aforesaid to them their Heirs and Assigns for ever. And I do hereby ordain and appoint my two Sons William Hendrickson and Tobias Hendrickson to be my true & lawful Executors to this my last Will & Testament. Item it is my Will and I do Order that my Executors first of all do pay to the Elder of the Presbyterian Church of Allentown ten pounds for the use of said church I do hereby revoke all other Wills by me heretofore made. IN WITNESS Whereof the said Guisbert Hendrickson have to this my last Will and Testament set my Hand and Seal the day and year above written.

   Guisbert Hendrickson (SEAL.)
Signed Sealed and Delivered by the said Guisbert Hendrickson as and for his last Will and Testament in the presents of us who were present at the signing & Sealing thereof.
  Tobias Polhemus
  Margaret Magaliard (w) her mark
  William Reynolds.

Tobias Polhemus, one of the witnesses ‡ to the within will being first sworn

‡ The old wills now on record in Secretary of State's office at Trenton, N. J., were originally recorded at Burlington, for West Jersey and numbered. While in East Jersey they were recorded at Perth Amboy and books lettered. Thus there are two sets of books covering the same period of time. Some of the Monmouth county wills, although in East Jersey, are recorded at Burlington, as is shown in this article.

on the Holy Evangelist of Almighty God doth declare and say that he was present and saw Guisbert Hendrickson the Testator in the within will named Sign and Seal the same & heard him Publish pronounce and declare the within Writing to be his last Will & Testament And at the doing thereof he was of sound and disposing mind and Memory as far as he knows and as he Verily believes and that Margaret Magaliard and William Reynolds were also present at the same time and Signed their Names as Witnesses to the Will together with this Deponent in the presence of each other and in the presence of the Testator.

Sworn the 28th day of April 1777 at Burlington before Robt Burcham.

The foregoing Will being prov'd probate was Granted by his Excellency Govr. Livingston unto William Hendrickson and Tobias Hendrickson Executors in the sd. Will named being first sworn truly to perform the same exhibit a true Inventory and render a true Accot. when thereto lawfully required Given under the Prerogative Seal the day and Year aforesaid.

      Cha. Pettit Regrr.

WILLIAM HENDRICKS AND WILLIAMPTJE LAEN HIS WIFE AND CHILDREN.

1. William, eldest son of Guisbert, married according to license granted February 22, 1768, Rachel Longstreet.

In Book I of deeds, page 496, Monmouth Clerk's office, is record of a deed dated February 2, 1778, from William Hendrickson and Rachel, his wife, of Upper Freehold, to Gilbert Longstreet of the same township. The grantors convey for £4,000 a tract of land in that township which Stoffel Longstreet had deeded to William Hendrickson, and "Peter Wecoff's" land, Albert Couwenhoven's lands, and Doctor's Creek are called for as monuments.

2. John, second son, married November 14, 1763, Anna Cox, and resided in what is now Ewing township, Mercer county.

3 Daniel, third son, was born about 1737; married Ann Stewart, and settled somewhere near what is now Hamilton Square. He was a zealous patriot and soldier of the Revolution.

4. Tobias, fourth son, married according to license dated March 21, 1762, Rebecca Coward, and died May 23, 1811, aged 70 years, 10 months, and 2 days, according to his headstone in Old Yellow Meeting House cemetery. His will is recorded at Freehold as heretofore mentioned with some of his descendants in Barkalow genealogy.

5. Cornelius, fifth son, is supposed to be the same person named in marriage license granted January 28, 1767, to Cornelius Hendrickson and Mary Thorn of Monmouth county. No other knowledge.

6. Jacob, the sixth son, married according to license dated May 2, 1771, Elizabeth Mount, and died July 24, 1831, aged 72 years, 6 months, 12 days, according to his headstone in the Old Yellow Meeting House cemetery. His wife is buried by him.

7. David, the seventh and youngest son, to whom his father left the homestead, which lay, I think, in what was then Nottingham township, Burlington county, but now part of Mercer county, lived and died on this farm, but I have no dates of his marriage or death.

One of the maternal uncles of these seven sons was John Polhemus, who lived in Upper Freehold township and died there without children. His will is dated June 7, 1788, proved 1793, and recorded at Trenton, N. J., in Liber. 33 of Wills, p. 234. This John Polhemus married Alice, daughter of Joseph Holmes and Elizabeth Ashton† his wife, of Upper Freehold. She died April, 1788, according to her headstone in Yellow Meeting House cemetery, aged 61 years, 10 months. Her husband died September 15, 1793, aged 72 years, and is buried by her. In his will he names his wife's cousins, Elizabeth and Sarah, daughters of Jonathan Holmes, and Elizabeth, daughter of John Holmes, and Elizabeth Wyckoff, daughter of Peter Imlay. He also mentions his own sister, Catherine, who married Matthias Laen (Lane). (They are named as members of Dutch church in 1750). If she is dead he orders legacy paid to her children. He mentions children of his brothers, Daniel Polhemus, Tobias Polhemus and Cornelius Polhemus, and children of his sisters, Nelly Couwenhoven and of Elizabeth Hendrickson. "My brothers' and sisters' children,"

---

† Joseph Holmes was the second son of Obadiah Holmes and Alice Ashton, his wife, and their son named in his will to whom he devised his lands at Crosswicks (Upper Freehold vicinity). Joseph Holmes was born in 1699; married Elizabeth, daughter of John Ashton, and lived on his farm in Upper Freehold, and died in July, 1777, He is buried in Ashton graveyard. His will is recorded in Liber. 19, page 7. He had the following seven children: Allis (Alice) born June 10, 1726, married John Polhemus, died without issue April 1, 1788, buried by her husband in Yellow Meeting house cemetery; Obadiah, born October 13, 1728; James, born March 6, 1732, died young; Mary, born September 17, 1733, married Peter Imlay; Joseph, born December 3, 1736, married Phoebe Wardell, died August 31, 1809, leaving only one child, a daughter, (his will was proved September 16, 1809, and recorded at Freehold in A of Wills, page 317. He leaves £300 to Baptist church of Upper Freehold); Jonathan, born December 4, 1738, married Lydia Throckmorton, died August 4, 1777, from exposure and hardships in American army during the war (he was a captain or lieutenant), buried in Yellow Meeting House cemetery by his wife; John, born March 29, 1744, married Deborah Leonard, died August 10, 1783, (his wife died May 6, 1811, also buried in Yellow Meeting House cemetery.)

are his words. His nephew, Jacob Hendrickson of Upper Freehold, and his brother, John Polhemus of Middletown, are appointed executors. The will is witnessed by Garret Wyckoff, Robert Imlay, and Samuel Imlay. It thus appears that the Polhemuses, Hendricksons, Longstreets, and Wyckoffs, settlers in Upper Freehold, were closely connected by blood or marriage.

Jonathan Holmes, the soldier of the Revolution, by his wife, Lydia Throckmorton, had a son Joseph, born 1772, married Mary Bruere, and died July 16, 1815. His youngest son, Joseph, born November 24, 1810, married Martha Ann Miers, and died August, 1897. They were the parents of Joseph Holmes, our present Chosen Freeholder from Upper Freehold township, and who still (1901) owns and resides on old Holmes homestead in that township. The Joseph Holmes who died July, 1777, and the progenitor of the Upper Freehold Holmes family, was a delegate to the Provincial Congress of New Jersey and a member of the Council of Safety in 1775-76. He was one of the most energetic and trusted of the patriot leaders of Monmouth county and his death at the very beginning of the war was a great loss. Col. Elisha Lawrence, who raised a battalion of Jerseymen to serve in the English army and who was very active on the royal side, was a near neighbor to Joseph Holmes. There were other very bitter and malignant Tories among his near neighbors. His dwelling on one occasion was attacked by the Refugees and plundered.

William Hendricks and Williamptje Laen, his wife, and their children:

Geesye, or Gezina, as spelled on page 87 of Wells' address at Brick church, where she and her husband are put down as members of the Dutch church in 1743, married Matthias Peterzon, or Pietersen and was the second child of William Hendricks. In the record of the baptism of his children, her name is sometimes entered as "Geesye Williamse," meaning Geesye, the daughter of William.

Matthias Pieterson, her husband, was a son of Peter Thys Laen VanPelt, and Barbara Houlton, his wife. He was known as Matthias, son of Peter, and so Pieterson became his surname. Some of his descendants, it is said, removed to Hunterdon and Somerset counties in this state, and others over into Bucks and Chester counties, Pa.

Matthias Pieterson and Geesye Hendricks had the following children:

Barbara, baptized May 26, 1717.
Peter, baptized November 23, 1718.

William, baptized January 13, 1723.
Mary, baptized January 10, 1733.
Daniel, baptized June 17, 1738.

Hans (John) the third child of William Hendricks, married Sarah Mosier, and died March 25, 1789, aged 89 years, according to his headstone in yard of Marlboro Brick church. His wife is interred by him and date of her death given as March 31, 1782, aged 80 years, 24 days. On page 86 of Wells' address her name is spelled "Sarah Meser" and she became a communicant in 1731. John Hendricks, as he wrote his name, made his will May 18, 1785, proved April 15, 1789, and is on record in Trenton in Book 30 of Wills, page 178, etc. He orders his executors to sell his land at Imlaystown, Upper Freehold township, and one half of his mill where his son, Abraham Hendricks, now lives in that township, and all other lands owned by him. He gives his old Dutch Bible and £10 to his son Abraham. He mentions his granddaughter Charlotte, and four children of his deceased son William. He also mentions his grandsons, Jacob and John Vanderbilt, children of his deceased daughter Elizabeth. He speaks of two children of his son Conradt, appoints his son Abraham Hendricks, and his two grandsons, Jacob and John Vanderbilt, executors. The will is witnessed by Mary Vanderbilt and Lewis Forman. Seven of the children of John Hendricks and Sarah Mosier, his wife, are buried in the yard of the old Brick church at Marlboro. All have the Hendricks surname. Some of his descendants removed to Easton, Pa., and to Rockingham and other counties in Virginia.

By Sarah Mosier he had the following children:

Johannes, baptized April 8, 1733, married, according to the license granted October 31, 1759, Phoebe Smith, and died, according to his headstone, July 13, 1760, aged 28 years, 5 months, 1 day. His will is dated July 2, 1760, proved July 26, 1760, and recorded at Trenton in Book 9 of wills, page 258, etc. He described himself as a resident of Middlesex county, New Jersey. I think it was in that part of Middlesex county taken off in 1838 to form Mercer county. He mentions his wife Phoebe, but had no children. He gives his brother William, six shirts and two beaver hats, and to his brother Guisbert (Gilbert) the remainder of his wearing apparel. He also mentions his brother-in-law, John Vanderbilt. The will is witnessed by John Hendricks, Andrew Forman and Lewis Forman. This John Hendricks, the witness, I think was a son of Gilbert Hendrickson and Elizabeth Polhemus, his wife, already mentioned, and residing in what was Nottingham township, Burlington county, but now Ewing township, Mercer county.

Elizabeth, baptized August 25, 1734, married according to license dated May 20, 1754, and recorded in office of Secretary of State at Trenton, N. J., John Vanderbilt of Staten Island, N. Y., and died August 13, 1760, aged 26 years, 1 month, 13 days, according to her headstone in Brick church cemetery. She left two sons, who are the executors named in her father's will made 25 years later, or in 1785. Under this will they sold and conveyed away his real estate, as appears from deeds recorded in Monmouth Clerk's office.

William, baptized December 25, 1736, married, according to license granted December 21, 1756, Charity Robinson of Monmouth county and died before his father, leaving four children surviving. One child named Charity, died December 23, 1761, and is buried in Brick church cemetery with a headstone giving her name and age. He also had a son John, baptized November 19, 1757, who was his firstborn. As no others are buried in Brick church yard it is likely that they removed to some other place or colony.

Conradt, baptized August 27, 1738, married first, according to license dated June 18, 1759, Mary English. She died October 26, 1762, aged 27 years, leaving one daughter, Elizabeth, baptized at Tennent church November 22, 1761. He married for his second wife Mary Knott. This license is dated June 17, 1763. During the Revolution he sided with the King and enlisted in the company raised by Capt. Thomas Crowell which served in the battalion under Col. Elisha Lawrence, the ex-sheriff or last of the Kings' Sheriffs in Monmouth county. This battalion was in Skinner's Brigade and was stationed much of the time on Staten Island. On page 12 of Book A of Executions in the Monmouth Clerk's office is record of an execution issued May 1, 1779, against Thomas Crowell of Middletown township who had been found guilty under an inquisition of joining the King's army. On the next page, No. 13, is record of an execution against Conradt Hendricks, who had also joined the King's army. The real estate of these men was sold under these executions. They, however, never returned to this county, so far as I can learn. They may have removed to Nova Scotia.

Guisbert (Gilbert), baptized May 24, 1741, died single March 25, 1785, aged

44 years, 1 month, 2 days, according to his headstone in Brick church cemetery at Marlboro.

Mary, baptized April 7, 1744, married Thomas Hendricks, who, I think, resided somewhere near Hopewell, N. J. She died November 5, 1768, aged 24 years, according to her headstone in Brick church cemetery. Her husband is not buried in this yard and I do not know what became of him or whether she left any children.

Sarah, baptized June 28, 1747, died single February 28, 1772.

Abraham, born ——, married, according to license dated December 17, 1754, Mary, daughter of William Wyckoff and Agnes VanDoren, his wife. She was born October 1, 1733, and died February 12, 1796, and is buried in Brick church cemetery. Abraham Hendricks may have been the oldest of the eight children of John Hendricks, but there is no record of his birth or baptism unless the "Old Dutch Bible," which his father mentions in his will, be found. Neither do I know where Abraham died or where he was buried. He seems to have resided in Upper Freehold and run a grist mill at or near Imlaystown or Allentown. During the Revolution he was an earnest and energetic patriot and a soldier.

I have no information or knowledge of his children, if any. His father's selection of him as executor and gift of family Bible to him leads me to think he was the oldest son. Jannetje, the fourth child of William Hendricks and Willaimpe Laen, his wife, married Christopher Warmsley, and moved to some other part of New Jersey or some other colony. She had, however, three of her children baptized in our Dutch church while visiting her parents, viz: William, baptized May 3, 1719, and two others unnamed, one October 25, 1724, and the other April 16, 1732.

Hendrick, the fifth child of William Hendricks, was born November 11, 1706, married about 1728, Altje, daughter of Albert Couwenhoven and Neiltje Schanck, his wife, and died July 28, 1783, aged 76 years, 8 months, 6 days. His wife was born January 20, 1709. Her father and mother are both buried in Schanck-Couwenhoven yard, and dates of their deaths from headstone inscriptions show that the printed statements heretofore given are incorrect. Albert Couwenhoven died September 13, 1748, aged 72 years, 9 months, and 6 days. Neiltje Schanck, his wife, died July 27, 1751, aged 70 years, 6 months, and 4 days. Hendrick Hendrickson and Aeltje Couwenhoven, his wife, had two sons baptized in the Dutch church, viz: Hendrick, June 20, 1730, and Albert, July 16, 1732. There may have been other children born and not baptized. Hendrick, according to license granted April, 1751, married Sarah Tomson or Thompson. Both are put down as residents of Middletown township. They had the following children baptized: Hendrick, May 3, 1752; William, February 26, 1757; Albert, July 8, 1759; Arrinthia, September 6, 1761. Albert, the second son of Hendrick, married, according to license dated January 3, 1755, Johanna Mills. Both are named as residents of Monmouth. This couple had the following children:

Hendrick, born June 27, 1756; Altje, born July 12, 1758, Elaxander Clark, as his christian name is spelled on church records, and had seven children baptized between 1776 and 1794, viz: Rebecca, November 29, 1761; Catherine, September 21, 1766; Mary, August 25, 1768; Nelly, February 3, 1777; John, February 3, 1777; William, February 3, 1777; Sarah, April 22, 1778. I do not know of any of the male descendants of Hendrick Hendrickson and Altje Couwenhoven, his wife, now residing in Monmouth county. I think some of them settled in Gloucester and Salem counties and others removed to New York and Pennsylvania. Daniel, the youngest son of William Hendrickson and Willaimpe Laen, his wife, is so named in his will and is also named in the will of his uncle, Daniel Hendricks, published heretofore in full. He removed from this county.

I find Daniel Hendrickson running a grist mill on the Millstone river, in Somerset county, N. J., in the year 1741. This may be the same person. His grandfather, Hendricks Hendrickson, with Peter Cortelyou, Stoffel Probasco, Theodore Polhemus, Hendrick Lott, Jacques Cortelyou, Dionje Denyse, and Cornelius Wyckoff, purchased in 1701, of John Harrison ten thousand acres of land in Franklin township, Somerset county, N. J. This land extended from Millstone river over to the old Indian path which ran from the falls of the Delaware River across New Jersey to a point about three miles from the mouth of the Raritan river. Here the river was crossed and the path ran over to Mount Pleasant and from there to Crawford's Corner, and from there over the hills by the residence of Daniel Hendricks, the pioneer settler to Ruckman's Hills at Middletown village, and here intersected the old Indian path from Freehold to the bay shore and to Sandy Hook.

The eight purchasers divided this tract into eight parts. Now Daniel

Hendrickson, the youngest son of William, had an opportunity to learn the miller's business in his father's mill on Mahoras brook, heretofore mentioned. His uncle Daniel, left him by will a small lot of land at Perth Amboy. This would indicate that Daniel had removed to this town or vicinity at the mouth of the Raritan river. His grandfather, Hendrick, owned lands on the Millstone River which afforded a good site for grist mills, a business which he understood. Neither is Daniel Hendricks, the youngest son of William, named in any of our county records after the probate of his uncle Daniel's will. There is a probability from these considerations that the miller of this name on the Millstone river in 1741 may have been this man.

This concludes the family records of some of the Dutch settlers of Monmouth county. I have not written these articles to gratify any foolish family pride or vanity, or to instill notions of superiority; for "birth is an accident," and transmits neither brains nor virtues of parents to children. The plodding, industrious, and economical habits of our Low Dutch ancestors are worthy of remembrance and imitation. Their ardent love of liberty, independence, and truth was a mighty factor in the establishment of this great Republic. Their descendants are bound by every principle of right and duty to carry forward their beneficent work, until mankind is freed from caste kings, priests and all other forms of hereditary bondage or oppression. The following lines by Lowell express the truth:

"Let those who will, claim gentle birth,
   And take their pride in Norman blood,
The purest ancestry on earth,
   Must find its spring in Adam's mud.
And all, though noble now or base,
   From the same level took their rise,
And side by side with loving grace,
   Leaped crystal clear from Paradise.

"Among our sires no high born chief,
   Freckled his hands with peasants' gore;
No spurred or coronetted thief,
   Set his mailed heel upon the poor.
No! We are come of a purer line,
   With nobler hearts within the breast;
Large hearts, by suffering made divine
   We draw our lineage from the oppressed.

"There's not a great soul gone before,
   That is not mentioned in our clan,
Who, when the world took side with power,
   Stood boldly on the side of man.
All hero spirits plain and grand,
   Who for ages ope the door,
All labor's dusky monarchs stand
   Among the children of the poor.

"Let others boast of ancestors,
   Who handed down some legal right,
To stand behind their tyrant's horse,
   Or buckle his spurs before the fight.
We, too, have our ancestral claims
   Of marching in the van;
Of giving ourselves to steel and flame,
   When aught is to be achieved for man.

"And is not this a family tree,
   Worth keeping up from age to age;
Was ever such ancestry
   Gold-blazoned on the herald's page?
In old Monmouth let us still,
   Maintain our race and title pure,
The men and women of heart and will,
   The people who endure."

ERRORS AND OMISSIONS.

Page 2, column 1, line 25:—Date of Albert VanCouwenhoven's death should be Sept. 13, 1748.

Page 2, column 1, line 30:—Date of Jacob VanCouwenhoven's death should be June 4, 1744.

Page 6, column 2, lines 19 and 20:—Strike out "or Ogburn" after "Peter" and substitute "Rhoda Ogbourn" for "Anna Ogden."

Page 10, column 2, line 43:—Date of Catharine Schenck's birth should be March 17, 1762.

Page 11, column 1, line 4:—Elleanor Schenck's marriage to George Crawford should be January 27, 1799.

Page 15, column 2, line 8:—Insert after "John R." "the third child of Ruliff and Sarah Schenck."

Page 20, column 1, between lines 29 and 30:—Insert "Aletta, born about 1752;" a child omitted.

Page 25, column 2, lines 24 and 26:—Date of Roeleff's birth should be Oct. 5, 1706, and his death Aug. 20, 1786. The dates printed were dates of his wife's birth and death.

Page 26, column 2, line 36:—"Catherine" was married to Daniel Hendrickson, Dec. 22, 1743.

Page 27, column 2, line 19:—Date of Sarah's marriage to John VanCleaf should be June 14, 1739.

Page 30, column 2, lines 49 and 50:—For "Antje Hendrickson, his second wife," substitute "Jannetje Wyckoff, his first wife."

Page 37, column 2, line 9:—Col. Elias Conover and Joseph Conover are said to be descendants of William VanCouwenhoven, the only brother who remained on Long Island, and one or more of his sons settled at Penns Neck or vicinity, and it is claimed was the progenitor of the above named persons and not John Couwenhoven as stated. I do not know which version is correct.

Page 41, column 1:—Among the jurymen named were other Scotchmen besides those marked with a star.

Page 44, column 1, line 4:—After "Jacob" insert "Couwenhoven."

Page 44, column 2, line 36:—After "Engeltje" insert words "the second child of Jacob VanDorn and Marytje Bennett."

Page 46, column 1, line 12:—Date of Peter's baptism should have been "Sept. 2, 1711."

Page 48, column 2, line 5:—Date of Antje VanDorn and Jan Clerk's marriage should be 1744.

Page 48, column 2, line 40:—Date of David VanDorn and Mary H. Crawford's marriage should be 1844.

Page 68, column 1, line 32:—"That he died in Monmouth county" is uncertain. He is said to have been an Indian trader in the Shenandoah Valley, Va.

Page 79, column 2, line 54:—Substitute "better" for "little" before "covenant."

Page 109, column 2, lines 36 and 37:—I should have said that John left children but I have no definite information about them.

Page 112, column 1, lines 9 and 10 of foot note:—The Burlington path began to diverge from Main street about where residence of late Joel Parker stands, and not where the Presbyterian stone church stands.

Page 139, column 1, lines 56 and 57:—Substitute "grandson" for "son" of Samuel Forman.

Page 139, column 1, in last line, strike out "Brigadier General of our Monmouth Militia" and substitute "Sheriff of Monmouth county."

Page 140, column 1, line 15:—Strike out "Gen." and substitute "Sheriff" before "David Forman."

Page 144, column 2, on line 37:—After word township, add "and another son named Edgar who served with credit during the great rebellion as a soldier of the Union."

Page 154, column 2, line 18:—After date "July 12, 1758" insert word "married."

INSCRIPTIONS TAKEN FROM HEADSTONES IN SCHENCK-COUWENHOVEN CEMETERY, PLEASANT VALLEY.

Albert Couwenhoven, b. December 6, 1676; d. Sept. 13, 1748, aged 72 y., 9 m., 6 d. Son of William Garretse Couwenhoven and Jannatie Monfort.

Neeltje Schenck, b. Jan. 23, 1681; d. July 27, 1751, aged 70 y., 6 m., 4 d. Wife of Albert Couwenhoven and daughter of Roelof Martense Schenck and Annetje Wyckoff.

Neltje Couwenhoven, b. Feb. 7, 1719; d. Apr. 22, 1738, aged 19 y., 2 m., 15 d. Daughter of Albert and Neltje Couwenhoven.

Christopher, b. Feb. 21, 1774; d. Mar. 16, 1775, aged 1 y., 25 d. Son of Cornelius Albertse Couwenhoven and Mary Logan.

John, b. June 1, 1777; d. Apr. 4, 1783, aged 5 y., 10 m., 3 d. Son of Cornelius Albertse Couwenhoven and Mary Logan.

Cornelius C., b. May 18, 1771; d. Dec. 20, 1814, aged 43 y., 7 m., 2 d. Son of Cornelius Albertse Couwenhoven and Mary Logan.

John C., b. Nov. 10, 1799; d. Nov. 26, 1852, aged 54 y., 16 d. Son of Cornelius C. Covenhoven and Elizabeth Covenhoven.

Elizabeth, b. Sept. 11, 1804; d. Jan. 30, 1860, aged 55 y., 4 m., 19 d. Daughter of John A. VanDerbilt and Mary McKildoe, and wife of John C. Conover.

Cornelius I., b. Mar. 11, 1826; d. Oct. 1, 1852, aged 27 y., 6 m., 20 d. Son of John C. Conover and Elizabeth Vanderbilt.

Emily I., b. Aug. 13, 1830; d. Feb. 14, 1856, aged 25 y., 6 m. Wife of Charles K. Butler and daughter of John C. Conover and Elizabeth Vanderbilt.

Isabella, d. Aug. 31, 1858, aged 4 y., 5 m., 5 d. Daughter of Charles K. Butler and Emily Conover.

Aaron, b. Nov. 29, 1838; d. Mar. 4, 1840, aged 1 y., 3 m., 5 d. Son of John C. Conover and Elizabeth Vanderbilt.

Eliza, b. Feb. 19, 1824; d. May 9, 1827, aged 3 y., 2 m., 20 days. Daughter of John C. Conover and Elizabeth Vanderbilt.

Mary, b. Feb. 14, 1792; d. Nov. 1, 1801, aged 9 y., 9 m., 18 d. Daughter of Cornelius C. Covenhoven and Elizabeth Covenhoven.

Sarah Jane Honce, wife of Henry D. Smock, d. Jan. 7, 1860, aged 24 y., 2 m., 15 d.

Jacob, son of Isaac and Caroline Smock, d. July 18, 1826, aged 2 y., 8 m., 7 d.

William I. Schanck, d. Aug. 12, 1860, aged 55 y., 8 m.

Denice D., son of David K. and Jane Schenck, aged 10 m., 2 d.

Jane, wife of David K. Schenck, and daughter of Denice Schenck and Margaret Polhemus, d. Apr. 5, 1823, aged 31 y., 3 m., 28 d.

Elizabeth Covenhoven, b. Mar. 7, 1769; d. Nov. 16, 1837. Wife of Cornelius C. Covenhoven and daughter of Harmen Covenhoven and Phoebe Baylee.

Daniel I. Schenck, b. Dec. 26, 1778; d. Oct. 23, 1858, aged 79 y., 9 m., 29 d. Son of Capt. John Schenck and Mary Denise.

Elleanor Schenck, b. Jan. 16, 1783; d. July 15, 1858, aged 75 y., 5 m., 29 d. Wife of Daniel I. Schenck and daughter of Garret G. Schanck and Sarah Covenhoven.

Col. John Schenck, d. June 19, 1864, aged 89 y., 11 m., 23 d. Son of Capt. John Schenck and Mary Denise.

Micha VanNuyse, d. Oct. 1825, aged 48 y. Wife of Col. John Schenck.

Elleanor Schenck, d. 1823, aged 21 y. Wife of Asher Carlile and daughter of Col. John Schenck and Micha VanNuyse.

Infant son of Elleanor Schenck and Asher Carlile d. 1823.

Garret, son of Col. John Schenck and Micha VanNuyse, aged 3 years.

Anne Maria, daughter of Col. John Schenck and Micha VanNuyse, aged 1 y., 11 m.

Anna, daughter of Col. John Schenck and Micha VanNuyse, aged 2 y.

Jacob Smock, d. Sept. 11, 1826, aged 30 y., 8 m., 24 days.

William I. Schenck, d. Aug. 12, 1860, aged 55 years, 5 m.

William C., son of Hendrick Covenhoven and Ann Bowne Crawford, b. June 23, 1808, d. Aug. 8, 1817, aged 9 y., 1 m., 25 d.

Dr. William Johnson Conover, son of John I. Conover and Lydia Johnson.

John I., son of Dr. William J. Conover and Catharine S. Conover.

Anna Rebecca, daughter of Dr. William J. Conover and Catharine S. Conover, d. Feb. 20, 1844, aged 2 y., 9 m.

A. S., d. Aug. 11, 1742.

Jacob Covenhoven, b. June 19, 1746; died Oct. 18, 1825, aged 79 y., 8 m. Son of Garret Jacobse Couwenhoven and Neeltje Rolofse Schenck.

Mary Schenck, born Mar. 17, 1757; d. Mar. 7, 1818, aged 60 y., 11 m., 20 days. Wife of Jacob Covenhoven and daughter of Hendrick Schenck and Catharine Holmes.

Hendrick Covenhoven, d. Sept. 17, 1835, aged 62 y., 5 m., 9 d. Son of Jacob Covenhoven and Mary Schenck.

Ann Bowne Crawford, b. June 25, 1788; d. Feb. 10, 1832, aged 43 y., 7 m., 14 d. Wife of Hendrick Covenhoven and daughter of William and Rebecca Patterson Crawford.

Mary Schenck, d. Feb. 2, 1773, aged 4 m., 21 d. Daughter of Garret G. Schenck, II., and Sarah Covenhoven.

Garret, minor son of Garret G. Schenck, II., and Sarah Covenhoven, d. Jan. 27, 1784, aged 3 y., 4 m., 15 d.

Rulif G. Schenck, b. Apr. 27, 1697; d. Aug. 22, 1768, aged 71 y., 3 m., 25 d. Son of Garret R. Schenck, I., and Nelke Voorheese.

John Schenck, b. Dec. 7, 1717; died Feb. 18,

1775, aged 57 y., 2 m., 11 d. Son of Garret R. Schenck, I., and Nelke Voorheese.

Nelly, daughter of Capt. John Schenck and Mary Denise, d. Sept. 23, 1773.

Garret G. Schenck, II., d. Sept. 29, 1797, aged 53 y., 11 m., 5 d. Son of Garret G. Schenck and Jannetje Couwenhoven.

Sarah Couwenhoven, b. July 23, 1744; d. Nov. 16, 1805, aged 61 y., 3 m., 24 d. Wife of Garret G. Schenck, II., and daughter of Rulif C. Couwenhoven and Sarah Voorheese.

Rulif C. Schenck, b. Feb. 28, 1778, d. Mar. 26, 1815. Son of Garret G. Schenck and Sarah Covenhoven.

Anne Schenck, d. Mar. 25, 1807, aged 42 y., 5 m., 25 d. Daughter of Garret G. Schenck, III., and Sarah Couwenhoven.

Garret G. Schenck, III., d. Aug. 25, 1779, aged 16 y., 5 m., 30 d. Son of Garret G. Schenck and Sarah Covenhoven.

Garret R. Schenck, b. Oct. 27, 1671; d. Sept. 5, 1745, aged 73 y., 10 m., 8 d. Son of Rolof Martense Schenck and Neeltje Garretse Couwenhoven.

Neeltje Voorheese, b. Oct. 1, 1675, d. Aug. 4, 1750, aged 74 y., 10 m., 4 d. Wife of Garret R. Schenck and daughter of Koert Voorheese.

Garret G. Schenck, b. Nov. 2, 1712; d. Aug. 20, 1757, aged 44 y., 11 m. Son of Garret R. Schenck and Neeltje Koerten Voorheese.

Janetje Couwenhoven, b. Oct. 6, 1714; d. Feb. 14, 1792. Wife of Garret G. Schenck and daughter of William W. Couwenhoven and Antie Lucasse Voorheese.

Mary, d. Jan. 29, 1758, aged 1 y. Daughter of Garret Jacobse Covenhoven and Neeltje Rolfese Schenck.

Aarie VanDoorn, d. Dec. 4, 1748, aged 52 y., 8 m. Son of Jacob VanDoorn and Marytje Bennett.

Jacob, d. Sept. 9, 1785, aged 52 y., 9 m., 9 d. Son of Aarie VanDoorn and Antje Jan Schenck.

Elleanor VanDoorn, d. Feb. 11, 1834, aged 91 y., 10 m., 8 d. Widow of Hendrick Smock and Garret Hendrickson and daughter of Aarie VanDoorn and Antje Schenck.

Mary Jane, daughter of Elisha and Jane Holmes.

Ann Golden, daughter of Elisha and Jane Holmes.

Daniel, son of Elisha and Jane Holmes.
Isaac, son of Elisha and Jane Holmes.
Peter, son of Elisha and Jane Holmes.
Joseph, son of Elisha and Jane Holmes.

John Walter, d. Oct. 11, 1775, aged 45 y., 9 m.

Jane, d. Jan. 6, 1774, aged 22 y., 7 m., 5 d. Wife of John Walter and daughter of Peter Janse Schenck and Janatie Hendrickson.

John, d. Oct. 13, 1837, aged 66 y., 11 m. Son of John Walter and Jane Schenck.

John Schuyler, d. Jan. 4, 1838, aged 7 y., 5 m., 22 d. Son of Charles O. and Sarah E. Walter.

Cornelius, d. Dec. 9, 1789, aged 3 m., 5 d. Son of Abraham VanHorn and Anne Covenhoven.

Samuel Bowne, died Mar. 11, 1799, aged 77 y. Husband of Patience (Eliase) Covenhoven.

Alfred Theodore, d. Oct. 15, 1803, aged 1 y., 9 m., 26 d. Son of Conover and Elizabeth Bowne of New York.

Elisha Holmes, d. June 17, 1866, aged 69 y., 11 m., 4 d. Son of Joseph Holmes and Nelly Schenck.

Jane, born Apr. 29, 1799; d. Sept. 27, 1837, aged 37 y., 4 m., 28 d. Wife of Elisha Holmes and daughter of Peter VanDorn and Jannatie Williamson.

Arintha, b. Nov. 24, 1798; d. Oct. 30, 1854, aged 55 y., 11 m. Second wife of Elisha Holmes and daughter of Schuyler Schenck and Margaret Covenhoven.

Sarah, d. June 30, 1768, aged 13 y., 1 m., 4 d. Daughter of Hendrick Schenck and Catharine Holmes.

Daniel Conover, b. Dec. 20, 1742; d. Feb. 18, 1821, aged 78 y., 1 m., 28 d.

Jacob Conover, b. Nov. 25, 1779; d. Sept. 9, 1846, aged 66 y., 9 m., 14 d.

Ensign Elias Covenhoven, b. Sept. 12, 1706; d. Dec. 25, 1750, aged 44 y., 3 m., 13 d. Son of Peter Couwenhoven and Patience Daws.

Willemsee, b. Mar. 24, 1709; d. Mar. 24, 1759, aged 50 y. Wife of Ensign Elias Couwenhoven, and daughter of John Wall and Mary Hubbard.

Catharine H., b. Mar. 17, 1762: d. June 5, 1816. Daughter of Hendrick Schenck and Catharine Holmes.

Rulif H., b. Apr. 17, 1753; d. Oct. 12, 1800, aged 47 y., 5 m., 5 d. Son of Hendrick Schenck and Catharine Holmes.

Sarah, b. Feb. 13, 1759; d. Apr. 13, 1811, aged 52 y., 2 m. Wife of Rulif H. Schenck and daughter of John Schenck and Neltje Bennet.

Hendrick, b. June 13, 1777; d. Dec. 12, 1812. Son of Rulif H. and Sarah Schenck.

Jacob, b. Sept. 13, 1793; d. Dec. 22, 1859. Son of Rulif H. and Sarah Schenck.

Johnathan, b. July 19, 1761; d. Apr. 4, 1771, Son of Hendrick Schenck and Catharine Holmes.

Rolof, b. Feb. 21, 1692; d. Jan. 19, 1766, aged 73 y., 10 m., 28 d. Son of Jan Schenck and Sarah Couwenhoven.

Gesye, b. Oct. 9, 1696; d. Sept. 20, 1747, aged 50 y., 11 m., 11 d. Wife of Rolof Schenck and daughter of Daniel Hendrickson and Catharine VanDyke.

John, b. Jan. 22, 1720; d. June 27, 1749 aged 29 y., 5 m., 5 d. Son of Rolof Schenck and Gesya Hendrickson, daughter of Sheriff Daniel Hendrickson.

Hendrick, b. July 29, 1731, d. Aug. 24, 1766, aged 35 y., 25 d. Son of Rolof Schenck and Gesye Hendrickson.

Catharine, b. May 11, 1731; d. May 12, 1796, aged 63 y., 1 d. Widow of John and Hendrick Schenck, and daughter of Johnathan Holmes and Senniche Hendrickson, daughter of ex-Sheriff Daniel Hendrickson.

Cornelius R., b. July 29, 1740, d. July 12, 1796, aged 55 y., 11 m., 14 d. Son of Rulif C. Couwenhoven and Sarah Voorheese.

Jane, b. Aug. 19, 1740; d. Mar. 26, 1799, aged 58 y., 7 m., 7 d. Wife of Cornelius R. Covenhoven, and daughter of Tunis Denise and Francinka Hendrickson.

Teunis, b. Mar. 10, 1761; d. Oct. 30, 1787, aged 26 y., 7 m., 20 d. Son of Cornelius R. Covenhoven and Jane Denise.

William C., born July 20, 1700; d. Nov. 10, 1755, aged 55 y., 3 m., 21 d. Son of Cornelius Couwenhoven and Margaratta Schenck.

Jannatie, b. Jan. 26, 1702; d. June 22, 1743, aged 41 y., 4 m., 27 d. First wife of William C. Couwenhoven and daughter of Peter Wecof and Willempe Schenck.

Cornelius W., b. Feb. 11, 1746; d. Oct. 10,

The Burrowes house, at Middletown Point, where the company was formed described by Major S. S. Forman. Here, also, occurred the raid of "the Greens" in the early June morning, the 5th, 1778. The object was to capture the son, Major John, at home for a few hours. He was alarmed in time to jump from his bed, reach the lower story, escape through a window, swim the creek and find safety through his knowledge of the country.

The picture to the right shows the fine old hall of the Burrowes house. The chair on the first landing marks the spot where Mrs. Burrowes was met and sabred by the brutal officer for refusing her shawl to bind the wounds of a raider—a wound resulting in blood poisoning and death in very early life. The burning of the mills owned by Burrowes & Forman is recorded in local histories. The taking of John Burrowes, Sr., to a prison ship, the seizure of two prominent Tories of Middletown by Colonel Henderson and William Wikoff, bringing them to Monmouth jail as hostages, and that securing Burrowes' release.

APPENDIX.

1806, aged 60 y., 7 m., 27 d. Son of William C. Covenhoven and his second wife, Annetje Hendrickson.
Mary, b. Dec. 6, 1740; d. Jan. 3, 1806, aged 64 y., 27 d. Wife of Cornelius Covenhoven and daughter of Hendrick Hendrickson and Neltje Garretse Schenck.
William Hendrick, d. Sept. 26, 1805, aged 22 y., 6 m., 12 d. Only son of Cornelius Covenhoven and Mary Hendrickson.
Cornelius, b. Nov. 29, 1671; d. May 16, 1736, aged 64 y., 5 m., 17 d. Son of William Gerritse Couwenhoven and Janattie Monfort.
Margaratta, b. Feb. 9, 1678; d. Dec. 6, 1751, aged 73 y., 9 m., 27 d. Wife of Cornelius Couwenhoven and daughter of Rolofe Martense Schenck and Annetje Wychof.
Rulif, b. Oct. 5, 1706; d. Aug. 20, 1786, aged 79 y., 10 m., 15 d. Son of Cornelius Couwenhoven and Margaratta Schenck.
Sarah, b. Apr. 12, 1710; d. Dec. 12, 1789, aged 79 y., 8 m. Wife of Rulif Couwenhoven, and daughter of Cornelius Voorheese and Marytje Ditmars.

RE-INTERMENTS FROM SCHENCK-COWENHOVEN CEMETERY TO HOLMDEL CEMETERY.

John Schenck, b. Feb. 10, 1670; d. Jan. 30, 1753. Son of Roelof Martense and Neeltje Garretse Couwenhoven Schenck.
Sarah Couwenhoven, b. Jan. 6, 1675; d. Jan. 31, 1761. Wife of John Schenck and daughter of William Garretse and Jannetje Monfoort Couwenhoven.
John Schenck, b. June 27, 1722; d. Dec. 24, 1808. Son of John and Sarah Couwenhoven Schenck.
Nelly Bennett, b. Nov. 29, 1728; died June 1, 1810. Wife of John Schenck and daughter of Jan Bennett and Eyke VanMater Bennett.
Mary Schenck, b. Jan. 23, 1769; d. May 12, 1772. Daughter of John and Nelly Bennett Schenck.
Chrineyonce Schenck, b. Sept. 18, 1753; d. young. Son of John and Nelly Bennett Scnenck.
Chrineyonce Schenck, b. Dec. 29, 1760; d. Mar. 15, 1840. Son of John and Nelly Bennett Schenck.
Margaret Polhemus, b. Mar. 11, 1766; d. Jan. 13, 1857. Wife of Chrineyonce Schenck and daughter of John and Mary VanMater Polhemus.
Daniel P. Schenck, b. May 12, 1805; d. Dec. 29, 1834. Son of Chrineyonce and Margaret Polhemus Schenck.
Lydia H. Longstreet, b. Dec. 18, 1809; d. Apr. 7, 1838. Wife of Daniel P. Schenck and daughter of Hendrick and Mary Holmes Longstreet.
Chrineyonce Schanck, b. Feb. 21, 1838, d. Feb. 17, 1839. Son of Daniel P. and Lydia H. Longstreet Schenck.
John C. Schenck, b. June 2, 1797; d. Aug. 22, 1799. Son of Chrineyonce and Margaret Polhemus Schenck.
Eliza Schenck, b. Mar. 2, 1799; d. Dec. 2, 1799. Daughter of Chrineyonce and Margaret Polhemus Schenck.
Margaret Schenck, b. May 12, 1801; d. Mar. 10, 1835. Daughter of Chrineyonce and Margaret Polhemus Schenck.
Abigail Schenck, b. Apr. 28, 1808; d. May 31, 1825. Daughter of Chrineyonce and Margaret Polhemus Schenck.
John C. Schenck, b. June 6, 1803; d. Aug. 13, 1858. Son of Chrineyonce and Margaret Polhemus Schenck.
Margaret Schenck, d. Jan. 16, 1831, aged 1 y., 2 m., 28 d. Daughter of John C. and Margaret Polhemus Schenck.
Sarah Schenck, d. Sept. 9, 1834, aged 2 y., 5 m., 21 d. Daughter of John C. and Margaret Polhemus Schenck.
Catherine Schenck, d. Feb. 23, 1840; aged 11 m., 5 d. Daughter of John C. and Margaret Polhemus Schenck.
Chrineyonce Schenck, d. Mar 10, 1861; aged 16 y., 7 m., 14 d. Son of John C. and Margaret Polhemus Schenck.
Charles Schenck, b. Sept. 1, 1856; d. Dec. 30, 1856. Son of Daniel P. Schenck, Jr., and Lavenia Conover Schenck.
Cornelius R. Covenhoven, d. Apr. 11, 1817 aged 33 y., 11 m., 8 d. Son of Cornelius R. and Jane Denise Covenhoven.
Mary Stontenburg, d. Apr. 29, 1861; aged 74 y., 24 d. Wife of Cornelius R. Covenhoven.
Holmes Conover, d. May 22, 1860; aged 52 y., 4 m., 13 d. Son of Cornelius R. and Mary Stontenburg Conover. Twice sheriff of Monmouth county.
Caroline Crawford, d. Aug. 28, 1843; aged 24 years. Wife of Holmes Conover and daughter of James A. Crawford.
Garret R. Schenck, d. May 28, 1866; aged 65 y., 5 m., 12 d.
Conover Schenck, d. July 26, 1840; aged 10 y., 3 m., 20 d.
Mary Jane Schenck, d. Aug. 12, 1833; aged 10 m., 3 d. Children of Garret R. Schenck.
Garret D. Schenck, d. Nov. 9, 1850, aged 51 y., 2 m., 25 d.
Sarah Ann Schenck, d. Jan. 5, 1851, aged 56 y., 2 m., 1 d. Wife of Garret D. Schenck.
Sarah Schenck, d. Dec. 29, 1848, aged 24 y., 1 m., 27 d. Daughter of Garret D. and Sarah Ann Schenck.
Daniel G. Schenck, d. Nov. 2, 1838, aged 4 y., 1 m., 7 d. Son of Garret D. and Sarah Ann Schenck.
George Rappleye, d. Apr. 25, 1869, aged 75 y., 3 m., 18 d.
Jane Ann Rappleye, d. July 30, 1838, aged 15 y., 8 m., 4 d. Daughter of George and Elizabeth Smock Rappleye.
Garret Smock, d. Mar. 30, 1856, aged 90 y., 7 m., 26 d.
Jane Schenck, u. Mar. 23, 1850, aged 82 y., 11 m., 30 d. Wife of Garret Smock.
Capt. John Schenck, d. Aug. 28, 1834; aged 89 years. Son of Garret and Jane Conover Schenck.
Mary Denise, d. July 15, 1829, aged 79 y., 6

d. Wife of Capt. John Schenck and daughter of Teunis and Francinke Hendrickson Denise.
David Schenck, b. May 10, 1783; d. Apr. 23, 1872. Son of Capt. John and Mary Denise Schenck.
Sarah Smock, d. Feb. 2, 1832, aged 32 y., 2 m. Wife of David Schenck and daughter of George and Margaret VanDeventer Smock.
John Schenck, b. June 26, 1828; d. Feb. 5, 1859. Son of David and Sarah Smock Schenck.
Jane Schenck, d. April 23, 1791, aged 1 y., 7 m., 11 d. Daughter of Capt. John and Mary Denise Schenck.
William Schanck, d. Mar. 5, 1844; aged 71 y., 8 m., 21 d. Son of Capt. John and Mary Denise Schenck.
Garret G. Smock, b. Oct. 31, 1815; d. Jan. 5, 1859.
George G. Smock, b. May 8, 1788; d. Apr. 21, 1868.
Sarah Smock, b. Jan. 17, 1793; d. Apr. 13, 1832. Wife of George G. Smock.
John O. Stillwell, b. Apr. 25, 1763; d. Nov. 17, 1847.
Mary Schenck, b. Apr. 19, 1775; d. Sept. 29, 1864. Wife of John O. Stillwell and daughter of John and Nelly Bennett Schenck.
Capt. Daniel I. Schenck, b. Apr. 1, 1771; d. Aug. 9, 1845. Son of John and Nelly Bennett Schenck.
Catharine Smock, b. Mar. 7, 1775; d. June 8, 1839. Wife of Capt. Daniel I. Schenck and daughter of Hendrick and Nelly VanDorn Smock.
John Schenck, d. Dec. 8, 1798, aged 4 y., 9 m., 12 d. Son of Capt. Daniel I. and Catharine Smock Schenck.
John S. Schenck, d. Jan. 18, 1833, aged 22 y., 4 m., 29 d. Son of Capt. Daniel I. and Catharine Smock Schenck.
Aaron Longstreet, b. June 9, 1753; d. Oct. 19, 1800.
Willempe Hendrickson, b. Feb. 2, 1761; d. Oct. 21, 1837. Wife of Aaron Longstreet and daughter of Hendrick Hendrickson and Lydia Covenhoven Hendrickson.
Hendrick H. Longstreet, b. May 4, 1785, d. Feb. 26, 1860. Son of Aaron and Willempe Hendrickson Longstreet.
Nelly S. Longstreet, b. Apr. 4, 1783; d. Sept. 27, 1803. Wife of Obadiah Schenck and daughter of Aaron and Willempe Hendrickson Longstreet.
Ann Longstreet, b. Mar. 29, 1812; d. May 28, 1814. Daughter of Hendrick and Mary Holmes Longstreet.
John I. H. Longstreet, b. Feb. 22, 1826; d. June 14, 1851. Son of Hendrick and Mary Holmes Longstreet.
Hendrick H. Smock, b. Dec. 1, 1805; d. Oct. 8, 1841. Son of Barnes B. and Lydia Longstreet Smock.
Johnathan I. Holmes, b. Dec. 23, 1791; d. Aug. 12, 1866. Son of Joseph and Nelly Schenck Holmes.
Ann Eliza Holmes, b. Dec. 13, 1827; d. Sept. 1, 1851. Wife of Daniel S. Conover, and daughter of Johnathan I. and Ellen Schenck Holmes.
Joseph Holmes, b. Mar. 29, 1822; d. Aug. 22, 1825. Son of Johnathan I. and Ellen Schenck Holmes.
Elleanor Hendrickson, b. May 20, 1824; d. Feb. 28, 1844. Wife of John S. Longstreet and daughter of Garret D. and Jane Hendrickson.
Peter Schenck, d. June 6, 1837, aged 71 y., 10 d. Son of John and Nelly Bennet Schenck.
Rhoda Ogbourne, d. Aug. 21, 1848, aged 83 y., 1 m., 24 d. Wife of Peter Schenck.
Rhoda Schenck, d. Jan. 28, 1821, aged 20 y., 5 m., 4 d. Daughter of Peter and Rhoda Ogbourne Schenck.
Sarah Schenck, d. Dec. 22, 1823, aged 27 y., 20 d. Daughter of Peter and Rhoda Ogbourne Schenck.
John P. Schenck, d. Feb. 10, 1863, aged 57 y., 6 m., 23 d. Son of Peter and Rhoda Ogbourne Schenck.

SCHENCK-COUWENHOVEN MARRIAGES FROM RECORDS OF FIRST DUTCH CHURCH OF MONMOUTH COUNTY.

Nelly Schenck and Derk Sutphen, Feb. 10, 1743.
Garret Schenck and Neltje Voorhees, Oct. 19, 1744.
Mary Schenck and Aert Sutphen, Nov. 23, 1744.
Ellener Schenck and Edmund Harris, Jan. 4, 1765.
Geesye Schenck and Aaron (Arie) VanDoorn, May 9, 1765.
Cornelius Schenck and Margaret Taylor, July 3, 1765.
Kort Schenck and Rebecca Rogers, Jan. 20, 1767.
John Schenck and Mary Denise, July 31, 1767.
Mary Schenck and Tobias Polhemus, Oct. 21, 1768.
Jane Schenck and John Walter, Dec. 5, 1769.
Jane Schenck and Daniel Denise, Apr. 18, 1771.
Rulif Schenck and Sarah Schenck, Dec. 22, 1774.
Lea Schenck and John VanCleaf, Nov. 30, 1775.
Garret Schenck and Mary VanMater, Aug. 3, 1778.
William Schenck and Marya Tyse (Tice). Dec. 20, 1778.
Roelof Schenck and Martha Buckalew, June 28, 1779.
Nelly Schenck and Joseph VanCleaf, Dec. 19, 1782.
Nelly Schenck and Joseph Holmes, Oct. 20, 1785.
Anne Schenck and Denyse Hendrickson, Dec. 28, 1786.

APPENDIX.

Garret Schenck and Jane VanKirk, Dec. 12, 1787.
Rulif Schenck and Sarah MacMullen, Feb. 13, 1788.
Nelly Schenck and Thomas Shepherd, Oct. 22, 1790.
John Schenck and Polly Quackenbush, Feb. 24, 1791.
Geeshe Schenck and Isaac Harris, May 5, 1791.
Teunis Schenck and Altie VanDeveer, Dec. 13, 1792.
Nelly Schenck and Garret Denise, Jan. 16, 1793.
Peter Schenck and Sarah Shepherd, Oct. 26, 1793.
Nelly Schenck and Thomas Shepherd, Jan. 19, 1795.
Rulif Schenck and Sarah Bennet, Jan. 28, 1798.
Denye Schenck and Margaret Polhemius, Oct. 31, 1798.
Daniel Schenck and Ellener Schenck, Feb. 10, 1801.
Gitty Schenck and Jacob VanDoorn, Feb. 4, 1802.
Ellenor Schenck and William Denyse, Feb. 23, 1802.
John Schenck and Sarah Laen, Dec. 20, 1802.
Francyntie Schenck and William Nicolas, Feb. 5, 1803.
Ellener Schenck and Daniel Stoutenburg, Oct. 13, 1805.
Mary Schenck and Joseph Dorsett, Oct. 27, 1805.
Mary Schenck and John Stilwell, Mar. 25, 1806.
Catharine Schenck and Peter VanKirk, Dec. 16, 1803.
John K. Schenck and Anne VanCleaf, Dec. 14, 1808.
Mary Schenck and John Whitlock, Feb. 20, 1810.
Cryonce Schenck and Mary Schenck, Jan. 31, 1811.
Iendrick Schenck and Sarah Schenck, Dec. 2, 1812.
Anne Schenck and John S. Walter, Sept. 27, 1814.
Jonathan G. Schenck and Ellener Schenck, Feb. 9, 1815.
Garret Schenck and Lydia Schenck, Apr. 4, 1815.
Jane Schenck and Aaron Lane, May 15, 1816.
Catharine Schenck and Joseph Combs, Dec. 23, 1816.
David Schenck and Sarah Schenck, Nov. 12, 1818.
Elisha Schenck and Idah Schenck, Dec. 18, 1818.
Garret Schenck and Sarah Ann Schenck. Dec. 22, 1820.
William Schenck and Abby Polhemus.
Pieter Couwenhoven and Neltje Polhemius, Nov. 7, 1737.
Sarah Couwenhoven and Johannes VanClef, June 14, 1739.
Aeltje Couwenhoven (widow) and Cornelius Middah, Feb. 3, 1740.
Pieter Albertse Couwenhoven and Willempe Voorhees, May 19, 1741.
Helena Couwenhoven and Benjamin VanCleaf, July 2, 1741.
Roelof Couwenhoven and Jannetje Hendrickson, Aug. 12, 1741.
Jacob Couwenhoven and Margaret Couwenhoven, Dec. 21, 1742.
Sarah Couwenhoven and Arie Laen, May 17, 1743.
Catharine Couwenhoven and Daniel Hendrickson, Dec. 22, 1743.
William Couwenhoven and Antje Hendrickson, (widow) Mar. 17, 1744.
John Couwenhoven and Catharine Voorhees, Oct. 19, 1744.
Arintha Couwenhoven and Cornelius Leister, (Luyster) May 19, 1746.
Catharine Covenhoven and David VanDerveer, Feb. 28, 1765.
Albert Covenhoven and Patience Covenhoven, Dec. 1, 1765.
Jane Covenhoven and Peter Longstreet, Dec. 3, 1765.
Cobatje Covenhoven and Cyrenius VanMater, Apr. 6, 1766.
Cornelius Covenhoven and Mary Hendrickson, Jan. 13, 1767.
Sarah Covenhoven and Joseph Thompson, Feb. 19, 1767.
Cornelius Covenhoven and Mary Logan, July 12, 1770.
Nelly Covenhoven and Barrent Smock, July 12, 1770.
Ghasie Covenhoven and Hendrick Covenhoven, Mar. 19, 1772.
Elias Covenhoven and Catty Forman, Oct. 2, 1774.
Catharine Covenhoven and Samuel Buckalue, Jan. 26, 1775.
Roelof Covenhoven and Altje Voorhees, Feb. 1, 1775.
Sarah Covenhoven and Derrick Barkalo, Mar. 28, 1775.
Agnes Covenhoven and William Remsen, Mar. 18, 1778.
Aeltje Covenhoven and Mathys Laen, Apr. 29, 1778.
Anne Covenhoven (widow) and Benjamin Griggs, Nov. 26, 1778.
Geartrury Covenhoven and Jacob Allen, Jan. 14, 1779.
William Covenhoven and Mary Wall, Nov. 4, 1779.
Jane Covenhoven and Abraham Golden, Nov. 25, 1779.
Sarah Covenhoven and Johannes DeGraef, Mar. 9, 1780.
Nelly Covenhoven and Hendrick Williamsen, Mar. 23, 1780.
Lea Covenhoven and William Combs, Aug. 31, 1780.
Francinke Covenhoven and Hendrick Hendrickson, May 13, 1781.
Arintha Covenhoven and Joseph Willet, Feb. 13, 1782.
Catharine Covenhoven and Hendrick Laen, May 14, 1782.
Nelly Covenhoven and George Laen, May 14, 1782.
William Covenhoven and Elizabeth Mount, Jan. 1, 1783.
Sarah Couwenhoven and Robert Ashton, June 21, 1783.
Teunis Covenhoven and Hannah VanBrakle, Mar. 19, 1783.
Jane Covenhoven and Hendrick VanDerbilt, Apr. 10, 1783.
John Covenhoven and Anne Smock, May 23, 1783.
Anne Covenhoven and Isaac VanDoorn, July 3, 1785.

Anne Covenhoven and Abram VanHorn, Oct. 13, 1785.
Euphame Covenhoven and John Willet, Jan. 19, 1786.
Jacob Covenhoven and Jemima Williamsen, Dec. 13, 1787.
Mary Covenhoven and Thomas Shields, Mar. 23, 1788.
Teunis Covenhoven and Martha VanDerhoef, Dec. 7, 1788.
Garret Covenhoven and Mary Covenhoven, Dec. 18, 1788.
Roelof Covenhoven and Sarah VanDerveer, Jan. 12, 1789.
Mary Covenhoven and Samuel Forman, Mar. 12, 1789.
John Covenhoven and Anne VanBrunt, Nov. 25, 1789.
Nelly Covenhoven and Cornelius VanHorn Dec. 14, 1790.
Catharine Covenhoven and John VanDerveer, Apr. 7, 1791.
Garret Covenhoven and Mary Schenck, Jan. 12, 1792.
Hannah Covenhoven (widow), and Aron Krane or Crane, May 16, 1792.
Garret Covenhoven and Nelly Heyer, June 26, 1794.
Nelly Covenhoven and Aaert Wycof, Oct. 4, 1794.
Nelly Covenhoven and Caleb Stillwell, Dec. 7, 1796.
Albert Covenhoven and Elizabeth Shepherd, Dec. 27, 1796.
Margaret Covenhoven and Teunis Hubbert, (Hubbard) Jan. 5, 1797.
Peter Covenhoven and Sophia DuBois, Mar. 19, 1797.
Nelly Covenhoven and Daniel Little, Mar. 22, 1797.
Cornelius Covenhoven and Margaret Hans, Nov. 26, 1797.
Nelly Covenhoven and Caleb Stillwell, Decc. 10, 1797.
Sarah Covenhoven and Daniel G. Hendrickson, Dec. 21, 1797.
Peter Covenhoven and Mary Rue, Feb. 17, 1799.
Peter Forman Covenhoven and Jane Denise, Nov. 27, 1799.
Elleanor Conover and William Herbert, Jan. 31, 1801.
William Conover and Jane VanDerveer, Feb. 19, 1801.
Ghasey Conover (widow) and David Gordon, Aug. 20, 1801.
Elizabeth Conover and Daniel Dubois, Feb. 9, 1803.
Sarah Conover and Albert (Elbert) VanDoorn, Mar. 14, 1803.
Martinus (Matthias) Conover and Jane Conover, Jan. 10, 1804.
William Conover and Catharine Sutphen, Jan. 16, 1805.
Mary S. Conover and Joseph Sutphen, Apr. 24, 1805.
Jane Conover and Jonathan R. Gordon, Oct. 23, 1805.
Lewis Conover and Catharine Denise, May 28, 1806.
Anne Conover and Sidney Denise, Nov. 18, 1806.
Mary Conover and James Patterson, Dec. 31, 1806.
Cornelius Conover and Mary Stoutenburg, Mar. 9, 1807.
Ebenezer Conover and Mary Lefferson, Dec. 17, 1807.
Mary Conover and John VanDoorn, Jan. 30, 1809.
Elizabeth Conover and John G. Taylor, Mar. 8, 1809.
Jane Conover and Stacey Prickott, June 15, 1809.
Rulif Conover and Pamilla Wallen, (Walling) July 17, 1809.
John Conover and Ann Smock, Feb. 8, 1814.
George Conover and Mary Dubois, June 19, 1815.
Peter Conover (widower) and Patience Scott, June 12, 1816.
Jacob Conover and Elleanor Smock, Nov. 13, 1816.
Elleaner Conover and Daniel West, Dec. 6, 1817.
Catharine Conover and John Frost, Jan. 12, 1818.
Anne Conover and William Jackson, Oct. —, 1819.
Jane Conover and Peter Garretsen, Feb. 3, 1820.
Willempe Conover and Garret VanDoorn, Feb. 26, 1821.
Arintha Conover and Johnathan Pierce, Dec. 17, 1821.
John Conover and Elleanor Peacock, Mar. 17, 1822.
John G. H. Conover and Gertrude VanDerbilt, Dec. 31, 1823.
Rachael Conover and Adam Conrow, Feb. 25, 1835.
Jane Conover and Levi Solomon Sutphen, Feb. 24, 1836.
Sarah Ann Conover and William Statesir, Apr. 20, 1836.
Mary Conover and John Taylor, Jan. 29, 1838.
William Conover and Mary Otterson, Oct. 10, 1838.
John Schuyler Conover and Emeline Heyer, Nov. 4, 1840.
Mary Louiza Conover and James VanKirk, Nov. 8, 1840.
Mary Ann Conover and Aaron Sutphen, Nov. 23, 1841.
Ellen Conover and Isaac G. Smock, Dec. 23, 1841.
John Schenck and Cobatje Covenhoven, Oct. 14, 1769.
Mary Schenck and Jacob Covenhoven, Apr. 25, 1771.
Jan Schenck and Jacomina Covenhoven, Nov. 26, 1741.
Neltje Schenck and Garret Covenhoven, Oct. 12, 1744.
Anne Schenck and Rulif Covenhoven, June 22, 1777.
Peter Schenck and Elizabeth Covenhoven, Jan. 1, 1775.
Jane Schenck and John Covenhoven, Aug. 22, 1778.
Nelly Schenck and Jacob Covenhoven, Dec. 19, 1782.
Mary Schenck and Garret Covenhoven, Jan. 12, 1792.
Garret Schenck and Nelly Covenhoven, Aug. 24, 1797.
Schuyler Schenck and Margaret Covenhoven, Feb. 18, 1798.
Mary Schenck and Elias Covenhoven, July 1, 1798.

APPENDIX. vii

Catharine Schenck and Jacob I. Covenhoven, Sept. 26, 1799.
De Lafayette Schenck and Nelly Covenhoven, Dec. 17, 1805.
Sarah Schenck and Garret Conover, Jan. 6, 1807.
James Schenck and Anne Conover, Dec. 21, 1809.
Peter Schenck and Nelly Conover, Apr. 3, 1811.
William Schenck and Anne Conover, Mar. 11, 1812.
John H. Schenck and Jane Conover, (widow) Aug. 2, 1812.
Ephraim Loree Schenck and Nelly Conover, Sept. 15, 1812.
Marya Schenck and Troley Conover, Dec. 9, 1812.
Mary Schenck and Garret Conover, Dec. 14, 1814.
Arintha Schenck and William Conover, Feb. 5, 1816.
Anne Schenck and Martinus (Matthias) Conover, (his second wife) Apr. 18, 1822.

TOMBSTONE INSCRIPTIONS.

Old Tennent Cemetery, Tennent, N. J.

Anna Denise, wife David Forman, and daughter of Teunis Denise and Francinke Hendrickson, d. Sept. 9, 1798, aged 63 y.
William Forman, d. Jan. 31, 1823, aged 71 y., 5 m., 5 d.
Francinka Hendrickson, wife William Forman, and daughter of Garret Hendrickson and Catharine Denise, d. June 19, 1815, aged 56 y., 4 m., 5 d.
John Covenhoven, d. Nov. 3, 1824, aged 79 y.
Mary Covenhoven, wife John Covenhoven, d. Nov. 14, 1826, aged 86 y.
John Covenhoven, Jr., son of John and Mary Covenhoven, d. Oct. 3, 1804, aged 29 y.
Elizabeth Hendrickson, wife of John R. Schenck, d. Nov. 15, 1831, aged 26 y.
Joseph L. Covenhoven, elder of this church, d. Apr. 3, 1853, aged 71 y., 2 m., 17 d.
Gertrude Covenhoven, wife Joseph L. Covenhoven, d. Jan. 19, 1853, aged 75 y., 6 m.
Charles Covenhoven, son of Joseph L. and Gertrude Covenhoven, d. Jan. 6, 1838, aged 22 y., 8 m., 16 d.
Rulif P. Schenck, d. Apr. 8, 1854, aged 18 y., 10 m., 16 d.
Rulif R. Schenck, b. June 20, 1784; d. June 28, 1860.
David Covenhoven, d. Sept. 20, 1822, aged 62 y.
Esther Covenhoven, wife David Covenhoven, d. July 1, 1829, aged 61 y.
Ann Covenhoven, daughter of David and Esther Covenhoven, d. Mar. 2, 1868, aged 73 y., 10 m.
William Covenhoven, d. Aug. 12, 1852, aged 78 y., 1 m., 20 d.
Jane VanDeveer, wife William Covenhoven, and daughter of David VanDeveer and Catharine Covenhoven, d. Jan. 16, 1858, aged 83 y., 3 m., 17 d.
Jacob Conover, d. Dec. 24, 1846, aged 31 y., 8 m.
Ellen L. VanDevere, wife Jacob Conover, d. Sept. 24, 1846, aged 29 y., 9 m., 22 d.
Wycof Conover, d. May 3, 1833, aged 49 y., 4 m., 21 d.
Ely Conover, wife of Wycof Conover, d. Nov. 11, 1880, aged 90 y., 2 m.
William B. Covenhoven, d. Aug. 15, 1807, aged 55 y., 2 m., 12 d. Son of Benjamin Covenhoven.
Elleanor Forman, wife William B. Covenhoven, daughter Peter Forman and Elleanor Willemsen, d. Aug. 20, 1823, aged 71 y.

Capt. Benjamin W. Covenhoven, d. Nov. 27, 1849, aged 61 y.
Margaret Covenhoven, wife Capt. Benjamin W. Covenhoven, d. Feb. 3, 1869, aged 85 y., 3 m., 26 d.
Peter Forman, Esq., son of Jonathan Forman and Margaret Wycoff, d. Sept. 8, 1785, aged 66 y., 8 m., 10 d.
Elleanor Williamsen, wife Peter Forman, and daughter of Aert Willemsen and Anatie Covenhoven, d. Nov. 6, 1771, aged 51 y., 1 m., 13 d.
Garret Covenhoven, son of Peter Forman Covenhoven and Jane Denise, d. Sept. 8, 1823, aged 17 y., 2 m., 6 d.
Daniel D. Covenhoven, son Peter Forman Covenhoven and Jane Denise, d. May 4, 1841, aged 41 y., 20 d.
Margaret Covenhoven, wife Daniel D. Covenhoven, d. Oct. 2, 1882, aged 83 y.
Garret B. Covenhoven, son of Benjamin Covenhoven, d. Dec. 18, 1824, aged 63 y., 11 m., 18 d.
Lydia Forman, wife Garret B. Covenhoven, daughter of Peter Forman and Elleanor Willemsen, d. Feb. 15, 1840, aged 78 y., 1 m., 29 d.
Benjamin G. Conover, son of Garret and Lydia Covenhoven, d. May 22, 1834, aged 46 y., 10 m., 12 d.
Elleanor Herbert, wife Benjamin G. Conover, d. Jan. 15, 1863, aged 78 y., 11 m., 1 d.
William B. Conover, d. Feb. 22, 1837, aged 21 y., 6 m.
Catharine Covenhoven, daughter of Garret B. Covenhoven and Lydia Forman, d. Nov. 13, 1830, aged 40 y., 26 d.
Mary F. Covenhoven, daughter of Garret B. and Lydia Forman Covenhoven, b. Dec. 10, 1795; d. Sept. 1, 1883.
Allice Conover, b. Oct. 18, 1800; d. May 18, 1864.
Robert Covenhoven, d. Apr. 1, 1826, aged 45 y.
John M. Covenhoven, d. Sept. 13, 1828, aged 70 y., 7 m.
Ann Covenhoven, wife John M. Covenhoven, d. Aug. 24, 1855, aged 91 y., 2 d.
Elizabeth Conover, wife Joseph Preston, d. Feb. 24, 1871, aged 57 y., 7 m., 15 d.
Rulif Vandevere, son David Vandevere and Catharine Covenhoven, d. Sept. 13, 1801, aged 36 y., 4 m., 24 d.
Catharine Vandevere, daughter of Rulif Vandevere and Nelly Lloyd, d. Nov. 20, 1808, aged 14 y., 6 m., 21 d.

Sarah Covenhoven, wife Garret H. Covenhoven, d. Mar. 15, 1856, aged 71 y., 11 m.
Joseph W. Covenhoven, d. May 2, 1849, aged 62 y., 9 m.
Allice Conover, d. Feb. 22, 1864, aged 75 y.
Richard Conover, d. Sept. 20, 1851, aged 81 y., 5 m., 12 d.
Hannah Conover, d. Sept. 6, 1810, aged 66 y., 6 d.
Mary Conover, d. May 23, 1850, aged 40 y., 2 m., 13 d.

Old Yellow Meeting House Cemetery, Imlaystown, N. J.

James Holmes, d. Mar. 6, 1825; aged 20 y., 7 m., 29 d.
Sarah Bruere, wife of John H. Bruere and daughter of Joseph and Mary Holmes, d. June 20, 1831, aged 23 y.
John H. Bruere, b. July 13, 1803; d. Sept. 15, 1864.
Joseph Holmes, son of Joseph and Mary Holmes, b. Nov. 24, 1800; d. Aug. 1, 1897.
Deborah Holmes, wife of John Holmes, d. May 6, 1811, aged 64 y., 6 m., 24 d.
John Holmes, son of Joseph and Elizabeth Holmes, d. Aug. 10, 1783; aged 39 y., 5 m.
Jonathan Holmes, d. Aug. 4, 1777 (or 1,) aged 38 y., 8 m., 2 d.
Lydia Holmes, d. Feb. 14, 1783, aged 38 y.
Joseph Holmes, Esq., d. Aug. 31, 1809, aged 72 y., 8 m.
Phoebe Holmes, wife of Joseph Holmes, d. Feb. 25, 1786, aged 49 y., 6 m.
Joseph Holmes, d. July 16, 1815, aged 43 y., 5 m., 16 d.
Mary Holmes, wife of Joseph Holmes, d. June 28, 1833, aged 59 y., 3 m., 25 d.
Forman Hendrickson, b. 1836; d. 1889.
Elizabeth Grover, widow of Daniel Hendrickson, d. Nov. 7, 1851, aged 87 y., 10 m., 6 d.
Gilbert Giberson, d. Dec. 21, 1843, aged 91 y., 2 m., 29 d.
Rachael Giberson, wife of Gilbert Giberson, d. June 23, 1833, aged 80 y., 3 m.
Allice Holmes, daughter of Jonathan and Lydia Holmes, d. Mar. 16, 1790, aged 14 y., 3 m., 2 d.
Mrs. Eliza Ellis, consort of Rowland Ellis, a merchant of Philadelphia; d. May 9, 1795, aged 20 y., 4 m., 9 d.
John Polhemius, d. Sept. 15, 1793, aged 72 y.
Allis Holmes, wife of John Polhemius and daughter of Joseph and Elizabeth Holmes, d. Apr. 10, 1788, aged 61 y., 10 m.
Sarah Throckmorton, daughter of John and Sarah Throckmorton, d. Mar. 8, 1805, aged 47 y., 2 m., 25 d.
Peter Wykoff, d. July 10, 1854, aged 48 y., 10 m., 23 d.
Harriet Wykoff, widow of Peter Wykoff, d. Mar. 31, 1861, aged 51 y., 10 m., 14 d.
John Salter, d. Aug. 29, 1723, aged 28 y., 10 m., 7 d.
Samuel Hendrickson, son of Tobias and Rebecca Hendrickson, d. Mar. 13, 1813, aged 44 y., 1 m., 3 d.
Alckey Hendrickson, wife of Samuel Hendrickson, d. Mar. 2, 1828, aged 58 y., 1 m., 17 d.
Tobias Hendrickson, d. May 25, 1811, aged 70 y., 11 m., 2 d.
Rebeka Coward, widow of Tobias Hendrickson, d. June 6, 1815, aged 72 y., 7 m., 10 d.
Gilbert Hendrickson, son of Tobias and Rebeka Hendrickson, d. Feb. 21, 1837, aged 72 y., 6 m., 13 d.
Allis Hendrickson, relict of Gilbert Hendrickson, d. Jan. 23, 1852, aged 84 y., 2 m.
Rev. John Coward, d. July 30, 1760.
Allis Coward, wife of Rev. John Coward, d. Oct. 30, 1766.
Idah Hendrickson, wife of Tobias Hendrickson and daughter of David and Easter Covenhoven, d. Oct. 27, 1815, aged 26 y., 4 m., 12 d.
Tobias Hendrickson, son of Gilbert and Allis Hendrickson, d. Dec. 22, 1833, aged 11 y., 6 d.
Samuel Hendrickson, d. May 8, 1848, aged 52 y., 9 m., 15 d.
George W. Cox, d. Aug. 8, 1874, aged 64 y., 6 m., 27 d.
Francinke Hendrickson, wife George W. Cox, daughter of William and Elleanor Hendrickson, d. Apr. 29, 1854, aged 31 y., 8 m., 11 d.
Peter Perrine Hendrickson, son of Tobias and Margaret I endrickson, d. Feb. 13, 1839, aged 7 m., 6 d.
Easter Ashton, d. Jan. 6, 1825, aged 73 y., 4 m., 4 d.
Garret Covenhoven, d. Dec. 21, 1831, aged 56 y., 7 m., 1 d.
Allice Hendrickson, wife Garret Covenhoven, d. Aug. 20, 1855, aged 80 y., 5 m., 7 d.
Jacob Covenhoven, son of Garret and Allice Covenhoven, d. May 10, 1828, aged 28 y., 3 m., 10 d.
Rebeka P. Covenhoven, wife Jacob Covenhoven, b. Oct. 13, 1802; d. June 2, 1858.
Catharine Covenhoven, wife William Meirs, and daughter of Garret and Allice Covenhoven, d. Nov. 17, 1828, aged 20 y., 5 m., 21 d.
Richard H. Covenhoven, b. July 16, 1819; d. Oct. 11, 1892.
Allice H. Covenhoven, daughter of Richard and Elizabeth Covenhoven, d. Feb. 27, 1850, aged 6 y., 11 m., 23 d.
Thomas S. Meirs, d. Aug. 11, 1859, aged 60 y., 11 m., 17 d.
Martha Polhemus, b. Apr. 23, 1838; d. Aug. 31, 1854.
Job Polhemus, b. Oct. 20, 1807; d. Jan. 28, 1897.
Mary Hodson, wife of Job Polhemus, b. Dec. 8, 1816; d. May 21, 1894.
Tobias Polhemus, b. Nov. 5, 1795; d. Mar. 10, 1878.
Sarah Meirs, wife Tobias Polhemus, b. July 28, 1802; d. Sept. 30, 1880.
Arthur Polhemus, son of Tobias and Sarah Polhemus, d. Jan. 22, 1863, aged 22 y., 10 m., 22 d.
Sarah A. Embley, d. Jan. 15, 1878, aged 33 y., 10 m., 3 d.
Jacob Hendrickson, d. Aug. 15, 1810, aged 66 y., 5 m.
Elizabeth Mount, wife Jacob Hendrickson, d. July 24, 1832, aged 76 y., 6 m., 12 d.
Michael Mount, d. Feb. 4, 1805, aged 85 y.
Mary Mount, wife Michael Mount, d. Sept. 2, 1809, aged 70 y.
Samuel Forman, d. Aug. 4, 1817, aged 78 y., 9 m., 7 d.
Margaret Forman, wife Samuel Forman, d. July 17, 1824, aged 74 y., 4 m., 1 d.
Ezekiel Forman, son of Samuel Forman and Mary Wilbore, d. Oct. 3, 1746, aged 39 y., 11 m., 2 d.
Elizabeth Seabrooke, wife Richard Mount, formerly wife Ezekiel Forman, d. Mar. 16, 1791, aged 79 y.

APPENDIX.

Richard Hendrickson, b. Sept. 6, 1800; d. Mar. 16, 1873.
Mary Thomas, wife Richard Hendrickson, b. Dec. 10, 1808; d. Jan. 15, 1880.
Michael Hendrickson, son of Jacob and Elizabeth Hendrickson, b. Mar. 2, 1776; d. July 11, 1811.
Sarah Horsfull, wife Michael Hendrickson, d. Aug. 4, 1854, aged 71 y., 10 m., 6 d.
Samuel M. Hendrickson, d. Aug. 29, 1819, aged 38 y.
Richard Horsfull, d. Oct. 4, 1859, aged 55 y., 5 m., 21 d.
Elizabeth Hendrickson, wife Richard Horsfull, d. Feb. 7, 1859, aged 55 y., 5 m., 5 d.
William J. Hendrickson, d. Feb. 15, 1893, aged 70 y.
Peter G. Hendrickson, d. Dec. 30, 1862, aged 76 y., 17 d.
Catharine Hendrickson, widow of Peter G. Hendrickson, d. Jan. 8, 1868, aged 81 y., 5 m., 25 d.
Gilbert P. Hendrickson, d. May 14, 1861, aged 45 y., 5 m., 19 d.
Hannah W. Hendrickson, d. Dec. 11, 1865, aged 62 y., 3 mo., 6 d.
William E. Hendrickson, son of Gilbert and Hannah Hendrickson, d. Dec. 23, 1866, aged 19 y., 5 m., 17 d.
Mary E. Hendrickson, daughter of Anthony and Lydia Hendrickson, b. Sept. 23, 1863; d. May 13, 1867.
Charles H. Polhemus, b. Feb. 6, 1834; d. Nov. 10, 1871.
Mary Polhemus, wife George Hendrickson, b. May 29, 1836; d. May 28, 1888.

First Church, Cranbury, N. J.

Peter Wyckoff, d. Mar. 29, 1855, aged 68 y., 28 d.
Elizabeth Wyckoff, wife Peter Wyckoff, d. Dec., 1895, aged 95 y., 9 m., 12 d.
William Schenck, d. Apr. 11, 1821, aged 44 y., 1 m., 28 d.
Sarah Schenck, wife William Schenck and daughter of Thomas Wetherel, d. Nov. 10, 1858, aged 75 y., 9 m., 28 d.
James Gaston, son of Hugh and Jane Gaston, d. Oct. 20, 1738, aged 33 y., 1 m., 18 d.
William Covenhoven, d. Mar. 10, 1813, aged 47 y.
Sarah Covenhoven, wife William Covenhoven, d. Apr. 28, 1853, aged 87 y.
Peter Covenhoven, d. Feb. 9, 1816, aged 23 y.
Mary Dey Covenhoven, d. Dec. 7, 1817, aged 23 y.
Phoebe Covenhoven, d. July 8, 1815, aged 17 y.
Lammetie Remsen, wife Luke Schenck, d. Jan. 31, 1780, aged 58 y., 8 m., 10 d.
Martin Schenck, d. Nov. 2, 1818, aged 35 y., 8 m., 16 d.
Samuel Longstreet, d. Dec. 21, 1829, aged 94 y.
William W. Covenhoven, d. May 9, 1803, aged 61 y., 2 m., 7 d.
Elizabeth, wife William Covenhoven, d. May 13, 1807, aged 61 y.
William W. Covenhoven, son of William and Elizabeth Covenhoven, b. Aug. 14, 1783; d. Jan. 23, 1837, aged 54 years.
Catharine, wife William W. Covenhoven, d. July 21, 1852, aged 64 y., 7 m., 15 d.
Ann Covenhoven, wife John P. Bergen, daughter of William and Elizabeth Covenhoven, d. Nov. 24, 1860, aged 90 y., 5 m., 14 d.

John P. Bergen, d. Jan. 11, 1850, aged 84 y., 3 m., 11 d.
John W. Covenhoven, d. July 16, 1854, aged 64 y., 6 m.
Phoebe Covenhoven, wife of Peter Covenhoven, d. May 14, 1826, aged 78 y., 5 m., 24 d.
John P. Covenhoven, d. Apr. 12, 1835, aged 57 y.
Lydia Dunkin, wife John P. Covenhoven, d. Aug. 2, 1851, aged 75 y.
Stephen Covenhoven, d. Sept. 8, 1837, aged 36 y.
Ann Covenhoven, wife Johnson Covenhoven, d. July 13, 1841, aged 54 y.
Elias J. Conover, d. Sept. 29, 1861, aged 49 y., 11 m., 9 d.
Arthur and Elleanor Wyckoff; he died Aug. 1784, aged 67 y.; she died Mar. 1788, aged 68 y.
Jane Lane, wife of Aaron Lane, d. Aug. 20, 1836, aged 44 y.

Second Church, Cranbury, N. J.

Richard G. Konover, d. Aug. 11, 1865, aged 60 y., 8 m., 28 d.

Penn's Neck Cemetery.

Richard Schenck, d. July 22, 1854, aged 52 y., 18 d.
John J. Schenck, son of Capt. John Schenck and Mary VanDorn, d. Feb. 3, 1857, aged 77 y., 8 m., 6 d.
Elizabeth Schenck, wife John I. Schenck, d. Mar. 9, 1857, aged 76 y., 8 m., 6 d.
James F. Schenck, d. July 11, 1865, aged 53 y.
Richard R. Schenck, d. Sept. 3, 1878, aged 49 y., 11 m.
Nathaniel Schenck, d. Oct. 6, 1886, aged 73 y., 11 m.
Kitty Schenck, wife John D. Schenck, b. Apr. 20, 1747; d. July 10, 1880.
William Schenck, b. Apr. 22, 1823; d. Mar. 23, 1891.
Lydia A. Stults, wife William Schenck, b. Feb. 19, 1827.
John A. Schenck, d. Sept. 18, 1839, aged 75 y., 9 m., 29 d.
Margaret Schenck, wife John A. Schenck, d. Oct. 8, 1842, aged 77 y., 7 d.
William Kovenhoven, b. Dec. 2, 1767; d. Sept. 24, 1838, aged 70 y., 3 m., 8 d.
Mary Kovenhoven, wife William Kovenhoven, d. Jan. 4, 1817, aged 38 y., 9 m., 6 d.
Voorhees Kovenhoven, d. Aug. 26, 1843, aged 33 y., 6 m.
Deborah Kovenhoven, daughter of William and Mary Kovenhoven, d. Feb. 14, 1859, aged 53 y., 5 m., 11 d.
George F. Kovenhoven, d. Nov. 2, 1815, aged 2 m., 21 d.
Anna F. Kovenhoven, d. Aug. 24, 1815, aged 12 d. Children of William and Mary Kovenhoven.

Old Penn's Neck Yard,

one-quarter mile from village of Penn's Neck, one and a half miles from Princeton, between Princeton Junction and Princeton, N. J.:

Eve Schenck, widow of John R. Schenck, d. Nov. 21, 1810.
Albert G. Schenck, d. May 21, 1786, aged 65 y., 1 m., 2 d.
Cornelius Couwenhoven, d. 1787, aged 51 y.
Chrystena Couwenhoven, wife William Cou-

wenhoven, and daughter of
d. June 24, 1787, aged 78 y.
Harmon Couwenhoven, d. Jan. 4, 1804, aged 63 y., 7 m.
Phoebe Baley, wife Harmon Couwenhoven, d. Feb. 2, 1832, aged 87 y., 9 m., 16 d.
Elias C. Schenck, d. Nov. 5, 1800, aged 6 y., 7 m., 17 d.
Elizabeth Schenck, d. May 5, 1785, aged 7 m.
Joseph Schenck, son of Jan Schenck and Mary Johnson, d. Oct. 25, 1822, aged 66 y., 5 m., 5 d.
Peggy Schenck, wife Joseph Schenck and daughter of William and Elizabeth Covenhoven, d. July 18, 1804, aged 38 y., 4 m., 8 d.
Anney Schenck, daughter of Joseph and Peggy Schenck, d. Oct. 25, 1776.
Margaret Schenck, d. Aug. 5, 1816, aged 70 y.
Mary Schenck, d. Sept. 12, 1769.
Garret Schenck, d. May 11, 1810, aged 68 y.
Jacob R. Schenck, son of Ruleph and Engeltie Schenck, d. Dec. 19, 1786, aged 60 y.
Mary Schenck, wife William P. Schenck, d. July, 1829, aged 70 y.
William Kouwenhoven, d. Oct. 7, 1777, aged 35 y., 4 m., 9 d.
Garret A. Schenck, d. Mar. 8, 1794, aged 41 y.

Baptist Church Yard, Holmdel, N. J

Leah Bown, widow of Daniel Holmes, d. Mar. 15, 1813, in 77th year.
James Holmes, Esq., d. Friday, Aug. 13, 1762, aged 66 y., 6 m., 4 d. This man was a member of the Colonial Legislature of New Jersey.

Old Red Meeting House Yard,
near residence of late Dr. Cook. Holmdel, N. J. Here was site of first Dutch church in old township of Middletown.

John C. VanMater, b. Jan. 30, 1793; d. Sept. 8, 1867.
Lucy, wife John C. VanMater, d. Jan. 23, 1861, age 63 y., 3 m.
Cyrenius Bennet, d. Apr. 20, 1850, age 70 y., 9 m., 17 d.
Albert Bennet, d. June 17, 1857, age 81 y., 11 m., 7 d.
Rebecca, wife Albert Bennet, d. Feb. 1, 1858, age 83 y., 1 m., 8 d.
William V. Bennett, d. Oct. 13, 1853, age 47 y., 5 m., 7 d. Wife, Ann S. Schenck, d. Nov. 8, 1879, age 76 y., 7 m., 13 d.
Alchey, wife Isaac I. Conover and daughter of John W. and Elizabeth Bennet, d. Feb. 19, 1846, age 47 y., 7 m., 16 d.
Alchey Snider, wife of Derrick Zutphen, d. Sept. 30, 1837, age 76 y., 2 m., 25 d.
Derrick Zutphen, d. Feb. 18, 1832, age 77 y., 9 m., 6 d.
Mary, wife of Derrick Zutphen, d. Apr. 18, 1824, age 51 y., 4 m., 16 d.

From Smock Grave Yard,
on farm of late Peter R. Smock at Holmdel:
Cornelia Stillwell, wife of William R. Smock, d. May 26, 1853, age 37 y., 5 m., 29 d.
Barnes. B. Smock, d. Sept. 26, 1854, age 80 y., 3 m., 13 d.
Lydia Longstreet, wife of Barnes B. Smock, d. Feb. 17, 1865, age 84 y., 1 m., 6 d.
Rulif Smock, d. Sept. 24, 1834, age 65 y., 10 m., 4 d.
Mary VanDoorn, wife Rulif Smock, d. Aug. 11, 1865, age 87 y., 5 m., 21 d.
Sarah Couwenhoven, wife of George .Smock, Sen., d. Mar. 30, 1794, age 88 y., 11 m., 6 d.
Mathias Laen, d. Jan. 15, 1824, age 75 y.
Catharine Smock, wife Mathias Laen, d. Oct. 12, 1837, age 78 y.

MARRIAGES SOLEMNIZED BY ELDER JOHN D. BARKALOW.

The following list of marriages was taken from a book kept by John D. Barkalow. Many of them are not recorded in Monmouth clerk's office, and there is no other record except this book, now in possession of William B. Hulse. On the first page, the following entry appears in the handwriting of John D. Barkalow:

"A book of records of marriages by John D. Barkalow, Elder of the Methodist Independent Church, Monmouth County,* New Jersey, August 12, 1812."
1. Married on the 3rd day of August, 1812, Mr. Samuel Young to Miss Elizabeth Williamson. Both of the county of Monmouth.
2. November 4th, Mr. Garret Hulshart, Sr., to Miss Allice McCabe.
1813.
3. January 28th, Mr. Daniel Emmons, Jr., to Miss Esther Fulshart.
4. February 6th, Mr. John G. Hulshart to Miss Mary Chapman.

* Ocean county was then part of Monmouth county.

5. August 1st, Mr. Jacob Lain to Miss Jane Hulshart.
1814.
6. March 12th, Mr. David Applegate to Miss Alice Hendrickson.
7. 24th, Mr. John I. Brewer to Miss Elize Jeffrey.— All the above of Monmouth county.
8. Married on 2nd day of April, 1814, Mr. Peter Gravat to Miss Hannah VanCleafe, both of the county of Monmouth.
1815.
9. June 24th, Mr. John G. Bartholf of the city of New York to Miss Christianna Haring of Monmouth county, New Jersey.
10. September 16th, Mr. Stephen Bills to Miss Mary Thompson, both of Monmouth county.
1816.
11. January 1st, Mr. John D. Oakerson to Miss Eliza Voorhees.
12. March 3rd, Mr. John W. Taylor to Miss Idah Covenhoven.
13. March 3rd, Mr. Aaron Hires to Miss Gertrude Cottrell.—These four above all of the county of Monmouth.

APPENDIX. xi

14. July 11th, Mr. Fenwick Thompson of the city of New York, to Miss Mary Mount of Monmouth, New Jersey.
15. December 7th, Mr. Gilbert Matthews to Miss Catharine Emmons, both of Monmouth.
16. December 11th, Mr. John Conine to Miss Rachel Bennett.

1817.
17. January 23rd, Mr. Tylee W. Lefetre to Miss Catharine Harring.
18. February 8th, Mr. John Errickson to Miss Allice Matthews.
19. March 5th, Mr. Uriah White to Miss Nancy Oakerson.
20. May 21st, Mr. Peter Applegate to Miss Maria Covenhoven.
21. December 27th, Mr. Joseph C. Thompson to Miss Ann Hulshart.

1818.
22. January 3rd, Mr. Joseph Combs to Miss Mary Patterson.
23. January 7th, Mr. William Snyder to Miss Eleanor Laen.
24. Married on the 22nd day of January, 1818, Mr. Abraham P. Hunt of the city of New York, to Miss Margaret Neaflea of Monmouth, New Jersey.
25. September 6th, Mr. William Houghman to Rebecca Nivison, both of Monmouth.

1819.
26. January 6th, Mr. Charles Fowler to Miss Mary Buckalue.
27. January 21st, Mr. Joseph Buckalue to Miss Nancy Valentine.
28. March 13th, Mr. Hezakiah Smith to Miss Ezilpha Lemmon.
29. March 20th, Mr. Robert Fielder to Miss Hannah Brown.
30. May 18th, Mr. Richard Stepe to Miss Elizabeth Robes or Jobes.
31. November 29th, Mr. Abraham Goodenough to Miss Mary Brown.

1820.
32. August 30th, Mr. John K. VanHouten to Miss Sarah C. Meeks, both of the city of New York.
33. November 18th, Mr. James Vincent to Miss Sarah Ann Kenaghan, both of Monmouth.

1821.
34. March 9th, Mr. James Hankins to Miss Sarah Wainright.
35. April 9th, Jonathan Errickson to Miss Julia Ann Rogers.
36. May 3rd, Mr. Robert Harbert to Miss Elizabeth Seebrooks.
37. At the same time and place, Mr. Jacob Cooper to Miss Hannah Daviss.
38. September 15th, Mr. John Hough to Miss Γariet Borden.
39. October 26th, Anthony Richmond to Miss Catharine Holmes.
40. December 15th, Mr. William W. Layton to Miss Catharine Voorhees.
41. Married on the 29th day of December, 1821, Mr. John Oakerson, Sr., to Miss Caty Buckelue.
42. On the same day Mr. Gidion Hulshart to Miss Catharine Thompson, all of Monmouth.

1822.
43. April 4th, Mr. Gilbert Miller of Burlington county to Miss Rebecca Oakerson of Monmouth.
44. May 7th, Mr. William Evens to Miss Mary Cob, Monmouth.
45. December 18th, Mr. Samuel D. Hayes to Miss Sarah Stricklin.

1823.
46. January 9th, Mr. Benjamin VanCleaf to Miss Rachel VanCleaf.
47. April 20th, Mr. Gilbert Brewer to Miss Hannah Voorhees.
48. October 4th, Joseph Brewer to Miss Hannah Hankins.
49. December 24th, James Layton to Miss Charlotte Ayres.

1824.
50. January 10th, Albert H. Voorhees to Miss Lydia H. Covenhoven.
51. April 3rd, Mr. Thomas VanHorn to Miss Rebeccah Pittenger.
52. August 12th, Mr. Peter G. Nickels to Miss Elizabeth Bennett.
53. August 23rd, Thomas Hulshart to Miss Ann Doshe Hulshart.
54. September 25th, Mr. John Voorhees to Miss Elizabeth Stricklin, both of Monmouth.
55. October 30th, Mr. Robert Skidmore to Miss Hannah Holeman.

1825.
56. May 7th, Capt. John S. Cowdrick to Miss Jane Barkalow.
57. June 13th, Mr. George Maxson to Miss Esther Fish.
58. August the 21st, Mr. William Duncan of Monmouth, New Jersey, to Miss Jane Story of NewBurgh, state of New York.
59. Married the 20th day of November, 1825, Mr. David Matthews, Sr., to Miss Ann Preston, both of Monmouth county.

1826.
60. March 26th, Mr. Ruliff Smith to Miss Catharine Hendrickson.
61. July 1st, Mr. John I. Clayton to Miss Altia Hulshart.
62. 8th, Mr. Jonathan C. Stricklin to Miss Nancy Voorhees.
63. August 26, Mr. William Bills to Miss Catharine Oakerson.

1827.
64. March 3rd, Mr. Richard Hagerman to Miss Maria Heaviland.
65. 22nd, Mr. William W. Sale of the city of New York, to Miss Elizabeth Patterson of Monmouth county.
66. June 2nd, Mr. Jacob Hagerman to Miss Lydia Heaviland; both of Monmouth county.
67. September 20th, James Oakerson to Miss Rhoda Attison.
68. October 20th, Samuel Werden to Miss Mary Ann Hendrickson.
69. December 22nd, John Hartsgrove to Miss Catharine Clayton.

1828.
70. January 5th, Forman Palmmer to Miss Phebe Cottrell.
71. February 23rd, Mr. John T. Hall to Miss Rebecca Patterson.
72. April 5th, Samuel Matthews to Miss Catharine Emmons.
73. September 27th, Mr. William Chapman, to Miss Eleanor Heaviland.
74. October 2nd, Mr. Joseph Perrine to Miss Amy Thompson.
75. Married on 16th day of October, 1828, Mr. A. Evernham to Miss Altia Hendrickson, both of Upper Freehold, Monmouth county, New Jersey.
76. 29th, Mr. Lewis Ayres to Miss Jane Layton.

77. November 8th, Mr. Samuel Painton to Miss Mary Snyder.
78. On the above same day, William R. Cottrell to Miss Lucy Woodward.
79. December 24th, John Henry Mount to Miss Nancy Boude.

1829.
80. June 17th, Mr. Isaac Lobb of the city of New York, to Miss Catharine Hamilton of the city of Trenton, Hunterdon county, New Jersey.
81. 28th, Mr. Stephen Hulshart to Miss Sarah Matthews, both of Monmouth county, New Jersey.
82. September 17th, Mr. Miles Reynolds to Miss Lydia Cottrell.
83. October 7th, Mr. Joseph VanCleaf to Miss Martha Lawrence, (Blackpeople).

1830.
84. Capt. Garret P. Hyers to Miss Williampe Conk, both of Monmouth county, New Jersey.
85. July 21st, George W. Bennett to Miss Annjeletty Clayton.
86. September 22nd, Joseph L. White to Miss Lydia Patterson.

1831.
87. May 28th, Tunice V. Voorhees to Miss Eleanor Stricklin.
88. September 24th, John Boude to Miss Lydia Emmons.
89. October 28th, Cornelius D. Clayton to Miss Catharine Giberson.
90. Married on 30th October, 1831, Mr. David D. Matthews to Miss Mary Emmons, both of Monmouth county, N. J.

1832.
91. January 19th, Mr. Joseph G. Hulshart, Esq., to Miss Agnes M. Ely Bennett. †
92. August 23rd, Mr. Benjamin Matthews to Miss Rhoda Ann Lewis.
93. September 29th, John J. Applegate to Miss Esther Hankins.
94. October 12th, Mr. Jacob Miller to Miss Ann Matthews.
95. December 1st, Mr. William Donaldson to Miss Eliza Bills.
96. 6th, Mr. William Stoney of the township of Middletown, to Catharine Matthews of the township of Freehold.

1833.
97. January 19th, Mr. John Reid to Miss Ann Hulshart.
98. 23rd, Mr. Charles J. Mathews to Miss Sarah Ann Robbins.
99. 31st, Mr. David T. Thompson to Miss Mary Anderson.
100. May 5th, Mr. Francis Duncan of Howell, to Miss Margaret Kernaghan of Freehold.
101. May 19th, Mr. William Clayton to Miss Eleanor Voorhees.
102. May 25th, Mr. James J. Clayton to Miss Alice Ann Covenhoven.
103. On same day, Mr. Samuel Forman Matthews to Miss Jane Boud, all of Freehold.
104. Married on the 1st day of January, 1834, Mr. Henry Reynolds to Miss Hannah Ann White.
105. At same time and place, Mr. John Marriner to Miss Abigil White, all of the township of Howell.

† These were the parents of John W. Hulse, Esq., one of the police justices of Freehold at this time.

106. April 12th, Mr. Charles Hankins to Miss Sarah Hulshart, both of Monmouth county.
107. October 19th, Mr. Calvin H. Gardiner of city of New York, to Miss Content Bills.
108. November 8th, Mr. Joseph W. Lewis of Freehold, to Miss Mary Ann Macelvey of the township of Howell.

1835.
109. February 28th, Mr. Anderson Chambers to Miss Amy Matthews.
110. March 26th, Mr. John J. Errickson of Freehold, to Miss Sarah Ann Youngs of Howell.
111. August 12th, Mr. John L. Patterson to Miss Mary Hannah Clayton.
112. August 13th, Mr. John Patterson to Miss Mary Ann Patterson.
113. November 5th, Mr. Matthias C. Barkalow to Miss Elizabeth Emmons.
114. December 5th, Mr. Abram Lefinge of the city and county of New York, to Miss Catharine Bills of the township of Freehold.
115. Married on the 28th day of August, 1836, Mathias Applegate to Miss Margaret Emmons, both of the county of Monmouth.
116. December 31st, Robert Ireland to Miss Margaret Voorhees.

1837.
117. January 7th, William Francis to Miss Sarah Voorhees.
118. January 14th, John P. Reynolds to Miss Eliza Ann Luker, both of Monmouth county.
119. July 30th, John Lokerson to Miss Alice Clayton.
120. November 12th, Mr. Aaron Borden to Miss Sarah Ann Emmons, both of township of Howell.

1838.
121. January 1st, Mr. Hampton Herbert to Miss Mary Kernaghan.
122. March 31st, Mr. William Allen of Eastville, Upper Freehold to Miss Ann Hendrickson of Freehold.
123. May 12th, Mr. Jacob Patterson to Miss Caroline Lorkerson; both of Monmouth county.
124. June 19th, Mr. Garret Voorhees to Miss Rebecca Ann White.
125. October 15th, John Boud to Miss Sarah VanKirk.
126. November 3rd, David Southard to Miss Rhoda Emmons.
127. December 16th, John J. Clayton to Miss Esther Emmons.
128. Married, 26th of January, 1839, Mr. James T. Thompson to Miss Amy Ann Hendrickson, both of Freehold township.
129. February 7, Mr. Moses Patterson to Miss Elea White; both of Howell township.
130. 9th, Mr. John W. Reynolds to Miss Susan Cottrell; both of Freehold township.
131. March 31st, Mr. Jacob Horner to Miss Sarah Applegate, both of Upper Freehold township.
132. April 3rd, David Hulsart of Freehold, to Miss Lydie Jane Patterson of Howell township.
133. 29th, Mr. Elias J. Anderson to Miss Hannah Cottrell; both of Freehold township.
134. November 14, Mr. Job M. Kerr to Miss Ann Shutts; both of the county of Monmouth.

1840.
135. April 29th, Mr. Jonathan More to Miss Sarah VanNote.
136. December 19th, Mr. Cornelius Hankins to Miss Nancy White.

APPENDIX. xiii

137. December 22nd, Joseph E. Lewis to Miss Elizabeth Wilkins.
1841.
138. January 2nd, David Clayton to Miss Lettia Voorhess; both of the county of Monmouth.
139. April 24th, Hendrick Eulshart to Miss Esther Patterson.
140. June 19th, Mr. Joseph Voorhees to Miss Rachel Lucas.
141. October 23rd, Mr. Daniel Hankins to Miss Hannah Ann Clayton.
142. Married on the 18th of November, 1841, Mr. Lloyd Robbins to Miss Maria Hall; both of the township of Howell.
1842.
143. June 12th, Mr. Orsen Miner to Miss Esther Applegate.
144. August 21st, Samuel Lake of Monmouth county, N. J., to Frances Ann Mount of state of New York.
145. October 16th, James Britton Patterson to Miss Sarah Maria Smith.
146. November 5th, Johnson Bills to Miss Ann Thompson; both of the county of Monmouth.
1843.
147. April 22nd, Hendrick Oakerson of Mercer county, to Miss Catharine Leiya Clayton of Monmouth, N. J.
148. August 5th, Thomas Debow to Miss Phebe Hankins; both of the township of Freehold.
149. December 2nd, John H. *Barkalow of the township of Freehold, to Miss Martha Worden of the township of Dover.—All of Monmouth county, N. J.
1844.
150. March 18th, John M. Clayton of the township of Howell, to Miss Alice Kernaghan of the township of Freehold.
151. May 2nd, Joseph T. Matthews to Miss Ann Reynolds, both of the township of Howell.
1845.
152. May 26th, Mr. William Thompson to Miss Mary Applegate.
153. October 5th, Mr. William Lake of the township of Howell to Miss Mary Ann Painton of the township of Freehold.
154. Married on 2nd day of December, 1845, Mr. Joseph Lake of the township of Howell, to Miss Lydia Megill of the same township.
1846.
155. Mr. Warington Fields of Yellow Hook, Long Island, state of New York, to Miss Sarah Lake of the township of Howell, Monmouth county, N. J.
156. June 20th, James C. Hankinson of the township of Freehold, to Miss Adaline Thompson of the same township.
157. November 29th, David D. Applegate to Miss Caroline Dey, both of Freehold township.
1847.
158. March 20th, Mr. Robert Graham to Miss Amy Ann Thompson, both of the township of Millstone, county of Monmouth.
1849.
159. Mr. Thomas Conk to Miss Eleanor Finch, both of Freehold township.
1850.
160. January 20th, Hiram Cottrell of Jackson township to Miss Nancy M. Worth of the township of Dover.
161. March 2nd, John Hendrickson to Miss Elizabeth Ann Buck, both of Jackson township, Ocean county. ‡
162. August 31st, Stephen Thompson of the township of Jackson, Ocean county, to Miss Mary Parent of the township of Millstone, county of Monmouth.
163. October 9th, Edward W. Worth of the township of Freehold, to Miss Hannah Wagner of the township of Howell.
1852.
164. January 8th, Michael Lewis to Miss Sarah C. Maxson, both of the county of Monmouth.
165. May 16, William H. Williams to Miss Catharine Brewer, both of the township of Marlborough, Monmouth county.
166. Married, 20th day of June, 1852, Mr. David Errickson to Miss Catherine Emmons, both of Freehold township.
1854.
167. February 16th, John Corneu of Mercer county, to Miss Ann Wilson of the township of Freehold.
168. September 27th, William B. Hulshart to Miss Alice H. Barkalow, both of Freehold township. §
1857.
169. October 18th, Mr. Asher Applegate to Miss Rhoda Hulshart.
170. October 28th, Mr. William Ayres of the township of Howell to Miss Catharn Magintia of the township of Ocean.
1858.
171. April 3rd, Thomas Wilson of Freehold township, to Susan Reynolds of the township of Jackson, Ocean county.
1859.
172. April 1st, I married David D. Southard to Miss Rhoda Ann Hulshart, both of Freehold township.
1860.
173. February 5th, William H. Hendricks of the township of Manalapan, to Miss Eliza Chambers of the township of Freehold.
174. At same time and place, Cornelius M. Barkolow to Miss Deborah Chambers, both of Freehold township.
175. September 4th, Tunis Emmons of the township of Howell, to Miss Mary E. Hulshart of township of Freehold.
176. November 11th, James J. Malsbury of the township of Millstone, to Miss Mulindy Worth of the township of Freehold.
1861.
177. March 31st, Edward Stephens to Miss Margaret Cottrell, both of Freehold township.
178. Married, August 24, 1861, William H. Bills of Freehold township, to Miss Mary H. Wolcott of Ocean township.
179. August 27, David D. Applegate to Miss Amy Chambers, both of Freehold township.
180. November 8; Job Smallwood of township of Dover, Ocean county, to Miss Ursula Hulshart of Freehold township.
1862.
181. September 25th, Archibald Appleget of the township of Freehold, to Miss Hannah Ann Benson of the township of Millstone.
1863.

---

‡ Ocean county was set off from Monmouth in 1850.

---

§ This was Preacher Barkalow's own daughter.

182. May 3rd, John H. Hulshart of the township of Freehold, to Miss Jane Ann Boud of the township of Howell.
1864.
183. January 20th, Joseph F. Carr of Hightstown, Mercer county, to Miss Sarah Elizabeth Bowne of Jackson township, Ocean county.
184. November 27th, James McLaughlin and Miss Amelia Cottrell, both of Freehold township.
185. December 8th, David Clayton and Miss Elizabeth Barkalow, both of Freehold township.
1866.
186. May 17th, Charles H. Cottrell of Middletown township, to Martha J. Anderson of Freehold township.

187. June 25th, William H. Patterson to Miss Catharine Malsbury, both of the city of New York.
1867.
188. April 21st, Gorden Reynolds of Freehold township, to Miss Sarah Elizabeth Reynolds of Jackson township, Ocean county.
1869.
189. October 20th, George W. Cottrell of Howell township, to Miss Margaret A. Voorhees of Jackson township, Ocean county.
1872.
190. November 6th, John H. Barkalow of the township of Lacey, Ocean county, to Ellen Pharo of Stafford township, Ocean county.
1873.
191. November 27th, Hiram Hulse to Miss Martha Anderson of the township of Jackson, Ocean county.

TOMBSTONE INSCRIPTIONS.

Presbyterian Church Yard, Allentown, N. J. taken June 18, 1901, by Mrs. Lydia H. S. Conover:

Derck Barcalow, d. Nov. 10, 1803, aged 58 y., 6 m., 22 d.
Sarah, wife of Arthur Barcalow and daughter of Tobias Polhemus, d. Jan. 7, 1799, aged 54 y., 2 m., 27 d.
John Sinclair, d. Sept. 22, 1801, in 38th year.
Hannah, his wife, d. June 5, 1819, in 56th year.
Samuel P. Forman, son of Peter Forman and Elleanor Williamsen Forman, d. Jan. 10, 1805, aged 47 y., 2 m., 4 d.
Rebecca, his wife, d. Nov. 2, 1840, in 79th year.
Forman, son of Peter and Hannah (Foman) Cowenhoven, d. Apr. 5, 1762, aged 1 y., 19 d.
* Gerrargus Beekman, son of C—— B——, d. Mar. 25, 1823, in 51st year.
Tobias Polhemus, d. Mar. 18, 1779, aged 71 y., 7 m.
His wife, Mary Leffertson, d. Jan. 3, 1781, aged 44 y.
Hannah Polhemus, daughter of Tobias Polhemus, d. Nov. 9, 1783, aged 87 y., 2 m.
Lefford, son of Tobias Polhemus, d. Feb. 19, 178–, aged 23 y., 6 m.
Margaret, widow of Peter Forman, d. Jan. 8, 1804, aged 77 y., 10 m.
Daniel Hendrickson, d. Feb. 5, 1840, aged 77 y., 2 m., 17 d.
Peter Imlay, d. Mar. 27, 1852, aged 62 y.
His wife Catharine, daughter of Daniel Hendrickson, d. Feb. 13, 1847, aged 50 y.
James L. Conover, d. Apr. 27, 1884, aged 68 y., 1 m., 7 d.
His wife Elizabeth, daughter of Jacob and Sarah (Vandeveer) Hendrickson, d. Apr. 10, 1874, aged 56 y.
John Jacob, son of James L. and Elizabeth (Hendrickson) Conover, d. Mar. 1, 1849.
Jacob Hendrickson, son of Jacob and Elizabeth (Mount) Hendrickson, d. Nov. 7, 1826, aged 40 y., 5 m., 26 d.
His widow, Sarah Vandeveer, b. Jan. 28, 1790; d. Dec. 3, 1878.
Michael Hendrickson, son of Jacob and Sarah Vandeveer Hendrickson, d. Dec. 8, 1814, aged 28 d.
Edward T. Hendrickson, b. Nov. 15, 1815; d. Sept. 9, 1894.
Richard Horsfull, Sr., d. Aug. 6, 1827, aged 50 y., 5 m., 13 d.
Margaret, wife of Stockton Pullen, d. Mar. 31, 1841, aged 57 y.
Samuel Wykoff, Esq., son of Garret and Aeltie Wikoff, d. Apr. 24, 1826, aged 95 y., 6 m., 1 d.
His wife, Gertrude, d. Feb. 15, 1820, aged 85 y.
Peter Wikoff, d. Mar. 21, 1847, aged 74 y., 11 m., 23 d.
His wife Mary, d. Nov. 4, 1857, aged 77 y., 1 m., 27 d.
William Croxon, d. July 10, 1857, aged 81 y., 10 m., 10 d.
His wife, Catharine Wikoff, d. Apr. 25, 1847, aged 74 y., 3 m., 6 d.
Vashti, wife of Samuel S. Forman, d. Jan. 16, 1813, aged 27 y., 21 d.
Samuel I. Wikoff, d. May 17, 1824, aged 58 y., 7 m., 10 d.
Stoffle Wikoff, d. July 19, 1823, aged 47 y., 9 m., 15 d.
Peter R. Wikoff, son of Aukey and Deborah, d. Mar. 24, 1833, aged 29 y., 7 m., 24 d.
Ann Eliza, wife of Michael Hendrickson, d. June 7, 1833, aged 23 y., 1 m., 6 d.
Aukey Wikoff, d. July 27, 1835, aged 58 y.
Emeline, daughter of E. I. and A. E. Hendrickson, d. Apr. 20, 1824, aged 2 y., 3 m., 24 d.
John, son of Garret and Elizabeth Wikoff, d. Oct. 5, 1793, aged 5 y., 5 m., 3 d.
Peter Wikoff, Esq., son of Garret and Aeltje Wikoff, d. Apr. 1, 1827, aged 87 y., 1 m., 6 d.
His wife, Allice Longstreet, d. June 16, 1820, aged 78 y., 5 m., 3 d.
Garret P. Wikoff, (of Allentown, N. J.) d.

---

* This christian name should have been spelled "Gerardus." He was a son of Christopher Beekman, and died unmarried. His will is recorded in Book B of Wills, Monmouth county Surrogate's office. He leaves his property equally to his four brothers and four sisters.

APPENDIX.

June 2, 1844, aged 82 y., 10 m., 23 d.
His wife Elizabeth, d. Jan. 4, 1839, aged 75 y., 4 m., 17 d.
Garret R. Wikoff, b. Jan. 16, 1805; d. Nov. 20, 1884.
His wife Allice, b. Mar. 1, 1797; d. Nov. 7, 1890.
Joseph Hendrickson, d. May 28, 1841, aged 53 y., 2 m., 14 d.
His wife, Elizabeth, d. June 20, 1855, in 71st y.
Mary A. Barcalow, wife of Joseph R. Conover, b. Jan. 22, 1843; d. Aug. 30, 1875.
Richard H. Wikoff, b. Jan. 18, 1804; d. Oct. 23, 1884.
His wife, Jane Forman, b. May 16, 1806; d. Aug. 18, 1891.
Their daughter, Ellen Wikoff, wife of A. B. VanNest, d. May 8, 1863, aged 22 y.
Samuel Hendrickson, d. May 18, 1871, aged 77 y., 2 m., 2 d.
His wife, Phoebe, d. Oct. 9, 1858, aged 62 y., 6 m., 2 d.
Forman Hendrickson, b. May 30, 1791; d. May 17, 1880.
His wife, Theodosia Hendrickson, daughter of Daniel and Elizabeth Grover Hendrickson, b. Nov. 2, 1795; d. Mar. 4, 1879.
Peter H. Wikoff, b. Nov. 26, 1794; d. Mar. 19, 1880.
His wife Ann, b. Mar. 28, 1799; d. July 11, 1881.
Allice Hendrickson, wife of William G. Hendrickson, and daughter of Samuel and Allice (Wikoff) Hendrickson, d. Oct. 27, 1883, aged 80 y., 7 m.
Hannah P., their daughter, and wife of Richard W. Burtis, d. Mar. 27, 1854, aged 21 y., 6 m., 22 d.
Gertrude Hendrickson, daughter of John Hendrickson and Allis (Wikoff) Hendrickson, d. July 12, 1875, aged 80 y.
William Disbro Konover, d. Sept. 21, 1890, aged 61 y.
Garret Conover, b. May 18, 1826; d. Oct. 27, 1890.
Eugenia, b. June 30, 1842; d. May 7, 1887.

Whitehouse, New Jersey,

old church yard; taken August 28, 1901:

Cornelius W. VanHorn, d. Oct. 8, 1862, aged 91 y., 1 m., 21 d.
Lukus Voorhees, d. Mar. 8, 1868, aged 80 y., 3 m., 3 d.
His wife, Ann Emery, d. Jan. 4, 1870, aged 80 y., 1 m., 8 d.
Benjamin VanDoren, d. Feb. 14, 1835, aged 38 y.
Abraham B. VanDoren, d. July 18, 1853, aged 21 y., 6 m., 4 d.
Elizabeth Wyckoff, widow of Roelof Covenhoven, d. Jan. 20, 1860, aged 83 y., 5 m., 26 d.
Garret Conover, d. Nov. 8, 1831, aged 67 y., 5 m.
His wife, Margaret Regar, d. July 8, 1840, aged 70 y.
Job Conover, d. Jan. 27, 1830, aged 23 y., 5 m.
Margaret, wife of Abraham Voorhees, d. May 12, 1843, aged 61 y., 5 m.

Whitehouse, New Jersey,

taken from oldest grave-yard there August 28, 1901:

David Covenhoven, d. Nov. 15, 1800, aged 51 y., 5 m., 11 d.
Cornelius VanHorn, d. Feb. 12, 1744, in 49th y.
Sarah, wife of Roelof Covenhoven, d. Apr. 5, 1801, aged 35 y., 6 m., 26 d.
Cornelius Cownover, (son of George and Alletta Luyster Conover) d. Oct. 31, 1805, aged 78 y.
John Vanderbilt, (son-in-law of Cornelius Cownover and son of John Vanderbilt of S. I., and Elizabeth Hendrickson of N. J.) d. Oct. 23, 1812, aged 55 y.
A daughter of Joris Cownover and Margaret Cownover, d. Jan. 12, 1765, aged 3 y.
Jacob Wyckoff, d. June 15, 1812, aged 71 y., 1 m., 15 d.
His wife, Elizabeth, d. Sept. 9, 1801, aged 50 y., 1 m.

Bound Brook, New Jersey,

Somerset county, High Street Cemetery, August 28, 1901:

Garret K. Schanck, son of Koert and Sarah Voorhees Schanck, d. July 1, 1809, aged 32 y., 3 m., 17 d.
Kortenius G. Schanck, son of Garret and Nelly Covenhoven Schanck), d. Nov. 27, 1878, aged 76 y., 11 m., 19 d.
Mary Conover, wife of Michael I. Field, d. Nov. 28, 1859, aged 80 y., 3 m., 22 d.
Catharine, wife of Roelof VanVoorheese, d. Nov. 10, 1795, aged 38 y.
Hannah, wife of Nickalus Covenhoven, d. Aug. 10, 1804, aged 31 y., 11 m., 20 d.

First Reformed Dutch Church Yard,

New Brunswick, Middlesex county, N. J., August 30, 1901:

William Morris Conover, d. May 6, 1811, aged 26 y.
Lewis Conover, d. Nov. 10, 1831, aged 55 y., 2 m., 27 d.
James Conover, b. Oct. 8, 1778; d. Feb. 12, 1861, in 83rd y.
His wife, Mary, d. Jan. 2, 1846, aged 80 y.
James S. Conover, son of James and Mary, d. Aug. 3, 1849, aged 39 y., 8 m.
Minnie I. VanVoorheese, Esq., d. Aug. 3, 1794, aged 41 y.
Michael Garrish, b. July 24, 1779; d. July 25, 1858.
His wife, Ariet Suydam, b. May 16, 1784; d. Aug. 26, 1874.
Their son, Michael Field Garrish, b. Feb. 27, 1807; d. Apr. 28, 1866.

Further inscriptions Schenck and Covenhoven,

Penns Neck, N. J.,

taken September 9, 1901, by Mrs. L. H. S. Conover:

Eve Schenck, widow of John R. Schenck, d. Nov. 21, 1810.
Albert Schenck, son of Garret Roelofse Schenck, d. May 21, 1786, aged 65 y., 1 m., 2 d.
William Couwenhoven, son of Jan and Jakoba (Vanderveer) Couwenhoven, d. Nov. 1764, aged 59 y.
His wife, Chrystenah, daughter of Cornelius Laen, d. June 24, 1787, aged 78 y.
Cornelius Couwenhoven, d. 1787, aged 51 y.

Harmen Covenhoven, son of William and Chrystenah Laen Couwenhoven, d. Jan. 4, 1804, aged 63 y., 7 m.

Phoebey Baley, wife of Harmen Covenhoven, d. Feb. 2, 1832, aged 87 y., 9 m., 16 d.

Elias C. Schenck, son of Joseph and Margaret (Covenhoven) Schenck, d. Nov. 5, 1800, aged 6 y., 7 m., 17 d.

Elizabeth Schenck, daughter of Joseph and Margaret Covenhoven Schenck, d. May 5, 1785, aged 7 m.

Joseph Schenck, son of Jan Garretse Schenck, d. Oct. 25, 1822, aged 66 y., 5 m., 5 d.

His wife, Margaret Kovenhoven, daughter of William and Elizabeth, d. July 18, 1804, aged 38 y., 4 m., 8 d.

Anney Schenck, d. Oct. 25, 1776, aged 6 y., 2 m., 20 d.

Margaret Schenck, d. Aug. 5, 1816, aged 70 y.

Mary Schenck, d. Sept. 12, 1769, aged 2 y., 8 m., 14 d.

Garret Schenck, d. May 11, 1810, aged 68 y.

Jacob Schenck, son of Roelof (the brewer) (and Engeltie VanDoren) Schenck, d. Dec. 19, 1786, aged 60 y.

Mary, wife of William I. Schenck, d. July, 1829, aged 70 y.

Garret A. Schenck, son of Albert Schenck, d. Mar. 8, 1794, aged 41 y.

William Kouwenhoven, (son of William and Margaret Garretse Schenck Kouwenhoven), d. Oct. 17, 1777, aged 35 y., 4 m., 9 d.

Mary, wife of John Slayback, d. Mar. 1829, aged 87 y.

William Smith Schenck, d. July 27, 1870, aged 67 y.

Margaret S. Schenck, d. July 19, 1863, aged 61 y.

William Kovenhoven, b. Dec. 2, 1767; d. Sept. 24, 1838, aged 70 y., 3 m., 8 d.

His wife, Mary Grover, d. Jan. 4, 1817, aged 38 y., 9 m., 6 d.

Joseph Grover, d. Mar. 26, 1856, aged 81 y., 9 m., 16 d.

His wife, Ruth, daughter of Harmen Covenhoven and Phoebey Baley, d. Mar. 12, 1859, aged 85 y., 8 d.

THE MONMOUTH ASSOCIATORS.

BY JAMES STEEN.

No county in the State of New Jersey suffered more during the Revolution than did Monmouth, and in no county did the citizens respond more nobly. The proximity to the shore and readiness of access by boat from New York rendered it peculiarly the prey of the British. There was super-added to that, a lawless element even more irresponsible and regarding less the rules of warfare, than the guerillas in our late Civil War. Tories and refugees, well acquainted with the county and knowing the inhabitants, preyed upon the aged and infirm who had property that they could take or destroy, and committed all sorts of excesses and outrages, shooting children and old men and hanging women, burning houses and barns, and destroying animals and other property that they could not conveniently carry off.

Notwithstanding, many of her able bodied men were in the Army, the large proportion of those that remained were to be found in the Militia. The Tories and pine robbers had no compunction against invading and destroying homes that were occupied only by the women and the feeble. So obnoxious did they become, aided as they were by the more cowardly neighbors of the patriots, who while committing no overt act, were in league with Tories and refugees, that the Monmouth patriots were forced to take action against traitors in their midst. Hence it is that there has come down to us a document, which while it adds to the history of the county a valuable chapter, is also a roll of honor for the descendants of those who thus banded themselves together in their country's defense. It was in the spring of the year 1780 that the patriots of Monmouth, tried beyond measure by repeated outrages and robberies, and realizing the assistance the non-combatant Tories still living unmolested in their midst were rendering the refugees, Tories and pine robbers, resolved on redress by retaliation. The document which follows is unique, and of the 436 names subscribed nearly one-half served either in the Continental Army or in the Monmouth Militia before the war was concluded. Every part of the county was represented, and the Committees of Safety of the various townships are represented among the names of those who were not only willing to associate but also to have that fact advertised in the New Jersey Gazette.

The Articles of Association are as follows:—

Monmouth Articles of Association.

Whereas from the frequent incursions and depredations of the enemy (and more particularly of the refugees) in this county, whereby not only the lives but the liberty and property of every determined Whig are endangered, they, upon every such incursion, either burning or destroying houses, making prisoners of, and most inhumanly treating aged and peaceable inhabitants, and plundering them of all portable property, it has become essentially necessary to take some different and more effectual measures to check said practices, than have ever yet been taken; and as it is a fact, notorious to every one, that these depredations have always been committed by the refugees (either black or white) that have left this country, or by their influence or procurement, many of whom have near relations and friends, that in general have been suffered to reside unmolested among us, numbers of which, we have full reason to believe, are aiding and accessory to those detestable practices. We, the subscribers, inhabitants of the county of Monmouth, actuated solely by the principles of self-preservation, being of opinion that the measure will be strictly justifiable cn the common principles of war, and being encouraged thereto by an unanimous resolve of the honorable the congress, passed the 30th of Oct., 1778, wherein they in the most solemn manner declare that through every possible change of fortune they will retaliate, do hereby solemnly associate for the purpose of retaliation, and do obligate ourselves, our heirs, executors and administrators, and every of them jointly and severally, to all and every of the subscribers and their heirs, &c., to warrant and defend such persons as may be appointed to assist this association in the execution thereof; and that we will abide by and adhere to such rules and regulations for the purpose of making restitution to such friends to their country as may hereafter have their houses burned or broke to pieces, their property wantonly destroyed or plundered, their persons made prisoners of whilst peaceably at their own habitations about their lawful business not under arms, as shall hereafter be determined on by a committee of nine men duly elected by the associates at large out of their number; which rules and regulations shall be founded on the following principles, viz:—

FIRST—For every good subject of this state residing within the county, that shall become an associator, and shall be taken or admitted to parole by any party or parties of refugees as aforesaid, that shall come on the errand of plundering and man-stealing, the good subject not actually under or taken in arms, there shall be taken an equal number of the most disaffected and influential residing and having property within the county, and them confine within the Provost jail and treat them with British rigor, until the good subjects of this state taken as aforesaid shall be fully liberated.

SECOND — For every house that shall be burned or destroyed, the property of a good subject that enters with this association, there shall be made full retaliation upon or out of the property of the disaffected as aforesaid.

THIRD—That for every article of property taken as aforesaid from any of the associators, being good subjects, the value thereof shall be replaced out of the property of the disaffected as aforesaid. We do also further associate for the purpose of defending the frontiers of this county, and engage each man for himself that is a subject of the militia that we will turn out at all times when the county is invaded, and at other times do our proportionate part towards the defence thereof. We the associators do hereby direct that a copy of this association be, as soon as the signing is completed, transmitted to the printer of the New Jersey Gazette, for publication, and that the original be lodged in the clerk's office.

Also we do request, that the associators will meet at the courthouse on Saturday, the 1st of July, at 1 o'clock in the afternoon for the purpose of electing a committee of nine men, as before mentioned, to carry the said association into effect

Asher Holmes
Joseph Johnston
John VanSchoick
William Nivison
John Smock
Joseph Holmes
John Nivison
John Brown
Elisha Walton
Daniel Denise
John E. Leconte
Garrit Covenhoven
Thomas Thorn
Samuel Elliot
Matthias VanDeripe
James Holmes
John Schenck (capt)
John Covenhoven
Moses Sheppard
William Hulsart
John Schenck (lieut)
Joseph Willet
Benj'n Covenhoven
Jacob VanPelt
Wm. Schenck (lieut)
John Willet
Alex. VanTenycke
Benj. VanCleve
Barnes Smock (lieut)
Peter Johnston
James Hampton
Harmon Sneider
Jarrit Stilwell
George Hymes
John Alwood
Hendrick Sneider
Samuel Pearse
Joseph VanCleve
Elias Conover
William Sneider
Henry Stricker
Solomon Combs
Robert Laird
David Rhea, jr (adjt)
William Schenck
Samuel Dorsett
Berryan Covert
William Anderson
William Covenhoven
Godfrey Warner
Samuel Carhart
Daniel Hill
Jonathan Forman
John Sutphin
William Lane
Samuel Hayes
John Ludlow
Lewis Perine
John Reid
Richard Postens
Aaron F. Welsh
John Baird
William Forman
John Morford
John Rue
William Dewinney
David Baird
David Hance

Lewis Carlton
Matthias Mount
Matthew Anderson
Andrew Clark
Cornelius Barkalow
William Rue
Henry Berry
Peter Emmans
Henry Drake
David Sutphin
John Holmes, sen
Rutliffe Schenck
Joseph Clayton
Tunis VanDerveer
Garrit Wikoff
Tunis VanDerveer
Daniel Lane
Stephen Seabrook
Richard Pippinger
Peter VanDorn
Jacob Smith
Jacob Bennit
Timothy Gordon
Adam Stricker
John Tilton
William Sanford
Lewis Gordon
Matthias Conover
Elias Longstreet
Stephen Fleming
George Taylor
John Chasey
Joseph Bowne
Samuel Pease
Jonathan Forman
Peter Longstreet
Peter VanDerhoof
Patrick Bailey
David Forman
Joseph Wooley
Jacob Allen
Tunis Vanpelt
Samuel Clayton
John Sutphin
John VanBrocle
James Mash
Isaac Staates
Abra'm Hendrickson
Hendrick Hyer
Matthias Roberts
Benjamin VanMater
Hendrick Wiliamson
Corn. Covenhoven
Walter Vanpelt
Lambert Johnston
Rulif Covenhoven
Stout Holmes
Hendrick Vanpelt
Burrowes Norris
John Moore
David Forman
A. Zutphin
Joseph Broom
John Smith Hunn
Kenneth Hankinson
Edward Moore
Joseph Fleming

APPENDIX.

Thomas Stilwell	Joseph Covenhoven	Benjamin M'Donald	John Emmons
Ezekiel Lewis	David Brookes	John Willson	Richard Russel
John Walton	James English	Jacob Woolcott	Joseph Combs
Ebenezer Kerr	David Lloyd	William Hilsey	William Postens
Corn. T. Vanderhoof	Daniel Ketcham	Cornelius Clark, BS	Moses Mount
Nathan Nivison	Lewis M'Knight	Jacob Quackenbush	Job Throckmorton
David Baird	James Reid	James Green (capt)	Matthew Rue
John Longstreet	Isaac Johnston	Joshua Huddy	James Sickles
John Boman	Robert Francis	Cornelius Sutphin	James Runnels
Peter Tanner	Tunis VanDerveer	John Emmans	Samuel Forman
Nicholas VanBrunt	Joseph Sutphin	Joseph Vannoort	John Reid
John Schenck	Joseph Morford	Hendrick Voorhees	Jacob Vanderveer
Manasseh Dunham	Robert Sharp	Daniel Emmons	Richard Chew
William Aumack	James English	Peter Quackenbush	Wm. A. Covenhoven
Jacob Covenhoven	James Tapscott	Joseph Johnston	David Vanderveer
John Campbell	Jacob Lane	Samuel Dennis	John Covenhoven
Josiah West	Oukey Leffertson	John Berry	Albert Covenhoven
Thomas Morris	John Freeman	Abraham Emmans	John Cooke
Thomas Henderson	Jacob Wickoff	John Lake	Richard Tice
John Errickson	John Johnston	Daniel Hendrickson	Tunis Voorhees
Matthias Tice	John Truax	James M'Knight	John Barkalow
William Bowne	William Craig	John M'Mullin	Daniel Randolph
Benj. Covenhoven	David Craig	Francis Herbert	John Antonides
Joel Bedel	Adam Boice, sen.	Barnabas Bennet	Thomas Erickson
William Rowler	John Hulsart	John Simermore	Abraham Vangelder
Thomas Barber	Aaron Sutphin	John Wilkinson	Moses Robbins
William Johnston	Peter Gordon	William Hendrickson	John VanCleve
Nicholas Cottril	Thomas Walling	Benjamin VanCleve	George Clinton
Richard Laird	William Wilbert	John Hampton	William VanSchoick
Samuel Bray	Jonathan Clayton	John Johnston	Daniel Griggs
David Covenhoven	James M'Chesney	Thomas Smith	John Clark, B. S.
David Smith	Eleazer Cottril	Daniel Hampton	Ebenezer Hart
James Smalley	Alburtus Showber	Aaron Reid	Charles Gilmore
William Willcocks	James Hoagland	Jacob Degroof	William Jenkins
John Freeman	John Vanderveer	Samuel Forman	Hend'k Covenhoven
George Crookshank	Edmund Robinson	John Covenhoven	Abra'm Hendrickson
Henry Rue	Jacob Tilton	Jonathan Clayton	John Schenck
James Kinsley	Tunis Vanderveer	Cornelius Schenck	Reuben Potter
Derrick Sutphin	Charles Postey	James Craig	Samuel Hingry
John Nivisink, Jr	James Holmes	Dollance Hagerman	Richard Rogers
William Lewis	Jacob Lane	Joseph Emley	Garrit Vanderveer
Jacob Pippenger	James Jonner	Alexander Clark	William Brown
Moses Laird	Andrew Mains	John Craig	John Brindley
Nicholas Clark	Humphrey Willet	Thomas Chadwick	Arthur Williamson
David Craig	Samuel Bigelow	Joseph Knox	Hendrick Vounk
John Rouse	John Morford	Samuel Rogers	Thomas Smith
John Jewell	Derrick Sutphin	Thomas Seabrook	William Brindley
John Yeatman	Jonathan Pew	Hendrick Smock	Richard Sutphin
John Aumack	Aaron Buck	Jonathan Enobly	Tunis Forman
Benjamin Sutphin	Anthony Holmes	(Embly?)	Joshua Studson
Michael Johnston	Joseph Goodenough	Stephen Barkalow	John DeGraff
Alexander Eastman	Richard Pool	Peter Forman	William Covenhoven
Samuel Craig	John Tilton	William Wikoff	George Brindley
Alexander M'Donald	William Covert	William Voorhees	David Ray
Robert VanSchoick	Benjamin Tilton	William Currin	Richard Marlat
James Yeatman	Thomas Cottrill	Nathaniel Scudder	Abraham Sutphin
James Herbert	John Tilton, Jr	Hugh Newell	Elihu Chadwick
John Perine	James Dorsett	Josiah Holmes	Abel Aikin
Peter Smith	John Stilwell	Peter Vounk	Joseph Vanderveer
John Lane	James Wilson	William Craig	John Reid
Garrit Voorhees	Henry Vanderbilt	Cornelius Stewart	Elisha Shepherd
Aaron Davis	Cornelius Hance	John Covenhoven	David Crawford
Alexander Low	Timothy Hughes	Cornelius M'Mullin	William Cheeseman
William Gordon	Michael Sweetman	Thomas Edwards	Jonathan Reid
W. Laird	Albert Hendrickson	Timothy Dorsey	John Chadwick
Thomas West	Koert Schenck, Jr.	Cornel's Covenhoven	Cornelius Lane
John Jamison	Ken'th Anderson, sen	Richard Poling	Wm. Williamson, jr
Michael Errickson	Jaques Denise	Zebulon Baird	Peter VanCleve
John Davison	James Vankirk	John VanCleve	Daniel Herbert
James M'Duffee	John Morlat	Samuel Henderson	Hend'k VanDerveer
Henry Perine	Richard Jeffrey	Barzulla Baird	Elias Bowne
Nehemiah Tilton	Ephraim Buck	George Casler	John Aumack
John Parent	William Shelft	Gilbert Shearney	
David Gordon (capt)	James Willson	John M'Connill	
John Anderson	William Morrison	Koert VanSchoick	

The number of signers to this association is 436.

It must have been an earnest and determined set of men who met that day in Monmouth Court House—Memories of the battle, recollections of wrongs, many and wicked, thronged their minds and doubtless were recalled in conversation. The committee of nine were duly appointed, and while we do not read in the papers of the day, much or anything of their forceful retaliation, still they doubtless accomplished much in the way of redressing wrongs and inspiring a healthy respect for the rough and ready justice of Monmouth patriotism. The only other notice the writer has found appears in the New Jersey Gazette of March 5th, 1783, and has a grim significance, which was doubtless appreciated by the Tory sympathizers throughout the county. It is as follows:—

"N. J. Gazette, March 5, 1783—Whereas the time of the Committee of the Associators of retaliations of the County of Monmouth expires; and it being necessary for a new one to be chosen, as there remains some business unsettled: The associators are requested to meet at the Court house on 15th March, as well to determine on said business and to be prepared for future depredations.

By order of the committee

Kenneth Hankinson,
Feb. 18, 1783   Chairman,

Kenneth Hankinson, who signed the foregoing, was a captain in Col. Forman's battalion, "Heard's Brigade," June 16th, 1776, and also captain in the First Regiment of Monmouth, 1717. His son, James Hankinson, was the father of Governor William A. Newell's mother.

www.ingramcontent.com/pod-product-compliance
Lightning Source LLC
Chambersburg PA
CBHW030550080526
44585CB00012B/328